PROGRAMMED
TO KILL

PROGRAMMED TO KILL

══

Lee Harvey Oswald,
the Soviet KGB, and
the Kennedy Assassination

══

ION MIHAI PACEPA

IVAN R. DEE
CHICAGO 2007

www.ivanrdee.com

Library of Congress Cataloging-in-Publication Data:
Pacepa, Ion Mihai, 1928–
    Programmed to kill : Lee Harvey Oswald, the Soviet KGB, and the Kennedy assassination / Ion Mihai Pacepa.
      p. cm.
    Includes bibliographical references and index.
    ISBN-13: 978-1-56663-761-9 (cloth : alk. paper)
    ISBN-10: 1-56663-761-9 (cloth : alk. paper)
    1. Kennedy, John F. (John Fitzgerald), 1917–1963–Assassination. 2. Oswald, Lee Harvey. 3. Soviet Union. Komitet gosudarstvennoi bezopasnosti. 4. Espionage, Soviet–United States–History. I. Title.
E842.9.P33 2007
364.152'4092–dc22

                                                        2007011654

In memory of John Fitzgerald Kennedy

ACKNOWLEDGMENTS

NO ADEQUATE WORDS can express my gratitude to the American government for granting me political asylum and giving me an opportunity to begin my life over again from scratch. This new existence has opened my eyes to the reality of the dictatorship I left behind, and allowed me to see my Communist-intelligence past through American eyes. Without this experience I could never have written this book.

My wife, Mary Lou, has introduced me to the marvels of American democracy and of the English language. She has also spent years of her life helping me document the knowledge I brought with me about Moscow's secret involvement in the assassination of President Kennedy. Without her help this book would never even have been conceived.

Assassination researcher Edward Jay Epstein—who interviewed some four hundred people who had been associated with Oswald, most of whom had never been interviewed by the FBI or the Warren Commission—uncovered a wealth of raw facts confirming my own information about the Soviet manipulation of Oswald. Without the evidence he obtained, mostly from people now long dead, my analysis of the Soviet hand in the assassination would not have been as well documented.

My good friends Dr. Radu Ioanid, director of International Archival Projects at the United States Holocaust Memorial Museum, and Professor Vladimir Tismăneanu, director of the Center for the Study of Post-Communist Societies at the University of

Maryland, have given me invaluable help in verifying the historical facts of Soviet-bloc communism. This book would have suffered without their meticulous research and attention to detail.

Last but not least, my editor and publisher Ivan Dee deserves my warm thanks for understanding the complicated intelligence story I was trying to tell and for putting it into attractive language accessible to the average American reader. Without his interest this book would quite simply never have seen the light of day.

I. M. P.

April 2007

CONTENTS

PREFACE

THIS IS A BOOK about Soviet espionage at the height of the cold war, and about the recruitment and manipulation of a difficult loner, Lee Harvey Oswald, the young American Marine who defected to Moscow and four years later assassinated the president of the United States, John Fitzgerald Kennedy. It is also about a successful Soviet-bloc disinformation effort to convince the rest of the world that Moscow never had the slightest interest in Oswald—an effort in which I invested fifteen years of my other life as a Communist intelligence general. Recalling that the 1914 assassination of the Archduke Franz Ferdinand by Serbian terrorists had set off World War I, Moscow feared that Oswald's involvement in the JFK assassination might ignite the first nuclear war.

In 1978, when President Jimmy Carter granted me political asylum, no one in Washington considered, either in print or in conversation, the possibility that Oswald might have been a Soviet agent. I was not surprised. Just a few months before I defected, President Carter had publicly praised the Romanian tyrant Nicolae Ceausescu as "a great national and international leader." In those days U.S. intelligence relied heavily on technical means, and not even the most sophisticated CIA satellite could read the minds of Soviet-bloc despots and their spy chiefs. In any event, for the time being I was preoccupied with more immediate matters. I had to build a new life for myself and help the Romanians get rid of Ceausescu, who was destroying Romania and terrorizing my daughter who was kept hostage there.

After the Soviet Union collapsed, I hoped the new leaders in Moscow would reveal the Soviet hand in the assassination of JFK. Instead, officers of the former Soviet political police, the KGB, took over the Kremlin itself, and Moscow has continued to wash its hands of Oswald ever since. Hangmen do not incriminate themselves.

By 1990 I was an American citizen, and I considered it my duty to help my adoptive country know the truth. Yes, Oswald acted alone when he pulled the trigger of his Mannlicher-Carcano rifle and ended the life of the popular American president. But ultimately it was Khrushchev and his spies who were responsible. In my other life, when we, the leaders of the Soviets' surrogate intelligence services in their satellite countries, learned of JFK's assassination, our Soviet bosses of course admitted nothing to us about any involvement in it, and we knew better than to ask questions. But we knew.

Let me suggest an analogy. In 1970, while I was still living in Bucharest, I was diagnosed with cancer of the lymph nodes—Hodgkin's disease—and given six months to live. Twenty-one leading Romanian doctors and two prestigious West German clinics concurred with the diagnosis. Since the cancer had allegedly infested most of my lymph nodes, the Romanian minister of health decided against removing a couple of them for biopsy. He was afraid that might spread the cancer, and I held too high a position in Romania for him to consider such a risk.

The only person to suspect another diagnosis was the world's leading expert in rare tropical diseases, Dr. Werner Mohr of Hamburg, West Germany. When he had me tested at a firing range and learned that I—an excellent shot in those days—could not hit the bull's-eye even once, he realized that in fact I had toxoplasmosis. That was a little-known tropical disease with symptoms identical to Hodgkin's except for impaired vision. Dr. Mohr even matched my toxoplasmosis with the strain of that disease found in Calcutta chickens, and I confessed that I had indeed recently eaten chicken in that city. Three months later I was cured.

After November 22, 1963, when those of us at the top of the Soviet-bloc intelligence community began learning the details of JFK's murder, we were as certain that his assassin had worked for Soviet espionage as Dr. Mohr had been sure that I had toxoplasmosis, not Hodgkin's disease. All of us bloc intelligence leaders had spent at least twenty years concentrating on recruiting American servicemen assigned outside the United States, and all of us could recognize the elements of Oswald's intelligence handling even in our sleep—just as Dr. Mohr had realized I had toxoplasmosis before he met me face to face. It was crystal clear to us that Oswald had been recruited by Soviet espionage while he was a Marine stationed in Japan, just as Dr. Mohr knew that I must have caught my toxoplasmosis in Calcutta.

It is one thing to know something like that in your bones, but proving it is an entirely different matter. In 1990 I began examining the documents on the Kennedy assassination published by the U.S. government, to see if I could find facts to support what I knew from Romania. As I tried to sift the wheat from the chaff in going through the stacks of reports, I became increasingly fascinated by the wealth of Soviet operational patterns visible throughout the material on Oswald that had been turned up by U.S. government investigators—who had not recognized them as such, owing to their lack of an insider's familiarity with Soviet intelligence operations.

Soviet intelligence, like the Soviet government, had an unusually strong penchant for patterns. All Soviet-bloc countries were called "people's republics"; all their police forces were rebaptized as "militia," and all militia personnel were dressed in blue uniforms indistinguishable from those of the Soviet militia; all Soviet-bloc espionage services were identically organized and had an identical modus operandi. "Everything you'll see here is identical to what I saw in your service," Sergio del Valle, Cuba's chief of both domestic security and foreign intelligence, told me in 1972, when he introduced me to the managers of the Cuban espionage service, the DGI.

Soviet espionage operations, like toxoplasmosis infections, can easily be identified by their particular patterns, if you are familiar with them. By its very nature, espionage is an arcane and duplicitous undertaking, and in the hands of the Soviets it developed into an entire philosophy, every aspect of which had its own set of tried and true rules that followed a prescribed pattern. To understand the mysteries of Soviet espionage, it will not help to see a spy movie or read a spy novel, as entertaining as that might be. You must have lived in that world of secrecy and deceit for an entire career. Even then you may not fathom its darker moments unless you are one of the few at the very top of the pyramid.

Eventually I developed an approach that has never before been used in any of the many studies of the Kennedy assassination. Taking the factual material on Oswald developed by official and private U.S. investigators, I stacked it up against the operational patterns used in Soviet espionage—patterns little known to outsiders because of the utter secrecy endemic to that community.

It took me many years to complete this process, but when I finished I was amazed at the wealth of information that dovetailed with Soviet operational patterns. In fact it was a perfect fit—to a point. As I will demonstrate, everything suggests the Soviet recruitment of Oswald when he was assigned as a young Marine in Japan. In the available documents I also uncovered clear evidence that his mission upon his return to the United States was to assassinate President Kennedy, who had forced Khrushchev to erect the Berlin Wall in 1961 and hastily to withdraw his nuclear missiles from Cuba in 1962. Never before had a Soviet leader been so egregiously humiliated.

For the last ten years of my intelligence career I also supervised Romania's ultra-secret equivalent of the U.S. National Security Agency, thus becoming familiar with Soviet ciphers and codes. Analyzing the innocuous-sounding letters from Oswald and his Soviet wife to the Soviet embassy in Washington (made available to the U.S. government), I realized that they constituted veiled intelligence messages. In them I even found evidence that Oswald had been dispatched to the United States on a *temporary mission*, and that he planned to return to Moscow after accomplishing his task. In fact, just before killing Kennedy, Oswald had requested a reentry visa to return to the inscrutable Soviet Union.

Then, when Oswald was already in place to carry out his mission, the political climate in Moscow abruptly changed, and Khrushchev no longer wanted the president killed. Why not? At the close of 1962 the West German Supreme Court had mounted a public trial of Bogdan Stashinsky, a Soviet intelligence officer who had been decorated by Khrushchev himself for having assassinated two enemies of the Soviet Union living in the West. This trial had publicly revealed Khrushchev to the whole world as a callous political butcher. By 1963 the once flamboyant dictator was already a crippled ruler gasping for air. The slightest whiff of Soviet involvement in the Kennedy assassination could have been fatal to Khrushchev.

Moscow therefore tried its best to deprogram Oswald, but without success. Available documents show that, in order to prove he was capable of securely carrying out the assigned assassination, Oswald even conducted a dry run by shooting at, and narrowly missing, American general Edwin Walker. Oswald put together a package, complete with photographs, showing how he had planned this operation, and he took this material to Mexico City to show Comrade Kostin, his KGB case officer, what he was capable of. Even though he had pulled off this improvised near-assassination without being identified as the perpetrator, Moscow remained adamant. In the end, Oswald stubbornly went ahead on his own, utterly convinced he was fulfilling his "historic" task.

Since Oswald already knew too much about the original plan, however, Moscow arranged for him to be silenced forever—if he should go on to commit the unthinkable. That was another Soviet pattern—seven of the eight first chiefs of the Soviet political police itself were secretly or openly assassinated to prevent them from incriminating the Kremlin.

At the end of this book, for the reader's convenience and guidance, I have put together an addendum entitled "Connecting the Dots," which contains the pertinent events of Oswald's story. At points where I have inferred a Soviet connection, I have placed the explanatory notes in brackets based on my own experience or other instructive material, so that the reader may visualize the overall Soviet intelligence pattern.

Programmed to Kill is a factual and painstakingly documented analysis, not the exciting spy story one might wish to take along to the beach. Then again, if there had been a simple solution to the Kennedy assassination, the case would not have remained essentially unsolved since 1963.

PRINCIPAL FIGURES IN THE BOOK

UNITED STATES CONTINGENT

JOHN FITZGERALD KENNEDY, president of the United States, 1961–1963. U.S.-Soviet relations had reached a low point during the Eisenhower presidency, and Moscow was afraid that if Richard Nixon were elected in 1960, he would continue Eisenhower's policies. Therefore Soviet propaganda machinery let the world believe that the handsome young Kennedy would bring fresh air into the tense standoff between the two countries. After Kennedy took office in January 1961, Khrushchev marked the occasion by releasing two downed American reconnaissance pilots. Then everything changed. In mid-March 1961, Kennedy approved the invasion of Cuba, and Khrushchev turned violently against him. A June 1961 meeting in Vienna ratcheted up Khrushchev's hatred for his new adversary. Afterward, Khrushchev sent a letter to Romanian ruler Gheorghe Gheorghiu-Dej characterizing Kennedy as a warmongering fanatic manipulated by the CIA–for him to call anyone a "CIA puppet" was the equivalent of a death sentence. In the author's presence Khrushchev asserted that, if JFK continued to rely on military might to maintain the "bourgeois occupation" of West Berlin, he would end up in even worse shape than he had been at the Bay of Pigs in Cuba. Within days Khrushchev announced that he would "free" West Berlin. On July 25, 1961, Kennedy firmly declared that the freedom of West Berlin was not negotiable, and the United States began a rapid buildup of American combat troops in Europe. Khrushchev was forced to erect the Berlin Wall, though he pretended it was a victory. As for Kennedy, his fate was sealed.

LEE HARVEY OSWALD, 1939–1963. Growing up without a father, being moved around the country by his dysfunctional, lower-middle-class mother who paid little attention to him, this lonely boy early learned to fend for himself and to spend his free time reading in local libraries. There he came across Marxism and soon persuaded himself that the Soviet Union enjoyed an ideal form of society. Following the example of his two older brothers, he escaped from his mother at age seventeen by joining the Marines. In September 1957 he was assigned as a radar operator at Atsugi Base in Japan, which also housed a U-2 spy plane unit. As a self-proclaimed Marxist studying Russian by himself, Oswald almost immediately came to the attention of Soviet foreign intelligence (PGU) agents swarming around the local bars, and he must have been quickly recruited by the PGU's Tokyo station. For the first time in his life, someone–the PGU–cared about him, and he was hooked. After a time as an obedient agent, he decided he wished to defect and spend the rest of his life in the workers' paradise, and he never deviated from that goal. Once in the Soviet Union, he was treated royally, particularly after the Soviets downed a U-2 on May 1, 1960, and he was undoubtedly told that Khrushchev himself was grateful to him for having provided the U-2's flight altitude specifications. In the fall of 1961 he was persuaded by the PGU to accomplish one last mission for his hero, Khrushchev, after which he could return to the Soviet Union as an even greater hero. Oswald accepted the wife the PGU gave him and the two children he would have with her, and in his way he tried to care for their future; but his real passion was for his political mission and for his own future as an honored Soviet citizen. After settling back in the United States in anticipation of his important assassination mission for the PGU's Thirteenth Department, he was devastated in late 1962 when the PGU instructed him to place everything on hold. Unwilling to sit around doing nothing, he decided to proceed with his mission anyway, by himself, confident that in the end Khrushchev would welcome him back. Oswald did his best to obtain weapons in an inconspicuous way and to fabricate identity documents, using the techniques the PGU had taught him. Until the very end he followed the emergency instructions he had originally been given–admit to nothing and ask for a lawyer. All in vain. He was a liability to the Soviets and had to be silenced. He was just twenty-four years old when Jack Ruby killed him.

MARINA OSWALD, Lee's Soviet wife. Very little is factually verifiable about her background, but she seems to have been a very compliant young Leningrad woman whom the PGU hastily selected for Oswald. After their marriage in the Soviet Union in about April 1961, the PGU gave her a few weeks of training in clandestine communications and told her to keep her husband happy and support him in every way. She depended totally on him, and the stories about their fights were most likely invented, so that he could be left alone to take care of PGU matters. She was unaware of Oswald's specific mission. At his death she was a very frightened twenty-two-year-old with two babies, stranded without money in a strange country where she did not even speak the language. Marina did know that she had to keep her mouth shut or the PGU would get her, and she has done so to this day.

GEORGE DE MOHRENSCHILDT, Oswald's "best friend" in the United States. The "aristocratic" de Mohrenschildt has been an enigma for most assassination researchers and even for his friends. In fact he was a longtime Soviet illegal officer whose biography was forever changing to accommodate his Soviet intelligence tasks. De Mohrenschildt became an American citizen in the 1930s, during the Nazi era, when he was documented as Baron George *von* Mohrenschildt, son of a German director of the Swedish "Nobel interests" in the Baku oilfields. Toward the end of World War II, when it became clear that the Nazis would be defeated, the German baron became the French George *de* Mohrenschildt, who had attended a commercial school in Belgium founded by Napoleon. After World War II he claimed that his father had been a Russian engineer in the Ploesti oilfields in Romania, captured there by the Soviet army and executed. Probably beginning as early as 1958, when Oswald was assigned to a Marine base in California, the PGU directed de Mohrenschildt to provide him with logistical support, but de Mohrenschildt was never aware of Oswald's specific mission. Although upset when he learned that the PGU had used him to support Kennedy's assassin, he accepted a quarter-million dollars from the PGU, agreed to keep a low profile, and even tried to promote the Soviet propaganda line. In 1977, however, unable to face hostile U.S. grilling scheduled by an American researcher and from the House Select Committee on Assassinations regarding his own contradictory background, he chose suicide.

JEANNE DE MOHRENSCHILDT, also a longtime Soviet illegal documented as an American. After divorcing an earlier husband who had publicly accused her of being a Soviet spy, in 1959 she married George de Mohrenschildt. She supported him in his operational activity.

JACK RUBY (né RUBENSTEIN), a Dallas nightclub owner with police and criminal contacts. He was a Cuban intelligence (DGI) agent engaged in arms smuggling. In anticipation that Oswald might—contrary to orders—carry out his mission, the PGU asked the DGI to prepare Ruby to kill Oswald in that event. The DGI coerced Ruby into doing so, telling him that Oswald was a CIA agent being used by reactionary American elements to murder Kennedy, and that Oswald had to be prevented from alleging that the Soviet Union and Cuba were involved. Ruby was promised a short prison sentence and afterward a good life in another country. After being sentenced for killing Oswald, he died in jail in 1967, just as his release was being considered. His death from a virulent form of cancer was probably induced by the PGU to silence him forever. (In 1957 the KGB had unsuccessfully tried to kill PGU defector Nikolay Khokhlov by using irradiated thallium to induce a fast-growing cancer. The following year the PGU gave the Romanian DIE a perfected irradiation weapon.)

RUTH PAINE, a naive housewife living in Irving, Texas. She was a Quaker who had become involved in Russian-American student exchanges sponsored by the Quakers, and that had led her to study Russian. She met Marina Oswald at an international gathering and struck up a friendship with her, based on Russian conversation and the fact that both had young children. A compassionate woman, Paine frequently invited Marina to stay with her when it appeared that Oswald was abusive, and, when he appeared to be destitute, she even helped Oswald find a job at the School Book Depository—from which he shot Kennedy. In fact Oswald was neither abusive nor destitute but was single-mindedly preparing to complete his mission and then take his family safely back to the Soviet Union. Both Oswalds took advantage of Paine's naiveté.

MAJ. GEN. EDWIN A. WALKER, Dallas resident who gave public speeches defending the views of the extreme right. After hearing him speak, Oswald selected him as a "fascist" target in order to prove to the PGU that he could securely carry out an assassination. In the event, Walker moved his head just in time and escaped the shooting unharmed, but from Oswald's perspective the operation was a success, as he was not identified as the would-be assassin.

FRANCIS GARY POWERS, U-2 pilot and CIA employee. The Soviets shot down his U-2 spy plane over the Soviet Union on May 1, 1960. Powers survived and was later exchanged. Back in the United States, he claimed that Oswald, based on his assignment as a radar operator at El Toro Air Base in California, had been able to provide the Soviets with the technical information—particularly the flight altitude—needed to bring down the U-2.

YURY NOSENKO, Soviet domestic counterintelligence (VGU) officer, who defected to the United States in 1964. He was a bona fide defector, but as an officer of the VGU's Tourist Department he reviewed only the disinformation file the PGU provided the VGU to conceal the fact that Oswald was in fact an important PGU agent. Nosenko's information provided to Washington confirms the false information that the PGU wished to disseminate—that Oswald was of no interest to the Soviets.

SOVIET-BLOC CONTINGENT

NIKITA KHRUSHCHEV, leader of the Soviet Union, 1953–1964. A crude, boorish peasant, he vociferously upheld Stalin's "Great Purge," becoming one of only three provincial party secretaries to survive. As reward, in 1938 Stalin appointed him first party secretary of Ukraine, where Khrushchev carried out Stalin's wishes with savagery and brutality. The habit of solving political matters through political assassinations remained with Khrushchev for the rest of his political career. He seized the Kremlin leadership by assassinating his domestic rival, Lavrenty Beria, and went on to conduct foreign policy by attempting to assassinate his international adversaries. In August 1961, Kennedy forced him to erect the Berlin Wall, thus abruptly ending the long-held Soviet dream of reuniting Marx's Germany under communism, and the American president became Khrushchev's main enemy. In June 1962, Khrushchev ordered the PGU to send Oswald to the United States to assassinate Kennedy, but then the political climate suddenly changed for Khrushchev. In October 1962 he was revealed as a political murderer at a spectacular West German public trial, and he was forced to renounce political assassinations, at least temporarily. Therefore the PGU told Oswald to stand down. That same month Kennedy again humiliated Khrushchev, this time over the Cuban missile crisis. Khrushchev had wished to be recorded in history as the Soviet leader who had exported communism and Soviet nuclear power to the Americas. Instead Kennedy forced him to withdraw his missiles. Oswald decided to go ahead on his own, and the Soviets were hard put to avoid international repercussions. Eleven months after Kennedy's assassination, Khrushchev was accused of harebrained schemes and ousted from power.

ALEKSANDR SAKHAROVSKY, chief of Soviet foreign intelligence (PGU). After World War II he was the chief Soviet intelligence adviser to Romania, going on to become the head of the entire PGU for a record-breaking fifteen years, 1956–1971. He was also the author's de facto boss for thirteen years (1951–1964). A coldly dynamic man virtually unknown in the West, Sakharovsky was the chief architect of Khrushchev's foreign policy and one of the fathers of the cold war. He continually spoke of "our historic task," which became a constant refrain within the PGU and the satellite services; the phrase is reflected in the title of Oswald's "Historic Diary," which he brought with him when he returned to the United States in 1962.

IVAN AGAYANTS (alias AVALOV), head of the PGU's disinformation component from its creation in 1959 until his own death in 1968. An educated Armenian, he was responsible for numerous bogus memoirs and other highly successful forgeries. He introduced the use of diaries as an operational instrument to help PGU agents sent abroad remember their fictitious biographies–both Oswald and Marina brought such documents with them when they left the Soviet Union in 1962.

VALERY KOSTIKOV (alias KOSTIN), identified officer of the PGU's Thirteenth Department (assassination and sabotage). He evidently trained Oswald in the Soviet Union for his assassination mission, where Oswald knew him as "Comrade Kostin." In September 1961, Kostikov was assigned under consular cover to the Soviet embassy in Mexico City, so as to be available for clandestine personal meetings with Oswald. Oswald is known to have met him there in September 1963, and they must have also met earlier, in April of that year.

VITALY GERASIMOV, identified PGU officer assigned under consular cover to the Soviet embassy in Washington, D.C. The PGU's Thirteenth Department evidently made him responsible for keeping track of Oswald in the United States, though personal meetings there were not allowed. The contact was maintained through letters and publications sent to Oswald's various post office boxes, and through letters from both Oswalds addressed to another consular official and then routed to Gerasimov.

GHEORGHE GHEORGHIU-DEJ, Communist leader of Romania, 1952–1965. He was a close collaborator of Khrushchev's. They were together in Bucharest and Moscow during the most important episodes of the Berlin and Cuban crises. Gheorghiu-Dej told the author he was convinced that Khrushchev would eventually kill Kennedy.

NICOLAE DOICARU, head of Romanian foreign intelligence, 1959–1978. A Russian speaker and confidant of Sakharovsky's, he was well aware of the PGU's involvement with Oswald. In August

1978 (following the author's defection), Doicaru was arrested and then retired. After Romanian president Ceausescu was executed in 1989, Doicaru offered to reveal whatever he knew about PGU operations, and to build a new Romanian espionage service directed against Russia. A few months later he died in a "hunting accident."

FIDEL CASTRO, Communist leader of Cuba since 1959. He was not involved with the Oswald case until after April 1963, when the PGU realized it might be unable to prevent Oswald from going ahead with his original mission. Castro approved the use of Jack Ruby by the DGI to silence Oswald, should that become necessary. After the Kennedy assassination, Castro publicly helped Moscow direct suspicion at the CIA and President Lyndon Johnson.

SILVIA TIRADO DE DURÁN, local employee at the Cuban embassy in Mexico City. She was completely unaware of who Oswald was when he walked into the Cuban embassy in September 1963. At first impressed by his pro-Communist and pro-Cuban credentials, she checked with the Soviet embassy and understood that the Cubans should have nothing to do with him.

BOGDAN STASHINSKY, officer of the PGU's Thirteenth Department, who defected to West Germany in 1961. He confessed to having assassinated two leading Ukrainian émigrés in 1957 and 1959 at Khrushchev's order, for which he was afterward personally decorated by Khrushchev. Stashinsky's trial in October 1962 generated worldwide publicity, and the West German judge declared that the Soviet government was the primary guilty party. After this fiasco, the Soviet-bloc intelligence services were enjoined from committing assassinations, at least for the time being.

CHORUS OF THE UNWITTING

Oswald's extended family, U.S. Marines, State Department and FBI officials, Russian émigrés, and the owners and employees of small businesses in the United States.

PROGRAMMED
TO KILL

1

KENNEDY KILLED BY A *"SERZHANT"*

W HEN President John Fitzgerald Kennedy was shot to death on November 22, 1963, I was living in my native Bucharest, one of three deputy chiefs of the Romanian espionage service, called the DIE (*Departamentul de Informatii Externe*, Department of Foreign Intelligence). In those days the DIE was neither more nor less than a subsidiary of the Soviet espionage service, the PGU (*Pervoye Glavnoye Upravleniye*, First Chief Directorate of the KGB). The DIE even paid its officers their salaries on the 20th of the month, just as the PGU did, to commemorate the founding on December 20, 1917, of the Cheka, the ancestor of the entire Soviet political police organization that later became the KGB.

At the DIE of those days, most of the management level consisted of "Romanianized" Soviet, Bulgarian, German, or Hungarian Communists who had once worked for the Soviets in Moscow or abroad and had been recruited by the PGU. On top of these undercover PGU officers posing as Romanians were undisguised Soviet PGU officers, who were called *razvedka* (Russian for "foreign intelligence") advisers. They were not paid by the DIE and had no official rank or position in it, so that they could not be influenced by the Romanians. Their activity went far beyond mere counseling, though. The chief *razvedka* adviser acted as the DIE's autocrat and uncrowned tsar. In all, there were more Russian speakers than native Romanians running the DIE, although a few of the latter, like

3

me, were beginning to occupy responsible positions. It was still generally true that the thicker a person's Slavic accent, the higher his seat in the hierarchy of all the Soviet-bloc "sister" services, the operations of which were geared almost exclusively toward filling requests received from the Soviet Union.

During the night of November 22, 1963, a few hours after the news had reached Bucharest that President Kennedy had been assassinated, our chief *razvedka* adviser, whom we knew as Gen. Ruslan Sergeyevich Romanov (this was an operational alias–in PGU practice the advisers to the DIE were not allowed to use their true names), summoned DIE chief Nicolae Doicaru and his deputies to DIE headquarters. Ruslan Sergeyevich told us that he had just been called by the PGU center in Moscow on the secure telephone line connecting it with the DIE, and had been ordered to begin immediately sending Moscow every scrap of information the DIE could obtain about the assassination, no matter how trivial it might seem. Thereupon we in the DIE sent out a circular book cable passing on that request to all our stations in the United States and Western Europe. (The DIE had adopted Romanianized Russian terms in all its professional vocabulary. The PGU's word for an intelligence station abroad, *rezidentura*, became the DIE's *rezidenta*–pronounced "rezidentsa"–an awkward word with no meaning in Romanian.)

No sooner had we sent out those instructions than Ruslan Sergeyevich received a new call from Moscow. After hanging up, he feverishly instructed us to put the DIE on "code C alert," which meant calling the chiefs and deputies of all the DIE desks to headquarters. All the foreign intelligence services in the entire Soviet bloc were being put on emergency alert, he added. An hour or so later, at Moscow's request, the Romanian Ministry of Foreign Affairs ordered its embassies in the United States and Western Europe indiscriminately to report everything their personnel could learn about Kennedy's assassination. According to the chief *razvedka* adviser, all Soviet and East European embassies in those areas of the world had been instructed to take similar measures. (Many years later, Soviet diplomatic defector Arkady Shevchenko, who in 1963 had been assigned to the Soviet Mission to the United Nations in New York, wrote in his memoir: "Almost immediately [after the assassination] Moscow cautioned us to be vigilantly circumspect, and to report anything, no matter how small, about what was going on.")

That same night the chief *razvedka* adviser informed us that Lee Harvey Oswald, the man who had just been arrested in Dallas for shooting Kennedy and a local police officer, was an American Marine who had defected to the Soviet Union in 1959 and returned to America some three years later. A few hours after that, the chief *razvedka* adviser received yet another order from Moscow, this time requiring that our *rezidentury* in the United States, Western Europe, and Japan temporarily suspend all contact with our foreign agents. (The writer Edward Jay Epstein, investigating events surrounding President Kennedy's assassination, learned that at this same time the Cuban espionage service, the DGI, had "instructed its officers around the world to remain within their respective embassies and to segregate and seal all DGI files.")

Of course, we in the DIE thought we understood the situation. In that Communist nightmare in which we lived it would have been the most natural thing in the world for Oswald, as an American Marine with contacts to the Soviet Union, to have been a PGU agent.

"A *serzhant*," Doicaru whispered in my ear. (Although he was the first native Romanian to become chief of the DIE, Doicaru had been appointed to his position by the Soviets and enjoyed their trust—just as I did.) In those days, *serzhant* was the broken record being played by our *razvedka* advisers, who placed a high priority on recruiting American servicemen. As early as April 1957 we had received a PGU directive signed by its newly appointed chief, Gen. Aleksandr Mikhaylovich Sakharovsky, requiring the DIE and other "sister" services to concentrate their efforts on recruiting American servicemen. According to the directive, current Soviet experience had established that Japan and West Germany, where the United States located its principal postwar occupation forces, now offered the best conditions for the accomplishment of this goal. American soldiers assigned to those two countries exhibited an increasingly relaxed attitude toward American laws and ethical standards, were more amenable to entering into conversation with East European representatives, and could consequently be approached operationally with much greater ease than in the United States.

Of course the PGU wanted us to recruit high-ranking American officers, but, according to the Sakharovsky letter, Soviet experience had proved that sergeants were much easier to approach and recruit. PGU experience had also shown that such *serzhanty* were able to provide extremely valuable intelligence. Hunting for a *serzhant* had therefore become my priority during the three years (1957–1959) I had been assigned as *rezident* in West Germany, and it was still a priority in 1978 when I finally broke with communism.

On that memorable November 22 we stayed up all night waiting for news from Moscow and from our stations abroad. The chief *razvedka* adviser never told us in so many words that the assassination of President Kennedy had ever been part of a PGU operation for "destabilizing" the United States, but we found Soviet reticence on the subject entirely understandable. Any indiscretion in that connection might have led to a nuclear cataclysm. Nevertheless we had few, if any, doubts that it was a PGU operation. Until shortly before Kennedy's assassination, we in the DIE had been involved in supporting various PGU operations designed to throw mud on the "Pig," the code name the PGU had assigned to Kennedy in March 1961 when it learned that he had approved CIA plans to invade Cuba, and we had no doubt that the American president had become one of the PGU's targets for removal. Moreover, in 1962 the DIE chief and I had with our own ears heard Nikita Khrushchev violently curse out the "millionaire's kid" (his scathing pejorative for Kennedy), who had made him suffer such indignity as no other Soviet leader had ever endured.

Assassination operations carried out abroad by the PGU were not a subject openly discussed in the Soviet foreign intelligence community, though we all knew that, soon after Khrushchev was enthroned in the Kremlin, he had adopted political murder abroad as a way of life. In 1953, when he came to power, Khrushchev found a relatively tranquil domestic scene, with the Soviet population too cowed by Stalin's security forces to cause political trouble. He therefore decided it was time to concentrate on the Soviet Union's foreign enemies. We at the top of the DIE were told that Stalin had made one inexcusable mistake, that of aiming the cutting edge of his security apparatus against the Soviet Union's own people; and that

Khrushchev, in his famous "secret" speech criticizing Stalin, had intended only to correct that aberration. So after Khrushchev had brutally crushed the 1956 Hungarian revolution and caused Imre Nagy and its other principal leaders to be kidnapped into Romania and later killed, he ordered the PGU to create components for "wet affairs" (*wet* was the PGU's euphemism for *bloody*) in all its "sister" services in the rest of the Soviet bloc. In the beginning these new operational units targeted anti-Communist émigrés living in the West, whom the Kremlin always considered as falling under the jurisdiction of their countries of origin regardless of their current citizenship.

In 1959, however, Khrushchev aimed these new units at the West itself, ordering the PGU and its "sisters" to be prepared to "destabilize" the United States and its main allies in case of international crisis by secretly killing off some of their political leaders, by selectively contaminating their drinking water with germ weapons, and by disabling some of their key installations such as power plants, airports, and maritime harbors. (PGU officer Oleg Adolfovich Lyalin, who defected from the PGU *rezidentura* in London in 1971, confirmed that in the 1960s the PGU department for "wet affairs," where he worked, had contingency plans "for the sabotage of foreign public services, transportation, communications, and the nerve centers of government at the outbreak of war and in some crises short of war.") With that, DIE management suddenly saw the door cracked open onto the most closely held secret in Soviet foreign intelligence operations–assassinations.

We in DIE management received new operational rules, reportedly drawn up by Khrushchev himself, requiring that henceforth political assassinations in the West be handled strictly orally and kept forever secret. Moscow's new rules for such operations also directed all "sister" services to spread "evidence" in the West accusing the CIA or other convenient "enemies" of having done the deed, and never to acknowledge their own involvement in political assassination abroad, no matter what evidence Western authorities might claim to have obtained. One of the first experimental operations conducted under Khrushchev's new rules was jointly carried out by the PGU, the DIE, and the East German *Stasi* in September

1958, when the anti-Communist Romanian émigré leader Oliviu Beldeanu was secretly kidnapped from West Germany. Official East German and Romanian newspapers placed the onus for this crime on the CIA's shoulders by publishing official communiqués stating that Beldeanu had been arrested in East Germany after having been secretly infiltrated there by the CIA in order to carry out sabotage and diversion operations. We even became aware of a few PGU targets, though the Soviets never directly acknowledged their paternity in any "wet operations" abroad. We understood that they wished to avoid indiscretions that could generate international conflicts.

We knew, for instance, that in February 1962 the PGU had narrowly missed assassinating the shah of Iran owing to the failure of a remote-controlled device that was to set off an explosion. The shah had committed the unpardonable "crime" of having prevented the Kremlin from taking over his country—he had removed a Communist regime installed in the northwestern part of Iran and had turned his government to face the West. Our *razvedka* advisers never told us in so many words that the PGU had failed to kill the shah, but that very night Ruslan Sergeyevich called DIE management together for an emergency meeting at DIE headquarters. The chief *razvedka* adviser, by nature a calm and reserved man, now seemed unusually agitated. He asked us to order the DIE station in Tehran to destroy all its compromising documents, to suspend all its agent operations, and to report everything, including rumors, about an attempt on the shah's life. A few days later our *razvedka* adviser canceled the DIE plan to kill its own defector Constantin Mandache in West Germany using a bomb mounted in his car because, the adviser told us, the remote control, which had been supplied by the PGU for this operation, might malfunction. (In 1990 Vladimir Kuzichkin, a PGU officer who had been directly involved in the failed attempt to kill the shah and who had later defected to the West, published a book in which he described the operation. According to Kuzichkin, the shah escaped because the remote control used to set off a large quantity of explosive in a Volkswagen car had malfunctioned.)

On November 24, 1963, Oswald's own death as good as confirmed in our minds the PGU involvement in the JFK assassination—

and, as we later learned, in the minds of our Hungarian, Bulgarian, and Yugoslavian counterparts, with whom we were in close liaison. To us, Oswald's murder seemed fully consonant with the implacable Soviet rule that anyone who could testify to a crime incriminating the Kremlin must be silenced. That imperative was so deeply rooted in the Kremlin's practice that even the chiefs of the political police themselves were secretly or openly assassinated after they had completed their bloody tasks of office. Only one of the first eight consecutive chiefs of the Soviet state security service (which over the years had various names—Cheka, NKVD, KGB) who served between 1917 and 1954 is known to have died a natural death—Semen Ignatyev, who vanished into thin air in 1953, then reappeared at a provincial post and died of natural causes in 1983. Feliks Dzerzhinsky, founder of the organization, suspiciously died of a stroke after an argument with Stalin in 1926. The rest either were poisoned (Vyacheslav Menzhinsky in 1934) or were executed as Western spies (Genrikh Yagoda in 1938, Nikolay Yezhov in 1939, Lavrenty Beria and Vsevolod Merkulov in 1953, and Viktor Abakumov in 1954).

Furthermore, if we DIE chiefs had had any lingering doubts that the PGU must indeed have been behind Oswald's death, they would all have been dissipated on November 25, 1963, the day after Oswald was killed. On that evening Ruslan Sergeyevich told General Doicaru that on the day of the Kennedy assassination a Dallas newspaper had published a full-page statement, bordered in black, which he said was in fact a transparent threat to Kennedy's life made by American extremists. The statement welcomed President Kennedy to "Dallas, the city that rejected his philosophy and policy in the year 1960 and that will reject them again in an even more expressive way than before." The adviser gave Doicaru a text about that story and asked that it be published the following day in a major Romanian newspaper. Doicaru reported that demand to Romanian leader Gheorghe Gheorghiu-Dej, and the text, which did in fact contain a transparent threat to Kennedy's life, appeared on page four of the November 26, 1963, *Scinteia* (the official party newspaper) as a bulletin "from Washington."

Having been schooled in the PGU's operational methods, we at the top of the DIE believed that General Sakharovsky, the chief of the PGU, must have expected Oswald to kill President Kennedy during his visit to Dallas, and that he had therefore directed the PGU experts in bogus letters and memoirs to put together something that would specifically divert suspicion toward extreme-right groups in the United States should the assassination indeed take place. The black-bordered statement entitled "WELCOME MR. KENNEDY TO DALLAS," which actually appeared in the November 22 *Dallas Morning News*, looked to us exactly like something the PGU disinformation service would have created, for the arguments in it were the familiar ones propounded by PGU propaganda. "WHY has Gus Hall, head of the U.S. Communist Party praised almost every one of your policies and announced that the party will endorse and support your re-election in 1964?" the statement asked, among other things. "WHY has the Foreign Policy of the United Sates degenerated to the point that the C.I.A. is arranging coups and having staunch Anti-Communist Allies of the U.S. bloodily exterminated[?]" That last question was, almost word for word, one of the PGU's (and therefore the DIE's) favorite disinformation themes of that day. Later we learned that Bernard Weissman, the man whose name was published under the black-bordered statement, had served in the U.S. Army in Munich. We strongly suspected him to have been another *serzhant* case.

2

===

MOSCOW'S
OPERATION DRAGON

O N THE evening of November 26, 1963, General Sakharovsky, chief of the PGU, unexpectedly landed in Bucharest. That day I attended a reception given by the Mongolian ambassador in Bucharest celebrating the thirty-ninth anniversary of the People's Republic of Mongolia—my first and last contact with Mongolian matters. When I returned to DIE headquarters, my chief executive officer told me that Doicaru and the chief *razvedka* adviser were waiting for me. They had just come back from the airport, where they had welcomed General Sakharovsky to Bucharest.

"Is *khorosho* see old friend," Sakharovsky said, greeting me in that distinctive intermingling of Romanian and Russian I knew so well. Although I had worked under him for many years, it is more accurate to describe him as a friend of my father's, who had occasionally acted as a German interpreter for Marshal Rodion Malinovsky. The marshal had been the Soviet gauleiter of Romania during the years Sakharovsky was her chief intelligence adviser, and he was now the Soviet Union's powerful minister of defense.

"Let's get something to eat," Doicaru decreed. He was also a disciple of Sakharovsky's. The four of us moved into the dining room behind Doicaru's office, where a silent waiter rushed over to serve us Sakharovsky's favorite food: caviar and *bubliki* rolls.

It turned out that Bucharest was Sakharovsky's first stop on a blitz tour of the main sister services. His task was to instruct the

11

management of these services to unleash a diversionary intelligence effort aimed at directing world attention away from the Soviet Union and focusing suspicion for the killing of President Kennedy on the United States itself. Sakharovsky brought with him a "directive" containing the main points of this offensive, which were too secret to have been sent even via enciphered radio traffic.

During dinner Sakharovsky told us that "the Comrade" himself—Khrushchev—wished to make it clear to "our sister services" that diverting attention away from the Soviet Union in connection with Kennedy's killing was now our first and most important task. (In the highest circles throughout the Soviet bloc, the term "the Comrade" colloquially designated a given country's leader.) "The Comrade" was afraid, Sakharovsky told us, that if the American media and public opinion were to begin pointing the finger at Moscow, it might end in a nuclear confrontation. Unfortunately there were some facts that could make the Americans mad if they came to light, the Soviet visitor added.

We learned from Sakharovsky that Oswald had never had a father, that he had been raised in orphanages and had lived a life of misery during his youth, that he had developed a deep-seated hatred for American capitalism and its social injustices, that he had become a self-taught Marxist, and that he had spoken quite good Russian when he defected to Moscow. Those things alone, Sakharovsky explained, were enough to subject the Soviet Union and its sister countries to "Western provocations." There was, however, a lot more to Oswald's story than we could imagine, he added. "His wife is a Soviet citizen."

"A wife," Doicaru whispered into my ear. Another PGU operational formula that our *razvedka* advisers were constantly harping on was that the DIE should provide Romanian "wives" for its *serzhanty* in order to keep them "tied to us forever." One of my priority tasks at that very moment, in fact, was to put the finishing touches on "Annette," a twenty-one-year-old Romanian girl of German origin selected to become the wife of "Konrad," a Marine sergeant at the American air base in Wiesbaden, Germany, who had been an operational acquaintance of my station in West Germany while I had still been the chief there. Now we had no doubt that the

PGU must have had a hand in Oswald's getting a Soviet wife while he was in the Soviet Union—nothing in the world could have made the PGU pass up such a golden opportunity.

Then Sakharovsky went on to mention another potential problem related to Oswald, namely that, despite having a German name, Oswald's closest friend in America was in fact a Russian émigré. The Soviet general did not mention the émigré's name but did name the international organization that had once sent the man to Belgrade. Upon hearing what Sakharovsky said, Doicaru, who had a phenomenal memory for names, dashed downstairs to the DIE's operational archive, which was in an underground vault. He had remembered that the DIE station in Belgrade had once wanted to recruit an American with a German name who was assigned to Yugoslavia as a representative of the International Cooperation Administration. "I was right," Doicaru told us when he returned. "George de Mohrenschildt" was the name of the man who seemed to fit Sakharovsky's description. DIE archive records showed that in 1957, when de Mohrenschildt had been assigned to Belgrade, the DIE station there had spotted him as a target for recruitment. In those days, however, the rule was that, before trying to recruit a foreigner, the DIE first had to ask Moscow for a name check on the target individual. In this case the PGU had answered that de Mohrenschildt was already "taken." (It was normal for the PGU's answer to be vague about the nature of the relationship with an individual, and about whether it was the PGU itself or another bloc service that had a priority interest in him.)

"You see?" Sakharovsky murmured when Doicaru handed him the archive's trace report.

At that time our relationship with General Sakharovsky and his *razvedka* advisers was essentially open and cordial. There were, however, two subjects that were always strictly taboo in conversations with them: the identities of agents involved in PGU operations, and the true names of PGU officers and advisers. So as soon as Doicaru and I realized that Oswald must have been a PGU agent who had been supplied with a Soviet "wife" and a Russian émigré "friend," we knew that we should not push Sakharovsky for further information about him. Being familiar with his normal behavior, however, both Doicaru and I could easily see that Sakharovsky was acting as if Oswald had indeed been part of a PGU operation, and as if some unforeseen turn of events had now badly shaken the PGU.

After dinner we accompanied Sakharovsky to the airport because he wished to spend the night in Budapest. The next day we locked ourselves in the office of the chief *razvedka* adviser to get a translation of the ultra-secret directive that Sakharovsky had brought with him. Its bottom line was that we should immediately begin spreading the rumor in the West that President Kennedy had been killed by the CIA. Operational guidelines were included in the PGU center's directive, according to which the CIA hated Kennedy because, by toning down its plans to invade Cuba in 1962, he had compromised the CIA's presence around the world. Furthermore Kennedy had wanted to end the cold war, and that would have set the CIA adrift without a rudder. Hence, the PGU line went, the old CIA cold warriors had decided to get rid of Kennedy, and to do it in such a manner as simultaneously to increase the "imperialist hysteria" against the Soviet Union. Oswald, an enlisted Marine, was the instrument the CIA had chosen for carrying out this operation. Moscow instructed the DIE to represent Oswald as a CIA agent who had been dispatched to the Soviet Union in 1959 under cover as a defector, and who had been repatriated almost three years later after completing his espionage task there. The CIA used Oswald, the Center's directive stated, in order to make the world believe the assassination had been perpetrated by the Soviet Union.

Sakharovsky's directive did not surprise us, for it seemed entirely consistent with Moscow's new rules requiring that after each "neutralization" (the euphemism used for assassinations and kidnappings abroad) we should surreptitiously spread rumors in the West accusing the CIA of responsibility for the crime. As a matter of fact, the official Romanian newspaper, *Scinteia*, had shortly before accused the CIA of being responsible for the DIE's own "neutralization" of Oliviu Beldeanu, the anti-Communist émigré leader who had been secretly kidnapped by the DIE from West Germany.

Sakharovsky's directive was immediately transformed into a DIE operational plan, which received the code name Operation

Dragon. As was the case with all other super-secret DIE operations, the Dragon plan was handwritten in one copy only and kept in the DIE chief's safe. A few days later I also had to write out (my handwriting was considered the most legible) an attachment to Operation Dragon containing guidelines for another rumor that was to be circulated, that the assassination of Kennedy had been coordinated by Lyndon Johnson himself. In the words of a new directive from Moscow, the vice president had feared that Kennedy would replace him with a member of the "Kennedy clan" on the ballot for the 1964 elections. The bottom line of this interpretation was that Johnson had seen through the clan's plot and had lured Kennedy to Texas, where Johnson could play on his home turf. Although it was against the rules for the president and vice president of the United States to travel together, the PGU directive emphasized, Johnson had managed to accompany Kennedy to Texas so that he could personally coordinate the killing. According to Moscow, the fact that Kennedy's assassin had been shot two days later while in the very hands of the police fully proved that the mastermind behind both crimes could only have been someone who had been in a position to manipulate the Texas police—and who better than the legendary senator from Texas, who had now instantly become the president of the United States? Attached to the PGU's new directive, which had been sent by Sakharovsky through a special PGU courier, was the text of an article published in a Dallas newspaper on the day Kennedy was assassinated, which the DIE was to use as "evidence." (It was probably the article that had appeared in the November 22 *Dallas Morning News* concerning a visit to Dallas by former vice president Richard Nixon the preceding day. The paper's headline read: "Nixon Predicts JFK May Drop Johnson.")

This new PGU directive also contained a wealth of "documentary" data purporting to show that the "Kennedy clan" was taking possession of the entire United States: Robert Kennedy, the attorney general, had become the second most powerful man in the country; one of the president's in-laws, Sargent Shriver, had become the director of the newly formed Peace Corps, which was described in the Moscow directive as an undercover branch of the CIA created to spread American influence throughout the Third

World; another of the president's in-laws, Stephen Smith, was to manage the Democratic party's presidential campaign in the 1964 elections.

In early December 1963, Moscow shifted Operation Dragon into high gear. Behind Kennedy's assassination now allegedly stood also the "sharks" of the "military-industrial complex," who had learned that the American president had decided to make drastic reductions in the country's military presence abroad and consequently to cut its arms spending. The "boss" of these "sharks" was Secretary of Defense Robert McNamara, who had given up his job as president of the Ford Motor Company only in order to move the country into a series of local wars and thereby increase the need for new weapons and military equipment. The bloodiness, however, of the November 1, 1963, coup against the "unruly" South Vietnamese president Ngo Dinh Diem and his brother, which had been carried out by the Pentagon and the CIA–and in which McNamara was to be represented as having been deeply involved–had disgusted Kennedy to such an extent that he had wanted to withdraw U.S. military advisers from Vietnam. That, the PGU document stated, had unleashed the rage of McNamara and his "sharks." They had moved fast; fewer than three weeks after Kennedy had made it known that he wanted out of Vietnam, he was dead.

There was not much the DIE could do to support the PGU's Operation Dragon. For one thing, Dej called Doicaru and me in and asked us to go slow with Dragon. He was sure that Moscow's hand in the failed assassination of the shah of Iran and in the killing of President Kennedy would come out sooner rather than later, and he wished to keep Romania as clear of these crimes as possible. For another thing, at that time the DIE had no trusted high-level sources in the West who might have appreciably influenced the course of the U.S. investigation. Nevertheless for many years DIE officers and agents dutifully dropped hints to anyone who would listen, in accordance with Dragon instructions.

It seems, however, that the PGU did much more with this disinformation operation. In a 1994 book, retired PGU general Oleg Kalugin, who had been assigned to New York at the time of Kennedy's assassination, writes: "We began receiving nearly frantic cables from KGB headquarters in Moscow, ordering us to do every-thing possible to dispel the notion that the Soviet Union was some-how behind the assassination." According to Kalugin, "when Moscow wanted to hammer home its official line—as it did when ac-cusations arose of Soviet involvement in the assassination of Presi-dent John F. Kennedy—we in Political Intelligence were called upon to propagate the Soviet point of view."

As soon as it was revealed that Lee Oswald was a Marine who had defected to Moscow, Kalugin's station in New York was or-dered to launch the idea that when Oswald was living in the Soviet Union he "had never been trusted and was suspected of being a CIA agent," and "to put forward the line that Oswald could have been involved in a conspiracy with American reactionaries displeased with the president's recent efforts to improve relations with Russia."

Arkady Shevchenko, the Soviet diplomat who later defected to the United States, was also in New York at that time and recalls "widespread speculation among Soviet diplomats that Lyndon Johnson, along with the CIA and the Mafia, had masterminded the plot."

Just before I was granted political asylum in the summer of 1978, Fidel Castro also stepped into the fray. On April 3, 1978, a group of U.S. congressmen held a long interview with Castro on behalf of the House Select Committee on Assassinations. After strongly express-ing the view that the Soviet Union and Cuba would have stood only to lose from killing Kennedy, Castro put forth the basic line of Op-eration Dragon: "We suspect," he said, "that some CIA agent had to do with that terrorist act." Toward the end of the interview, Castro confidentially added: "Now, I am going to tell you something. . . . I apologize for that, but I would have not trusted [President] John-son. I may say sincerely, I sincerely believe that Johnson could have followed that line, on the attempts against people's lives, terrorism, subversion."

Kalugin has the last word, concluding: "In the end, our cam-paign succeeded, and subsequent investigations have shown that the KGB—despite some contact with Oswald in the Soviet Union and Mexico City—had nothing to do with Kennedy's assassination." Note the careful wording of this statement.

3

FIRST HARD EVIDENCE OF THE PGU'S HAND

THE KENNEDY assassination was one of the extremely rare cold war episodes in which both sides were vitally interested in hiding the truth. Many in the West still do not realize that by 1963 the once high-flying Nikita Khrushchev was already on the skids. Following his humiliating decisions to erect the Berlin Wall in 1961 and hurriedly to withdraw his nuclear missiles from Cuba in 1962, he had lost the confidence of the Soviet Union's governing elite. Also in October 1962 the West German Supreme Court mounted the public trial of Bogdan Stashinsky, the PGU officer stationed in East Berlin who had defected to the West and related that a couple of months earlier he had killed two leading anti-Communist Ukrainian émigrés in West Germany. After initially being heard with skepticism, Stashinsky ended up convincing the public of his sincerity and remorse.

What had begun as Stashinsky's trial was soon transformed into a questioning of Khrushchev. The flamboyant, impulsive, and unpredictable ruler in the Kremlin, whose "secret" speech unmasking Stalin's crimes was still fresh in everyone's memory, now appeared to the Karlsruhe courtroom to be just another odious butcher. And a liar. It was not at all true that after the Twentieth Party Congress Khrushchev had halted the KGB's killings—he had merely turned the focus abroad. It was not true that Khrushchev had forsworn crime—he had personally ordered the killings committed by

Stashinsky, and he had signed the decree that rewarded the perpetrator with the highest Soviet medal. At the end of his seven-day trial Stashinsky declared: "I wanted to give worldwide publicity to the way in which [Khrushchev's] 'peaceful coexistence' really works in practice."

Any revelation of a Soviet hand in the assassination of the widely popular American president could have now been fatal to Khrushchev.

With respect to the assassination, the interests of Lyndon Johnson, the new president, happened to coincide with Khrushchev's. President Johnson faced elections in less than a year, and any conclusion implicating the Soviet Union would have forced him to take unwanted political or even military action. To investigate the assassination and satisfy the electorate he therefore created a "high-caliber, top-flight, blue-ribbon group" that came to be called the Warren Commission after its chairman, Chief Justice Earl Warren.

This "investigating group" held only fourteen days of hearings, for its task was not really to investigate the Kennedy assassination but rather to invoke the collective integrity of its distinguished members to calm the people and delay other inquiries. The Warren Commission did indeed find "no evidence to indicate that either Lee Harvey Oswald or [his killer] Jack Ruby was part of any conspiracy, domestic or foreign, to assassinate President Kennedy." The commission accepted at face value the Soviet explanation that Oswald had defected to the Soviet Union on his own, and that the KGB had never been involved with him, despite a wealth of evidence proving exactly the contrary.

Ironically the Warren Commission Report was the first official U.S. investigative document providing us in the DIE with hard evidence that the PGU was indeed involved in that ghastly crime. In December 1964 our *rezidenta* in Washington sent us a copy of the thirteen-page document entitled "Historic Diary" that Oswald had brought back to the United States upon his redefection from the Soviet Union in 1962. According to the *rezidenta*'s report, this document had recently been released by the Warren Commission with the comment that, though the handwriting had been verified as Oswald's, there were serious doubts about the authenticity of its content. In fact the commission concluded that the diary was "not an accurate guide to the details of Oswald's activities" in the Soviet Union, noting that the accuracy of dates and names was questionable, and that many entries seemed to have been written long after the fact. But the Commission went no further.

A few weeks after we received Oswald's "Historic Diary," Col. Tigran Gregorian, who at that time was the DIE expert in English, presented us with a report concluding that the diary had in fact been drafted by the PGU. Gregorian discovered that the diary contained a number of British expressions and spellings. There was good reason for them, Gregorian's report stated. In those days DIE officers who were sent to Moscow for operational training, which included language lessons, learned only British English, as that was what the PGU instructors spoke—the PGU did not employ its first teachers of American English until 1964.

I do not recall the specific examples of Briticisms mentioned in Gregorian's report; but my wife, an American linguist, independently noted this anomaly in Oswald's diary. She pointed out that an uneducated American like Oswald would surely never have used expressions and spellings like "Alferd is a Hungarian chap," Rosa is "very merry," and Ella refuses Oswald's "dishonourable advanis." My wife also noted that another passage in Oswald's diary stresses a theme that would have been more familiar to the PGU than to Oswald and seems designed to strike a chord with an American audience: "I relize I am in the Insanity ward" at a Moscow hospital. Soviet misuse of insane asylums to punish dissidents was a political issue in the West during this period, but even if Oswald had actually been hospitalized, it is incredible that he would have accidentally been placed with the mentally ill. My wife too concluded that Oswald's diary must have been copied in great haste, as suggested by its many spelling inaccuracies. It was probably also drafted in a rush after Oswald applied to go back to the United States, judging by such anachronisms as giving a figure in new rubles for January 1960, when the ruble devaluation did not take place until a year later, and naming John McVickar as chief American consular officer in Moscow as of October 1959, when in fact he did not assume that position until almost two years later.

Subsequently I learned that an American handwriting expert estimated that the "Historic Diary" must have been written in one or two sittings, as will be discussed in a later chapter.

Personal diaries were all the rage at that time in PGU/DIE operations. As far back as I can remember, our illegal officers and agents sent to the West under a fictitious biography had needed to take along some kind of written memory aid so that they could remember exactly where they had supposedly been when, and what they had done in various periods of their alleged lives. Until the late 1950s, these notes had been taken abroad in the form of microdots or on soft film concealed in some everyday object. Of course they presented the potential risk of becoming incriminating evidence if ever found. Early in 1960 the PGU concluded that this practice was too dangerous from an operational standpoint, and it devised what it called a "legal and innocuous" way of keeping such data.

In January 1959, General Sakharovsky had created a new disinformation department within the PGU, specializing in creating false letters, newspaper articles, and other documents. The head of that department, Gen. Ivan Agayants, was an urbane Armenian who owed this appointment "to his success in sponsoring a series of bogus memoirs and other works" by such supposed authors as White Russian commander General Vlasov and Soviet foreign commissar Maksim Litvinov, and even a collection of fraudulent correspondence between the Yugoslav leader Tito and Stalin himself. A year later the PGU instructed all sister services that the fictitious biographies of illegal officers and agents sent to the West should be taken abroad in the form of diaries, drafts of books, personal letters, or autobiographical notes. These were drafted by disinformation specialists, copied out by hand by the illegal or intelligence agents concerned, usually just before leaving for the West, and then carried across the border openly.

"Eureka!" Doicaru exclaimed when I gave him the Romanian translation of Oswald's diary. "That's Sakharovsky's hand," he explained, pointing his finger to the title "Historic Diary." I had anticipated Doicaru's explosion, for "historic" was General Sakharovsky's favorite expression. The *Securitate* had the "historic task" to weed out the bourgeoisie from Romanian soil, he would constantly preach when he was the *Securitate*'s chief Soviet adviser. The "historic duty" of the PGU and its "sisters" was to dig the grave of the international bourgeoisie. *Dogonyat i peregonyat* was our "*monumentalnaya*, historic task," he told us, just after Khrushchev had launched his famous slogan about catching up with the West and overtaking it in the space of ten years.

"And look at that," Doicaru exclaimed again, pointing to a passage of the diary in which Oswald acknowledged that in the Soviet Union he had received money from the Soviet Red Cross. "What better proof do you want?" (Oswald's diary states that on January 5, 1960, he received "5000 rubles [roughly five hundred dollars] a huge sum!!" from the "Red Cross" in Moscow, and that later, when he was assigned to work at a Minsk radio factory, his salary of seven hundred rubles a month was augmented by an equal amount given to him as a subsidy from the Red Cross.)

I had expected Doicaru's outburst. For many years the PGU had used the Soviet Red Cross to fund espionage operations in the West. Following this Soviet pattern, the DIE had also appointed an undercover officer, Col. Marcel Popescu, as vice president of the Romanian Red Cross and used that organization to cover the source of funds paid to Westerners recruited as DIE agents who for various reasons had to take refuge in Romania, and to émigrés repatriated by the DIE. (An authoritative book on the KGB published in the United States in 1985 provides proof that from the time of its establishment by Lenin, the Soviet Red Cross was used by the organs of state security to fund espionage activities in the West.)

The "Historic Diary" was not the only manuscript that Oswald brought back with him from the Soviet Union. Our station in Washington also sent us a fragmentary manuscript describing life in the Soviet Union, particularly in Minsk, where Oswald supposedly lived for almost two and a half years. In these notes, which had also been released by the Warren Commission, Oswald himself admits that the monies he received from the Soviet Red Cross had in fact come from "the M.V.D.," though he remarks that he did not realize this fact "for almost two years." For us, Oswald's use of the term *MVD* was also revealing. The MVD, meaning the Ministry of Interior (*Ministerstvo Vnutrennikh Del*), was at one time the popular designation for the state security organization, which then fell under that ministry's administration. In 1954 that organization was removed from the ministry and made into an independent committee, the KGB—but old hands continued to use the epithet MVD.

The fact that Oswald had brought so many manuscripts out of the Soviet Union, in defiance of the regulations imposed on others who emigrated at that time, gave us further evidence of the PGU's hand.

The Warren Commission held only a few hearings, which were conducted in a superficial manner. Norman Redlich, the Warren Commission staff lawyer in charge of preparing the questioning of Marina Oswald, recorded in a memorandum that she had "lied to the Secret Service, the FBI and this commission repeatedly on matters which are of vital concern to the people of this country and the world."

Eventually Marina admitted to the FBI that she had destroyed a photograph of Oswald and his weapon the day after Kennedy was assassinated; that she had withheld evidence indicating that Oswald had attempted to shoot American general Edwin Walker seven months before killing Kennedy; and that she had falsely denied knowing about Oswald's trip to Mexico City in the fall of 1963. Chief Justice Warren, however, ruled out any attempt to test Marina's sincerity by using a lie detector because, as he explained to his staff, it would make little sense for the commission to impugn the credibility of its chief witness on Oswald's character.

On June 15, 1964, the commission announced that it had completed its hearings, and most lawyers working for it returned to their private firms. The commission's final report was written by three lawyers (Redlich, Alfred Goldberg, and Lee Rankin) who had no experience in foreign counterintelligence and who worked under constant urging from the commission to close doors rather than open them because of the pressure to complete the report before the coming presidential election.

The commission concluded that President Kennedy had been killed by shots fired from the Texas School Book Depository by Lee Harvey Oswald, and that Oswald had been killed two days later at the Dallas Police Department by Jack Ruby. The commission found no evidence to indicate that either Oswald or Ruby was part of a conspiracy, domestic or foreign, to assassinate the president, and it resolved that there was no credible evidence that Oswald had been an agent of the Soviet government, nor had he received unusually favorable treatment in entering or leaving the Soviet Union or in returning to the United States. The commission could make no definitive determination of Oswald's motives, though it did discuss some of his asocial and anti-American character traits that might have contributed to his actions.

The Warren Commission report was published by the Government Printing Office on September 24, 1964. It consists of twenty-six volumes of haphazardly assembled testimony to the commission and documents obtained primarily from federal and state authorities and from the Soviet government, plus one volume containing the summary report. The summary report (republished by several publishers) is a disorganized hodgepodge of material assembled by various staff members, to which is attached an unsatisfactory index.

In 1965 our *rezidenta* in Washington sent us the complete Warren Commission Report. Our experts, who spent months studying its investigative documents, found in them a wealth of factual but essentially raw information clearly showing the Soviet hand to an informed analyst with inside Soviet intelligence experience. Our analysts thus assumed that President Johnson was eager to prevent speculation about "international complications" involving Khrushchev or Castro. After all, it had been three years since the Cuban Missile Crisis had almost triggered a nuclear war with the Soviet Union. U.S. relations with the Soviets had been steadily improving, and the Soviet government went to great lengths to appear genuinely distraught over Kennedy's death. Senior Politburo member Anastas Mikoyan had come to Washington for Kennedy's funeral and thoughtfully brought with him an innocuous file purporting to be everything the Soviets had on Oswald. In hindsight, our intelligence experts proved right.

In 1976 the House of Representatives established a Select Committee on Assassinations and conducted its own investigations, in 1979 publishing twelve volumes of documents and hearings and one summary volume on the Kennedy assassination. Although the

House originally suspected the CIA of involvement in the assassination, that was found to be not likely. In the end the committee concluded that there had probably been a conspiracy, but it could not specify by whom. For some members, the Mafia was a prime suspect.

The committee's report does contain some important new material in the form of documents that had come to light after 1964 and interviews conducted by the committee, pointing even more suggestively toward Moscow than the Warren Commission's materials had. But because of its unfamiliarity with Soviet intelligence, the House could not properly evaluate what it had uncovered.

In its final report the committee excluded a Soviet hand in the assassination by simply stating that "the reaction of the Soviet Government as well as the Soviet people seemed to be one of genuine shock and sincere grief. The committee believed, therefore, on the basis of the evidence available to it, that the Soviet Government was not involved in the assassination."

Such credulity showed that the House committee, like the Warren Commission, understood nothing about the degree to which the Soviet government had routinely relied on deception in its conduct of foreign and domestic affairs, even to the point of falsifying Moscow street maps and telephone books. Apparently no one recalled that Khrushchev had boldly lied to President Kennedy, through Ambassador Anatoly Dobrynin, in denying that the Soviets were putting missiles in Cuba.

4

===

RECRUITING A *SERZHANT*

F UNDAMENTAL to understanding what the Soviet involvement
with Oswald must have been is the sense of what the PGU
meant when it directed the bloc intelligence services to look for a
serzhant. In the 1950s, when the PGU began its campaign to recruit
American servicemen outside the Soviet Union, it found that sergeants were much more accessible than higher-ranking officers and
could provide excellent information if given the right guidance.
That was why *serzhanty* became a top priority during the fifteen
years that Sakharovsky directed the activities of the Soviet-bloc foreign intelligence services. The PGU ran many successful cases of
this kind.

Sgt. Robert Lee Johnson is a good example. In the 1950s he was
stationed in West Germany, where, like Oswald, he became infatu-
ated with communism and decided to spend the rest of his life in
the Soviet Union. In 1953, Johnson surreptitiously entered East
Berlin and went to a Soviet military unit, where he asked for political asylum. There he was theoretically granted his request, but he
was also recruited by the PGU and persuaded to return temporarily to his military unit to carry out a "historic task" before starting
his new life in the Soviet Union. By 1959 *serzhant* Johnson was in
a position to supply the PGU with valuable classified documents on
American cipher systems and cryptographic equipment.

In Berlin the PGU also recruited Johnson's friend, Sgt. James
Allen Mintkenbaugh, who was instrumental in providing the PGU
with samples of American rocket fuel–a Soviet intelligence priority

at that time. In another case, in 1960, Sgt. Jack E. Dunlap walked into the Soviet embassy in Washington, D.C., and thereafter provided the Soviets with highly classified materials from the National Security Agency, where he was assigned.

These sergeants would never be colonels or even captains, but they were extremely productive intelligence agents. That was why Sergeant Johnson, for instance, was secretly awarded the rank of Red Army major and received written congratulations from the Soviet Council of Ministers and from Khrushchev himself. Vitaly Sergeyevich Yurchenko, a high-ranking PGU officer who defected to the CIA in 1985 (and then soon redefected), reported that the PGU regarded the case of Chief Warrant Officer John Anthony Walker—another *serzhant*—as the greatest in the PGU's history, "surpassing in importance even the Soviet theft of the Anglo-American blueprints for the first atomic bomb," with "devastating consequences for the United States" in the event of war. John F. Lehman, secretary of the navy when Walker was arrested, agreed.

I became directly involved in recruiting *serzhanty* in 1957 when I was appointed chief of Romania's espionage station in West Germany. The PGU spelled out for me the pattern for recruiting them. Away from home, the PGU instructions stated, these low-ranking American servicemen hungered for companionship and usually spent most of their free time hanging around the bars and night-clubs that sprang up like mushrooms around the U.S. bases, especially in West Germany and Japan. There they could be approached operationally with much greater ease than in the United States. Thus the DIE stations in West Germany and Japan were to become actively involved in recruiting agents from among the barflies and prostitutes who frequented the joints that catered to the enlisted men stationed nearby.

The main task of such agents, called "spotters," was to finger "ideologically motivated" targets, that is, American servicemen who were sympathetic to the Soviet Union or to liberal and leftist movements. At the other extreme, the spotters were to be on the lookout for servicemen with vulnerabilities: men with character weaknesses, such as drinking and gambling problems; skirt chasers; sexual perverts; men with debts or criminal records; men without scruples about how they earned money, especially if it was "tax free," that is, unreported. Finally, when conditions seemed ripe, the spotters were to contrive some way for their officer handlers to meet the targeted Americans. The instructions declared that by using this new operational pattern the PGU had recently achieved "astonishing" successes.

"A *serzhant*!" Ruslan Sergeyevich told me before I left for my assignment in West Germany. "You give party *serzhant*, and party give you Gold Star"–that was the highest Soviet-bloc medal.

As it turned out, my station's first agent at an American military base was not even a *serzhant*. On one of the countless evenings that the DIE's Capt. Ivan Bichel, who was responsible for recruiting a *serzhant*, spent in one of the bars clustered around an American base near Munich, he met a Romanian-born German man who used to stop by there almost every day after work to enjoy a drink or two in the company of American servicemen. Bichel had no problem learning that this *Volksdeutscher*, as Romanian-born Germans were called, was employed at the American base. The two of them quickly became buddies, and soon Bichel succeeded in "lending" his new friend five hundred German marks to make the down payment on a Volkswagen van. The only operational problem was that the *Volksdeutscher* was a low-level janitor at the American base, with little access to information of value.

Nevertheless DIE headquarters reacted enthusiastically to the news. It assigned the code name Balthasar to the case, approved giving the target another "loan" to buy furniture for his new house, and ordered that Balthasar be gradually involved in spotting American targets at his place of work. Before long Balthasar was registered in the DIE records system as a "spotting agent" who had been recruited on the basis of ideological affinity combined with financial remuneration.

Long after midnight on one rainy night in September 1958, Bichel knocked at the door of my apartment on the second floor of the mission complex. "I have something for you in the garage," he whispered, unusually excited. That morning Bichel had left for Munich to see Balthasar, and, as always, I had been waiting up for him to give me a brief report on his meeting. I was not expecting anything spectacular, but I wanted to be sure that nothing had gone wrong. Opening the doors and trunk of his car, Bichel announced: "It's all from him!" The Mercedes was bulging with large canvas duffel bags. "Nothing but military documents," he said softly, untying one of the bags.

It turned out that Balthasar was still in the same janitorial job, but, following Bichel's instructions, he had gained his employer's confidence and had been put in charge of using the furnace to burn operating manuals for weapons and military equipment that, for one reason or another, were being discarded in favor of new manuals. Instead of burning them, though, Balthasar had loaded up his new Volkswagen van with as many of the manuals as it would hold. The documents were not highly classified, most of them being marked "For Official Use Only," but they were the first original American military documents we had ever seen.

A few days later a DIE plane took me and my booty to Bucharest, where I had my first lunch with Col. Aleksey Rudenko, the DIE's *razvedka* adviser for Germany—it was also the first time I had ever eaten *malosol* caviar with a tablespoon. "Our colonels are there waiting for us," he said, after we had finished lunch. Opening a hidden door in the paneled wall of his office, he shoved me into his adjacent conference room. Around a conference table sat four men, all puffing away like smokestacks. "Our best experts on American arms and weapons systems," Rudenko explained, introducing me to the four KGB officers, who awkwardly got to their feet and revealed their identical, ill-fitting grey civilian suits.

"Good stuff!" rumbled the most senior of them.

In the spring of 1958 I again found myself in Rudenko's office. A PGU general, who had just flown in from Moscow, announced without preamble that the Kremlin considered Balthasar an extremely valuable agent and wanted no more personal meetings held with him in West Germany. Balthasar was to be brought clandestinely to a PGU safe house in Austria, where he would be trained to take secret photographs of his military documents and use dead drops (hiding places) to pass the rolls of film. For special reports and conditions, he was to be trained to use strip film, the rolls of which he would bury in the bindings of books, which he would mail to addresses in the West. The PGU general also said that Moscow had decided to pay Balthasar a monthly salary as well as a bonus for every document he provided, ranging between five and twenty West German marks (at that time the equivalent of between $1.20 and $4.80). Soon Balthasar became one of the most important cases in the DIE. (His intelligence work came to an end soon after I was granted political asylum. In 1981 the American press reported that he had been arrested by the West German police.)

In mid-1958 my station finally began working on a real *serzhant*, who received the code name Konrad and Rudenko's even higher attention. One of my officers had cast his eye on him, abetted by one of the women DIE headquarters had sent to Wiesbaden to hang around the bars and make friends with the servicemen from the large American air base in that city. Konrad was an avid skirt chaser and fell easy prey to "Mimi." My station recorded most of their amorous encounters. In the long run, however, Mimi had no luck at building any serious relationship with Konrad, who flitted from one girl to the next, so I proposed blackmailing him with the audiotapes we had. Instead Rudenko decided to send the tapes to Moscow, where KGB experts would use them to draw a psychological portrait of Konrad's sexual appetites. Using that study, Rudenko would supply the "custom-designed" profile of a female agent who would be capable of keeping Konrad between her legs, as the saying went, and who might even become his wife.

5

A "DEFECTOR"

I N RETROSPECT, both Doicaru and I realized that we had first learned about the PGU connection with Oswald long before he killed President Kennedy. At the end of 1958, while I was the chief of Romania's espionage station in West Germany, I was unexpectedly called to East Berlin for an emergency meeting. Doicaru and Rudenko were waiting for me at our embassy.

"We've gotten a special task for you from Moscow," Rudenko explained. He did most of the talking. The PGU colonel set a Romanian translation of an American document on the table in front of me. It was a press release (dated April 30, 1956, as I have since established) that had been distributed by the U.S. National Advisory Committee for Aeronautics (NACA), the forerunner of NASA (the National Aeronautics and Space Administration). The document reported that NACA had received a new type of airplane, the Lockheed U-2, which would make it possible to obtain meteorological data needed for jet transports that would fly at altitudes far higher than used at the time, except by a few military aircraft.

"Even the American media knew it was a lie," Rudenko added, handing me a newspaper clipping. It was an article (from the *Los Angeles Times* of April 14, 1957) concerning the same Lockheed U-2 plane that the U.S. government was claiming would be used to conduct scientific research. In fact, that article said, the U-2 was purely a spy plane, which was now flying out of Europe and Japan under top-secret classification. The fact that the U-2 planes themselves were heavily guarded day and night was hard proof that they were highly classified and were being used for extremely secret missions.

"CIA's latest tool," Rudenko concluded, giving me a Russian document and its Romanian translation. It was a requirement issued by the Soviet military intelligence service, the GRU (*Glavnoye Razvedyvatelnoye Upravleniye*, or main intelligence directorate of the Soviet General Staff), which asked for data on the U-2 plane. After listing what the GRU had already learned about the U-2, the requirement asked for "everything," including rumors about the flight altitude of this "black lady of espionage." The Soviet Defense Ministry knew that U-2 planes had flown over the Soviet Union several times, but its Air Defense Command (the *Voyska protivovozdushnoy oborony*, or v-pvo) had been unable to track them positively because of their ultra-high altitude.

Acknowledging that the flight altitude of the U-2 must be a highly classified secret known to very few people, the GRU indicated an indirect way of obtaining this information: by learning the maximum operating range of American radar gear used to monitor U-2 flights. The GRU indicated that most U-2 flights over the Soviet Union were originating at the U.S. Air Force bases in Wiesbaden, West Germany, and Atsugi, Japan, both manned by the Marine Corps, and asked for any information on the radar gear existing at those airports.

"'Balthasar' goes to Wiesbaden," Doicaru said, finally making it clear why I had been summoned to Berlin.

"And 'Konrad,'" Rudenko added. "He *is* in Wiesbaden."

Of course I protested that Balthasar was just a low-level janitor who could not wander freely through all the American bases in Germany, and that Konrad was just an "operational acquaintance" who was far from having been recruited. Neither Doicaru nor Rudenko had ears for my excuses. If Balthasar and Konrad could not get their hands on the flight altitude of the U-2, I simply had to recruit another *serzhant* to service this requirement.

In the summer of 1959 I received a new request from DIE headquarters. Based on "unconfirmed" information just obtained by the PGU, the request stated, it was believed that the U-2 spy plane could fly at altitudes of "about 30,000 meters" (roughly ninety thousand feet). My station was asked to make a special effort to confirm that information and report to headquarters.

I had already sent headquarters a few data obtained from the U.S. base in Wiesbaden, all of which clearly showed that the U-2's flight altitude was one of the most highly classified American military secrets, known only to persons directly involved in its flights and to a few specially cleared air-traffic controllers and radar operators at that base. Unless an unexpected miracle occurred, I was sure that my station could produce nothing more on the subject. From the new request I realized that the PGU must have been luckier. Evidently one of its stations has been able to get its hands on a traffic controller or radar operator assigned to the Marine Air Force base in Wiesbaden or in Atsugi. Another *serzhant*, I thought.

It would not take long for me to learn that the new *serzhant* was in fact a defector. On June 19, 1960, Nikita Khrushchev landed in Bucharest as head of a large party delegation to attend the Third Congress of the Romanian Communist party (at that time called the Workers party), and he remained there for eight days. Khrushchev's expert in Romanian affairs, General Sakharovsky, came with him, though he was not formally included in the party delegation.

In a five-hour speech, Gheorghe Gheorghiu-Dej, Romania's ruler, presented a vast plan for the rapid industrialization of his country. As a Marxist, Dej based his new policy on the Soviet principle that the per capita production of steel was the main indicator of progress in a modern society. He therefore provided that a quarter of the country's budget for the next five years (1960–1965) be invested in the development of a large metallurgical industry. Far and away the main objective of Dej's new industrial program was the construction of the "largest metallurgical complex in the world," to be erected in the city of Galati on the Danube.

The Galati complex was planned to be built by a consortium of German and French engineering companies. Dej, however, wanted to sign a contract with these firms, steal their blueprints, and then build most of the equipment in Romania. Mill was the code name of this operation, which was Dej's latest espionage infatuation, and I was its "chief engineer" in my new position as head of Romanian industrial espionage.

That same evening after Dej's speech I stood at attention before Khrushchev at his waterfront villa. "You mean you're not really going to buy it from the West?" Khrushchev asked suspiciously, after I had finished briefing him on what Dej had instructed me to say about the Mill operation.

"We're going to steal it, of course," Dej explained, "but how could I have said that in front of the plenum?" Unctuously, Dej told Khrushchev that he had learned the tactic from the Soviet leader. *"Dogonat i peregonat,"* Dej added piously, tossing out Khrushchev's slogan about catching up with and overtaking the West. "And we're not going to catch up with capitalism by making it rich. We'll overtake it by stealing from it. Galati will be a monument to your genius, Nikita Sergeyevich, not to capitalism."

Khrushchev spent the rest of the evening sipping vodka and telling stories about the downing of the American U-2 plane on May 1, 1960, and about the subsequent Paris summit meeting, where he had just finished "humiliating" Eisenhower. Both Khrushchev and Sakharovsky took great pleasure in bragging about the incident; no matter what subject was under discussion, they always managed to turn the conversation back to the U-2.

According to what I learned during those eight days in June 1960 when I was constantly in Khrushchev's and Sakharovsky's company, the Soviets had been able to shoot down the U-2 only because the PGU had obtained reliable information on the plane's flight altitude. I understood that the intelligence had been received somewhere toward the end of the preceding year, but that the Soviet Air Defense Command had for some time found no opportunity to verify it, because there had been no more U-2 flights until April 9, 1960. Observing that flight, Air Defense became convinced that the PGU intelligence was accurate, and it therefore adjusted its radars and missiles so as to be prepared when the next flight occurred. That happened on May 1–"the most valuable May Day present we've ever given the Comrade," Sakharovsky said.

From the moment the U-2 entered Soviet airspace until it was shot down, Sakharovsky said he had been in constant contact with the Air Defense commander, Marshal Biryuzov. That evening

Sakharovsky had dined with the Comrade, and a couple of weeks later he had received the Order of Lenin.

Naturally I toasted Sakharovsky on his success. "Bottoms up to the *serzhant* too," Doicaru joked, raising another glass.

"Well, he wasn't even a *serzhant*," the Soviet general said, after emptying his glass.

Sakharovsky did not elaborate on the details of the PGU operation that had ended with the downing of the U-2 and the capture of its pilot, Francis Gary Powers. But Doicaru and I remembered that a few weeks after the incident, our *razvedka* advisers to the DIE added a new wrinkle to their constant refrain about our need to recruit a *serzhant:* now we were also told to look for a "defector."

According to the advisers, a growing number of idealistic, peace-loving enlisted men in the U.S. armed forces were disappointed with the inequalities of American society and with the warmongering American government, and those young men could not envision a future for themselves in the United States. Recent experience showed, the advisers claimed, that some of those men, especially shy, introverted ones who did not mix with their fellow enlisted men, could be persuaded to defect to the Soviet Union. Despite their low military rank and position, such defectors could often supply valuable, even sensational, intelligence.

At the time we were not interested in the *razvedka* advisers' demand—what American *serzhant* would defect to Romania anyway? Soon after President Kennedy was shot, though, we began concentrating on the advisers' defector tale. To our surprise we learned that, before defecting to Moscow, Lee Harvey Oswald had been stationed as a radar operator at the super-secret Atsugi Air Base outside of Tokyo, and that some of the U-2 planes that flew over the Soviet Union took off from that Marine base.

6

RECRUITMENT IN JAPAN

O N September 12, 1957, the *USS Bexar* docked at Yokosuka, Japan, carrying a group of enlisted men who were being assigned as radar operators to the Marine Air Control Squadron No. 1 (MACS-1) at Atsugi Air Base outside Tokyo. Pvt. Lee Harvey Oswald was one of them. The function of MACS-1 was to direct U.S. military aircraft by radar, to communicate with the pilots by radio, and to scout for straying enemy aircraft, such as Soviet or Chinese, which would be intercepted by American planes. The base also included a cluster of some twenty buildings identified by signs as the Joint Technical Advisory Group, in reality an operational base belonging to the CIA, as well as a hangar housing the highly secret U-2 reconnaissance planes. The Marine Corps radar operators learned in their classified briefings that the strange utility plane, called the U-2 for short, was a reconnaissance project that was not to be discussed with anyone outside the radar unit. They also realized that the pilot requests for wind speeds aloft at 90,000 feet came in over the radio soon after a U-2 had disappeared off their radar screens, though their radars read up to only 45,000 feet. The world altitude record in those days was 65,889 feet.

For all these reasons, Atsugi Air Base was a "closed" military unit, and its personnel had special security clearances. For precisely the same reasons, the Soviet PGU considered Atsugi its most important military target in Japan. I learned this in November 1957 when I was summoned to East Berlin by DIE chief Doicaru and the

PGU's Colonel Rudenko to be briefed on the latest PGU requirements for information on the CIA's U-2 program.

At that time the PGU and its sister services were fully consumed with the *serzhant* hysteria, leading to recruitments in the bars and nightclubs clustered around American bases. One of the main DIE jobs in the 1950s was to infiltrate those bars with loose young women recruited as agents, and one of my principal tasks as station chief in West Germany was to use those women and other agents to spot approachable American servicemen and entrap them in love affairs or appeal to other vulnerabilities. That was the general avenue of approach that my DIE station in West Germany had used for Konrad, the *serzhant* assigned at the U.S. air base in Wiesbaden spotted for recruitment.

What happened to Oswald when he reached Atsugi? The investigative documents concerning that period of his life describe him as a quiet and shy young man who liked to read nonfiction books "like *Mein Kampf* . . . or *The Decline and Fall of the Roman Empire*," and who enjoyed discussing his interest in Marxist political theory. At first he would spend his liberties in the television room at the barracks, earning the derision of the rougher Marines who called him "Mrs. Oswald" and once threw him in the shower fully dressed. A few of the Marines, however, liked him for his blunt honesty and even admired him for his intelligence: "You could show him how to do something once and he'd know how to do it, even if it was pretty complicated." There was a touch of arrogance in Oswald, a belief in his unrecognized intellectual superiority, but, as one Marine put it: "Hell, we [enlisted men] all thought we were smarter and better than any of the officers, and Ozzie was just like the rest of us." Gradually Oswald found a camaraderie that he had never known before. His friends began taking him with them on their excursions to the bars in nearby Yamato and Yokohama, teaching him to drink and cheering him on when he finally had his first sexual experience with a Japanese bar girl. After a time, though, Oswald would occasionally "disappear to Tokyo on a two-day leave and refuse to discuss these trips with even his closest friends."

Would the PGU station in Tokyo have been as interested in this American *serzhant* as the Romanian DIE would have been? Certainly. U.S. Navy yeoman Nelson C. Drummond was just an ordinary *serzhant* assigned to a nondescript job when he was recruited by the Soviets in London at about this time, but by the time of his arrest in 1962 he had betrayed so many Navy secrets that he received a life sentence. Oswald was not only a *serzhant* working inside a base that was a PGU priority target but he was also a radar controller, and that was exactly what Colonel Rudenko asked me to look for at the end of 1958, when he summoned me to that emergency meeting in East Berlin to tell me that the PGU had made the U-2 a priority.

Could it really have been possible for a U.S. serviceman who often spent his evenings socializing in bars around his base and loudly proclaiming his sympathy for Marxism to escape the spider's web stretched across such target areas by the Soviet-bloc espionage community? Possibly, but not likely. Based on my twenty-seven years' experience with Soviet intelligence, I am convinced that the PGU's eye fell on Oswald soon after he began frequenting the bars surrounding his base. There, after a couple of drinks, he would almost certainly have launched into his favorite subject, the virtues of theoretical Marxism. Balthasar, the janitor at the U.S. base near Munich, was not even an American, but the DIE station had managed to snare him because he would often visit a bar after leaving work at the American base. The data reviewed by the Warren Commission, supplemented by Edward Jay Epstein's interviews, show that Oswald clearly fell into the same pattern used by the DIE to hook Balthasar in West Germany.

Zack Stout, one of the Marines who was stationed at the Atsugi Air Base with Oswald, testified that Oswald had gotten involved with an attractive Japanese girl who "worked" as a hostess at the Queen Bee, one of the three most expensive nightclubs in Tokyo and one that catered to American senior officers and U-2 pilots. To take out a hostess from that club required paying not only for the girl but also for the business lost by the nightclub and its bar during her absence. Stout and other enlisted Marines frequently saw Oswald with this girl at their own cheap bars close to the base. They marveled that such a high-class hostess would go out with Oswald at all, and they wondered how he could afford her, since an evening with such a girl should have cost Oswald roughly the equivalent of a month's pay. Such an expense was also totally out of character for Oswald, who was consistently described throughout his life as a pennypincher.

Who, then, would have paid for Oswald's girl from the Queen Bee? To me there is no other answer but that the PGU must have been financing and manipulating that Queen Bee hostess who began spending her days and nights with Oswald, just as the DIE had paid for Konrad's girl Mimi. With the help of that Queen Bee girl, the PGU officer responsible for that night spot could assess Oswald for vulnerabilities and simultaneously smooth the way for his recruitment by making him the envy of his admiring fellow Marines, with free sex with a beautiful Japanese girl thrown into the bargain. The scenario follows the usual PGU pattern.

In fact Oswald seems to have been a PGU officer's dream come true, and there can be little doubt that he must have been rapidly recruited. In effect he had probably already recruited himself. The PGU would have had only to reach out and grasp his outstretched hand. Later Oswald himself would drop oblique hints that he had been recruited soon after arriving in Japan. In interviews he gave in Moscow in November 1959, shortly after he defected, to two sympathetic American journalists, Aline Mosby and Priscilla Johnson, Oswald said he had been planning that step for two years. Under the date of October 21, 1959, he also wrote in his "Historic Diary": "I have waited for 2 year [sic] to be accepted." Sometime after returning to the United States from the Soviet Union, Oswald would claim in a radio debate on the subject of Cuba that, as later reported by the New Orleans journalist William Stuckey, "it was in Japan that [Oswald] made up his mind to go to Russia and see for himself how a revolutionary society operates, a Marxist society." He also is said to have confided to George de Mohrenschildt, the Russian émigré who would befriend Oswald in Dallas after his return from Moscow, that "I met some Communists in Japan and they got me excited and interested, and that was one of my inducements in going to Soviet Russia, to see what goes on there."

Oswald's mention of the "Communists" he met in Japan at first seems disconcerting, particularly in view of his earlier statement in the Mosby interview that he had never met a Communist before arriving in Moscow, unless it was an old lady in New York who when he was a child had handed him a pamphlet on the Rosenbergs. It can, however, be supposed that in telling de Mohrenschildt about his contacts with Communists in Japan he was simply using an impromptu euphemism to describe his PGU contacts in talking to a politically broad-minded friend. (Or, as we shall see, Oswald may well have known that de Mohrenschildt would understand he meant the PGU.) In connection with Oswald's red herring of an old lady in New York, it is interesting to note that when the British government was in 1955 forced—from momentary lack of evidence for prosecution—to clear the famous PGU agent Kim Philby of charges brought against him by the House of Commons, Philby gave a triumphant press conference and told the assembled journalists that the last time he had knowingly spoken to a Communist had been in 1934.

On October 18, 1957, Oswald learned that his unit was to be shipped out to the South China Sea and the Philippines because the civil war in Indonesia was heating up. According to Stout, Oswald seemed unhappy about having to leave Japan. According to George Wilkins, another Marine serving with Oswald at Atsugi, on October 27, just before departure, Oswald shot himself in the arm with a derringer pistol he said he had ordered from a mail-order house in the United States, against regulations. The wound did not appear to be serious, and several of the Marines believed that Oswald had deliberately shot himself in order to remain in Japan. He stayed in the hospital for almost three weeks but was released just in time to board the *USS Terrell County* with his unit on November 20 and head for the Philippines.

By then Oswald was certainly fully engaged with the PGU and might, for the first time in his life, have felt appreciated for his intelligence and cleverness. He had found someone he could talk with about his passion for Marxism. It is no wonder that he might have tried to keep such a good thing going. In an attempt to force the Marine Corps to change his assignment, he may have injured himself just enough to get himself into the hospital but not enough to cause any lasting damage. The ploy did not quite succeed, but almost. With minor variations, it was a tactic that Oswald would use over and over again.

After three months at sea, Oswald and his unit returned to Atsugi, where he was court-martialed for having had an unregistered weapon, the derringer with which he had shot himself the previous October. He was sentenced to twenty days at hard labor, forfeiture of fifty dollars in pay, and reduction to the rank of private (thus nullifying his having passed the examination for corporal). Although he received a suspended sentence, he was placed on mess duty instead of being returned to radar duty. Immediately he put in for a hardship discharge, hoping, according to the other Marines, to be discharged in Japan, where he had made friends. His request was denied, whereupon he picked a fight with the sergeant who had put him on mess duty, and that landed Oswald in the brig for nearly a month. When he was finally released, on August 13, 1958, several of the Marines found him to be a changed man: cold, withdrawn, and bitter. According to Joseph Macedo, a fellow radar operator, Oswald complained: "I've seen enough of a democratic society here in MACS-1. When I get out I'm going to try something else." After that Oswald seemed to associate more infrequently than ever with the other Marines, often disappearing on passes to Tokyo.

It was perhaps at this point that Oswald conceived the idea of defecting to the Soviet Union. He must have felt that his friends were the Soviets, who loved and appreciated him, whereas his relationship with the Marine Corps had deteriorated badly. His prospects for accomplishing much of anything by staying in the Marines must have seemed slim. Far from encouraging his defection, however, his PGU handlers would certainly have pressed Oswald to stay just where he was, with the Marines in Japan, because that would have been where the PGU's Tokyo *rezidentura* would get the credit for his case. But remaining in the Marine Corps was probably not the future that the introverted and serious-minded Oswald envisioned for himself. In his bitterness and frustration with his life on the earthly soil of Japan, he may well have viewed defection to the workers' paradise of the Soviet Union as his just reward for being a faithful disciple of Marxism.

On November 8, 1959, then, after finally reaching Moscow, Oswald would write to his brother Robert, "Do you know . . . that I have waited to do this for well over a year[?]"

7

AN IDEAL AGENT

O NE OF the important keys to comprehending why Lee Harvey
Oswald put his life in the Soviets' hands lies in understanding him. What kind of a person was Oswald, and what made him vulnerable to recruitment by the Soviet PGU? Into what kind of agent might the PGU have wanted to mold him? Finally, of course, why did Oswald kill the president?

Lee Harvey Oswald was born in New Orleans on October 18, 1939, two months after the death of his father, a collector for an insurance company. His mother, Marguerite Oswald, was apparently neither financially nor emotionally capable of raising her three sons by herself. Her two older boys, John Pic, born in 1932 during a previous marriage, and Robert Oswald, born in 1934, were essentially brought up in a children's home, and they entered military service as soon as they turned seventeen. The younger Lee spent most of his youth tagging along with his mother as she moved from place to place, seeking to make a life for herself. Except for a brief period spent near Fort Worth, Texas, during an unsuccessful remarriage, throughout most of Lee's childhood Marguerite lived in New Orleans and worked at a succession of low-paying jobs, leaving Lee largely to amuse himself at home alone during the hours when he was not in school.

After Robert had followed John into military service, in August 1952 Marguerite took Lee with her to New York City, where John, by then married, was assigned to duty with the Coast Guard. At first Marguerite and Lee stayed with John and his wife, and when that caused friction they moved into a place of their own. Although Lee had not had problems with school in either Texas or New Orleans, in New York he did not get along with the other children and began playing hooky, watching television at home alone or later roaming the city by himself. Because of his truancy, on April 16, 1953, the Children's Court in the Bronx—where Lee and his mother were then living—remanded him for psychiatric observation and diagnosis to Youth House, where he remained until May 7. There he was given psychological tests, which, according to house psychologist Irving Sokolow, indicated "present intellectual functioning in the upper range of bright normal intelligence." All his scores were average or better for his age group. The chief house psychiatrist, Dr. Renatus Hartogs, found him to be shy, insecure, and withdrawn, with a "vivid fantasy life turning around the topics of omnipotence and power, through which he tries to compensate for his present shortcomings and frustrations." Dr. Hartogs recommended that he be released, since there was no indication of "neurological impairment or psychotic mental changes."

Years later, upon his defection to Moscow in 1959, in his interview with Aline Mosby, Oswald said he had first become interested in Marxist ideology at the age of fifteen, when he was living in New York. He explained that "an old lady handed me a pamphlet about saving the Rosenbergs," adding rather theatrically for Mosby's benefit, "I looked at that paper and I still remember it for some reason, I don't know why."

Julius and Ethel Rosenberg had been convicted of treason in 1951 and sentenced to death. As loyal and disciplined agents for the Soviet government, they never confessed but instead claimed consistently and eloquently to be "the first victims of American Fascism," right up to the time of their execution in June 1953. Possibly in New York the young Oswald might have run across anti-American propaganda connected with the Rosenbergs, but it is unlikely that sympathy for two Americans who steadfastly denied being Communist spies would have been enough to turn an introverted and naive young man toward Marxism. Oswald's mention of the Rosenbergs is doubly suspect because, as we shall see, by the time of the 1959 interview he had surely been carefully coached by the PGU in how to behave with the American press, and because the Rosenberg case remained for years the PGU's favorite all-purpose vehicle for anti-American propaganda.

In January 1954, Oswald and his mother returned to New Orleans, where he remained the same loner he had been before. People who knew him remembered a "quiet, solitary and introverted boy who read a great deal and whose vocabulary made him quite articulate." He completed ninth grade, then just before his sixteenth birthday dropped out of tenth grade after forging a note from his mother saying that she and her son were moving to San Diego. "San Diego" was evidently Oswald's private euphemism for the Marine Corps, where he dreamed of joining his brother Robert. He even went so far as to persuade his mother to sign a false affidavit stating that he was seventeen, and he used it to try to join up. But the Marine Corps was not fooled by it and sent him away to wait another year. Meanwhile, according to his mother, Oswald devoured the Marine Corps manual his brother had given him.

Instead of returning to school, Oswald spent the next year working at a succession of jobs as an office messenger or clerk, and it was during this period that he began reading Marxism at the public library. At one point he became somewhat friendly with Palmer McBride, a fellow messenger at a dental laboratory who shared his interest in classical music. According to McBride, Oswald, who was always extolling the virtues of communism, tried to persuade McBride to go along with him in trying to join the Communist party in order "to take advantage of their social functions," or alternatively to make contact with the Youth League of the Socialist party. Oswald also wrote to the Socialist Party of America asking for literature and information on youth groups he might join.

The picture one gets is of a lonely young man just waking up to the excitement of abstract ideas and eagerly seeking a support group of like-minded friends. There is no indication that he found one. Instead he was again uprooted by his mother, who took him along on her next move in the summer of 1956, back to Fort Worth, Texas.

On October 18, 1956, Oswald turned seventeen. With his mother's written consent, six days later in Dallas he enlisted in the

Marine Corps and requested training to become a radar controller, a field for which only young men of higher-than-average intelligence were chosen. He passed the physical, did fairly well on the aptitude tests, and was sent to San Diego for basic training.

After Oswald's enlistment he spent almost a year at various bases in California, Florida, and Mississippi, receiving first basic training and then instruction as a radar operator. In accordance with standard Marine procedures, as one of the first priorities he received intensive training in marksmanship. On December 21, 1956, Oswald qualified with two points to spare as a sharpshooter, the middle of three levels on the Marine scale of marksman–sharpshooter–expert. That placed him slightly above average in the Marine Corps and thus made him an excellent shot compared with the average civilian male his age. He was, however, still only seventeen, and his level of marksmanship at that age is essentially irrelevant to his later prowess. More important is the fact that Oswald liked guns, and that his Marine training showed him to be a good student when it came to learning how to use them. Not only would he later sometimes go squirrel and rabbit hunting with his brother Robert, but there was a thread of fascination with guns running throughout his life. "He always did like hunting and fishing," his brother Robert would write after the assassination.

In fact, Oswald bought a rifle with some of the first money he ever earned, after getting a job as a messenger in the fall of 1955.

During his Marine training Oswald continued to be a shy and introverted young man who did not mix easily with others. While assigned to Keesler Air Force Base in Biloxi, Mississippi, for radar training, his classmates assumed he was visiting his mother when he used most of his weekend passes to travel the roughly one hundred miles to New Orleans; but in fact his mother was then living in Texas, and his relatives in New Orleans remember getting only a single call from him at the time. Nevertheless, there is no factual basis for supposing that he was doing anything more on those weekends than just exploring by himself, as he had done in New York and would continue to do throughout his life. No wonder he would go off on his own: when he was with his classmates from the radar operator course, they teased him for his meekness, nicknaming him

"Ozzie the Rabbit" after a contemporary cartoon character. In the end he surprised them, though, by finishing seventh in his class of thirty.

Let us pause here to recall the Soviet pattern for recruiting agents. Until 1956 the PGU bible defined three ways to recruit foreign agents: through ideological affinity, through compromising materials, or through financial remuneration. Before World War II and for a decade thereafter, ideological affinity proved to be the most successful method, producing valuable agents such as the Rosenbergs and the famous British traitors Kim Philby, Donald Maclean, and Guy Burgess. After the 1956 Soviet invasion of Hungary the ideological means became obsolete, having lost its practical appeal in the West. That forced the bloc intelligence community to replace it with what was called "gradual enticement," which entailed having the case officer develop a friendly relationship with the target and then cement the recruitment with a payment of tax-free money after it had become too late for the target to back out of the relationship and report where his sudden affluence had come from.

Oswald, on the other hand, must have been a real surprise for the PGU, because of both his devotion to Marxism and his lack of interest in money. How would the PGU have reacted after reading Oswald's biography? The defector Oleg Gordievsky, a former PGU station chief in London, cites the following statement by Konon Molody, a highly acclaimed PGU "illegal resident" (or undercover operator) running agents in England in the late 1950s and early 1960s, as being a good description of the perfect PGU recruitment target at that time.

> A good agent is one whose vital statistics are the following: he works, for example, in a military department and holds a middle-ranking but key position giving him access to information; he doesn't aspire to higher office, has a chip on his shoulder about being a failure (let's say that ill health prevented him [from] finishing studies at the general staff college; he drinks (an expensive habit); he is critical of his own government. . . . [Agents with] a firm ideological base [are] of course preferable [but sadly have become] a very rare breed.

With only a ninth-grade education, Oswald could scarcely have aspired to a much higher position in the military than he had already attained. He had a chip on his shoulder because he believed that his intellectual abilities were not sufficiently recognized, and he harbored resentments over his family's poverty. He was beginning to develop a taste for drink and women (though later he would be abstemious on both counts). Best of all, from the PGU's point of view, he was not only critical of the American government but was well on the way to becoming firmly indoctrinated in Marxism (such as he understood it). By the time he arrived in Japan, where he would also be accessible, Oswald certainly represented an intelligence dream for the PGU.

What tasks would the PGU have given Oswald after recruiting him? In those days the PGU's primary emphasis was on documentary materials, and I am sure that Oswald would have been asked to turn over any operating manuals he could get his hands on, especially those for radar equipment, and to copy the contents of all code books. That was what the PGU asked from Balthasar and Konrad at that time, and I see no reason for it to have treated Oswald differently. In fact it appears that the PGU never slackened its interest in such documents. John Walker, the *serzhant* recruited by the PGU in 1968, supplied exactly the same kinds of materials until he was arrested by the FBI seventeen years later. At the 1986 sentencing of Walker's son and espionage accomplice, the twenty-three-year-old Michael Walker, who had been an operations clerk aboard the U.S. carrier *Nimitz*, it was disclosed that Michael had stolen "more than fifteen hundred secret documents" on weapons systems and defense planning from the U.S. Navy and sold them to the PGU through his father.

Apart from obtaining documentary materials, Oswald's case officer must also have carefully debriefed him on the capabilities of American radar and on his knowledge of Soviet aircraft. Oswald should also have been asked to provide personality sketches of all the American servicemen he knew. And he was certainly instructed to keep his eyes and ears open for anything he might learn about the mysterious U-2 plane. The PGU apparently told him to buy a camera and take pictures at his base, for George Wilkins, a Marine serving with him at Atsugi, said he taught Oswald how to use the camera he had bought, and that Oswald would then walk around the base "taking pictures of the various objects that apparently interested him—such as the radar height-finding antennas." Oswald is also reported to have shown a keen interest in the briefings on classified material given by his unit's intelligence officer at Atsugi.

8

WORKING FOR THE PGU

I N September 1958, a year after Oswald arrived at Atsugi, the Communist Chinese stirred up a new international crisis over the Nationalist islands of Quemoy and Matsu in the Taiwan Strait, and Oswald and his unit boarded the *USS Skagit* for Formosa. There Oswald evidently felt homesick for Japan—and probably for the meetings with his PGU case officer who, as was the standard PGU procedure for such cases, must have smothered Oswald in the praise he had spent his whole life seeking. One midnight he was found shaking and crying and slumped against a tree at his guard-duty post, having fired his rifle several times at an alleged group of men in the woods. Charles Rhodes, the Marine who found him, be-lieved Oswald had planned the shooting incident to get himself sent back to Japan: "Oswald liked Japan and wanted to stay." On Octo-ber 6 he was returned to Atsugi for medical treatment. This time it seems he succeeded in forcing the hand of the Marine Corps.

After a few days in the hospital, instead of rejoining his unit in Formosa Oswald was assigned to general radar duty at Iwakuni Air Base, located some 430 miles from Tokyo. There Owen Dejanovich, who had gone to radar school in Mississippi with him, found that Oswald had in the interim grown extremely bitter and now went around spouting slogans about American imperialism and capitalist exploitation. His fellow Marines occasionally saw him at a local bar in the company of an attractive Eurasian girl, described by one, Dan Powers, as a half-Russian who was teaching Oswald the Russian language, according to what Oswald had told him.

It is difficult to imagine that Oswald the loner had by himself been able to find a Russian teacher in that remote area where he certainly knew no local residents. More likely the PGU decided it was now time to encourage Oswald's desire to learn Russian. At that time it was a priority for the PGU and its sister services to penetrate the units of the U.S. Department of Defense's NSA working in West Germany, Italy, and Japan. These units specialized in intercepting secret Soviet transmissions and decoding their contents, and the PGU anxiously wished to open a window into one of them. Strict instructions from the PGU required the sister services to persuade their *serzhant* agents to agree to learn foreign languages and to apply for a job at one of the NSA posts abroad. A knowledge of Russian would not only help Oswald get into such a unit, it should also land him a job on its Soviet desk. Oswald apparently liked the pretty language instructor and jumped at the chance to learn Russian in preparation for his intended defection to the Soviet Union, the country where it seems he had by then set his heart on spending the rest of his life.

Oswald finally left Japan on November 2, 1958, on board the *USS Barrett*. Upon arrival in San Francisco he took thirty days' leave to visit his mother and go squirrel hunting with his brother, then on December 22 he reported for radar duty at the Marine Air Control Squadron No. 9 (MACS-9) at El Toro Air Base in Santa Ana, California. John Donovan, the officer in command of Oswald's radar crew at El Toro, described him as "competent, very competent" in any job he saw him handle. Like the other Marines assigned there, Oswald had a much higher than average IQ–but unlike the others Oswald was almost solely interested in international affairs, not in women and sports. He liked to ask a passing officer about some matter of foreign affairs, then afterward remark to Donovan: "If men like that are leading us, there is something wrong–when I obviously have more intelligence and more knowledge than that man." He knew the names of many philosophers, but his knowledge did not go much beyond the names. He expressed particular interest in Hegel and the subject of social revolutions. When he talked with people, however, he did not seem to be seeking information but rather showing how much he knew–"He had his mind made up and was willing to discuss that point of view with anyone."

According to the Marines in his unit, the work at El Toro was not demanding, and Oswald spent much of his free time studying Russian by himself. He subscribed to a Russian-language newspaper and would answer with *da* and *nyet* when his fellow Marines teased him about his interest in the Russian language and in communism. He seemed to enjoy having the nickname "Oswaldovich" and being jokingly called a "Russian spy." On February 25, 1959, he took a test in the Russian language and received an overall grade of "poor." Yet he had apparently achieved some proficiency in that difficult language.

While he was stationed at El Toro, Oswald's contact with the PGU should have been essentially impersonal. Although the PGU had officers stationed at the Soviet consulate in San Francisco at the time, the extent of FBI coverage of their movements made the PGU reluctant to use officers under official cover to hold *personal* meetings with agents anywhere in the United States. During those years the PGU operational pattern required that the communications plan for every important DIE agent in the United States be based on *impersonal* means of receiving their information. The PGU favored the use of dead drops for agents who were able to provide intelligence on unprocessed film. In the few cases where agents had large volumes of documents to deliver, such as agents involved in scientific and technological intelligence (S&T), the PGU also used lockers at train and bus stations. The agent had to dead-drop the locker key to the PGU by some simple means, such as by taping it underneath a predesignated park bench, where it could be retrieved unobtrusively, usually by an officer under illegal cover. Personal meetings with valuable agents living in the United States were to be held in third countries. Mexico was considered the most desirable place for contacts with the bloc's most important agents from the United States, because the PGU considered the Mexican counterintelligence service weak, corrupt, and inefficient. Even the communications plan for the DIE's agent Balthasar, who lived in West Germany, forbade his attending personal meetings there—he had to travel to Austria every six months to meet with his case officer.

The one specific indication of the nature of Oswald's contact with the PGU during this period came from Nelson Delgado, Oswald's bunkmate at El Toro. Delgado recalled that toward the end of Oswald's tour of duty there, he noticed a stack of "spotter" photographs showing front and profile views of a fighter plane among Oswald's papers. Oswald stuffed the photographs into a duffel bag along with some other things, and Delgado agreed to deposit the bag in a locker at the Los Angeles bus station for him and bring him back the key. For this Delgado believed Oswald had given him two dollars. Assuming Delgado's recollection is accurate, there can hardly be any explanation other than espionage for a duffel bag containing classified material to be placed in a public locker.

Quite possibly Oswald also included in such duffel bags some of the new information on the height at which the U-2 planes were flying in their practice runs over that part of southern California. According to Francis Gary Powers, the U-2 pilot whom the Soviets shot down, at El Toro Oswald had access "not only to radar and radio codes but also to the new MPS-16 height-finding radar gear," and the height at which the U-2 flew was the most highly classified secret about it. On the other hand, it is equally possible that Oswald might have saved his best information for personal meetings with his PGU case officer held across the border in Tijuana, Mexico. Or he might even have used it as his ticket to the Soviet Union, intending to turn it over to the PGU only when he was safely in Moscow. As a defector myself—though in the opposite direction—I can easily imagine Oswald's wanting to arrive in Moscow bearing some spectacular piece of information. Specific details on the height flown by the U-2 would have more than qualified, for that was then the number one Soviet intelligence priority.

During the long and uneventful radar watches at El Toro, Delgado, a Mexican American, began teaching Oswald Spanish, finding him a willing and able student. Oswald also bought a Spanish-English dictionary so he could learn vocabulary on his own. Once, the two of them went to Tijuana for the weekend, but there Oswald soon went off on his own, allegedly to meet "friends." It is highly unlikely that in that short time the solitary Oswald had been able to make any outside friends whom he might have been meeting in Tijuana. John Donovan also recalled that Oswald "took a couple of trips down to Tijuana." Only a few miles from Oswald's base, Tijuana must have been selected by the PGU as a place to hold personal meetings with Oswald while he was assigned at El Toro. Such meetings would have helped the PGU instruct Oswald periodically in new tasks and arrange his eventual travel to the Soviet Union.

According to Delgado, at El Toro Oswald showed great interest in Fidel Castro's movement and then in the Cuban revolution itself when it occurred in January 1959. Later that year, in August, Oswald tried to interest Delgado in running off to Cuba with him to emulate Maj. William A. Morgan, a former sergeant in the U.S. Army who had joined Castro in Cuba. Oswald also expressed interest in visiting the Cuban consulate in Los Angeles. The Cuban revolution was evidently something new and exciting for a person like Oswald who was generally intrigued with Marxism. In the end, though, he remained consistently loyal to the Soviets.

Describing what information Oswald could have compromised, John Donovan recalled: "He had access to the location of all bases in the west coast area, all radio frequencies for all squadrons, all tactical call signs, and the relative strength of all squadrons, number and type of aircraft in a squadron, who was the commanding officer, the authentication code of entering and exiting the ADIZ, which stands for Air Defense Identification Zone. He knew the range of our radio. And he knew the range of the surrounding units' radio and radar." Although some of the codes were routinely changed or would have been changed after Oswald's defection, according to Donovan there was no way of changing some things, "such as the MPS-16 height-finding radar gear, [which] had recently been integrated into the Marine Corps system, . . . [and the] TPX-1, which is used to transfer radio–radar and radio signals over a great distance."

With Oswald's service in the Marine Corps coming to an end at the close of 1959, the PGU had to begin working on his future intelligence career. It is noteworthy that on March 19 that year Oswald applied to Albert Schweitzer College in Churwalden, Switzerland, a small, new liberal arts school—certainly unearthed by the PGU, just as the DIE had found a similar college for Konrad when he was nearing the end of his term in the Marine Corps. On his own

Oswald could not have found that unknown college in a remote Swiss town. Nor by himself could he have afforded to attend it, his savings after serving three years in the Marine Corps totaling only some $950. After paying for his passage to Europe, when he arrived in England he declared to customs that he had a mere seven hundred dollars. Moreover, nothing in his past indicated that he cared about formal education, and in fact he complained to Donovan that the Marine Corps "ought to be able to recognize talent such as his own, without a given magic college degree." On the other hand, an honorably discharged Marine Corps veteran with a college degree from Switzerland and a knowledge of Russian and German would have certainly been favored for employment at NSA.

As reasons for wanting to attend that college, Oswald wrote (surely with PGU coaching, though with his own erratic spelling): "In order to acquire a fuller understanding of that subject which interest me most, Philosophy. To meet with Europeans who can broaden my scope of understanding. To receive formal Education by Instructors of high standing and character. To broaden my knowledge of German and to live in a healty climate and Good moral atmosphere." On March 23, 1959, Oswald passed tests at El Toro that gave him the equivalent of a high school diploma and would allow the Churwalden school to accept him. The facts of Oswald's actual application to Churwalden, the high-flown wording of that application, and the twenty-five-dollar deposit he sent to the school on June 19, 1959, after being accepted, suggest that he was following the path the PGU intended in preparation for a future career as an agent.

After he was accepted by the Albert Schweitzer College, Oswald wrote to his brother Robert, "Pretty soon I'll be getting out of the Corps and I know what I want to be and how I'm going to be it."

9

A SECRET TRIP TO MOSCOW

THE PGU had little personal contact with Oswald after his return to the United States from Japan. By the time he left the Marine Corps, the PGU may have found it difficult to keep him motivated in the direction it wanted rather than the direction he wanted. Unable to wean him from his defection fixation, the PGU appears to have humored him momentarily by offering him a visit to Moscow. The trip would have had to be made clandestinely so as not to compromise the future activities that the PGU had in mind for Oswald. The Moscow visit could have been described to him as a reward for the information he had so far provided.

It was common practice within the Soviet-bloc foreign intelligence community to reward ideologically motivated agents with secret trips inside the bloc. Because such agents usually refused to take money for their intelligence cooperation, they were often provided with secret savings accounts in the local currency, which they could draw upon during their trips inside, and with lifetime annuities for such time as they might eventually decide to retire to a bloc country. For example "Hans," a West German employed at the Hoechst chemical firm who had offered his services to the DIE for ideological reasons, refused to accept payment for the valuable technological intelligence he provided. Therefore in 1958 the DIE rewarded him with a free trip to Romania so that he could enjoy a week of luxurious living there. To protect his future as an intelligence agent, Hans's trip to Romania was, of course, arranged "black," that is, with no overt record of its having taken place. His case officer instructed him to tell his friends and family that he was planning to visit Spain for a week. Hans's case officer also gave him a stack of picture postcards from Spain and asked him to write greetings on them and address them to his relatives, friends, and fellow workers. Hans traveled on his own to Vienna, where he was given a Romanian passport and boarded a Romanian Tarom flight for Bucharest. At the same time a DIE illegal officer documented as Hans spent a week at various Spanish hotels, from where he mailed the postcards Hans had written earlier and turned over to his case officer.

Three separate events convince me that by mid-1959 Oswald must already have provided the PGU with information on the U-2's flight altitude, and that he therefore deserved to be rewarded with a secret trip to Moscow. First, when the DIE assigned me to West Germany as chief of station in 1957, the annual package of PGU requirements included only general references to U.S. high-altitude reconnaissance planes, indicating that Moscow knew something about their existence but had no specific technical data. The requirements at that time therefore asked for anything at all, including rumors, about their shape, technical characteristics, and operational flight altitude. The new PGU requirements on the American reconnaissance planes that the DIE station in West Germany received in the summer of 1959, however, contained the notation that, according to unconfirmed information, the U-2 could fly at altitudes of "about 30,000 meters" (the altitude noted by the men in Oswald's radar unit at Atsugi). The DIE station in West Germany was asked to make a special effort to confirm that information.

Second, almost one year before the U-2 was shot down, approximately in the early summer of 1959, Petr Semenovich Popov, an officer in the Soviet GRU who was cooperating with the CIA, passed the CIA a message indicating that the Soviets had "definite knowledge of specifics of the U-2 program." Evidently the Soviets' knowledge of the U-2 was at that time not yet sufficient to enable them to shoot one down, but after October 1959 the CIA suspended all U-2 flights anyway. The suspension was probably ordered because of a few crashes, but the CIA was perhaps also influenced by Popov's report as well as by a threat Oswald made on a visit to the U.S. embassy in Moscow on October 31, 1959, when he said he would tell the Soviets "all information concerning the Marine Corps and his specialty therein, radar operation, as he possessed." (Popov himself was arrested by the KGB in October 1959, having been compromised by George Blake, a PGU penetration of British foreign intelligence, who knew about the case.) In my view, Popov's report to the CIA on the U-2 can be seen as independent confirmation that the PGU indeed had specific information on the U-2's flight altitude by the time of Oswald's trip to Moscow in early October 1959.

The third point is that, a few weeks after the U-2 was shot down, the PGU began hammering the DIE to obtain *a defector*. This new slogan convinced DIE management that a defector, not an agent in the field, had provided the intelligence that had enabled Moscow to shoot down the U-2. Since as far as I know Oswald was the only defector in PGU hands at that time who had knowledge of the U-2, he must have been the source of that highly prized information—as even Powers, the downed U-2 pilot, also suspected. Such valuable intelligence would have more than entitled Oswald to a trip to the Soviet Union and probably also to an eventual retirement pension and even a Soviet medal.

There were other reasons for the PGU to bring Oswald to Moscow. In those days the PGU was under strong pressure to provide the Soviet Air Defense Command with intelligence that would allow it to curb secret American flights over Soviet territory, and it would have been extremely useful to have Oswald minutely debriefed by military experts on American reconnaissance flights. Every new U-2 flight threatened to compromise Khrushchev's efforts to persuade the world that the Soviet Union had acquired air superiority over Washington's capabilities. For the PGU, time was of the essence.

If it is likely that a PGU officer met with Oswald in Tijuana, there is good reason to believe that there they set up a plan for the operational trip to Moscow with its combined purposes. Oswald's service in the Marine Corps was scheduled to end on December 7, 1959, but on August 17 he applied for a dependency discharge, claiming that his mother needed his support and submitting documents from her confirming her injury the previous December, when a large candy jar had fallen on her nose at work. In early September Oswald applied for a new passport, stating that he intended to "attend the College of A. Schweitzer, Switzerland, and the University of Turku, Turku, Finland," and might travel to England, France, Switzerland, Germany, Finland, Russia, Cuba, and the Dominican Republic. His passport was issued on September 10, 1959.

Oswald was discharged on September 11, and on September 14 he arrived in Fort Worth, where his mother was then living. He clearly had no intention of staying around to help her financially. After two days he left for New Orleans, to embark on the journey that would take him to Moscow. On September 20, just before sailing, he wrote his mother from New Orleans: "Well, I have booked passage on a ship to Europe. . . . Just remember above all else that my values are very different from Robert's or yours." From that statement it can be supposed that by then Oswald had no intention of attending the school in Switzerland and following through on the PGU's career plans for him. He hoped to defect and live out the rest of his life in the workers' paradise.

Arriving in New Orleans, Oswald immediately went to a travel agency and booked passage for France on the *SS Marion Lykes*, a freighter with ten cabins. He paid $220.75 for the one-way ticket, and on the steamship company's application form he described himself as a "shipping export agent" going abroad for two months. The freighter sailed on September 20, two days behind schedule. During the eighteen-day crossing Oswald and the three other passengers ate at the same table in the evening. George B. Church, a retired lieutenant colonel in the U.S. Army who had boarded the freighter together with his wife, recalled that during the voyage Oswald had vaguely mentioned plans to study "philosophy or psychology" in Europe, and that, unlike the other passengers, he had avoided being photographed. "Whenever I got my camera out to take some pictures, he would head in the other direction. He told us he didn't want his picture taken," Mrs. Church testified. When she asked Oswald for his home address so that she could send him a Christmas card, Oswald looked suspiciously at her, asked why she cared, and when he eventually gave her his mother's address he misspelled his name as "Oswalt." The other passenger on board, Billy Joe Lord, a young student who was Oswald's cabinmate, recalled that Oswald did not wish to talk about himself. After the first few days he spent most of the voyage alone in his cabin, not even appearing for meals. On October 8 the freighter docked at Le Havre, where its passengers disembarked.

These three passengers from the *SS Marion Lykes* were the last reliable witnesses to identify Oswald before October 31, 1959, when he visited the U.S. embassy in Moscow. What, then, can we assume happened to Oswald after he arrived in Le Havre? The Warren Commission report states flatly that Oswald "went directly to Helsinki, Finland, by way of Le Havre, France, and London, England, arriving at Helsinki on Saturday, October 10, 1959." The report goes on to state that "Oswald probably arrived in Helsinki too late in the evening to have applied for a visa at the Soviet Union Consulate that night. In light of the rapidity with which he made connections throughout the entire trip, he probably applied for a visa early on Monday, October 2, 1959. On October 14, he was issued Soviet Tourist Visa No. 403339 good for a 6-day visit in the U.S.S.R. He left Helsinki on a train destined for Moscow on October 15."

When we in the DIE's management read the Warren Commission report, we were stunned by that body's naiveté in matters of intelligence. There is no single independent confirmation to substantiate the commission's conclusions, which were based on passport stamps and travel records that the PGU could easily have falsified. And there is good reason to question those conclusions. The only record of Oswald's travel in this period that the PGU could not have falsified outright is the British passport control report showing that *a* Lee Harvey Oswald entered the United Kingdom at Southampton on Friday, October 9. He declared that he was carrying seven hundred dollars on him and intended to spend one week in England before going on to college in Switzerland. The British report says nothing about his intending to transit Finland or visit the Soviet Union.

The other three passengers on the freighter, who upon arrival at Le Havre immediately took the boat train to Southampton, did not recall seeing Oswald on that train. A stamp in Oswald's passport indicates that on that same day he took an international flight from London's Heathrow Airport, and another stamp shows that he arrived in Helsinki the following day, or apparently very late that night. There was, however, no direct flight from London to Helsinki during this period. Moreover, Oswald's name did not appear as passenger on any flight that took off from Heathrow that day, or on any flight arriving in Helsinki from other European cities within this travel window.

There are also no independent records or witnesses to confirm that Oswald left Helsinki by train on October 15, or that he arrived in Moscow the following day, as the Soviets would later claim and his passport would show. His name was found in the registration records of two four-star hotels in Helsinki, the Torni for the night of October 9, and the Klaus Kurki for the next five days. Both hotels were very expensive luxury accommodations, not the kind of place the frugal Oswald always selected for himself. In New Orleans he had stayed at the inexpensive Liberty Hotel, but six days at those Helsinki hotels would have set him back more than the cost of his entire Atlantic crossing. The steward of the *Marion Lykes* remembered Oswald for not having left the customary tip when he disembarked. When Oswald later traveled to Mexico in 1963, he stayed in a very inexpensive hotel costing him only $1.28 a night.

The Helsinki hotel registrations could have been forged by the PGU, which in those days operated with virtually a free hand in Finland. The country's president, Urho Kaleva Kekkonen, was a highly regarded PGU agent. This may also explain why Oswald's 1959 passport application listed the University of Turku as a possible destination, in addition to the school in Switzerland. Because Oswald had been accepted at the Swiss school for a term beginning in April 1960, the PGU might have considered the Turku school as a possible fallback destination for him until then, using its connections there to get him accepted on short notice.

There is no doubt in my mind that the PGU planned to bring Oswald into the Soviet Union clandestinely, for during those years there were few things the PGU emphasized to its case officers more strongly than the need to cloak their *serzhanty* in the utmost secrecy. It is also likely that the PGU planned to keep Oswald in Moscow no more than the customary one week, because it was operationally difficult to cover a longer absence. At the end of the week the PGU would have brought Oswald back to light and sent him perhaps first to the University of Turku and then to his designated college in Switzerland, with the long-range goal of having him qualify for a job at a target facility such as an NSA monitoring unit in West Germany. It is doubtful that the PGU, which would have wanted Oswald in its hands as soon as possible, would have allowed him to wander around Helsinki by himself for almost a week, as the hotel records indicated.

The simplest and most likely way for the PGU to have brought Oswald quickly and secretly to Moscow was to smuggle him onto a Soviet ship or airplane using a false passport or an entrance visa issued on a separate sheet of paper. Both these methods were widely practiced at that time by the PGU and its sister services. All Soviet Morflot (sea travel) and Aeroflot (air travel) representatives in the West were intelligence officers or cooptees (as were their Romanian counterparts), and it would have been child's play for the PGU to carry out such an operation. The week that the British passport records showed that Oswald wished to spend in England was probably originally intended as the cover story for the week the PGU intended to have Oswald in Moscow. Particularly in the absence of any witness reports of Oswald's travel to Southampton with the other passengers from his ship, it is quite possible that a PGU illegal officer, documented as Oswald, took the boat train and entered England that day. That was another common practice within the Soviet-bloc intelligence community at that time, and it continued for many years.

The case of Wladimir (Vlado) Dapcevic is relevant here. Based on information the Yugoslavs had obtained and passed on to the Romanians at this time, Dapcevic was working for the PGU, which had charged him to assassinate Josip Broz Tito, Yugoslavia's renegade Communist leader, with whom the Soviets had their differences. (Dapcevic's brother was the chief of Tito's protective security service, giving Dapcevic potential access to the leader.) At Tito's personal request, Romanian leader Nicolae Ceausescu had ordered the DIE's anti-terrorist unit secretly to kidnap Dapcevic, who was lured to Bucharest by the Yugoslavian espionage service, and to hand him over to Drasko Jurisic, the Yugoslavian federal secretary for internal affairs, who together with a small staff had come to Bucharest for that purpose. The DIE obliged. To divert attention from Romania, the day after Dapcevic had been secretly taken to Belgrade, a DIE illegal officer carrying the passport of the kidnapped man flew on a Sabena plane from Bucharest to Brussels—from where he later returned to Romania using a different passport. That move prompted Belgian authorities to believe for years that Dapcevic had not disappeared during his visit to Romania but had returned to Belgium.

The simplest and fastest way for the PGU to bring Oswald into Moscow "black" would probably have been to pick him up in Le Havre, drive him to Paris, and put him on an Aeroflot flight for Moscow using another identity. At the end of Oswald's week of meetings with the PGU in Moscow, the plan was probably to bring him back to Western Europe "black" while having an illegal using his documents exit from London for the Continent at the same time. This would allow Oswald to resume his own identity and perhaps continue on to the University of Turku.

When Oswald not only refused to leave the Soviet Union but compromised his presence there by appearing at the U.S. embassy on October 31, 1959, the PGU obviously had to change its cover story. Now Oswald would have to be shown as a young student who took a brief tourist trip to the Soviet Union before starting college in Finland. In other words, I suggest that the stamps in Oswald's passport showing his flight to Helsinki, his registration at the Helsinki hotels, and the record of his train trip from Helsinki to Moscow must all have been fabricated quickly after the fact, when the PGU saw that the planned cover story of his week in England was no longer viable.

10

SOVIET CITIZENSHIP DENIED

WHAT, then, was Oswald's reception in Moscow? Based on my knowledge of other cases run by the PGU and the Romanian DIE at about that time, he should have been quartered in a PGU safe house located away from downtown Moscow. There, according to the routine PGU procedure also instituted at the DIE, he would have been welcomed by one or two PGU officers, and his arrival would have been celebrated at a dinner given in his honor—just as the CIA celebrated my arrival in the United States. For the next couple of days Oswald should have been debriefed in great detail on his knowledge of the U-2 and other military matters, with breaks in the routine for some sightseeing in Moscow. After that a higher-ranking officer from the PGU's American Department should have come to join him for another festive dinner at the safe house, in anticipation of his new assignment. At this point Oswald would have been praised for all he had contributed thus far to the Communist cause, and the PGU would have outlined its plans and hopes for his future.

As he wrote to his brother Robert, however, Oswald—now that he had finally reached the land of his dreams and had so clearly earned his reward—seems to have been genuinely determined to become a Soviet citizen and never leave the Soviet Union. There is reason to believe that he refused his handler's proposals for returning to the West as a PGU agent and, when the PGU insisted, threatened to kill himself. That would have been fully consistent with his past behavior, as when he had shot himself or had staged an incident to get out of a Marine assignment.

How would Oswald's handlers have reacted in such a situation? Probably the same way I reacted when Hans, the West German agent at Hoechst, placed me in a similar situation. During Hans's secret 1959 visit to Romania, I brought Mihai Petri, then acting minister of foreign trade, to Hans's safe house. Petri expressed the gratitude of Romania's leader, Gheorghe Gheorghiu-Dej, for Hans's admiration for Romania's independence and added his own warm thanks for Hans's "extremely valuable" cooperation with "my men" in the Romanian Commercial Mission in Frankfurt. During the meeting Petri, who was in fact a deep-cover DIE officer, further tried to flatter Hans by expressing regret that he did not have people like him among his own advisers.

To our consternation, Hans took this casual remark literally, and a few hours later he told his DIE handlers that he had decided to repatriate to Romania and work for Petri. When I reported this new development to Colonel Rudenko, he directed that Hans be immediately moved from the safe house to a hotel, and that the DIE's technical operations department be asked to apply a tourist visa and an airport entrance stamp on his passport. "We must avoid any suspicion that 'Hans' might have been brought in 'black' or kidnapped into Romania," Rudenko explained. His plan also included organizing a press conference at the hotel, where Hans was to praise Romania's independence and announce his decision to move to Romania and work for its government. Hans was immediately moved to the Athénée Palace, a hotel for Westerners, and his passport was counterfeited to reflect that he had entered Romania legally. Just hours before the scheduled press conference, however, I was able to change his mind about moving to Romania. Evidently the PGU was not able to change the stubborn Oswald's mind.

It seems that when Oswald obstinately refused to leave the Soviet Union, his PGU handlers acted more or less the way the DIE did in Hans's case. They moved Oswald from the safe house to a hotel, in order to avoid the suspicion that he had been brought in "black" to Moscow, and they fabricated stamps and documents to "legalize" his entrance into the Soviet Union and tried to cover the period between his arrival in Le Havre on October 8, 1959, and his alleged arrival in Moscow a week later. I truly believe it was only now that the PGU built the legend that Oswald had walked into the Soviet embassy in Helsinki asking for a tourist visa, and that he had arrived in Moscow by train on October 16.

It was probably also then that the PGU applied in Oswald's passport a tourist visa (number 403339 of October 12, 1959) allegedly issued by the Soviet embassy in Helsinki. Helsinki was a good choice. At that time the PGU used Helsinki and Vienna as operational centers for smuggling people into the Soviet Union. In each city the PGU had a permanent team charged only with such operations. Their tasks ranged from taking Western businessmen engaged in illegal deals with Moscow, or Westerners recruited as agents who needed special training, and secretly slipping them into the Soviet Union. Occasionally they forcibly kidnapped people and secretly transported them across the border into the Soviet Union. The teams in both cities were subordinated to the PGU's Thirteenth Department ("wet affairs," kidnappings, etc.), had quite a large number of safe houses at their disposition, and were supplied with all the paraphernalia needed for such operations: specially modified cars, diplomatic license plates, seals for diplomatic pouches, etc. They also employed illegal officers infiltrated onto the staffs of several hotels, who were mainly used for the false registration of PGU agents or targets in order to cover the period of time they secretly spent in the Soviet Union. For operational and prestige reasons, the PGU–like the DIE–used only first-class hotels for this kind of operation. It was certainly no problem for the PGU to insert Oswald's name in the registration documents of the Torni and Klaus Kurki hotels.

While taking these measures, Oswald's PGU handlers probably continued their efforts to persuade him to return to the West, just as I did with Hans. Oswald, however, was not Hans. When Oswald realized that he could not instantly become a Soviet citizen, he tried to force the PGU's hand by slightly slashing his left wrist, in much the same way as he had tried to force the hand of the Marine Corps by marginally injuring himself. The doctors who performed the autopsy on Oswald's body in 1963 stated that, though there was a wound on the inside of his left wrist, it was in any case "not very deep." A confirmation that this was indeed the case is the fact that when he visited the U.S. embassy in Moscow on October 31, 1959, Oswald did not give American consular officials "any indication that he had recently received medical treatment," in spite of his supposed stay at the Botkin Hospital from October 21 to 28, as alleged in documents the Soviet government provided to the Warren Commission after Kennedy's assassination.

How would the PGU have handled Oswald's tantrum, besides treating the physical wound? From approximately October 16, when he was probably scheduled to return to Western Europe after the customary week of debriefings and briefings, until the moment he rebelled, the PGU would have used all its persuasive arguments to get him to agree to its plans. As a final step in winning Oswald over, the PGU evidently gave in to his insistence that he be allowed to visit the U.S. embassy and announce his intention to defect and to renounce his American citizenship. The PGU may have helped him write out the statement of intent that he brought to the embassy with him on October 31—the statement is undated, suggesting that the PGU may have wanted to allow itself some leeway in choosing the date he would be allowed to go. The statement shows an awareness of the formal conditions for renouncing one's citizenship, but in fact it had no effect on the process, which would have had to have been accomplished by a document prepared by an American consular officer.

According to his "Historic Diary," on October 31 Oswald took a taxi to the embassy; that was probably true, since he might have been observed at either the hotel or the embassy. The taxi was perhaps one of the many owned by the PGU (the DIE also had quite a few in Bucharest, for surveillance purposes). It was a Saturday afternoon, when the embassy was officially closed, as the PGU would of course have known. In order to placate him, the PGU probably took the calculated risk of letting Oswald visit the embassy, believing he would probably not be able to talk to anyone that day and certainly would not be able to complete the formalities for renouncing his citizenship. (Oswald's future usefulness to the PGU depended largely on his retaining his American citizenship.)

The stubborn, unruly Oswald did, however, at least succeed in meeting American consul Richard E. Snyder, who took Oswald's written statement but asked him to return the following Monday, when the embassy would be open and he would be able to process his request. Then, while talking with Snyder, Oswald got carried away, telling him "that he had been a radar operator in the Marine Corps, intimating that he might know something of special interest, and that he would give the Soviets any information concerning the Marine Corps and radar operation which he possessed."

Oswald's PGU handlers must have had a near heart attack on receiving the report of what Oswald had told Snyder. The PGU would have instantly recognized that his slip regarding his intent to betray Marine Corps secrets to the Soviets—which would have been routinely picked up by Soviet implanted microphones covering the embassy—might well jeopardize the future the PGU was planning for him as its agent in the West. (As of 1960 there were 134 listening devices mounted in key sections of the U.S. embassy in Moscow. From my own knowledge of Soviet-bloc domestic security services, I can say that the consular sections of the leading Western embassies were the prime target location for microphones, so as to cover contacts of local citizens with those embassies.) The PGU's first reaction was to stop Oswald from returning to the embassy. He was allowed to mail the embassy a letter dated November 3, giving the Hotel Metropole as his return address, in which he angrily protested his treatment at the embassy. He ended the letter by saying that, in the event he was granted Soviet citizenship, he would "request my government to lodge a formal protest regarding this incident." Thereafter the U.S. embassy was unable to talk with him or deliver any message to him at his hotel.

After Oswald's misbehavior at the embassy, the PGU's next step was to arrange for him to be interviewed by a few sympathetic foreign journalists, in order to eliminate any suspicion that he might have been kidnapped into the Soviet Union or was being held there against his will. Making the best of an unwelcome situation, the PGU presumably also wished to generate a little sympathetic propaganda in the West for Oswald's defection and his idealistic view of communism—just as the DIE had planned to do with Hans.

There is no independent confirmation that Oswald was actually moved into the Hotel Berlin, though he may have been, as the first step in making public his wish to defect, and in allowing the domestic KGB to become aware of his presence. (Ordinarily the PGU would have intended to keep the domestic KGB completely unaware of this case.) Oswald may or may not have actually been treated at the Botkin Hospital after the wrist-slashing incident. In any case, before he was allowed to visit the U.S. embassy he was moved to the larger and more American-tourist-oriented Hotel Metropole. Two American reporters who had been alerted to his case by the U.S. embassy on October 31 were unable to reach him at the hotel that day, however. The PGU needed almost two weeks to ensure that only kindly disposed journalists would see him, and to coach the restive and unpredictable Oswald on what to say at a press interview. He was presumably told to represent himself as a student, as that was the legend he had used for his trip to Europe, and not to mention his military service, so as not to raise suspicions that he was being or might be used for intelligence purposes. Oswald had just turned twenty, so the student story would have been perfectly credible.

On November 13, Aline Mosby, representing United Press International, was the first American journalist who succeeded in interviewing Oswald, talking to him in his hotel room. According to her notes, he told her: "I think you may understand and be friendly because you're a woman." Regarding his status, he said he had been told that he could remain in the Soviet Union and that job possibilities were being explored; the authorities thought it would probably be best, he said, to continue his education. The only other interview Oswald ever gave in the Soviet Union was to Priscilla Johnson, a representative of the North American Newspaper Alliance, whom he agreed to meet in her room at the Metropole on November 16. Johnson later described herself as being, in those days, an idealistic young woman who had majored in Russian and become a World Federalist. She found Oswald "very, very young and touching in his eagerness to stay in Russia," and she was impressed by his "extraordinary" commitment to communism in light of his age. Regarding his status, Oswald told Johnson that on that very morning a Soviet official had come to his room and "informed him that he could remain until a decision had been made what to do with him. It was virtually a promise that he could stay, and Lee was vastly relieved."

After these two interviews, Lee Harvey Oswald suddenly disappeared without a trace into the depths of the Soviet Union. On November 26 he wrote his brother Robert: "I want to, and I shall, live a normal happy and peaceful life here in the Soviet Union *for the rest of my life.*" Asking himself why "I and my fellow workers and communist's would like to see the present capitalist government overthrown," Oswald answered rhetorically that the U.S. government supported an economic system "which exploits all its workers. . . . America is a dieing country, I do not wish to be a part of it, nor do I ever again wish to be used as a tool in its military aggressions."

Oswald wrote his brother once more that year, on December 17, saying he would not write again and did not wish to hear from Robert. He explained, "I am starting a new life and I do not wish to have anything to do with the old life."

11

BOGUS DOCUMENTS

FOR THE entire period between Oswald's entrance into the Soviet Union sometime in October 1959 and his final departure (accompanied by the wife and child that he had meanwhile acquired) on June 2, 1962, there is very little factually verifiable information about his activities. With confidence it can be stated only that he visited the U.S. embassy in Moscow once in 1959 and four more times in 1961 and 1962; he was observed at the Hotel Metropole in Moscow on October 31, 1959, by a few American journalists and a couple of weeks later gave interviews to two of them; and in March and again in August 1961 he was seen in Minsk by American tourists. Russian émigrés living in Dallas who later met the Oswalds confirm that Marina Oswald knew Leningrad and spoke with a Leningrad accent, and that both Oswalds were familiar with the city of Minsk, where Oswald allegedly lived after his defection. The autopsy of Oswald's body performed in 1963 "showed that he had a scar on his left wrist and that it was of the kind that could have been caused by a suicide attempt"; this tends to confirm Oswald's alleged suicide attempt soon after his arrival in Moscow.

Everything else reported about Oswald's stay in the Soviet Union cannot be independently corroborated. Thus all other information cannot be taken at face value and must be considered to have been potentially subject to Soviet manipulation.

In 1964 the CIA drafted a set of questions for the Soviet government, designed to elicit data from the Soviets about the procedures under which Oswald had been processed and controlled during the two and a half years he had spent in the Soviet Union. The draft was, however, rejected by the Warren Commission. A commission memorandum dated February 24, 1964, explained that, according to the State Department, the CIA's draft would have provoked serious adverse diplomatic effects, and that the State Department "feels that the CIA draft carries an inference that we suspect that Oswald might have been an agent for the Soviet Government and that we are asking the Russian Government to document our suspicions." Instead the State Department proposed that the commission send to Moscow "a very short and simple request for whatever information the Russian authorities" had available on Oswald. The Warren Commission complied. It also asked the Soviet Union for statements from Soviet citizens who might have met Oswald during his residence in that country, but none were ever provided. Later, in response to a request from the House Select Committee on Assassinations relayed by the State Department, the Soviet government "informed the committee that all the information it had on Oswald had been forwarded to the Warren Commission, a statement that the committee greeted with skepticism, based on the advice it had received from a number of sources, including defectors from the KGB."

In 1977 Edward Jay Epstein, in the process of writing his book on Oswald, asked permission from the Soviet Foreign Ministry to interview some alleged witnesses to Oswald's life there. After a wait of nearly six months, "the request was turned down by [Foreign Minister] Andrey Gromyko on the grounds that none of the witnesses I requested to see desired to be interviewed."

According to the House Select Committee on Assassinations, the Soviet government turned over to the Warren Commission only "routine, official papers. None of them appeared to have come from KGB files, and there were no records of interviews of Oswald by the KGB, nor were there any surveillance reports." Among the documents received were copies of the postal correspondence between the Soviet embassy in Washington, D.C., and the Oswalds after their arrival in the United States in 1962. In my experience, that was in accordance with standard Soviet practice, based on the premise that the local security service (in this case the FBI) already had copies of all such correspondence anyway. A few other Soviet documents were supplied, such as the purported record of Oswald's treatment at the Botkin Hospital in Moscow. But neither the Warren Commission nor the House Select Committee was allowed to undertake any investigation on Soviet territory in connection with the contents of those documents.

When Oswald came from the Soviet Union, he also brought out with him a fragmentary manuscript describing life there, particularly in Minsk, where he supposedly lived for almost two and a half years. There were two other documents: a handwritten statement of Oswald's political philosophy and a question-and-answer paper that he seems to have written to prepare himself for a possible press conference upon arrival in the United States, though none took place. These two papers appear to have been copied from notes during the crossing to the United States on the *SS Maasdam* in June 1962. Handwriting analysis showed that both these documents, which are written on Holland America Line stationery, show evidence of having been written by Oswald "under conditions where wave and motor vibration existed."

The chief source of "information" about Oswald's stay in the Soviet Union is his "Historic Diary," which he brought with him to the United States in 1962. As already noted, even the otherwise credulous Warren Commission admitted that the diary was "not an accurate guide to the details of Oswald's activities" in the Soviet Union.

Edward Jay Epstein had the diary examined by Dr. Thea Stein Lewinson, "a psychologist who specializes in using handwriting as a diagnostic tool for determining states of mind," and her verdict was: "A microscopic examination of Oswald's handwriting in this diary indicates that the entire manuscript was written in one or two sessions." If so, it was probably written at approximately the time of the last entry, March 27, 1962, or at any rate shortly before Oswald's departure from the Soviet Union on June 1. It was also apparently copied in great haste, as suggested by the many spelling inaccuracies.

On the other hand, Oswald's "Historic Diary" is, in my view, interesting not for the "facts" it purports to relate but for the cover story and impressions that the PGU evidently wished Oswald to

take with him when he returned to the United States. Even the
early entries in the diary reveal little of the devout Marxist who arrived in the Soviet Union with his mind made up to stay there for
the rest of his life. In fact the entire diary seems to concentrate on
his eventual decision to redefect, even though his life in the Soviet
Union is pictured in relatively rosy terms, with lots of money,
friends, and parties. Almost nonexistent is the irascible real Oswald,
who upon arrival in the Soviet Union vowed he would "never return to the United States, which is a country I hate," as he wrote his
brother Robert.

Some of the locutions in the diary do sound like pure Oswald:
"I have waited for 2 year to be accepted," and "I am a Marxist, and
I waited two years for this I don't want to live in the U.S." More often, however, his Marxist convictions sound lukewarm at best, even
in entries dated in October 1959: "I explaine I am a communist,
ect.," and "I give vauge answeers about 'great Soviet Union.'"

In his "Historic Diary" Oswald writes that, as soon as he arrived
in Moscow on October 16, 1959, he went to the Hotel Berlin,
where his Intourist guide helped him write a letter to the Supreme
Soviet requesting Soviet citizenship. On October 21, however,
when his six-day visa was about to expire, he was told he had to
leave the country that evening. Alone in his hotel room, he decided
to end it all and slash his wrist; the guide arrived to find him bleeding into the bathtub, called an ambulance, and took him to the hospital, where he received five stitches and remained for six days.
Upon release, Oswald writes, he moved to the Hotel Metropole,
then visited the Soviet passport office to request Soviet citizenship
and permanent residence. After four days of sitting alone in his
room waiting for the telephone to ring, he took matters into his own
hands and visited the U.S. embassy to renounce his American citizenship, sure that "the Russians will except me after this sign of my
faith in them." There is, however, no indication whatsoever that Oswald ever applied for Soviet citizenship, nor did the Soviet government ever provide the U.S. government with any documents indicating such a step.

Oswald's diary claims that it was not until November 16, 1959,
that "a Russian official" came to his hotel room and notified him

that "I can remain in USSR till some solution is found with what to do with me." The date of this announcement, however, conflicts with what Oswald wrote about it in his first letter from Moscow to his brother Robert, dated November 8, 1959–in other words, eight days before the "Historic Diary" claims that it happened. In that letter, discussing "my decision to remain in the Soviet Union and apply for citizenship here," Oswald writes: "I have been told that I will not <u>have</u> to leave the Soviet Union if I do not care to. . . . I will not leave this country, the Soviet Union, under any conditions. . . . Someday, perhaps soon, and then again perhaps in a few years, I will become a citizen of the Soviet Union, but it is a very legal process, *in any event*, I will not have to leave the Soviet Union." Further in his diary, Oswald also claims it was only on January 4, 1960, that the passport office issued him "not the soviet citizenship as I so wanted, only a Residence document, not even for foringners but a paper called 'for those without citizenship.' Still I am happy. The offial says they are sending me to the city of 'Minsk.'" (As we shall see, it is unlikely that Oswald was sent to Minsk in 1960.)

From these conflicting statements about Oswald's status, all of which were potentially subject to Soviet control, it is clear that none of them can be taken as fact. Rather, Oswald's diary seems to have been indeed crafted by Soviet disinformation experts in accordance with the legend created by the PGU to cover the years he spent in the Soviet Union–as the DIE experts concluded after the assassination–and then copied out in Oswald's own hand. It was surely never intended that the diary would be made public and receive the close scrutiny it has. Its main purpose was simply to help Oswald himself remember who he was supposed to be and where he was supposed to have been, as well as who his supposed friends in the Soviet Union had been and what they were like. The title of the "Historic Diary" is particularly revealing. By the time Oswald left the Soviet Union, the PGU had probably assigned him the task that would indeed cement his place in history.

12

KHRUSHCHEV DECLARES WAR ON KENNEDY

O N November 9, 1960, John F. Kennedy was elected president. Khrushchev sent him a cordial message upon his election and another in January upon his inauguration, and he made it plain to the U.S. ambassador in Moscow, Llewellyn Thompson, that he was ready to meet the new American president. Khrushchev's other election present was his decision to free two downed U.S. airmen imprisoned virtually incommunicado in the Soviet Union. Captains Freeman D. Olmstead and John R. McKone, reportedly the only surviving crew of the RB-47 plane shot down by the Soviets on July 1, 1960, in the vicinity of Novaya Zemlya, were released five days after Kennedy took office.

Khrushchev's honeymoon with the new American president turned out to be brief. At the end of January 1961 the DIE received a letter from Moscow stating that President Kennedy had approved plans for an assault on Cuba to begin in two or three months. Trinidad, a city on the southern coast of Cuba, was to be the designated landing site. That letter was signed by the chairman of the KGB himself, Gen. Aleksandr Shelepin, and stated that Comrade Khrushchev had decided to help "the people of Cuba" defend their revolution.

In order to do so, however, Moscow needed a respite of six to seven months, allowing time quietly to provide Castro with the weapons and military advisers he would need to repel the invasion.

The point of Shelepin's letter was that the "socialist camp's" foreign intelligence community was to create a "diversion" in Washington that would delay Washington's "criminal plans" for Cuba. (As already noted, the PGU defector Oleg Lyalin confirmed that in the 1960s the PGU had contingency plans to sabotage the nerve centers of Western governments.)

In the end, though, there was no need for such a "diversion." In mid-March 1961 the PGU learned that Kennedy had moved the landing site in Cuba from Trinidad to the Bay of Pigs, which he believed would permit a quiet nocturnal operation, better disguise U.S. participation in the invasion, and avoid the appearance of a World War III assault. That produced an explosion of joy in Moscow. Its military experts unanimously agreed that the Bay of Pigs and its surrounding Zapata swamps were poorly suited for guerrilla warfare and provided "ideal conditions" for the Cubans and Soviets to wipe out the invaders. Therefore, the DIE was informed, Khrushchev had canceled his operation aimed at creating a "diversion" in Washington and was throwing his energies into creating a joint PGU–Red Army task force responsible for helping Castro "decimate" the CIA attack.

At that time the DIE was not involved in Moscow's new effort to protect Castro's revolution. I learned little about it until April 1971, when I visited Cuba as a member of a Romanian government delegation attending a ten-year celebration of Castro's victory at the Bay of Pigs. A military exhibit put together for that occasion and presented by Raul Castro showed quite convincingly, despite its propagandistic overtones, that Castro and his Soviet sponsors had been aware of the invasion plans down to the last detail and had been thoroughly prepared to confront it.

Even without the exhibit, however, standing there on the spot where the invasion had taken place, I could see that there would have been little hope for the survival of a relatively small invading force without air or naval support. The waters at the inhospitable Bay of Pigs were studded with coral formations, and its shores— offering no beachhead that could be occupied and controlled—had been packed with heavily armed and well-trained soldiers awaiting the attackers. The invasion indeed met swift defeat.

Even this success could not sweeten Khrushchev's bitterness. "The Pig betrayed me," I heard him tell Gheorghiu-Dej in June 1962. By that time Khrushchev was at the peak of his war with Kennedy, and "Pig" was also the code name for the American president used in PGU correspondence with the DIE.

Khrushchev's first personal meeting with Kennedy after he became president took place in Vienna on June 2 and 3, 1961, after the Bay of Pigs, and it only increased the Soviet leader's hatred for his new adversary. In a pugnacious report sent to Gheorghiu-Dej (and probably to other East European leaders) after the Vienna summit, Khrushchev characterized Kennedy as an arrogant millionaire who acted as if he owned the world.

The two-day discussion, Khrushchev wrote, had reinforced his suspicions that Kennedy was a warmongering fanatic manipulated by the CIA. He had told Kennedy to his face that his insistence on more than three on-site nuclear inspections a year under a new arms-control agreement could only be for espionage purposes. He had also made it clear, Khrushchev added, that if Kennedy attempted to rely on military power to maintain the "bourgeois occupation" of West Berlin, he would suffer an even worse consequence than what had happened in Cuba. Nothing on earth would stop Moscow from removing that splinter from the heart of Europe. If Kennedy wanted war, that was his problem—the Soviet Union would have no choice but to accept his challenge. But "our response," Khrushchev's letter declared, would be such that "no two stones will be left standing on top of one another in the West."

Although by now my job was to coordinate Romania's industrial espionage operations, I was still the country's chief expert on German matters, and I had therefore been fully involved in the new conflict between Khrushchev and Kennedy over Berlin. The escalation of the Berlin crisis was adding fuel to the fire. In his June 15, 1961, televised report to the Soviet people about the Vienna meeting, Khrushchev underlined his determination to "free" West Berlin before the end of the year. Soon after that, East German leader Walter Ulbricht made it clear that the day after a "peace treaty" was signed with the Soviet Union, East Germany would close West Berlin's refugee centers, its radio stations, and Tempelhof Airport.

That left Kennedy no alternative. In an emotional television address to the nation on July 25, he affirmed that the freedom of West Berlin was not negotiable. "We cannot and will not permit the Communists to drive us out of Berlin, either gradually or by force." That speech was accompanied by a rapid buildup of American combat troops in Europe and by Kennedy's demand that Congress approve an additional military budget of $3.2 billion and provide him with standby authority to call up the reserves.

As usual, Khrushchev answered with threats and lies: he would resume atomic testing, he would detonate a hundred-megaton bomb—which the Soviet Union did not yet have—and on August 7 he delivered a blistering speech asserting that the Soviet Union would not abandon the peace treaty, because were it to do so, the West would then demand the abandonment of the "socialist system" itself.

Khrushchev was already defeated, however. Intelligence obtained by the DIE confirmed PGU information that President Kennedy had ordered the Pentagon to prepare contingency plans for using nuclear weapons against the Soviet Union, should the Kremlin further escalate the Berlin crisis, and Khrushchev knew only too well that he had few if any ways to reach the United States with his nuclear weapons. That information propelled the Soviet leader into his first major, and most spectacular, failure.

On August 13, Khrushchev made the humiliating decision to end his three years of intensive effort to gain control of West Berlin: he closed East Berlin off and proclaimed that action a major victory. The Berlin Wall was the only trophy he could display for his supposed triumph.

Gheorghiu-Dej, who was prescient on the timing of his trips, returned on that same day from a two-week visit to Moscow with a different feeling: "The lunatic is so furious at Kennedy that he's ready to tear him limb from limb with his bare teeth!"

Today people remember Khrushchev as a down-to-earth peasant who corrected the evils of Stalin. But he was not. The Khrushchev I knew was a compulsive political chatterbox who had no objective appreciation of facts, and who had gotten a taste for the simple criminal solution because of his close association with Stalin's mass killings. In 1936, when Stalin unleashed his Great Purge, aimed at eliminating all competition and opposition to himself, some seven million people lost their lives in the ensuing slaughter, including most of the high-ranking Soviet Communists. Of the seven men who formed Lenin's Politburo at the time of the October Revolution, Stalin alone outlived the purges.

Among provincial party secretaries, only three who had zealously supported Stalin's *yezhovshchina* (the purges were popularly named for the hated political police chief Nikolay Yezhov) survived the executions. The flamboyant Khrushchev, who as Communist party boss in Moscow had ardently upheld Stalin's new purges from the first day, was one of those three. As a supplementary reward, in 1938 Stalin appointed him first party secretary of Ukraine and directed him to organize a similar purge in his new territory. There Khrushchev proceeded to carry out his master's wishes with savagery and brutality.

The habit of resorting to political assassinations remained with Khrushchev for the rest of his career. He even became ruler of the Soviet Union with the help of an assassination. A few days after Stalin died, Khrushchev plotted a palace coup aimed at killing off his main political rival to the Soviet throne, Lavrenty Beria. The coup was successfully executed during the June 26, 1953, meeting of the Presidium, following the plan devised by Khrushchev himself. According to his own account, Khrushchev came to that meeting with a gun in his pocket and played the main role from beginning to end: "I prodded [Premier Georgy] Malenkov with my foot and whispered: 'Open the session and give me the floor.' Malenkov went white; I saw he was incapable of opening his mouth. So I jumped up and said: 'There is one item on the agenda: the anti-Party, divisive activity of imperialist agent Beria.'" After Khrushchev moved that Beria be released from all his party and government positions, "Malenkov was still in a state of panic. As I recall, he didn't even put my motion to a vote. He pressed a secret button which gave the signal to the generals who were waiting in the next room." With Beria arrested and locked in a cell, Khrushchev easily managed to wrest the job of leader of the Soviet Union away from his closest ally, Malenkov. Afterward Khrushchev personally supervised the framing of Beria, who on December 24, 1953, was shot as a Western spy.

A few years ago Sergei Khrushchev published a lengthy book in which he tried to put a human face on his father. I found it sincere and convincing in its way, but it deals with a different Khrushchev— a serene, peaceful, loving one. Then again, if my daughter, who is now also an American citizen, should someday decide to write a book about her father, she would not know anything about my real intelligence career in Romania. Even though she visited me at my public office, and I often took her to the Generals' Club of the *Securitate*, I took pains never to allow her even a glimpse of my real work. That was another of the strictly enforced rules we inherited from Moscow.

13

MAY DAY IN MOSCOW

O N February 13, 1961, the U.S. embassy in Moscow received a letter from Oswald, the first time any Western source had heard from him since the fall of 1959. The letter was undated, but its envelope had been postmarked in Minsk on February 5. In it Oswald said he wished to return to the United States. What could have suddenly transformed Oswald's thinking? Only a little over a year earlier, on December 17, 1959, he had written his brother Robert to say that he was "starting a new life and I do not wish to have anything to do with the old life."

No valid factual or circumstantial evidence whatsoever explains what could have caused Oswald's change of heart. Not even his "Historic Diary" really attempts to explain it. According to the diary, Oswald left Moscow by train for Minsk on January 7, 1960. There, going by his own entries, he lived the life of a pasha, compared to anything he had ever experienced. In Minsk he occupied a fancy apartment located on the river Svisloch, was surrounded by a gaggle of girlfriends, and had more money than he could spend. (The "Historic Diary" states that his combined monthly salary from factory work and the "Red Cross" was "1400 R. about the same as the Director of the factory!") An entry in the diary for January 1, 1961, states: "New Years I spend at home of Ella Germain. I think I'm in love with her. She has refused my more dishonourable advanis, we drink and eat in the presence of her family in a very hospitable atmosfere. Later I go home drunk and happy. Passing the river homewards, I decide to propose to Ella." The next day Ella turns him down, and he then abruptly decides he does not like the Soviet Union. In the entry for January 4–31 he writes: "I am stating to reconsider my disire about staying. The work is drab the money I get has nowhere to be spent. No nightclubs or bowling allys no places of recreation acept the trade union dances I have had enough." (Besides the British spelling of *dishonourable*, note the–for an American– unnatural expressions *homewards* and *has nowhere to be spent.*)

Hundreds of books have been published on the assassination of President Kennedy, and each of them has portrayed Oswald somewhat differently. But nowhere has he ever been described as a spendthrift or a party-goer. He himself perhaps best described the real Oswald in his November 26, 1959, letter to his brother Robert:

> So you speak of advantages. Do you think that is why I am here? For personal, material advantages? Happiness is not based on oneself, it does not consist of a small home, of taking and getting. Happiness is taking part in the struggle, where there is no borderline between one's own personal world, and the world in general. I never believed I would find more material advantages at <u>this</u> stage of development in the Soviet Union than I might of have had in the U.S.

There is no reason to think he ever changed from that unsociable, nonmaterialistic idealist he was in 1959. After his return to the United States in 1962 there is voluminous testimony from his landladies, relatives, and émigré acquaintances that he did not go out in the evenings, certainly not to nightclubs and bowling alleys, and that he did not spend money on himself, his apartment, or even his wife.

Moreover there is good reason to believe that Oswald never for a moment wavered from his firm determination to spend the rest of his life in the Soviet Union. The fact, attested to by his relatives and émigré friends, that Oswald was strongly against his wife's learning English or acquiring any material possessions in the United States suggests that he considered his return there to be only temporary. For example, he told a New Orleans policeman that "he did not speak English in his family because he did not want them to become Americanized." He also told the same policeman that he was in America only temporarily and planned to return to Russia.

As we shall see, other data support the conclusion that Oswald was not sent to live in Minsk in January 1960, if at all. An address book found among Oswald's effects after his death indicates to me that even after he made his defection to the Soviet Union public in October 1959, the PGU still intended that he learn German and go to Switzerland to attend the Albert Schweitzer College, as planned. The book is paginated according to the Russian alphabet and appears to have been started in conformity with the cover story of his arrival in Moscow in October 1959, for it contains homemade calendar months from then (with the date of *October 16* emphasized) to April 1960. Under the letter A appears the entire German alphabet in rather carefully drawn printed capital letters in old German, along with a few words in German and Russian. Also found among Oswald's effects at the time of his arrest was a pack of flash cards for learning German.

Whether or not the PGU wished to prepare Oswald for a future assignment in the West, it would have been entirely out of character for the PGU to have sent him off to a provincial city a few weeks after he defected. Based on my experience, the standard practice at that time would have required that Oswald be taken back to a safe house as soon as he was interviewed by the two American journalists. There PGU officers and army experts would have continued to debrief him about the U-2 planes, his technical knowledge of CIA bases for high-altitude reconnaissance flights, and Marine Corps procedures and equipment. Other PGU debriefers would have probed for personality data about Oswald's fellow Marines.

It would also have been standard procedure for the PGU to provide Oswald with a Russian teacher and give him private instruction in Marxism and the history of the Soviet Union—for purposes of indoctrination, not resettlement. He would have been taken on pleasure trips to scenic areas of the Soviet Union, perhaps including the historic old city of Kiev, a place described in the manuscript material he brought out with him in 1962 that he is otherwise not known to have visited. Still probably hoping that Oswald could be persuaded to return to Western Europe to attend college, the PGU would have emphasized how he could continue to serve the Soviet Union.

Then something important happened, interrupting the PGU's debriefings of Oswald and preparations for his resettlement or possible reassignment. Perhaps the reason that Oswald's little handmade calendar in his address book stops after April 1960 is that his life underwent a dramatic change on May 1 that year. On that day the Soviet military shot down the U-2 piloted by Francis Gary Powers. Khrushchev's jubilation knew no bounds, as the whole world would come to see.

At that moment Oswald must have been praised and feted beyond his wildest dreams. Even if the PGU had other sources whose intelligence contributed to this success, Oswald was there, at hand, in Moscow. What does an eight-hundred-pound gorilla eat for breakfast? Anything he wants! So it must have been with Oswald after that triumphant Moscow May Day.

Overnight the downing of the U-2 became the central point of Soviet domestic and foreign policy. Although in the memoirs written after his fall from grace Khrushchev occasionally improves on the facts, his reflections on the events of that May Day ring genuine:

> At five o'clock in the morning of May 1 my telephone rang. I picked up the receiver, and the voice on the other end said, "Minister of Defense Marshal Malinovsky reporting." He went on to tell me that an American U-2 reconnaissance plane had crossed the border of Afghanistan into the Soviet airspace and was flying toward Sverdlovsk. I replied that it was up to him to shoot down the plane by whatever means he could. Malinovsky said he'd already given the order, adding: "If our antiaircraft units can just keep their eyes open and stop yawning long enough, I'm sure we'll knock the plane down." He was referring to the fact that already in April we'd had an opportunity to shoot down a U-2, but our antiaircraft batteries were caught napping and didn't open fire soon enough.

It appears that, after receiving the latest information on the U-2's altitude and radar pattern that Oswald must have brought with him to Moscow in October 1959, Khrushchev gave the order to shoot down the next U-2 caught in Soviet airspace. For half a year the Soviets did not have an opportunity to do so, however, because the United States suspended the program after that October,

resuming it only with the April 9, 1960, flight alluded to above by
Khrushchev.

Khrushchev continues:

> In the midst of the proceedings [the May Day parade], Marshal
> Biryuzov, commander in chief of our antiaircraft defenses, mounted
> the reviewing stand on top of the Mausoleum and whispered in my
> ear. He informed me the U-2 had been shot down; the pilot had
> been taken prisoner and was already under interrogation. Accord-
> ing to Marshal Biryuzov's report, several of our antiaircraft instal-
> lations had been arranged in a chessboard pattern, so that the U-2
> was bound to run into one or another. When the plane came within
> range of one battery, two missiles were launched. As I recall, the
> plane was hit by the first missile; the second was fired for good mea-
> sure, to make sure it couldn't escape.

Oswald apparently was taken to view that 1960 May Day parade in Moscow, as he would casually remark to a co-worker after
he returned to the United States. Taking an agent to view the parade was another pattern introduced into the PGU's modus
operandi by General Sakharovsky, who believed that nothing could
better motivate an ideologically sympathetic Westerner than the
"grandeur of the internationalist message of a May Day parade." In
Bucharest, not only did the DIE take its agents who happened to be
visiting Romania to view these parades, it also secretly brought
some agents into the country especially for the event.

Oswald's "Historic Diary" misleadingly places him in Minsk on
that date, however, adding the artificial-sounding comment: "I follow the Amer. custom of marking a Holiday by sleeping in in the
morning." This is exactly the sort of gratuitous remark a PGU disinformation expert would insert to show off his knowledge of
American mores.

The U-2 pilot was not interrogated by Soviet military intelligence, as would have been routine if the downing of the plane had
been the result of a military operation, as Khrushchev described it.
Powers himself would later write that he was secretly interrogated
at the Lubyanka, the jail at KGB headquarters, and that means to
me that it was in fact the KGB, not the Red Army, that played the
first violin in the whole operation.

According to Powers, his interrogation began the same day he was shot down, and it was witnessed by about a dozen people, some in uniform but most in civilian dress—the latter evidently important KGB officials who had come to see the show. The following day many of the same people were there, and it was not until May 3 that the interrogation began in earnest. During one session, conducted by a general rather than the usual two majors, "a short, thin, chain-smoking man of about forty monitored the proceedings." Powers later learned that he was Aleksandr Shelepin, chairman of the KGB.

Col. Oleg Penkovsky, a GRU (Soviet military intelligence) officer who was in clandestine contact with the CIA, reported on April 23, 1961, that, since Powers had been downed in a military operation, the GRU had selected him, Penkovsky, to talk to Powers because he spoke good English. But Shelepin had interfered with the GRU's plans because Shelepin himself wished to report personally to Khrushchev on the matter. "Shelepin got an interpreter and picked Powers up. The military people knocked Powers down and Powers was considered to be a military man. Therefore he should have been turned over to us, the General Staff [the GRU]. But the KGB seized him, took him to Dzerzhinsky Square [KGB headquarters], and made their own report." In other words, Penkovsky and the GRU were unaware that PGU intelligence had enabled the Soviets to shoot down the U-2, but KGB chairman Shelepin made sure Khrushchev knew whom to thank.

A substantial part of Powers's interrogation centered on the flight altitude of the U-2. He was asked if he had ever been stationed at Atsugi, and he answered truthfully that he had not. His interrogators specifically asked him about U-2s at Atsugi, showing him articles in Japanese about a U-2 that had crash-landed there. (The Soviets would not have wanted Powers to suspect they had a source at Atsugi, and newspaper articles could conveniently explain their interest in that base. In September 1959 the Japanese magazine *Air Views* had published a detailed account of a U-2's emergency landing at a glider-club strip near Atsugi and suggested that the U-2s might be conducting other reconnaissance besides weather.) Powers was also asked if he knew about American RB-47 reconnaissance flights, but he said he did not. (As noted earlier, the

Soviets would soon shoot down an RB-47 in the vicinity of Novaya Zemlya on July 1.)

While Powers was being secretly interrogated at the Lubyanka, and before the Soviets had announced their coup, Khrushchev gleefully set about trapping the United States into making false statements about the U-2. When Powers did not arrive at his destination in Norway, and believing that he must have been killed, on May 2 the public information officer at Incirlik Base in Turkey, from which Powers had set out on his flight, released a report saying that an unarmed weather reconnaissance plane of the U-2 type had vanished over Turkey after the pilot had reported trouble with his oxygen equipment. Khrushchev writes in his memoirs that the Soviets "smiled with pleasure as we anticipated the discomfort which the spies who cooked up this false statement would feel when confronted with the evidence we already had in our pocket." He decided that he would "announce that the plane had been shot down, but—and this was important—I would *not* reveal that the pilot had been captured alive." On May 5 he did exactly that. That same day the American government shifted its story to speculate that the pilot might have lost consciousness and allowed the plane to stray across the border into Soviet airspace, but the State Department categorically denied any deliberate attempt to violate Soviet airspace.

Khrushchev was enjoying himself immensely. "Two or three days later, after [the Americans] talked themselves out and got thoroughly wound up in this unbelievable story, we decided to tell the world what had really happened. . . . We laid out everything just as it occurred: the plane's point of origin, its route, its destination, and its mission. But the biggest blow for the Americans was the announcement that the pilot was in custody and that he was giving us evidence that we would reveal to the world."

On May 7, Khrushchev sprang his trap, announcing to the Supreme Soviet and the world that the U-2 pilot had confessed to being a CIA employee and to have been flying on a spy mission over the Soviet Union. The Soviets set up an exhibit in a building in Gorky Park to display the plane's wreckage and Powers's maps, clothes, survival gear, and his prominently featured poison-tipped suicide pin. They took Powers out of prison just to show him the display. Khrushchev himself went to Gorky Park to have a look ("I was curious to see the plane too") and happily talked to the foreign newsmen who gathered around him. In his remarks he followed the line taken by the American press, blaming the CIA and the American military but not President Eisenhower for the incident.

Secretary of State Christian Herter tried to shield the president by announcing on May 11 that the U-2 missions were not subject to presidential authorization. Eisenhower, however, preferred to show that he was in charge and acknowledged that he had personally approved the flights, explaining that espionage was a "distasteful but vital necessity." Khrushchev exults in his memoirs: "This was a highly unreasonable statement, not to say a foolish one. . . . [Eisenhower] had, so to speak, offered us his back end, and we obliged him by kicking it as hard as we could." Khrushchev did attend the summit conference in Paris later that month, but he effectively blew it up on the first day, using the U-2 incident as a pretext. He was, he would write, "proud that we gave a sharp but fully justified rebuff to the world's mightiest state."

Still more mileage was to be gotten out of the U-2 incident, however. On August 17, 1960, Powers was put on well-publicized public trial in Moscow's ornate Hall of Columns, allowing Khrushchev an opportunity to show himself as a skillful political leader and the United States as the enemy of peace. As Powers would relate, "this was no courtroom but an immense theater. Tall white columns flanked all four walls. Hanging between them and from the ceiling were more than fifty chandeliers, all brilliantly lighted. . . . The audience numbered close to a thousand. . . . This was like being tried in Carnegie Hall!" Hundreds of foreign journalists attended, and the entire proceedings were photographed for later showing on television and in movie theaters.

On August 19, Powers was sentenced to ten years' imprisonment. He was later released in February 1962 and exchanged for the PGU illegal officer Rudolf Abel. Abel had been arrested in New York in June 1957 and sentenced to thirty years in prison. He never broke, not even to the extent of admitting that he was a Soviet citizen. It was standard PGU advice to its officers and agents never to admit anything. When Oswald was arrested in Dallas on November

22, 1963, he confused his interrogators by denying everything, including many obviously true facts about himself.

Oswald was likely one of the people in the audience attending Powers's trial. On February 15, 1962, after having decided to return to the United States, Oswald wrote his brother Robert: "I heard over the voice of america that they released Powers the U2 spy plane fellow. That's big news where you are I suppose. He seemed to be a nice, bright american-type fellow, when I saw him in Moscow." It would have been standard procedure for the PGU to allow Oswald to observe the Powers trial as one of the rewards given him for helping the Soviet Union to shoot down the U-2.

Another special honor bestowed on outstanding PGU (and other Soviet-bloc) agents was to give them officer rank in the security or armed forces and photograph them in uniform, the photograph to be placed in their PGU files. This form of reward was strongly promoted by General Sakharovsky and was used especially for agents with a military background. The case of Sgt. Robert Lee Johnson, the PGU agent who when stationed in Paris furnished the Soviets particularly important cryptographic intelligence, is a perfect illustration. In recognition of his accomplishments, in 1962 he was "given the congratulations of Comrade Khrushchev and the Soviet Council of Ministers, told he had been awarded the rank of Red Army major, and presented with $2,000 to spend on a holiday in Monte Carlo." In Romania, for example, Ceausescu in 1977 ordered that a DIE agent code-named "Ionescu," who had defected from the Romanian army when he was a captain, gone to work for Radio Free Europe in Paris, and there for many years cooperated with the DIE, should upon his retirement from the radio be offered the rank and pension of a retired army general as an inducement to return to Romania.

Oswald's information had likely turned May Day 1960 into one of the few genuine and unalloyed triumphs of Khrushchev's entire career. Whatever form the PGU's gratitude may have taken, it was apparently sufficient to ensure forever Oswald's unswerving loyalty to the Soviet Union, and eventually persuade him to return temporarily to the United States.

14

ASSASSINATION BECOMES A TOOL OF FOREIGN POLICY

S OON AFTER the Soviets brought down the American U-2 plane on May 1, 1960, the triumphant Khrushchev declared war on the White House.

With the death of Secretary of State John Foster Dulles in the spring of 1959, President Dwight Eisenhower had assumed a more personal role in the conduct of foreign policy. He appeared ready to buy Khrushchev's new proposal for peaceful coexistence and to improve relations with the former archenemy. An international summit, attended by the leaders of the United States, the Soviet Union, Great Britain, and France, was scheduled to begin in Paris on May 16, 1960.

Khrushchev's handling of the 1960 Paris summit illustrates his nefarious nature. As I learned from Khrushchev himself, once in the air flying toward Paris, he began obsessing over the idea that Eisenhower had deliberately sent a U-2 mission over the Soviet Union a few days before the summit in order to sabotage any resolution of the Berlin crisis. En route to Paris, Khrushchev built up a "vitriolic hatred" for his adversary. He decided to withdraw an already accepted invitation for Eisenhower to visit Moscow, unless Eisenhower would declare from the summit's podium that he would cancel the U-2 program. Just as the summit meeting was about to open, moreover, the Soviet leader decided to demand an apology from Eisenhower. In the end, Khrushchev opened the four-power summit by publicly announcing that the Soviet Union would no longer have any dealings with Eisenhower, and that there would be no more summits as long as he was still president of the United States.

"I'm going to kill that cripple," Khrushchev told Gheorghiu-Dej a month later in Bucharest, when he and Sakharovsky arrived there on a visit. "Cripple" had become Khrushchev's nickname for Eisenhower, who in 1956 had suffered a heart attack that had left him with a slight speech impediment. According to Sakharovsky, Dej turned as white as feta cheese. The Romanian leader had good reason to be afraid. By that time Khrushchev had shifted from killing Russian émigrés to assassinating foreign leaders.

I first learned about Khrushchev's escalation of terror in October 1960, when Gen. Ivan Serov, head of the KGB, and General Sakharovsky, then a deputy chief of the PGU, unexpectedly paid a visit to the DIE. Both visitors were sporting flowered Ukrainian folkshirts, which they wore over baggy trousers. Even today it is still a mystery to me why most of the top KGB officers I knew would take such pains to ape whatever Soviet leader happened to be in power at the moment. Under Stalin they all wore military-style tunics buttoned to the neck, walked slowly, and spoke softly. Under Khrushchev they switched to either ill-fitting clothes or raucous tones of voice. It was a peculiarity of the Soviet form of communism that I have never been able to explain. As one might expect in the Balkans, under Gheorghiu-Dej Romania succumbed to a cult of personality even more flamboyant and idiotic than Stalin's, but I never knew any Romanian who tried to look like Dej. Nor did I later meet any who wanted to stutter like Ceausescu.

Serov and Sakharovsky had arrived in Bucharest the evening before, accompanying Nikita Khrushchev and Georgy Malenkov—who had just been replaced as prime minister but was still a member of the Politburo. The group had come to Romania for "consultations" about the "dangerous events" taking place in Hungary. At the DIE, Serov told us that Moscow had obtained "irrefutable evidence" that Hungary was being flooded with Western intelligence agents who were inciting "the dregs of Hungarian society" to rebel against the "people's government." The recent "rebellion" in Poland, which the previous June had forced the Soviets to send in tanks to put it down, had made Poland unfit to be used as a base for possible military intervention in Hungary. Therefore Khrushchev had decided to deploy a number of Red Army units to Romania and to mass them near the border with Hungary, ready to intervene.

Every "rabid dog" would be shot, Serov said. He added that the Romanian leader had offered to join in, but Khrushchev had insisted there was no need to internationalize the Hungarian crisis.

A few days later I heard Gheorghiu-Dej remark that Khrushchev had been "insane" during their meeting. Dej specifically mentioned his cries that the Hungarians "should be killed like rats" and that "only a bloodbath can bring Attila's Huns to heel again."

On November 4, 1955, Soviet military units did indeed attack Budapest, and Imre Nagy, the "rebellious" Hungarian prime minister, sought refuge in the Yugoslavian embassy. A week later Sakharovsky was back in Bucharest to present Gheorghiu-Dej with Khrushchev's demand that Nagy be lured out of the Yugoslavian embassy and secretly kept under arrest in Romania until a new Hungarian government was formed. Dej agreed, and on that same day Col. Wilhelm Einhorn, a deputy director of the DIE of Hungarian origin, was personally instructed by the Soviet ambassador to Hungary, Yury Andropov (the same man who would later become chairman of the KGB and then leader of the Soviet Union). After János Kádár, the new Hungarian ruler, pledged that no charges would be brought against Nagy if he would leave the country, Einhorn secretly escorted Nagy to Romania on November 22, 1956.

Nagy was put up in a large DIE safe house with microphones concealed in every nook and cranny. There General Sakharovsky showed Nagy a picture of a villa in Yalta, the most fashionable Soviet retirement area, and told him it would be his home if he would publicly apologize for his "past mistakes," which had so badly damaged not only his own country but also the whole Communist movement. "This is your historic duty," Sakharovsky reportedly told him again and again. But Nagy did not succumb to these blandishments.

In December 1956 Nagy's case was transferred to a specially created KGB group headed by Gen. Boris Shumilin, an expert in "counterrevolutionary affairs." A year later Nagy and the principal members of his cabinet were hanged after a show trial organized by the KGB in Budapest.

In March 1957, Gen. Ivan Anisimovich Fadeykin, chief of the PGU's newly created Thirteenth Department, responsible for assassinations and kidnappings in the West, landed in Bucharest with the task of creating a similar department in the DIE. Fadeykin was well known to the DIE from his years as head of the PGU *rezidentura* in East Berlin, which became a mechanism for kidnapping people from West Germany and other Western countries. He had also been instrumental in the brutal June 1953 suppression of anti-Soviet demonstrations in East Berlin, when his troops opened fire on the German demonstrators. Evidently that had been too much even for Stalin and Beria, for afterward Fadeykin was recalled to Moscow. But it was not too much for Khruschchev.

In 1957, General Fadeykin began his "exchange of experience" in Bucharest by playing Khrushchev's broken record, according to which Stalin had made an unpardonable mistake: he had aimed the cutting edge of the state security apparatus against the Soviet Union's own people. When Khrushchev delivered his "secret speech," Fadeykin said, the only thing he had in mind was to correct that aberration. In December 1917, when Lenin had established the Cheka, he had given it the emblem of a shield and a sword to symbolize its duties: to shield and protect the Communist revolution, and to put its enemies to the sword. Lenin never intended, Fadeykin said, to use "us" against "our own people." Ten million Soviet citizens had given their lives to defend "our" political system during World War II—what more evidence did one need to see their devotion to communism?

"Our enemies," Fadeykin explained, were not in the Soviet Union. The West's bourgeoisie and our own traitors who had defected from their motherland and were now attacking it from abroad—these were our "deadly enemies." The cutting edge of our sword must be directed against them, and only against them, in order that we might fulfill "our historic destiny" as the gravedigger of capitalism. When PGU illegal officer Ramon Mercader killed "our archenemy Leon Trotsky" in Mexico in August 1940, he had to use an ice axe to carry out the deed. We should change that kind of behavior, Fadeykin advised; we should create modern tools to carry out our new, historic task. That was what Nikita Sergeyevich had really wanted to tell us in his "secret speech."

In fact, Fadeykin explained, one of Khrushchev's first foreign policy decisions had been his 1953 order to have such a "deadly enemy" secretly assassinated. Fadeykin was referring to a PGU operation aimed at killing Georgy Okolovich, a Ukrainian émigré who was the leader of the National Labor Alliance (*Natsionalnyy Trudovoy Soyuz*, or NTS), one of the most aggressively anti-Communist Russian émigré organizations in Western Europe. Although born in the Crimea, Khrushchev considered himself a Ukrainian—he would soon incorporate the Crimea into Ukraine—and it was quite normal for him to plan to "neutralize" the leaders of anti-Communist organizations run by Ukrainian émigrés.

A PGU execution team thus arrived in West Germany in February 1954. Unfortunately, in Fadeykin's view, once there the team's leader, Nikolay Khokhlov, "betrayed his country" by defecting to the American CIA. Even worse, in April Khokhlov held a sensational press conference at which he displayed to the whole world the latest "neutralization weapon" created by the PGU: an electrically operated gun fitted with a silencer and concealed inside a cigarette pack, which fired cyanide-tipped bullets. Fadeykin added that, because trouble always comes in bunches, two other PGU officers familiar with the assassination component defected at about the same time: Yury Rastvorov and Petr Deryabin.

According to Fadeykin, all these setbacks led to drastic changes. First, Khrushchev ordered the PGU to spread the rumor worldwide that he had dismantled the PGU's assassination component. Then he baptized kidnappings and secret assassinations in the West with the euphemism "neutralization" operations. Finally, he rechristened the Ninth Section of the PGU—as the assassination component had been called until then—the Thirteenth Department, buried its existence in even deeper secrecy, and placed it under his own supervision.

Once this was accomplished, Khrushchev introduced a new pattern in the PGU's "neutralization" operations. In spite of the PGU's

penchant for bureaucratic paperwork, he ordered that assassinations abroad were to be handled strictly orally. They were never to
be committed to paper, and they were to be kept totally secret from
the Politburo and every other governing body. Fadeykin stressed
that "the Comrade, and only the Comrade," could now approve
"neutralizations" abroad. Regardless of any evidence that might be
produced in foreign police investigations, the PGU was never to acknowledge its involvement in assassinations and kidnappings
abroad; any such evidence was to be dismissed out of hand as a
ridiculous accusation. Finally, after each operation the PGU was
surreptitiously to spread "evidence" in the West, accusing the CIA
or other convenient "enemies" of having done the deed, thereby if
possible achieving a double objective.

Before Fadeykin left Bucharest, the DIE had acquired its own
component for kidnapping and assassinations in the West. The new
unit was given the name Group Z, because the letter Z was the final letter in the alphabet, representing the "final solution." We understood that its structure was virtually identical to that of its sister
units recently created in the East German, Hungarian, and Bulgarian foreign intelligence services. In accordance with another new
PGU pattern, all four sister units maintained operational components in East Berlin, and all were equipped by the PGU with a complete arsenal of supplies ranging from powerful soporifics to trusted
agents living in the West who had previously been used in terrorist
operations by the various bloc services, thus allowing for a stan-
dardization of operational methods.

In 1964, Khrushchev got rid of Aleksandr Panyushkin, Stalin's
chief of foreign intelligence. Panyushkin was a former ambassador to
the United States and China, and Khrushchev intended to replace
diplomacy with terror. Thus he appointed a terrorist to head the
PGU: General Sakharovsky, the former chief adviser of the Romanian political police between 1949 and 1953. He had been the brains
behind the wave of terror that had pounded Romania's "bourgeoisie," killing more than fifty thousand people in those years.

Since settling in the United States in 1978, I have religiously
scanned the most important American and European newspapers,
and recently the Internet, but I have never found a significant ref-

erence to General Sakharovsky. That is hardly surprising. For most of the twenty years I worked with him I did not even know his true name—he dealt with us under the name Aleksandr Zakharov. That was the Soviet reflection of the cold war when not even all members of the Israeli and British governments knew the identity of their spy chiefs.

Sakharovsky served fifteen years as head of the PGU, a record that has never been broken, and he played an extremely negative, though very secret, role in shaping our contemporary history. He authored the bloody Sovietization of Romania (1945–1952) and the brutal export of communism to Cuba (1958–1959). His nefarious handling of the Berlin crisis (1958–1961) forced Khrushchev on August 13, 1961, to close off East Berlin with barbed wire, which later became the Berlin Wall that protected tyranny from freedom during the next thirty years. Sakharovsky's dangerous handling of the Cuban Missile Crisis (1962) brought the world to the brink of nuclear war. In 1969 he transformed airplane hijacking—the terrorist weapon of choice as late as September 11, 2001–into an instrument of international terrorism. And in 1970 he established a "socialist division of labor" among the countries of the Soviet bloc to support his war of terror against the United States. (Twenty years later, Czechoslovakian president Vaclav Havel acknowledged that, under this division of labor, his country's Communist espionage service had developed a plastic explosive, Semtex-H, that could not be detected by sniffing dogs, and that it had secretly shipped a thousand tons of this odorless explosive to Palestinian and Libyan terrorists. According to Havel, a mere two hundred grams of this explosive was enough to blow up a commercial plane in flight. "World terrorism has supplies of Semtex to last 150 years," Havel estimated.) Documents found in the archives of the East German *Stasi* show that Sakharovsky's division of labor continued right up to the fall of the Berlin Wall.

Seen through the perspective of history, Sakharovsky's most terrible legacy is the assassination of President Kennedy and the PGU's subsequent *dezinformatzyia* efforts to portray American leaders as the ruthless and greedy killers.

15

TESTING THE WATERS

I T WAS a great surprise to find that Oswald's undated letter containing his intention to repatriate arrived at the U.S. embassy in
Moscow on February 13, 1961. That was just two weeks after the
DIE had received a KGB letter advising that Khrushchev was en-
trusting the bloc foreign intelligence community with the "historic
task" of creating a "diversion in Washington" during the Soviet
arms buildup in Cuba.

The coincidental timing of those two letters provides a strong
reason to believe that the PGU was considering Oswald for such a
diversionary task. He was a young and presentable native American
whose citizenship was probably still valid, and he should have been
able to integrate back into American life much more easily and
quickly than any Soviet-bloc illegal officer could ever hope to, no
matter how well documented he might be. Oswald was fanatically
devoted to the Soviet Union; furthermore the PGU had sufficient
compromising material on him to persuade him to do whatever it
wanted and to keep him quiet—a routine PGU precaution. In fact
Oswald must have seemed like a perfect candidate for such a difficult job.

Of course the stubborn and independent Oswald had to be indoctrinated and programmed by the PGU to the point that he
would perform the task assigned to him. The PGU always considered indoctrination and mental programming essential parts of any
foreign intelligence operation, but after Sakharovsky took over its
leadership in 1956, he transformed this kind of indoctrination into

a veritable obsession. All legal and illegal officers projected for assignment in the West but not scheduled to work in an official *rezidentura* had to be solidly programmed before being sent out.

"They'll be working alone behind enemy lines," Sakharovsky would explain to us in the DIE, "in that corrosive environment where even stainless steel can turn rusty." The first and most important step of this indoctrination process was to ensure that such an officer deeply despised the "bourgeoisie" and regarded its leaders as "rabid dogs." Even now my skin crawls when I remember Sakharovsky proclaiming in his soft, melodious voice: "There is just one way to deal with a rabid dog—shoot it!" The next step was solidly to implant in the officer's mind a future vision of the wonderful life he would live in the "proletarian paradise" after completing his mission abroad. Finally, we had to instill in him the firm idea that the very future of communism depended on the success of his mission.

Oswald's February letter to the U.S. embassy raises several interesting issues, inviting the conclusion that he had indeed been chosen by the PGU for involvement in the so-called diversion in Washington. Oswald writes that he would repatriate only "if we could come to some agreement concerning the dropping of any legal proceedings against me." One of the PGU's first concerns must have been to ensure that Oswald would be able to return to the United States without suffering any ill effects from his defection to the Soviet Union, and that he could move around freely in accomplishing his mission—whatever it might be—once he returned to the land of his birth. This letter, it should be noted, like Oswald's first communication to the embassy in 1959, was undated, so that the PGU could mail it when the time seemed right.

Oswald's letter begins with the statement: "Since I have not received a reply to my letter of December 1960, I am writing again asking that you consider my request for the return of my American passport." There is, however, no indication that he had written the embassy that December. The reference to an earlier letter has the ring of a common PGU tactic, in which the other person—in this case the embassy—is made to feel guilty and thereby somehow obligated to help. Oswald also writes that the Soviet authorities "have

at no time insisted that I take Russian citizenship," thus neatly fi-
nessing the fact that in October 1959 it was he who was insisting
on Soviet citizenship. Moreover he writes that he "cannot leave
Minsk without permission, therefore I am writing rather than calling in person." After the fiasco of Oswald's first visit to the embassy,
on October 31, 1959, the PGU was evidently reluctant to let him
out of its sight just yet.

The embassy replied to Oswald on February 28, saying that he
would have to come in for a personal interview before the status of
his American citizenship could be determined. That the embassy
did not dismiss Oswald's request out of hand was certainly an encouraging sign for his PGU handlers. Now it was important to
make sure that Oswald played his cards right.

Before Oswald would have been told to write that letter asking
the embassy to give him back his passport, the PGU's Thirteenth
Department would have had to create a legend for his stay in the
Soviet Union. And to support that story it would have had to find
some sympathetic individuals in the Dallas/Fort Worth area, where
Oswald might most easily settle upon returning to the United
States, who could be used to vouch for him and his experience in
the Soviet Union. Further events lend credence to the idea that the
eye of some Thirteenth Department officer may have landed on
George de Mohrenschildt, the flamboyant and gregarious Dallas
émigré employed in the oil industry who had descended from old
Russian nobility.

As noted earlier, de Mohrenschildt's file in the DIE archives
showed that in 1957–1958, when he was working with the International Cooperation Administration in Yugoslavia on assignment for
the U.S. Department of State, the PGU had prohibited the DIE
from targeting de Mohrenschildt for recruitment. That was a clear
and unmistakable sign that the PGU was already in contact with
him. His PGU file probably also contained an unexpected golden
nugget: de Mohrenschildt had for many years been close to the family of President Kennedy's wife, the Bouviers. Even his DIE file
showed that he would tell anyone who would listen that he had
known Jackie and her sister as little girls in New York. It was perhaps also known that in 1960 he had started a National Foundation

for Cystic Fibrosis with Jackie Kennedy as honorary chairman. Who could help Oswald to a better start in his new life, with a measure of protection, than this man who was so close to the American president's family?

Marina Oswald would later testify to the Warren Commission that de Mohrenschildt had told her about his connections with Jackie Kennedy. More significant is her testimony fourteen years later to the House Select Committee on Assassinations, by which time she mostly claimed to have difficulty remembering any details about her life with Oswald. Nonetheless she firmly stated: "I recall that George de Mohrenschildt told me once that when he was younger, I mean he knew Jackie Kennedy before she was married to John Kennedy."

De Mohrenschildt had grown up in Minsk, which is very likely why Minsk was chosen as the town where Oswald would ostensibly have spent his years in the Soviet Union. In fact de Mohrenschildt himself later confirmed that he had been attracted to Oswald because of the Minsk connection. After Kennedy's assassination he wrote that Oswald "had lived in Minsk, where I had spent my early childhood. And so I was curious to meet the [Oswald] couple and to find out what had happened to Minsk." Not only would Minsk give Oswald something in common with de Mohrenschildt, it would be generally helpful for cultivating contacts among the Russian émigré community in the Dallas/Fort Worth area. Minsk is the capital of Belarus (at that time called Belorussia), or White Russia, but among older Russian émigrés "White Russia" also connoted the opposite of Red, or Communist, Russia. In any case, Minsk projected the image of a conservative European cultural heritage. The city was also far enough away from Moscow to confine contacts between Oswald and the U.S. embassy mainly to written correspondence, which the PGU could closely monitor.

Sometime before February 13, 1961, when the embassy received Oswald's letter—which was postmarked February 5 in Minsk—the Thirteenth Department must have begun building a cover story for Oswald centered on the city of Minsk. Oswald would have been taken there so that he could begin familiarizing himself with the city. On March 10, Oswald was seen in Minsk by Katherine Mallory, a member of the visiting University of Michigan band. From the crowd of students gathered outside the Minsk Polytechnic Institute, where the band had been invited to a reception, a well-dressed young man stepped out and offered to interpret for her in conversation with others in the group. Although he did not give her his name, it was surely Oswald, for he mentioned that he was an ex-Marine from Texas now living in Minsk, adding that he despised the United States and hoped to spend the rest of his life in Minsk. Oswald's Thirteenth Department case officer was undoubtedly also in the crowd, and he would not have been happy to hear what Oswald said about himself after having just written the embassy to request re-entry to the United States. No wonder that Oswald's next letter to the embassy would claim that he could not possibly visit the embassy just then. Oswald is not known to have been seen by other American tourists in Minsk until August 10, when a Monica Kramer "accidentally" caught him in a photograph she snapped outside the Palace of Culture. They apparently did not exchange conversation.

On March 20, 1961, the U.S. embassy received a new letter from Oswald, dated March 12 and again posted from Minsk. In it Oswald stresses his inability to come to the embassy. He says he finds it "inconvenient to come to Moscow for the sole purpose of an interview," claims he cannot leave Minsk "without permission," and sees "no reasons for any preliminary inquiries not to be put in the form of a questionnaire and sent to me." Finally, he again implies that the situation is all the embassy's fault: "I understand that personal interviews undoubtedly make the work of the Embassy staff lighter, than written correspondence, however, in some cases other means must be employed." Unmoved, the embassy replied on March 24 and reiterated that he would have to come in for a personal interview, adding that the Soviet Foreign Ministry "has always assured the Embassy that it interposes no objections or obstacles to visits to the Embassy on the part of American citizens in the Soviet Union."

This answer from the U.S. embassy certainly put wings on the PGU's shoulders, because it clearly indicated that Oswald was still considered to be an American citizen. The U.S. government would have to take him back into the fold.

16

PRELUDE TO REPATRIATION

Having tested the waters and found that the U.S. government still considered Oswald an American citizen, the PGU would have set about in earnest to prepare him for his return to Texas. He would have spent weeks in Minsk familiarizing himself with the Minsk Radio Factory, where he was supposed to be working, and posing for photographs with a few carefully selected local figures who were supposed to be his close friends. That is exactly what the DIE would have done in order to authenticate the biography of an illegal officer or agent who was supposed to have spent a few years of his life in a remote Romanian town.

The next step the DIE would have made, had it been running Oswald's case, was to create at least one credible witness to this period of his life. Over the years I supervised well over a hundred cases of DIE officers documented with false identities, and I was directly involved in creating all kinds of witnesses for them, from parents, aunts, girlfriends, and fellow workers to sons and daughters. All were brought to life in strict accordance with the pattern established by the PGU, whose fingerprints I can readily discern all over the main witnesses for the years Oswald allegedly spent in Minsk.

In Marina Oswald's 1978 testimony to the House Select Committee on Assassinations, in which she claimed to have forgotten a great deal about the time she lived with Oswald, the only one of Oswald's Minsk friends Marina seemed to remember was Pavel Golovachev. She testified that "in Minsk Lee did not have very many friends. I do recall one young man working with him. His name was

Pavel Golovachev." She recalled that Golovachev liked to practice
his English with Oswald and was probably his closest friend there.
In an entry dated March 17–April 31, 1960, the "Historic Diary"
says: "I meet Pavil Golovacha. A younge man my age friendly very
intelligent a exalant radio techniction his father is Gen. Golovacha
Commander of Northwestenr Siberia. Twice hero of USSR in
W.W.2." (The general's existence was evidently confirmed by the
CIA.) Found among Oswald's effects after his arrest were at least
two photographs of Golovachev, including one showing him as he
"repairs a hi-fi." During her testimony to the Warren Commission in
1964, Marina was shown that photograph and stated that it "shows
Paul–Pavel Golovachev. He is assembling a television set. He sent
us this photograph. He is from Minsk. He worked in the same factory as Lee did."

Marina would also tell her biographer that Golovachev, who
worked at the radio factory with Oswald, belonged to the golden
elite and was far and away Oswald's "closest friend in Russia, and
probably the closest friend he ever had." In 1978, when asked if she
had heard from Golovachev since leaving Minsk, Marina testified:
"I do believe when we moved back to the United States, we did receive some letters from the Soviet Union, but I do not remember exactly from whom." In fact, some of the letters signed in Golovachev's name are available; Oswald's correspondence with him
could very possibly have also served as a kind of temporary, open-
code communication channel between Oswald and the Thirteenth
Department. The photographs of Golovachev himself, including
one together with Oswald, were apparently sent with a letter dated
September 15, 1962. (This will be discussed later in considering
clandestine communications between Oswald and the PGU after
his return to the United States.)

In regard to Pavel Golovachev himself, it is unlikely that such a
bona fide member of the Soviet elite would have become best
friends with a defector like Oswald, who was characterized as mentally unstable. Kim Philby, probably the most highly regarded defector the Soviet Union ever had, has often been described as not
having had any real friends except for fellow defectors after he settled in Moscow, and as having fallen into periodic fits of drunken-

ness and depression, though the PGU now and then engaged him for writing projects or training courses. "Golden youths" such as Golovachev were just what the DIE also used—without their knowledge—to document sensitive cases. Photomontage was no problem for the PGU—as it was not for the DIE—and the picture of Oswald with Golovachev and two girls looks especially stiff and unnatural. The fact that Golovachev was one of the persons whom the Soviet government refused Edward Jay Epstein permission to interview also suggests that my suspicion about him is well founded.

Once the Minsk story had been prepared, the PGU would have turned its attention to training Oswald for his new intelligence assignment. The DIE had no experience with Americans who were sent back to the West, but the author John Barron describes the case of "Anton Sabotka," a PGU agent whose case may serve as a good example of the type of training and instructions Oswald might have received. (Barron did not reveal Anton's real name in order to protect him in the new life he embarked upon after his arrest in 1972 by Canadian authorities, with whom he then fully cooperated.) Anton was born in Canada into a family of immigrants who in 1946 took him back to their native Czechoslovakia. His father, a fanatical Communist, became a party leader in a rural Slovak district. For his part, Anton cooperated with the Czechoslovak political police, the STB, truly believing that by doing so he would help his adoptive country. In the summer of 1957 he was taken over by the KGB's Thirteenth Department, which persuaded him to repatriate back to Canada, where he was to perform "special" tasks in a time of "crisis."

From an operational standpoint, Anton's case was almost identical to Oswald's. He spoke English like a native Canadian and was completely at home with Canadian habits and customs. His Canadian citizenship entitled him to a valid Canadian passport and legal residence in Canada. His past intelligence work for the STB constituted a guarantee that he would remain loyal in the future. Even his final task appeared identical: to carry out sabotage operations, which had just been added to the Thirteenth Department's responsibilities.

In 1958 the PGU secretly moved Anton to Moscow for operational training. There he was comfortably lodged in a safe house, whose housekeeper prepared his meals and kept the refrigerator stocked with food, vodka, and beer. Six days a week, between 9 a.m. and 5 p.m., Anton was drilled by a stream of PGU instructors. They started by training him in a variety of "methods of clandestine communications," such as "ciphers, codes, invisible writing, microdots, drops, recognition signals, and radio procedures." A couple of months later, when this part of Anton's training was finished, he also learned how to unload messages from agent dead drops and relay them to the PGU by radio, or deposit them in hiding places, from where they would be retrieved by persons unknown to him.

In Oswald's case there are valid indications that he too was trained in the techniques of clandestine communications. On returning to the United States in 1962, Oswald occasionally listed his occupation as "photographer," though he is not known ever to have been trained as one. For example, he told the employment office at the Louisiana Department of Labor on April 26, 1963, that he was qualified as a commercial photographer, and on September 17 of that year he listed his occupation as photographer when applying for a Mexican tourist card. Oswald did spend a few months in late 1962 and early 1963 working at the Dallas graphics firm of Jaggars-Chiles-Stovall, whose photocopying equipment he used to fabricate certain false identity documents for himself. There he once suggestively asked a fellow employee if he knew what a microdot was, proceeding to explain that it was a technique used in espionage whereby a number of documents could be reduced to a dot and hidden "under a postage stamp." Oswald also noted the word *microdot* in his address book, next to the entry for Jaggars-Chiles-Stovall. In the late 1950s and throughout the 1960s, microdots were all the rage among Soviet-bloc intelligence services. At first the PGU did indeed recommend hiding them under postage stamps as a way of sending messages to agents; but in the mid-1960s the technique was refined to employ bleached microdots that were virtually invisible and could be far better concealed—buried in the binding of a book or pressed onto the surface of a phonograph record. There is no evidence that Oswald ever received microdots from the PGU, but his knowledge of microdots as an espionage technique suggests he was trained in their use.

In order to equip Anton to handle any situation, he was also trained in marksmanship at a firing range that was ostensibly part of a "sporting club." When Anton saw the target, however, he understood he was not being trained for sport. "It consisted of the silhouette of the upper half of a man's body with target circles centered in the middle of the chest." Anton practiced mostly with American pistols, and he learned to fire both carefully aimed single shots and rapid point-blank fusillades. His target practice normally lasted one hour. By the time Anton left the Soviet Union he had become so proficient that he occasionally outshot his instructor. Perhaps Oswald was trained at the same firing range.

The DIE had a similar firing range contained in a large safe house located on May Day Boulevard, at the outskirts of Bucharest, where an illegal officer or agent who was being trained in kidnapping or sabotage operations could spend days or weeks, as required. The firing range had a screen on which were projected films simulating specific types of operations; the trainee fired at the screen, which would freeze at the sound of the shot and show what part of the target's body the bullet had hit.

For all Soviet-bloc cases who received this special training, there was a strongly enforced rule: they were forbidden to talk about it even if arrested. For disinformation purposes, they were also to represent themselves as being totally unfamiliar with firearms. An item that the defector Yury Nosenko reported about Oswald sounds just like part of such a disinformation operation. According to Nosenko—who was not part of the PGU team handling Oswald—a few weeks after the Kennedy assassination a friend told him that "the KGB had conducted an investigation of Oswald's activities in Minsk, in which it was learned he had occasionally gone hunting with members of a gun club. His fellow hunters had considered him such a bad shot, they often had to give him game."

There is no reason to believe Oswald was a poor shot, and in fact his assassination of Kennedy from a window of the Texas School Book Depository proved just the opposite. It is significant, however, that when Oswald left the Soviet Union he "was allowed" to take along a membership certificate in the Belorussian Society of Hunters and Fishermen and a gun permit, both issued in the summer of 1960, as well as a hunting license issued to him on July 18, 1960, by the party organization at the Minsk Radio Factory where Oswald was supposedly working, and valid for one year. That contradicts the customs regulations of the time, which prohibited people emigrating from the Soviet Union from carrying any identification papers with them besides those issued by the Soviet authorities for the purpose of emigration. After he returned to the United States, Oswald would repeatedly show his Belorussian hunting club papers to other people, and he would talk openly about his membership in that club. The documents were still in his wallet on the day of his arrest after the assassination. They had most likely been prepared by the PGU to accord with Oswald's cover story of residence in Minsk and to provide a documentary basis for launching the PGU rumor that his fellow hunters considered Oswald a poor shot, should such disinformation become desirable.

Anton's PGU instructors never clearly defined his mission in Canada, and whenever he asked he received vague answers. Over the months of his training, however, Anton came to realize what he would be asked to do. The subject most emphasized besides communications was the identification and evaluation of sabotage targets. He had to "report about factories, refineries and power plants: their location as fixed by three bearings; dimensions and shape; materials used in construction; nature of the facility; source of power; security measures in effect; capacity or output; sites from which it might safely be observed; its peculiar vulnerabilities to sabotage."

The DIE too had a special camp in which the students—DIE illegal officers and members of the Spanish and Greek Communist parties—were trained for sabotage operations. The camp was tucked away in the area of Snagov, a resort town north of Bucharest, and had its own firing range and fields for pyrotechnics. Except for one theoretical course on Marxism, the entire training program concentrated on practical studies, such as radio communications, ciphers, marksmanship, and the use of weapons and explosives. The camp's main goal was to produce experts in blowing up buildings, railroad stations, and bridges. All students were provided with false names to hide their real identities from one another and from their Romanian instructors.

No evidence has come to light to suggest that Oswald received similar training in sabotage. On the other hand, Anton never whispered a word about this part of his training before he was arrested and agreed to cooperate with Canadian counterintelligence. That was to be expected. Every day at the DIE's sabotage camp began and ended with lessons preaching the need for secrecy. It was drummed into the students' heads that the slightest allusion to such training could cause them to be suddenly suspected as terrorists. That would not only restrict their freedom of movement but would severely damage the Communist international they served.

Nevertheless certain evidence suggests that Oswald did have Thirteenth Department connections. Oswald himself indicated as much when on a visit to Mexico City in September/October 1963 he met with a Soviet embassy official named Kostikov, whom he also referred to in an apparently operational context as "comrade Kostin." Valery Vladimirovich Kostikov was an identified officer of the PGU's Thirteenth Department who at the time was assigned to Mexico City under consular cover and in fact had been there since September 1961. It is worth noting that Oswald was originally scheduled to leave the Soviet Union for the United States around October 1961–a month after Kostikov's arrival in Mexico City–but his departure was postponed for several months because the State Department delayed the entrance visa for his wife, Marina. It is possible that Oswald first met Kostikov as Comrade Kostin in the Soviet Union while Oswald was being trained by the Thirteenth Department for his special assignment. (PGU Thirteenth Department case officer Mikhail Mikhaylovich Antipov was, for example, assigned to the United Nations in New York after he had finished training the agent Anton. Although Anton had been dispatched back to his native Canada, he understood that he might sometime be given tasks in the United States.)

At that time Mexico was the PGU's (and the DIE's) preferred location for meeting its agents who lived in the United States, and it is quite possible that Kostikov was assigned to Mexico City in order to provide Oswald with personal contact and logistical support as needed. For such support purposes it was common for the PGU's Thirteenth Department (and the DIE's Group Z) to assign those officers to the Soviet (Romanian) embassies in the relevant Western cities who had previously met the respective agents and were familiar with their cases.

When an agent of the PGU's Thirteenth Department had completed his training, all he could normally expect to know about his future mission was that it would be "difficult but honorable," in the words of KGB chairman Aleksandr Shelepin when speaking on one occasion to an officer in training for assassinations. In the case of Anton, after more than a year of training he was "equipped with sufficient rudimentary knowledge to commit sabotage or kill on his own," if the PGU so ordered, and he understood that he might be required to perform "special" tasks in a time of crisis. In other words, Anton was programmed to do whatever the PGU wanted him to do. For the time being he was told that he should first go to Canada, from where he might be moved to the United States after several years. Anton was ordered to settle in Edmonton, where he was born and grew up. There he was to "find a job and a house, create a normal life, then simply wait." During his resettlement in Canada, Anton had only to keep the PGU "advised of his whereabouts and status." Sometime after he was fully settled, Anton was told, a man would approach him and identify himself as a PGU representative. Anton was to "obey whatever orders he conveyed."

Circumstantial evidence indicates that Oswald might have had a better idea about his mission than Anton did. In 1964, Marina Oswald testified to the Warren Commission that her husband had once said, "if someone had killed Hitler in time it would have saved many lives." I can easily hear Oswald's case officer hammering that thought into his head day after day, but substituting "Kennedy" for "Hitler." Marina also told her biographer that Oswald once complained that Kennedy's "papa bought him the presidency," a remark recalling Khrushchev's disdain for Kennedy as the "millionaire's kid." Paul Gregory, a young man who used to visit the Oswalds to practice his Russian soon after their arrival in Fort Worth, recalled that inevitably their conversations turned to politics. "As for Khrushchev, Lee described him as 'simply brilliant.' . . . He also liked John F. Kennedy. On their living room table the Oswalds kept, more or less permanently, a copy of *Life* magazine with a cover photo of the President."

One other important thing the PGU had to do before dispatching Oswald back to the United States was to ensure that he would not sell out to the enemy. After Khrushchev came to power, the PGU's Thirteenth Department was plagued by resounding defections that terribly damaged the Soviet Union's international prestige. Another compromised Thirteenth Department operation would have been too politically disastrous to contemplate. "A wife," was the broken record at that time of the DIE's *razvedka* adviser. "Give the *serzhant* a wife and a child. That will tie him to us for all eternity."

Anton landed in Montreal with his Czechoslovakian wife and six-year-old Czechoslovakian-born son on May 29, 1961. His child carried through customs a toy truck in which the PGU had concealed cipher pads, microdots containing communications instructions, a microdot reader, and a Minox camera. One year later, when Lee Harvey Oswald returned to the United States, he was accompanied by his Soviet-born wife and daughter. On June 13, 1962, was baby June Oswald clutching a toy when she went through customs in Hoboken, New Jersey?

17

MARINA

On May 5, 1961, Oswald wrote his brother Robert for the first time in "more than two years." He did not yet mention that he was trying to return to the United States, but he did announce: "On April 30 of this year I got married. My wife . . . was born in the city of Leningrad." In a letter postmarked May 16 in Moscow, he also informed the U.S. embassy that he had married since he had last written, saying, "My wife is Russian, born in Leningrad, she has no parents living and is quite willing to leave the Soviet Union with me and live in the United States." Again he said he could not come to Moscow and asked for "guarantees that I shall not, under any circumstances, be persecuted for any act pertaining to this case."

Oswald's "Historic Diary" records that he met "Marina N. Prosakoba" at a dance on March 17, 1961, married her on April 30 "at her aunts home," but did not tell her anything about his "desire to return to US" until "in the last days of [June 1961] I revele my longing to return to America. My wife is slightly startled. But than encourages me to do what I wish to do."

Soviet law at the time required that marriages between Soviet citizens and Westerners be approved by Moscow. (In Romania they had to be approved by the Council of State, the highest governmental forum, the chairman of which was the country's president.) As vice chairman of Romania's National Commission for Visas and Passports, which was the instrument behind the scenes for resolving such cases, I had a good picture of how the process worked. It was a bureaucratic nightmare that followed the Soviet rules to the letter and might drag on for years. Even if Oswald had requested this approval on the very first day he met Marina, there was no way on earth for him to have received it in six weeks. Shuffling his file from Minsk to Moscow would alone have certainly taken longer than that. There was only one exception to this sinuous process, and that was when some element of the government had a special interest in seeing the marriage expeditiously concluded.

Quite a few other facts strongly lead to the conclusion that Marina was selected by the Thirteenth Department to become Oswald's wife, and that the whole operation involving her was run against the clock. Marina seems to have been hastily selected. During the next few months before the couple appeared in person at the U.S. embassy, her biography seems to have been revised and improved upon. As noted earlier, in his May 1961 letters to his brother Robert and to the U.S. embassy in Moscow, Oswald wrote that his wife was born in the city of Leningrad. Her birth certificate, on the other hand, shows that Marina Nikolayevna Prusakova was born in "Molotovsk" (which later reverted to the name Severodvinsk), in "Archangel *oblast*" (district).

Not only is Severodvinsk in a remote northern area where it would be unlikely for anyone in the West to be able to confirm her birth record, but to émigrés in the West the Archangel area would have been favorably known as the site of many Stalin-era gulags holding anti-Soviet prisoners. The Thirteenth Department probably had second thoughts about allowing Marina to use Leningrad, which was perhaps her true birthplace, because people like George Bouhe, the unofficial dean of Russian émigrés in the Dallas/Fort Worth area where Oswald was to return, had originally come from there when it was called St. Petersburg and might still have connections there who could check on her background.

In fact Marina's whole family background story seems to have evolved a little too hastily. In the West she would claim that she knew nothing about her father, not even his name, and that she took the name of her stepfather, Aleksandr Medvedev. In this case, however, her patronymic should have been Aleksandrovna, not Nikolayevna. When challenged on that point, Marina replied with an involved story that even her sympathetic biographer found to be scarcely credible.

From an operational standpoint, Marina's case closely parallels that of "Andrea," the wife created by the DIE for "Malek," a civilian working for NATO. When the DIE selected and prepared Andrea, it strictly followed the PGU pattern for creating a "wife." I now find significant evidence that the same PGU pattern was applied to Marina. The first rule of that pattern was that there should be documented evidence that the proposed wife was very good at sex, so that she would have a firm hold on her husband. In Andrea's case the DIE had secretly filmed her making love with various West German businessmen, who had been wild about her sexual talents. Marina looks just like another Andrea in this respect. When she met Oswald, Marina was an attractive young woman of nineteen, who later, in intimate discussions with George de Mohrenschildt's wife Jeanne in Texas, nostalgically recalled the wild "sexual orgies" she had participated in before her marriage. According to Jeanne, Marina's passion for such orgies looked "like a degeneration, you know, definitely [moral] degeneration." Once, while being driven by Jeanne through a nightclub area full of "flashy pimps," Marina became extremely excited upon seeing a muscular, sexy male. "He is fantastic, fantastic!" she exulted. "Maybe the Cubans I met in Minsk were just as attractive."

Another PGU requirement was that the would-be wife have professional credentials that would make a good impression in the West. Andrea, who was actually a cabaret dancer, was documented as an executive secretary. Marina was documented as a pharmacist, but the people who met her after she came to the United States found it remarkable that nothing she did in her daily routine seemed to indicate any pharmaceutical training. Describing how Marina broke even the most elementary hygiene rules in caring for her first baby, Jeanne de Mohrenschildt concluded: "That is what didn't make sense, didn't make sense at all. After all, a pharmacist."

The PGU pattern also required that the biography of the designated wife show that she came from a family that had in some way been persecuted by the Communist government, so as to arouse the sympathy of the target, and later, of his relatives and friends in the

West. Andrea's father had been a political prisoner in Communist Romania, and his properties had been nationalized. Marina's biography showed her to have been brought up in an old-fashioned Russian environment, not by doctrinaire Communists. The émigrés in Texas were impressed with her background because, as George de Mohrenschildt would write, she "came from a fairly good family from our point of view, since her father belonged to a former tsarist officer group. After his death her mother married a man called Prussakov. . . . Russian refugees liked Marina only because her real father had been a prerevolutionary officer or some tsarist official." On top of that, Marina had also been "dropped" from the Komsomol (the Communist Youth Organization), allegedly "for nonpayment of dues." Coincidentally, Andrea's biography showed that for the same reason she had been excluded from the Union of Young Communists, Romania's equivalent of the Komsomol.

Another element of the PGU pattern required that the future wife have a "relative," usually an uncle, who was connected with the intelligence business in some way and who could later be used to explain how the target was able to obtain the marriage approval and exit visa for his new wife. Andrea's "uncle" was DIE Col. Cristian Scornea, who later recruited Malek. Marina, like Andrea, also had an uncle connected with the intelligence business. His name was Ilya Prusakov, and he was conveniently living in Minsk. Marina would testify to the Warren Commission that Prusakov was an MVD (Ministry of Internal Affairs) official, and that because of his position she had succeeded in getting through to another MVD official in late 1961 who had helped get her exit visa. According to Oswald's "Historic Diary," it was on December 25, 1961, that Marina was called in to the "passport & visa office" and told "we have been granted Soviet exit visa's." George de Mohrenschildt would write the version understood by the Texas émigrés: "Marina had an uncle, a colonel of special forces NKVD–KGB today. . . . Maybe this colonel for his own reasons helped his niece to get out of Russia."

Marina's uncle, the MVD or KGB colonel, was a stock character for many years in the KGB's VGU (domestic security and counterintelligence) and PGU scenarios taking place inside the Soviet Union. Sometimes he would appear on the scene to rail angrily at the poor Westerner who was having an amorous affair with his "niece," later perhaps to calm down and agree to intercede with the authorities on the culprit's behalf if the latter would agree to cooperate and provide certain information. The "uncle in the KGB" continued for many years to play various roles in VGU/PGU operations. Several Marines stationed at the U.S. embassy in Moscow in 1986 and carrying on affairs with local Soviet girls were eventually introduced to an "Uncle Sasha," who was actually a KGB officer who tried to recruit them.

In his 1987 statements to investigators, one of those Marines, Sgt. Clayton J. Lonetree (who was later sentenced for his espionage activity), described how his relationship with Violetta Aleksandrovna Seina, a Soviet translator for English, grew from what he described as a chance meeting in a Moscow subway station into a series of clandestine rendezvous in a house ostensibly owned by her Uncle Sasha. A few months later Violetta introduced Lonetree to her Uncle Sasha himself, at another meeting that also began "in a subway station." Another of those Marines, Cpl. Arnold Bracy, was accused by American authorities of failing to report personal contacts with an attractive Soviet cook and her Uncle Sasha.

In Marina's case, her "Uncle Ilya" apparently served the function of helping explain the relative ease with which she was able to obtain her exit visa.

The PGU formula also required that the designated wife become pregnant as soon as she had a hold on the target. In Andrea's case that happened a few months after she met Malek, who soon after that told "Uncle Scornea" that he had decided to divorce his wife and marry Andrea. In Marina's case that happened in 1961, just a few months after she met Oswald.

According to the "Historic Diary," in September or October 1961 Marina went away for four weeks to visit an aunt in "Khkov in the Urals," even though she was a newlywed who had just recently become pregnant. She would later tell her biographer that she had been due for a three-week vacation and had spent most of it visiting two aunts in Kharkov. (Kharkov, incidentally, is in Ukraine, not the Urals.) That was another rule of the PGU pattern: before leaving the country, the designated wife should be given an intensive training course—without the knowledge of her husband. In 1978, just before leaving Romania, Andrea also disappeared for a couple of weeks. She told Malek that she wished to say goodbye to her relatives in the Brasov area, but in fact she spent all that time in a DIE safe house undergoing intensive training for her future tasks in Austria. Andrea too was pregnant at the time.

When Marina left the Soviet Union, she carried a short "Autobiography" that shows not only the important dates in her own brief life but also the names and positions of her relatives. It reads remarkably like the kind of life story the DIE and other Soviet-bloc officers prepared for their agents to memorize. Except for names, places, and dates, Marina's "Autobiography" looks just like the one Andrea wrote out for herself in preparation for her departure for Vienna.

According to my own experience in such cases, Marina either should have already been a PGU agent—but probably one without compromising operational experience—or should have become one when selected to become Oswald's wife. In either case her main assignment would have been to support her husband in every way, from providing moral encouragement and sexual pleasure, to covering for him when operational tasks took him away from home, and supporting any cover story that explained his absence.

When Thirteenth Department illegal officer Bogdan Stashinsky fell in love with Inge, an East German girl, the chairman of the KGB himself, Aleksandr Shelepin, urged him to forget her and marry a KGB girl instead, "who could assist him on illegal assignments." When Stashinsky remained adamant, Shelepin acquiesced but insisted that Inge be trained and indoctrinated in Moscow. In August 1961 Inge did in fact cause her husband to defect. After that, the Thirteenth Department, and the DIE, were doubly concerned that the wives of its illegal officers and special agents who were being prepared for dispatch to the West should provide strong operational support for their husbands.

Investigators and researchers of the Kennedy assassination have encountered special difficulties in obtaining reliable information from Marina, which strongly suggests that she may have indeed been protecting her husband's operations. William Manchester, who in

1967 published a meticulous account of the Kennedy assassination, wrote: "Of all I approached only one, the assassin's widow, failed to respond to my request for cooperation."

In 1978, when Marina testified to the House Select Committee on Assassinations, she generally professed to have a very poor memory of almost all events in her life with Oswald. In exasperation one member of the House committee said to her, "You have told so many versions of this period, for various reasons. . . . At what point are we to believe what you are saying before this committee?" Marina responded, "May I consult with my attorney, please?" but did not answer the question.

Another intelligence task for Marina would have been that of helping Oswald circulate socially among the Texas émigrés who might unwittingly be used in the accomplishment of his mission. As it turned out, Marina made an excellent initial impression on the Russian émigrés in the Dallas/Fort Worth area. Upon meeting the Oswalds, George Bouhe, an aristocratic old gentleman and leader of the émigré community, was totally captivated by Marina's "pure Leningrad Russian, innocent of jargon or slang, that [to the émigrés] bespoke intelligence and education." Bouhe was particularly attentive and asked Marina numerous questions about Leningrad. Soon after meeting her, he went out of his way to help her and her husband. He also put them in contact with people who would play a crucial role in Oswald's future actions.

In spite of Marina's possible connections with the PGU, it was perhaps literally true that, as Oswald told his mother upon arriving in Texas: "Not even Marina knows why I have returned to the United States." Nor did Andrea know the specific nature of Malek's espionage work for the Romanian DIE.

Of course the ultimate question remains: If Marina was indeed at one time connected with the PGU, why did she not acknowledge that fact after Oswald had shot President Kennedy? Or why did she not at least come forward and tell her real story after the Soviet Union itself collapsed? Once again I look to Andrea for the answer. Before she left Romania her DIE case officer told her, at every meeting, that if she should ever divulge her connection with the DIE, the arm of the proletariat was long enough to reach her and her children anywhere on earth. Ceausescu's Romania collapsed in December 1989, but to the best of my knowledge Andrea has never yet breathed a word about her agent status, though she now lives in the United States and has been repeatedly questioned about it by the FBI and other Western counterintelligence services.

18

A FOOTHOLD IN TEXAS

WITHOUT advance notice, Oswald appeared at the U.S. embassy in Moscow on Saturday, July 8, 1961, to ask to be repatriated. He was persuaded to return to the embassy with Marina on Monday, July 10, and again the following day. The embassy gave him back his passport, stamped valid only for direct travel to the United States. (That one would actually expire before he could leave, but he would be issued a new one.) Procedures for Marina's immigration were initiated. Although Marina's Soviet exit visa was allegedly approved by the end of that year, State Department bureaucratic procedures held up the Oswalds' departure another five months. They did not visit the embassy again until May 24, 1962, to complete their final documents and get Marina's visa. Then they paid the embassy one last visit on June 1 to obtain a loan for their travel. They left Moscow that same day, accompanied by their daughter, June, who had been born on February 15. Their travel arrangements had been made by the embassy.

The Oswald family sailed from Rotterdam on the *SS Maasdam*, arriving in Hoboken, New Jersey, on June 13. The U.S. embassy in Moscow had arranged for someone from the Traveler's Aid Society in New York to meet their ship and help with the next leg of their journey. Thanks to a loan from Robert Oswald, the family flew on safely to Fort Worth on June 14. At first the family lived with Oswald's mother, but in August, once he had begun earning money, they moved into a furnished apartment of their own.

Oswald did not like it when his mother bought clothes for Marina and a high chair for the baby. Marguerite Oswald would testify that "he strongly put me in my place about buying things for his wife that he himself could not buy." That would be a theme running throughout the family's relationships with other Americans as well. Although Oswald never made much money and often reproved his wife for caring about material goods, the reason seems to have been less a feeling of shame that he could not himself afford to buy things for his family than a desire for them to remain spartan Marxists and not encumber themselves with things they would in any case not be able to take back to Moscow with them.

Oswald soon severed all relations with his mother, and after Thanksgiving also with his brother. Just as he had used his mother to gain an early discharge from the Marine Corps and then almost immediately cut his ties with her and his brother in order to get on with what was probably an earlier PGU assignment, so he must have again needed to be free of family restraints in order to start building an operational base for his current assignment.

The first thing Oswald did after arriving in Fort Worth was to visit the Texas Employment Commission and ask about work as a Russian translator. He also took his manuscript about life in the Soviet Union to a public stenographer and had her type up some of it, though as it turned out the manuscript would serve only as entrée to people he wanted to meet. To me these moves appear to have been part of the scenario prepared for Oswald in Moscow to further his contact with the Russian community, where the PGU certainly had sources that could indirectly help him and also keep an eye on him.

The employment commission gave Oswald the names of two people to consult about translating jobs: one led nowhere, but the other name was that of Peter Gregory, a petroleum engineer who in his spare time was teaching Russian at the Fort Worth Public Library. On June 19, 1962, Oswald met Gregory to talk about possible translating work, also chatting about his Russian wife and about his manuscript on life in the Soviet Union. Gregory became interested in him, and soon Oswald was on his way to meeting others in the local Russian émigré community.

Gregory's son Paul began visiting the Oswalds for Russian conversation practice with Marina. Paul suggested that Marina should in turn begin studying English, but Oswald would have none of it. "He did not want Marina to learn English, he justified, lest he lose his own fluency in Russian."

In January 1962, while he was still in the Soviet Union, Oswald received a letter from his mother telling him the Marine Corps had changed his discharge to "dishonorable"—actually it was changed to "undesirable." If Oswald had indeed been sent back to the United States on assignment for the PGU's Thirteenth Department, he would certainly have been told to try to change the status of his military records. It was a cardinal operational principle with the PGU and its sister services that an agent should look pristine and be scrupulous about remaining within the law in everything he did overtly, so that he would not come to the attention of the authorities for the wrong reason and thereby perhaps inadvertently compromise his clandestine activities.

As soon as Oswald received his mother's letter, while he was still in the Soviet Union, he wrote not only to his brother Robert for information but also to Texas governor John Connally, in the mistaken belief that he was still secretary of the navy, and later to Texas senator John Tower, in an effort to clear his record. The latter two names must have been given to Oswald by the PGU, for he would not have known them by himself or found them anywhere in faraway Minsk. The legalistic arguments he uses in his letters also strongly suggest PGU guidance. The undesirable record stood, however.

The desire to have his undesirable discharge corrected would be a constant theme running through the rest of Oswald's life. Upon arriving in Texas on June 14 and finally seeing his brother Robert again, this subject was one of the first things Oswald brought up. On June 18 he filed a petition with the Naval Discharge Review Board, but ultimately the navy refused to change its decision. Oswald periodically tried to do something about it, but when in the summer of 1963 he eventually learned it would cost money for a lawyer even if he should succeed, he seemed to give up and handle the matter in his own way. Starting with the first application he filled out for the Texas Employment Commission in Fort Worth, Oswald simply claimed that he had been honorably discharged, probably correctly figuring that no one would bother to check. That was what he also claimed when applying on October 15, 1963, for employment with the Texas School Book Depository.

Another PGU concern about Oswald's resettlement in the United States was apparently to create a publicly plausible reason for him and his family to wish to return to the Soviet Union at the end of his mission. In late July 1962, Oswald was hired as a sheet-metal worker by the Leslie Welding Company in Fort Worth. He remained there until he left voluntarily—though telling his wife he had been fired—on October 8, 1962, and moved to Dallas the next day. Oswald now set a pattern of changing jobs frequently, at first falsely claiming he had been fired and later seeming deliberately to start performing so poorly that he would be let go. (He would be fired from jobs on April 6 and July 19, 1963.) As we shall see, his loss of work always seemed to fit conveniently with his apparent operational plans. Beginning in the summer of 1963, when he started openly expressing interest in returning to the Soviet Union, his alleged difficulties in finding regular employment helped justify that intention. After July 19 he went on unemployment compensation until October while falsely claiming he had been turned down at job interviews.

It seems likely that Oswald gradually and deliberately began building a picture of himself as a persecuted man who could not find a job that would enable him to care for his family and whose wife did not speak English and was unhappy in this country. When he lost the job in April 1963, a fellow employee gave him names of places where he might look for work, but Oswald just laughed wryly and said that if he failed to find anything else he could "always go back to Russia." In October, before getting his final job at the Texas School Book Depository, Oswald looked, in the opinion of Ruth Paine, who was by then the Oswalds' only friend, "extremely discouraged because his wife was expecting a baby, he had no job prospects in sight, and he no longer had any source of income."

Such a picture of the miserable life that had been forced upon the Oswalds in the United States would have given them a perfectly plausible reason for suddenly deciding to return to the Soviet Union. The PGU's Thirteenth Department presumably gave Oswald the same kind of instructions it gave Anton, its Canadian-born agent: settle near your relatives, find a job and house, then wait until you receive your next assignment–or, if the agent already knew his assignment, wait for instructions about when and how to begin work on it. That was routine at that time, and there is no reason to believe that the PGU changed anything for Oswald.

The restive Oswald, however, had no time to waste. He was convinced, it seems, that Kennedy was a new Hitler who had badly humiliated the "brilliant" Khrushchev and his beloved Soviet Union before the whole world, and evidently he truly believed that the sooner he got rid of Kennedy the better it would be for mankind. At the same time Oswald must have thought that the sooner he accomplished his "historic" mission, the sooner he would be allowed to return to Moscow, where he would finally be able to start his real life.

Until late August 1962 the Oswalds met no one else among the Russian émigrés besides the Gregorys. But on approximately August 25 the Gregorys gave a small dinner party at which the Oswalds were introduced to a few other émigrés, including George Bouhe. He was very interested in talking to Marina because she had grown up in his birthplace. Having made a good first impression on Bouhe, the Oswalds soon began to meet other members of the Russian community, twenty-five of whom would testify to the Warren Commission or its staff. Some of the women gave Marina clothes and kindly took her into their houses when they believed Oswald was mistreating her, but the community's relationship with Oswald himself would never develop into real friendship. He objected to the assistance people tried to give Marina, and his espousal of Marxist and anti-American political positions alienated everyone. By the end of 1962 all the Russian émigrés had dropped the Oswalds, with the exception of the de Mohrenschildts.

George de Mohrenschildt would later write that when he heard rumors about the Oswalds from members of the Russian-speaking community in Dallas/Fort Worth in the summer of 1962, he became curious and looked them up. Oswald was "supposedly an ex-marine, an unfriendly and eccentric character, who had gone to Russia and brought back with him a Russian wife. He had lived in Minsk, where I had spent my early childhood." According to Marina's biographer, some people said Oswald was just one of the many "stray dogs" that the unconventional de Mohrenschildt and his wife Jeanne took in.

De Mohrenschildt remarked to Oswald that he had known Jackie Kennedy and all her family when she was still a girl. Until April 1963 the de Mohrenschildts tried to help the Oswalds, but once more Oswald resented efforts to coddle Marina or give her gifts of food and clothing, and he did not follow up on the better-quality job leads that de Mohrenschildt suggested to him.

19

THE COMMO PLAN

T HE FOREIGN intelligence community of the Soviet bloc always considered communications with its sources in the West to be the most sensitive aspect of its operations. PGU statistics sent to the DIE showed that some 80 percent of the community's operational failures (apart from defections) had been caused by inadequate contact arrangements with its agents. The meetings between an agent and a PGU officer with diplomatic cover—who was subject to local surveillance and monitoring—were always considered the most vulnerable point and a primary cause of compromise. In the mid-1950s the PGU therefore shifted toward using impersonal communications systems with its most important sources in the West. The PGU component that produced operational equipment for impersonal contact and serviced the PGU's impersonal communications systems with its illegal officers and agents gradually grew to the point that it became a behemoth, with its own laboratories, production facilities, broadcasting stations, radio communication centers, and a mail censorship unit. Soon the corresponding components in the sister services followed suit. In the DIE this component was called Brigade M, and it had the status of a *Securitate* headquarters directorate.

Toward the end of the 1950s a commo (communications) plan for an illegal officer or agent sent to the West on a special mission was usually based on impersonal contacts in the country where he was assigned, augmented by one or at most two personal meetings a year in a third country. These plans also included the so-called iron meeting—*zheleznaya yavka* in Russian—as a standard item for emergency situations, *iron* meaning ironclad or invariable.

"Johann," a DIE illegal officer who in 1959 was sent to West Germany to take action against the defector Constantin Mandache, was a good example. According to his commo plan, which was prepared by the PGU *razvedka* adviser for "wet" affairs, Johann received short enciphered messages from DIE headquarters via shortwave radio transmissions in Morse code broadcast from Romania, which he could pick up on a standard, high-quality portable radio receiver. Longer instructions were sent to him via microdots hidden under the postage stamps of letters and greeting cards mailed from West Germany to one of his post office boxes. All the instructions were enciphered—at that time a microdot could contain some four hundred groups of five digits. On his end, Johann reported on his relocation and his day-to-day nonoperational activity in open letters mailed to an accommodation address in Vienna. His operational reports were dead-dropped in West Germany in the form of unprocessed films (each dead drop being used only once). The films were made with a Minox camera, its standard carrying chain used as a guide for the distance the camera should be held above the document being photographed. In emergency or unexpected situations, Johann could mail encoded secret-writing messages on pages of a *Der Stern* magazine to another accommodation address in Austria.

When Johann left for West Germany he took with him a shaving brush containing his one-time cipher pads on soft film, a wooden clothes brush concealing a Minox camera, a wooden hairbrush concealing a microdot reader, a notebook containing carbon sheets for secret writing, and a specially modified Grundig radio receiver. He also openly carried a German book by Goethe, *Die Leiden des jungen Werthers* (The Sorrows of Young Werther), an identical copy of which was kept at DIE headquarters. That book was to be used as a cipher key in case something happened to Johann's one-time cipher pads. Johann also had an iron meeting for emergency situations, but that too was impersonal. Once a month he had to pass by an advertising column located in downtown Düsseldorf, where he was living, and look for signals from headquarters. A yellow dot glued on that column meant he was called to a personal meeting in Austria; a red one indicated he was in danger and should destroy all his commo gear.

The case of the British RAF corporal Geoffrey Arthur Prime, which coincided in time with Oswald's, shows that the PGU was using these same commo plans. At Karlshorst in East Germany, Prime was trained in "the receipt of radio transmissions, secret writing, encryption, use of ciphers and microdots, operation of a miniature camera, and the use of dead drops." Prime was told he would not be met in person in the United Kingdom, only in a neutral country; he was given the choice of Finland or Austria, and he chose the latter. At the end of his training Prime was sent off with a Minox camera on a chain, a set of one-time pads for encryption, and a writing tablet containing carbon sheets for secret writing, all concealed in the hidden compartment of a briefcase.

Assuming that Oswald had indeed been sent back to the United States on a PGU mission, he should have had a similar commo plan: reports mailed from and dead drops located in the United States; personal meetings in a third country, most conveniently Mexico, which borders on Texas; and occasional impersonal iron meetings. When he arrived in the United States in 1962, Oswald should have had with him more or less the same commo gear as Anton, who was trained by the Thirteenth Department and sent to Canada at about the same time: concealed cipher pads, microdots containing instructions, a microdot reader, and a Minox camera. Anton was also trained to use a burst transmitter, which could record five-digit groups on a magnetic tape and "squirt" the whole message "through the atmosphere in a few seconds." That transmitter was to be delivered to him "after he was securely established in Canada and had built a safe hiding place for it in a floor, wall, or dry cellar."

The PGU rule in cases like Johann and Anton prohibited the agents from using impersonal gear to send messages to the PGU during the first year of their resettlement, when they might be routinely surveilled and monitored by the local counterintelligence service. Anton later confirmed to Canadian counterintelligence that for more than a year after his return to Edmonton he informed the PGU of his situation by using only open-code phrases introduced in letters to his father in Czechoslovakia. The Oswalds had no parents they could write to in the Soviet Union, but after arriving in the United States they began corresponding with a few of Marina's relatives and friends, and particularly with Pavel Golovachev. Based on my experience, the real Golovachev would not have had to be involved in Oswald's case, with the possible exception of posing for the few photographs mentioned earlier, because the PGU could easily have handled the correspondence in his name.

The PGU did not provide U.S. authorities with Oswald's letters to Pavel Golovachev, obviously believing there was little if any chance that copies of them would be in the FBI's files. In Golovachev's first letter to the Oswalds, dated August 4, 1962 (found after Oswald's death in Marina's home), he sends some photographs of himself and of the Oswalds' old apartment, in an apparent attempt to support the Minsk portion of Oswald's biographical legend. Golovachev also promises to mail some magazines in the near future. In his next letter, dated September 15, Golovachev suggests that Marina subscribe to the official Soviet newspaper *Isvestiya*, the Sunday supplement of which, called *Nedelya*, would carry stories of interest to her. He says he has air-mailed one batch of magazines and will soon send more. This emphasis on receiving publications from the Soviet Union might indicate that the PGU was sending instructions via open-code messages in dummied-up issues of Soviet magazines and newspapers. This was a method used only in special cases, but if Oswald had indeed been working for the PGU, as a Marine he certainly qualified as a special case, to say nothing of the "historic" assignment he now may have had.

For more rapid open-code communication with the DIE, Malek, the West German coupled with Andrea, was instructed to use Andrea's letters to the Romanian embassy in Vienna. She was a Romanian citizen, and writing to the embassy would not have been unusual. That method not only enabled the DIE to receive Malek's information much more quickly, it also allowed the DIE to send him rapid open-code instructions in the form of answering letters from the embassy to Andrea. The DIE cipher department prepared a set of open codes on soft film and concealed it in a Pelikan fountain pen that Malek was to take with him when the time came for him to leave for Vienna with Andrea.

In Malek's commo plan, Andrea's first letter was to be trivial—
date of immigration and current address—and to be addressed to the
embassy without indicating the name of any particular diplomat.
This would avoid suspicion that she was sending a message or that
she had been given that name by Romanian authorities before leaving the country. Andrea's subsequent letters, however, were to be
nominally addressed to the Romanian diplomat who would sign the
embassy's answering letter to her—that would prevent their getting
lost within the embassy's bureaucracy. Chosen for Malek's case was
the Romanian consul general in Vienna, a DIE collaborator, who
was instructed to pass every letter he received from Andrea to the
DIE station chief. That was done in accordance with another PGU
pattern, that of having an agent write to the embassy using routine
channels to someone like the consul, rather than to a conspicuously
active intelligence officer.

Marina Oswald's status as a Soviet citizen could also serve
nicely as innocuous cover for letters to the Soviet embassy in Washington. One of the PGU's foremost concerns would have been for
Oswald to allay possible FBI suspicions and to clear the way for
Marina to correspond with the Soviet embassy. On June 26, 1962,
two FBI agents interviewed the newly arrived Oswald. Although he
appeared tense and a little bit insolent to the agents, he apparently
was able to convince them that he had had no contacts with Soviet
intelligence while in the Soviet Union—though he could not satisfactorily explain why he had gone there in the first place. Interestingly, Oswald took care to inform the FBI that as a Soviet citizen
his wife was required to notify the Soviet embassy in Washington of
her current address, and that he planned to contact the embassy for
that purpose in a few days. He refused to take a polygraph test or
answer questions about Marina's relatives. Later Oswald told his
brother that the interview had gone "just fine."

Marina's first letter to the embassy was dated July 1, 1962—five
days after Oswald's interview with the FBI. It is addressed only generally to the embassy of the USSR in Washington, rather than to an
individual, and it consists of a small formal announcement of bio-
graphic information from her passport, and her current address
(Robert Oswald's home). From the PGU's point of view, the impor-

tant information would have been that contained in the postscript: "P.S. Date of arrival in the United States June 13, 1962"; in other words, the Oswalds arrived on schedule and without mishap.

The copy of this letter supplied to the Warren Commission by the Soviets shows that it was routed to "Comrade Gerasimov." Vitaly Gerasimov was an identified PGU officer assigned under the cover of consular officer in Washington, and his activities were of particular interest to the FBI. Possibly he was the case officer assigned to handle Oswald in the United States.

A brief bureaucratic reply asking Marina to send in her Soviet passport for registration purposes and to fill out a form was sent to her on July 9 in the name of the chief consul, Nikolay Reznichenko. The copy retained at the embassy shows that it was again routed to Gerasimov. All future correspondence from the Oswalds would be addressed to Reznichenko, and most copies existing in the Warren Commission files show that they were internally routed to Gerasimov. Upon his arrest in connection with Kennedy's assassination, Oswald was carrying Reznichenko's name and address in his wallet.

In an undated letter to the Soviet embassy in Washington, apparently sent in early August 1962 just after the Oswalds moved into their own apartment, Oswald gives the new address and asks for the return of Marina's passport. He also asks for information about how to subscribe to "Russian language" publications such as *Pravda*, *Izvestiya*, and *Ogonek*, and ends with a request "for the Embassy to send us any periodicals or bulletins which you may put out for the benefit of your citizens living, for a time, in the U.S.A."

The phrase "for a time" supports the contention that Oswald considered himself on temporary assignment in the United States, and it was probably intended to remind his PGU handlers that he remained determined to return to live out the rest of his days in the Soviet Union. His letter to the Soviet embassy is also of interest because it signals the beginning of a steady stream of publications Oswald would receive, first at his home address and later at post office boxes. In August 1962 he subscribed to *The Worker*, a publication of the Communist party of the United States, and asked to be sent other party literature. Three months later he asked the Socialist Labor party in New York to send him literature. In addition to mail from Communist and Socialist organizations in New York, Oswald received other Soviet publications through a bookstore in Washington, D.C., known to be friendly to the Soviet embassy and, beginning in the spring of 1963, Cuban literature from New York. This illustrates another PGU practice in the case of an important agent—the more mail he received, the less possible it was for the local counterintelligence service to check it for secret writing and microdots.

During Anton's training in the Soviet Union he was also instructed by the PGU in receiving enciphered radio messages sent by Moscow, using a high-quality shortwave radio receiver that could be bought on the open Canadian market. In 1965, when Anton had his first personal meeting after leaving the Soviet Union, his case officer directed him to buy a "powerful radio receiver and handed him a schedule of broadcasts from Moscow" that would be beamed to him in Edmonton. Soon after, Anton began receiving Morse-code messages transmitted in the morning; in the evening he would lock himself in the basement of his house to decipher them.

Almost a year after he returned to the United States, Oswald too may have anticipated being instructed to buy such a radio receiver. Marina later told her biographer that her husband was particularly happy to move on March 2, 1963, to an apartment where he had his own little study that was "not much bigger than a double coat closet" but was a private place where he could lock the door and "do all of my own work there." Until then there is no indication that Oswald had had any personal contact with the PGU since leaving the Soviet Union, but the PGU could have told him to buy a receiver through an open code inserted in one of the newspapers or letters sent to him from Moscow or from the Soviet embassy in Washington. As we shall see, however, it is likely that in arranging a private workspace Oswald was simply applying the lessons of his Moscow training and getting ready for radio or other encoded messages—which in the event probably never came. Even Anton received no messages at all between his May 1961 arrival in Canada and March 1965, presumably because of the Kremlin's jitters during that period over Thirteenth Department activities.

20

OSWALD'S BEST FRIEND

S OON AFTER arriving at Fort Worth in June 1962, Oswald moved away from his brother and mother and sought contacts in the local Russian émigré community. By the end of that year, however, his vehement Marxism had alienated all of those staunchly conservative immigrants but one: the wealthy, aristocratic, handsome, well-educated, and well-traveled George de Mohrenschildt. Marina described him to another émigré as "Lee's best friend." In her 1964 testimony to the Warren Commission, Marina declared that Oswald hated all the Russian émigrés he had met in the United States. "He thought that they were fools for having left Russia; they were all traitors." Of all those émigrés, Marina asserted, "he liked de Mohrenschildt . . . but only de Mohrenschildt." The Warren Commission's summary report characterized de Mohrenschildt as "the only Russian-speaking person living in Dallas for whom Oswald had appreciable respect."

That flamboyant Russian émigré lady-killer with the titled name seemed to be a most unlikely friend for the puritanical, socially inept, introverted Lee Oswald. Nevertheless, after Oswald left the Soviet Union in 1962, de Mohrenschildt became the main figure in his life. De Mohrenschildt brought Oswald and his Soviet wife out of their shells by introducing them to sympathetic people, found temporary homes for them and looked for better jobs for Lee, buttressed their morale when things looked bleak, helped Oswald move out from under his relatives in Fort Worth and relocate in Dallas, and repeatedly helped Marina find shelter when he felt she needed to be away from her husband. Gary Taylor, an American college student who was married to de Mohrenschildt's daughter when Oswald returned to the United States, was impressed by the role his father-in-law had taken in "organizing all the support that Oswald needed for his new life in Dallas." Evidence also shows that de Mohrenschildt and his wife were the only persons besides Marina who knew that Oswald owned a rifle and had used it to take a shot at Gen. Edwin Walker on April 10, 1963.

In Oswald's relationship with de Mohrenschildt there are three principal points of controversy that have never been satisfactorily clarified: what stirred de Mohrenschildt to take such an unusual interest in Oswald, how did they first meet, and what did de Mohrenschildt know about the rifle with which Oswald killed President Kennedy?

After the assassination, de Mohrenschildt floated several versions as to why he had been so strongly attracted to Oswald. None of them, however, provides a credible answer, and their very number is another reason to disbelieve them. In one, de Mohrenschildt claimed that he and his wife became curious about the Oswalds because "it pleased us to know that here is a pretty girl from Soviet Russia that had arrived, because we all picture Soviet Russian women like a commando—big, fat women, working in a brick factory." In another, de Mohrenschildt said he found "a point of contact" with Oswald—"the fact that he lived in Minsk, where I lived when I was a child also, where my father was this marshal of nobility. And later on in life I lived in Poland, very close to that area. I was interested in how the peasants were getting along, what does he find in the forest there, what kind of mushrooms you find, that type of conversation." In still another version, de Mohrenschildt justified his interest in Oswald by saying he "liked animals. My dog was sort of friendly with him. When he would come, my dog would not bark. He liked walking. He told me that around Minsk he used to take long walks in the forest which I thought was very fine. Those are contacts that possibly brought a certain understanding between us."

De Mohrenschildt also tried to attribute his "attraction" to Oswald to the fact that Marina's father had been "a Czarist officer of some kind—you see what I mean?" In 1977, when the House Select Committee on Assassinations began looking into his connection with Oswald, de Mohrenschildt came up with a new version. In an interview with Edward Jay Epstein, he said "he had been asked to keep tabs on Oswald by the CIA officer in Dallas responsible for debriefing businessmen on their trips to Communist countries. Since Oswald was presumed to be unfriendly, the CIA officer suggested that it would be useful to place a 'friend' in Oswald's path." De Mohrenschildt told Epstein that "he agreed to talk to Oswald in hopes the CIA man might help him in future ventures. The Walker shooting, however, was more than de Mohrenschildt had bargained for; he immediately parted company with Oswald."

The House Select Committee on Assassinations established, however, that J. Walton Moore, the officer of the CIA's Domestic Contacts Division who had been in touch with de Mohrenschildt, reported that "according to his records the last time he talked to George de Mohrenschildt was in the fall of 1961," many months before Oswald returned to the United States. (By the time of the House investigation there were many allegations of a CIA connection with Oswald and the assassination, but the House committee established the absence of any CIA involvement.)

De Mohrenschildt first met Lee Oswald in the United States in the late summer of 1962, under circumstances he would never disclose. "I tried, both my wife and I, hundreds of times to recall how exactly we met Oswald," de Mohrenschildt told the Warren Commission in April 1964, but the Oswalds "were out of our mind completely, because so many things happened in the meantime." De Mohrenschildt could not even explain how he had learned Oswald's address in Fort Worth. "I don't recall that," de Mohrenschildt told the Warren Commission. Such statements sounded quite unnatural when compared with de Mohrenschildt's other testimony, in which he could remember even his childhood in minute detail. It was as if the two of them had first met in a whorehouse but did not care to say so. De Mohrenschildt's wife, Jeanne, also claimed to the Warren Commission that she was unable to explain how their strange relationship with the Oswalds had begun. "I would like to know, myself, now, how it came about," she said.

In de Mohrenschildt's first interview with the FBI, which took place in Haiti soon after Kennedy had been assassinated, he said he had met Oswald through either George Bouhe or Max Clark, another Russian émigré living in Fort Worth. Bouhe and Clark, however, said they had not been present at the original meeting between de Mohrenschildt and Oswald. In 1964, de Mohrenschildt told the Warren Commission that he had first met the Oswalds together with Col. Lawrence Orlov, an American oil speculator whose great-grandfather had come from Russia. "Lawrence and I were on some business in Fort Worth, and I told him let's go and meet those people, and the two of us drove to this slum area in Fort Worth and knocked at the door." Colonel Orlov, however, insisted that the only time he accompanied de Mohrenschildt to Oswald's home, "the two were already well acquainted." In another version, de Mohrenschildt told Jim Savage, a friend of his in the oil business in Houston, that he had met the Oswalds through the Dallas Aid Society—but no such organization existed at that time. Thirteen years after Kennedy's assassination, in an unfinished interview with Edward Jay Epstein, de Mohrenschildt was even more "vague, again suggesting that he had met the Oswalds in Orlov's company."

Then there is the matter of Oswald's rifle. In his 1964 sworn testimony to the Warren Commission, de Mohrenschildt asserted that he had not known that Oswald owned a rifle until his wife had accidentally seen it during a visit to the Oswald apartment. "Absolutely positive that personally I didn't know a damn thing about it, positive, neither did my wife," de Mohrenschildt told the Warren Commission under oath. "I didn't know he had the gun. I didn't know he was interested in shooting or hunting. I didn't know he was a good shot or never had any impression," de Mohrenschildt claimed. "I did not know even that he was interested in weapons . . . 'til the day . . . Easter, I think, when my wife saw his gun."

Before testifying to the Warren Commission, however, de Mohrenschildt told Jim Savage, his friend in Houston, that he had inadvertently given Marina the money Oswald used to buy the rifle. Marina reportedly said to him in the spring of 1963, "Remember the twenty-five dollars you gave me? Well, that fool husband of mine used it to buy a rifle."

De Mohrenschildt's testimony about Oswald's rifle is also filled with contradictions. According to his statement to the Warren Commission, he and his wife visited the Oswalds on Orthodox Easter Sunday 1963, to give a rabbit toy to their baby. He alleged that this was the first time they visited the Oswalds' new apartment on Neely Street in Dallas, and Marina gave Jeanne a tour of her home. "Oswald and I were standing near the window looking outside," when "Jeanne, who was with Marina in the other room, told me 'Look, George, they have a gun here.' And Marina opened the closet and showed it to Jeanne, a gun that belonged obviously to Oswald." Asked if he went in to look at the gun, de Mohrenschildt denied it: "No; I didn't look at the gun." He categorically stated that he "did not see the weapon" during that whole visit or at any other time before or after that. For this reason the Warren Commission decided not to show him Oswald's rifle for identification.

Jeanne de Mohrenschildt gave the Warren Commission similar testimony: "From what I remember George sat down on the sofa and started talking to Lee, and Marina was showing me the house—that is why I said it looks like it was the first time, because why would she show me the house if I had been there before? Then we went to another room, and she opens the closet, and I see the gun standing there." Jeanne also confirmed her husband's assertion that he had not seen the rifle: "I came back to the room, where George and Lee were sitting and talking. I said, do you know what they have in the closet? A rifle. And started to laugh about it." When Marina Oswald was specifically asked by the Warren Commission, "Did you ever show that rifle to the de Mohrenschildts?" she denied it. "I know that de Mohrenschildts [sic] had said that the rifle had been shown to him, but I don't remember that."

On April 1, 1977, three days after de Mohrenschildt committed suicide, Jeanne gave the House Select Committee on Assassinations a copy of a 315-page manuscript entitled "I Am A Patsy! I Am A Patsy!" that George de Mohrenschildt had been writing at the time he killed himself. It contained yet another version of that same event. In it de Mohrenschildt wrote that he had seen Oswald's weapon, which was in "a large closet, next to the balcony," where Marina kept "her wardrobe, which was considerable. On the bottom of the closet was [a] rifle standing completely openly. . . . I looked curiously. Indeed there was a military rifle there of a type unknown to me, something dangling in front." Jeanne asked, "what is that thing dangling," de Mohrenschildt wrote. "A telescopic sight," he explained. "Jeanne never saw a telescopic sight before and probably did no[t] understand what it was. But I did, I had graduated from a military school." According to this manuscript, Marina told George de Mohrenschildt and his wife that Oswald "likes shooting at the leaves." That "did not make much sense to us," de Mohrenschildt wrote, "but liking target shooting ourselves we did not consider this a crazy occupation."

De Mohrenschildt's contradictory accounts of how he learned that Oswald owned a rifle and where he saw it were contradicted once more by Marina. In her testimony to the Warren Commission she stated that Oswald kept his rifle only "in a small room where he spent a great deal of time, where he read—where he kept his things, and that is where the rifle was." Oswald "told me not to enter his room," not even for cleaning it, and "he tried to take care of it himself." Asked if the gun was at any time "placed in a closet in the apartment on Neely Street," Marina denied it, stating that Oswald's rifle had been only in that little room "either in a corner, standing up in a corner or on a shelf." She also denied that it had been openly exposed. "You must know that the rifle—it isn't as if it was out in the open. He would hang a coat or something to mask its presence in the room."

In his testimony to the Warren Commission, de Mohrenschildt recalled that he had heard his wife say Oswald had a rifle, and "really jokingly I told him: 'Are you then the guy who took a pot shot at General Walker?' And he smiled to that, because just a few days before there was an attempt at General Walker's life, and it was very highly publicized in the papers, and I knew that Oswald disliked General Walker, you see." De Mohrenschildt claimed he knew nothing about Oswald's attempt to kill General Walker, but "if somebody has a gun with a telescopic lens you see, and knowing that he hates the man, it is a logical assumption you see." (How de Mohrenschildt knew Oswald's rifle had a telescopic lens is another unclear point. De Mohrenschildt testified that his wife, upon looking at the gun in the closet, asked Marina in a voice that he could overhear, "What is that? That looks like a telescopic sight." Jeanne, however, testified that she saw the telescopic sight but "didn't know what it was" and only asked Marina "what on earth" Oswald was "doing with a rifle.")

Once again Marina contradicted de Mohrenschildt. She told the Warren Commission that, a few days after Oswald shot at General Walker, the de Mohrenschildts "came to us, and as soon as [George] opened the door he said, 'Lee, how is it possible that you missed?' I looked at Lee. I thought that he had told de Mohrenschildt about it. And Lee looked at me, and he apparently thought that I had told de Mohrenschildt about it. It was kind of dark. But I noticed . . . that his face changed, that he almost became speechless. You see, other people knew my husband better than I did. Not always—but in this case." Asked by the Warren Commission if he had ever made that remark to Oswald, de Mohrenschildt denied it: "Never. I don't recall that incident." Later on, however, he seemed to improve on Marina's testimony. In the manuscript of his book, de Mohrenschildt wrote that "Lee was a little scared of my extrasensory perception—which I believe I still have with my students. Had I known anything about [his attempt on Walker], I would have persuaded him not to try any such crazy foolishness." On March 29, 1977, just a few hours before he committed suicide, de Mohrenschildt told Epstein that he knew Oswald had taken the shot at General Walker "through some sort of ESP (extrasensory perception) which he had with Oswald."

The fact that de Mohrenschildt was the only known individual to whom Oswald gave an autographed copy of one of his now famous photographs showing him with a holstered pistol strapped to his waist, holding a rifle in one hand, and in the other copies of Communist publications, provides one more reason to believe that George de Mohrenschildt knew a lot more about that rifle and about Oswald's attempt to kill General Walker than he ever admitted. After Kennedy was assassinated, those photographs became a clearly touchy subject, which no one who knew about their existence wished to discuss. During the initial search following the assassination, the first two prints were found in the garage of Ruth

Paine, at whose home Marina Oswald was staying at that time. Oswald, when shown these pictures at Dallas police headquarters, insisted they were fakes. Later Marina claimed that after Oswald's arrest she shredded another photograph that Oswald had inscribed to their daughter June and put the torn pieces in an ashtray and lit a match. Oswald's mother, Marguerite, then flushed the burned remains of the picture down the toilet.

In her initial testimonies to the FBI and the Secret Service, Marina denied she had ever seen her husband with a rifle. When confronted with the two pictures shown to Oswald, however, Marina professed to remember that she had taken "two photographs" in the backyard of their home "on a Sunday . . . two, perhaps three weeks" before Oswald took a shot at General Walker on April 10, 1963. The Warren Commission concluded, based on Marina's statements and on expert testimony and the dates of the newspapers Oswald was holding in the pictures, that Marina had probably taken the two photographs on Sunday, March 31, using Oswald's Imperial Reflex camera. In her testimony to the Warren Commission, Marina first stated that she had taken only one photograph on that occasion, but she corrected it to two when confronted with two different views. She would later testify to the House committee that those were the only two photographs she had ever taken in her life to that time.

Robert Blakey, the Warren Commission's chief counsel, concluded that "Marina Oswald, in addition to giving two different versions of when the pictures were taken, gave different versions of the number of pictures taken" as well. "At first she testified that she took one picture. She later testified that she took two pictures. In addition, Marguerite Oswald, Oswald's mother, testified that soon after the assassination she and Marina destroyed yet another picture" in a motel in Irving, some fifteen miles from Dallas, where they were moved to be protected from reporters. In that picture, "Oswald was holding the rifle over his head with both hands. No copy of such a photograph has ever been uncovered."

On March 29, 1977, during an interview with Epstein, de Mohrenschildt told him he also had a photograph of Oswald holding his rifle, which he claimed he found after Kennedy was assassinated. Three hours later, however, de Mohrenschildt killed himself.

Three days after that, Jeanne de Mohrenschildt presented that photograph to the House Select Committee on Assassinations, together with the manuscript of her husband's book. It was a different photograph, one that had never been seen before, but one that had clearly been taken at the same time as the others. In his manuscript de Mohrenschildt claimed that Jeanne found it in February 1967, after they returned from Haiti, in one of the boxes they had placed in a warehouse in 1963, before departing. She "shouted excitedly . . . 'Look, there is an inscription here.' It read: 'To my dear Friend George from Lee,' and the date follow[s]—5 April 1963. . . . [T]hen I slowly turned the photograph and there was another epitap[h], seemingly in Marina's handwriting, in Russian. In translation it reads: 'this is the hunter of fascists! Ha! Ha! Ha!'" In his manuscript de Mohrenschildt claimed he had no prior knowledge of this picture, and he speculated that Oswald had in a sense left "a gift for us from beyond his grave."

Marina never mentioned the existence of this fourth version of Oswald's backyard photographs until she was confronted with it by the House committee in September 1978. Before being shown de Mohrenschildt's photograph, however, Marina was asked if she had ever written anything on the back of any of the pictures of Oswald with his guns. "No," she answered flatly. "Did you ever write a note or anything to George de Mohrenschildt on the back of the original or a copy?" she was asked. "No," Marina stated. "Are you sure of that?" she was asked once more. "Yes."

When she was shown an enlargement of the picture provided by Jeanne de Mohrenschildt, Marina admitted to having taken that picture as well, but she tried to persuade the committee that she had not written the Russian inscription on the back. "At first look I thought it was, but when I start to examine it, I don't think it is my handwriting." She also tried to exculpate Oswald: "I do not have much opportunity to compare his English handwriting to this photograph, but I cannot claim it was his handwriting." Committee experts, however, had already confirmed that the first text had been written by Oswald, that the picture had been taken with Oswald's Imperial Reflex camera, and that the rifle he was holding was probably the Mannlicher-Carcano he had used to kill Kennedy.

The only thing Marina eventually admitted was that Oswald might have shown such a picture to de Mohrenschildt. She told the House committee: "what strikes my memories, George de Mohrenschildt came—I am not trying to confuse you, you know, give you a false statement. I try to get my memory to go. What strikes me, I think I was surprised that he showed pictures to George de Mohrenschildt because I thought the rifle and the gun, first of all I was always against it so, if in my memory I remember being surprised at him showing pictures like that to George, so apparently I saw them at the apartment." She was asked if she remembered Oswald showing the pictures to de Mohrenschildt, and Marina said: "Something strikes my memory that how dare he show pictures like that to a friend."

In an early testimony, Jeanne de Mohrenschildt said that on April 4 or 5, 1963, she had stopped by the Oswalds' apartment on Neely Street for an afternoon visit. Later she retracted that statement, saying that she had visited the Neely Street apartment for the first time on "Saturday before Easter," that is, on April 13. "I completely mixed all the dates," she explained. It seems most likely, however, that both de Mohrenschildts did in fact visit the Neely Street apartment on April 5, and that they received the autographed photograph of Oswald on that day. That is the date on the back of the photograph, and it would have been natural for Oswald to autograph it in George de Mohrenschildt's presence and hand it to him, as Marina indicated. It also makes sense that the photograph with its ironic inscription about "hunter of fascists," would have been presented to de Mohrenschildt *before* Oswald attempted to kill General Walker on April 10, since after that those words would no longer have been amusing. (The same comment applies to de Mohrenschildt's statement in his manuscript, noted above, that Jeanne laughed when she told him Oswald had a rifle in the closet.)

From all these many facts and statements, it is clear that Oswald and George de Mohrenschildt must have had a special relationship, one that was strongly downplayed after Kennedy was assassinated. Given that de Mohrenschildt was in contact with the PGU in 1957—as I learned for a fact while I was still in Romania—his efforts to minimize and distort his contact with Oswald suggest that de Mohrenschildt was still acting under PGU guidance during the time he was in contact with Oswald in Texas.

A review of what he was doing in the years leading up to his friendship with Oswald shows that de Mohrenschildt frequently happened to be in just the right place at the right time in terms of the PGU's priority interests. In early 1957 the PGU was actively trying to kill Marshal Tito, whose violent condemnation of the 1956 Soviet invasion of Hungary had exacerbated Moscow's poor relations with Belgrade and fueled a Soviet Politburo cabal for overthrowing Khrushchev. By coincidence, it was just at that time that de Mohrenschildt arrived in Belgrade on an eight-month assignment as an oil and gas specialist. During his 1957 stay in Yugoslavia, he "tried twice to approach the private island of Marshal Tito by boat, and both times, was fired upon by security guards." When he was asked about this during his testimony to the Warren Commission, de Mohrenschildt replied that he had been shot at because "the Communists" believed "I was making sketches of their fortifications. Actually," he claimed, "I was making drawings of the seashore."

I recall that in 1958 the Soviet-bloc intelligence community inaugurated Operation Zácámânt (the Romanian word for "raw materials"). Its task was to identify new deposits of coal, minerals, and oil in Third World countries, and to influence the governments of those countries to use Soviet-bloc enterprises to develop such deposits. Coincidentally, according to Edward Jay Epstein, "in 1958 de Mohrenschildt went on an extended trip to Ghana, Togoland and Dahomey under the cover of being a philatelist, while he was actually gathering intelligence on the oil potential of the area." When the Warren Commission asked him why he had used the cover of a philatelist during that trip, de Mohrenschildt claimed he had been sent by a "wealthy man of American and Swedish origin, who owns, among other things, stamp concessions all over Africa," and who had "found out that there were some oil seeps in the northern part of Ghana, indications of oil. And he asked me to go there and investigate." He used this "trick," he explained, because "we did not want to let it be known to Shell Oil Co. that I was a consulting geologist."

Defeating the CIA's invasion of Cuba was another PGU priority at the beginning of 1961. Coincidentally, George de Mohrenschildt and his wife spent the first four months of 1961 in Guatemala, where the CIA was then training the Cuban invasion force. According to his testimony to the Warren Commission, de Mohrenschildt knew nothing about those invasion plans. Only in mid-April 1961, when he and his wife left Guatemala City, "we read the paper on the road about the Bay of Pigs invasion. That is all we knew about it." On Monday, April 11, the Cuban invasion force began leaving Guatemala from an airport improvised in Retalhuleu, near Guatemala City. The invaders were transported to Puerto Cabezas, in Nicaragua, from where they began their ill-fated attack on the Bay of Pigs on April 15.

In its final report, the Warren Commission concluded that its investigation had "developed no signs of subversive or disloyal conduct on the part of either of the de Mohrenschildts." Fifteen years later the House Select Committee on Assassinations declared: "Despite this disclaimer of any subversive or disloyal activity on the part of de Mohrenschildt by the Warren Commission, de Mohrenschildt was rumored to have had ties with the intelligence communities of several countries. Indeed, de Mohrenschildt himself admitted some involvement with French intelligence, but his actual role with them was never fully disclosed, and he emphatically denied any other intelligence associations."

Epstein, who clearly did not wish to take de Mohrenschildt's statements at face value, conducted an extensive investigation into his life in the United States, interviewing dozens of de Mohrenschildt's friends, business associates, and relatives and reading hundreds of pages of material on de Mohrenschildt that had been released by various intelligence agencies under the Freedom of Information Act. Epstein evidently concluded that de Mohrenschildt had in fact been Oswald's "handler," and he presumably sought to confront de Mohrenschildt with the results of his own investigation. A few hours after their unfinished discussion on March 29, 1977, de Mohrenschildt killed himself with a shotgun blast to the head. That afternoon he had also been issued a subpoena to testify before the House Select Committee on Assassinations. What terrible secret was de Mohrenschildt so eager to protect?

21

THE BACKGROUND OF
AN ILLEGAL OFFICER

W HEN I finished studying the available material on George de
Mohrenschildt, I was struck by the similarity of his background to that of the famous Soviet illegal Richard Sorge, who was
documented as a German journalist and ended up being attached
to the German embassy in Tokyo during World War II. The many
points of correspondence between these two cases suggest that de
Mohrenschildt may have had a lifelong career as a Soviet illegal officer, and that at some stage in that career the PGU involved him in
Oswald's case. That would explain de Mohrenschildt's evasive and
contradictory statements about how he first met Oswald and why
he was so intensely interested in him. It could also explain why de
Mohrenschildt chose to kill himself after learning that the U.S. government had begun reinvestigating his strange, unexplained connection with Kennedy's assassin.

Because in the 1930s and 1940s Soviet foreign intelligence had
no expertise to train illegals to speak a Western language with the
necessary fluency, it resorted either to foreign Communists who had
moved to Moscow after the October Revolution or to Russians of
foreign descent, molding their family histories to fit with their future
tasks. De Mohrenschildt's background suggests that he belonged to
the second group. Based on his testimony to the Warren Commission, he was born in Mozyr, Russia, on April 17, 1911, to a father "of
Russian, Swedish, German descent" who "spoke German at home

sometimes, sometimes Russian," and represented the landowning nobility in the tsarist government. Later his father served as a director of the Swedish "Nobel interests" in the Baku oilfields. His mother was a "Russian of Polish and Hungarian descent." "That was a mixed-up family, of which there were so many in Russia," de Mohrenschildt explained.

None of de Mohrenschildt's statements about his family history can be independently confirmed. All that is known for certain about his background before he immigrated to the United States is that he arrived "in May 1938 on the *SS Manhattan*, carrying a Polish passport issued in Belgium, which identified him as Jerzy Sergius von Mohrenschildt and stated that he had been born in Mozyr, Russia, in 1911." Three years later, when he was briefly detained by federal authorities for sketching a naval installation at Port Aransas, Texas, he "was carrying two different biographical sketches of himself." One identified him as being "of Swedish origin, born April 17, 1911," while the second described him as a "Greek Catholic" born in 1914.

To an intelligence analyst familiar with Soviet illegal operations, de Mohrenschildt's background sounds as if it had been designed by the same mentality that created Richard Sorge's. Sorge was allegedly born in 1895 in a small town near Baku, in the Caucasian oilfields, to a German father and a Russian mother. His father allegedly worked in the same Baku-area oilfields as de Mohrenschildt's father. Even more remarkable, Sorge's father was reportedly employed by the same Swedish Nobel enterprises as de Mohrenschildt's, suggesting that at one time the Soviet espionage service may have had a way of manipulating the Nobel personnel records in Baku. In another coincidence, Sorge allegedly left the Soviet Union as a child, just as de Mohrenschildt did, so that both supposedly received non-Communist educations and remained in the West. In real life, however, Sorge joined the German Communist party as a student in Hamburg and was sent to Moscow, where he worked for the Comintern and became a Soviet citizen. But that part was quietly dropped from his biography.

If de Mohrenschildt was indeed an illegal officer, his first assignment should have been to settle temporarily in a transitional country. There he could obtain a genuine foreign passport using forged documents supplied to him by the Soviet espionage service, and establish a Western cover profession for himself. It seems that is just what he did. Allegedly after an intermediate stay in Poland, where he became a citizen, at some point he went to Belgium, a country open to foreigners that the Soviet espionage service was using at about that time to legalize other illegals (including, notably, Leopold Trepper, organizer of the famed World War II Soviet spy ring the Red Orchestra). De Mohrenschildt claimed that it was 1931 when he arrived in Belgium, where he supposedly earned a master's degree equivalent in Antwerp and a doctor's degree in international commerce from the University of Liege. In 1938, supposedly after completing his studies, he left for the United States on a Polish passport issued by the Polish embassy in Brussels. Note that de Mohrenschildt came to the United States on a Polish passport issued in Belgium, not in Poland, even though he testified that from Belgium he had gone back to Poland from time to time in the summer. It was a general rule for a Soviet-bloc illegal to "legalize" himself, that is, to obtain a genuine passport, at an embassy in a third country, where the forged documents presented with the passport application were unlikely to arouse suspicion (and from which the illegal could easily escape in the event of a problem).

De Mohrenschildt told the Warren Commission that in 1922 he and his parents escaped from the Soviet Union to Poland and settled in Wilno, a small town on the border with the Soviet Union. There "it happened to be we had an estate, . . . 5,000 or 6,000 acres" in "Russia—which became Poland—in Czarist Russia, but which became Poland. Right on the border." That "estate was seized by the peasants and divided among themselves by themselves," but his father "was able to regain it . . . and eventually sold it back again to the peasants piece by piece. So we were not completely penniless." De Mohrenschildt claimed to have attended high school in Wilno and then, having become a Polish citizen, to have volunteered for the Polish army and been sent to an aristocratic Polish military school, financed by his father's sale of the estate. After graduating in 1931 as "sergeant candidate officer," he supposedly left for study in Brussels. None of this background could be checked because in the 1960s and 1970s, when de Mohrenschildt was investigated by

U.S. authorities, not only was Poland still in the Soviet bloc but Wilno (today's Vilnius, the capital of Lithuania) was in the Soviet Union itself. He did have an older brother living in the United States, but when de Mohrenschildt was asked, "Did your brother join you in Wilno, Poland?" he replied: "He immediately—it looks vague. I think he joined us for a little while, or he maybe went ahead of us and came to the United States." In fact the commission had established that the brother had come to the United States on August 29, 1920, directly from Russia, and had apparently lost all contact with his family, so that the brother would not have been able to confirm that his parents had ever moved to Poland or had ever owned an estate there. The parents themselves were also conveniently dead. According to George de Mohrenschildt, upon arrival in Wilno his mother had "almost immediately died from typhoid fever which she contracted during this escape," and his father had been killed in Germany at the end of World War II.

Richard Sorge's first intelligence task was also to get out of the Soviet Union, obtain a foreign passport, and find a job that would provide him professional cover in his targeted country, allowing him to justify the money he would receive from Moscow. In November 1929 he arrived in Berlin without leaving any trace that he had come from Moscow. In Berlin, using his and his father's real birth certificates, Sorge "obtained his [German] passport legally" and "established his cover as a writer for the *Soziologische Magazine*." Since Sorge really was a German citizen, he was one of the very few Soviet illegals who did not have to go to an embassy in a third country in order to obtain a legal passport.

The Warren Commission had heard, apparently from people who knew de Mohrenschildt, that a grandfather, Sergius von Mohrenschildt, had been born "somewhere in Pennsylvania, later went to Russia, entered the oil business." De Mohrenschildt first said it had been a "great grandfather, or great great grandfather," then said he did not remember him but did remember "some Baltic Swede, an ancestor of ours, who was an officer of the [American] Independence Army, . . . Baron Hilienfelt . . . who then went back to Europe and died there" and was buried in Sweden. De Mohrenschildt indicated his brother had told him that through the baron he would be eligible to join the Sons of the American Revolution. De Mohrenschildt also claimed kinship with a Ferdinand de Mohrenschildt, "my uncle, who was here in the United States for quite some time and died here . . . I guess in 1925 or 1924," who had been "First Secretary of the Czarist Embassy, the last Czarist Embassy here in Washington." There is, however, apparently no independent evidence to support his relationship to these remarkably convenient "ancestors" with American backgrounds.

For his first mission, Sorge's biography was similarly embellished by the Soviet espionage service. His first assignment was in the explosively revolutionary Shanghai, the seat of the underground Central Committee of the Chinese Communist party, where he arrived in January 1930 documented as a German journalist who wished to study agricultural conditions in China. His real task was to recruit local Communists for Soviet espionage. Consequently Sorge's biography was embellished to show him as the grandchild of a "father figure of Marxism," Friederich Albert Sorge, who was secretary of the First International and a close companion of Karl Marx. In fact there was no truth to the relationship except for the similarity of their names. Friederich Albert Sorge had had only one son, and in a December 1894 letter to Friedrich Engels he had written: "Our son is working in Chicago." According to "every other evidence," Sorge's father was at that time working in Baku, where Richard Sorge was born four months later.

Toward the end of World War II, when it was beginning to be clear that Nazi Germany would lose, the Baltic baron George von Mohrenschildt, who had circulated among conservative German émigrés in the United States, would become the untitled but still aristocratic George de Mohrenschildt, who would claim to be "more or less of a French orientation," and who had attended a commercial school in Belgium that had been founded by Napoleon. In his testimony to the Warren Commission, the only intelligence connection he admitted to was through Pierre Fraiss, a Frenchman working for the New York decorating firm of F. Schumacher and Company, whom he had allegedly helped "collect facts on people involved in pro-German activity" in 1941. "I was never an official member of [French intelligence]," de Mohrenschildt testified, "but I worked with Pierre Fraiss, and it was my understanding that it was French intelligence."

All these almost unbelievable similarities between Richard Sorge, that paragon of the illegal generation dominating the Soviet intelligence scene in the 1930s, 1940s, and 1950s, and George de Mohrenschildt, lead me to conclude that de Mohrenschildt must also have been a Soviet illegal officer of the same generation.

In earlier chapters I have occasionally used the term "illegal officer." Perhaps this is a good place to say a few words about that concept, which constituted one of the best-guarded secrets in the Soviet-bloc espionage community. In 1972, when I was appointed *the* deputy chief of the DIE, I was also given supervisory responsibility over the DIE component running illegal operations, called Brigade U. Brigade U was so hush-hush that the location of its headquarters was known to only four outside officers: the DIE chief, the DIE personnel director (who was also Ceausescu's brother), the DIE party secretary, and me. It was only after I assumed responsibility for this activity that I realized how little I had known about it until then, in spite of the twenty-two years I had already spent in the intelligence business.

The PGU training manual for illegal operations defined the illegal officer as a Soviet-bloc intelligence employee serving under nonofficial cover or "foreign flag," whose activities could not be attributed to the Soviet bloc. In other words, the Soviet-style illegal was a kind of "Potemkin village," in this instance one whose true background was intended to be kept forever secret. The general rule was that an illegal should have military rank in the security forces. When his background precluded his being a member of the officer corps (because of incompatible social origin, relatives in the West, etc.), he was made a civilian employee (called *referent* in the DIE, because such persons were usually hired to accomplish a specific, well-defined task). Irrespective of his military status, the illegal received a monthly salary and all the other perquisites enjoyed by a regular foreign intelligence employee, including retirement benefits. He was, however, prohibited from entering any intelligence service offices and from disclosing his intelligence affiliation to anyone except his case officer, his instructors, and their superiors, who were introduced to him by his case officer.

An illegal's training might last anywhere from three to eight years. It was conducted on an individual basis in safe houses, where the trainee was continuously monitored through concealed microphones—the DIE had some 150 safe houses used only for illegal officers. The general rule was that an illegal operating in a Western country should not be known to the official or "legal" *rezidentury* present in that country, and that communications with him should be conducted through traveling illegal officers specially trained for such duties. Another rule was that the contact with an illegal should always be through impersonal means in his country of assignment, and that personal meetings with him should take place only in safe third countries. Finally, every three or four years the illegal should be brought home clandestinely in order to "recharge his batteries" through political and professional indoctrination and to train him in the latest communications techniques. While an illegal was assigned abroad, his parents—and wife, if he had left one behind—would understand that he had been sent to work at some construction site in a remote corner of the Communist bloc, perhaps Mongolia or China, where he could not be reached by telephone. Letters from his family were always pulled out of the mails by the intelligence service, and some of them were shown to him at the end of his assignment, if he ever returned to his native country.

Historically there were three categories of Soviet-bloc illegals, colloquially called "generations." The first one was created in the early 1920s and comprised illegals who served abroad under their true identities but posed as militant anti-Communists in order to gain the confidence of their targets. This category was usually sent to the West for only a few months and was used almost exclusively to assassinate or kidnap anti-Communist White Russian leaders who had taken refuge in the West. Typical for this first generation was Sergey Puzitsky, who held the rank of "commissar of State Security" and played the key role in the 1930 kidnapping from Paris of Gen. Aleksandr Kutepov, the head of the White Guard movement in exile. Puzitsky acted under his own name but pretended to have been the leader of an underground White Guard organization in the Soviet Union. Nadezhda Plevitskaya, who was instrumental in the kidnapping of Kutepov's successor, White Russian general Yevgeny Karlovich Miller, was a typical civilian illegal of the same

generation. Known as the "Kursk nightingale," she sang her way
into the hearts of white Russian émigré communities throughout
Europe.

In the late 1920s Stalin ordered his foreign intelligence services
to create a new type of illegal who would be able to gather intelligence of military significance from potentially hostile countries
without compromising the new proletarian state if he were caught.
These "second-generation" illegals acted under their own identities
but were documented as citizens of other foreign countries. They
had their true backgrounds substantially embellished so as to make
them attractive to their target countries and even allow them to
pass nominal security checks there. Originally they were sent
abroad for several years, usually to establish illegal intelligence networks in their target countries for the purpose of collecting information on plans for hostile aggression against the Soviet Union.
This generation's father was Gen. Yan Karlovich Berzin, who between 1924 and 1935 was chief of the Soviet military intelligence
service, the GRU. Richard Sorge, who in the early years of world
War II worked out of the German embassy in Tokyo while also running a GRU illegal network, was considered by Moscow to be this
generation's most successful illegal. Soon the PGU's predecessor
also began sending out illegals of this kind, and between the two
services these illegals turned out to be the most productive Soviet
intelligence sources before and during the war, when their efforts
were directed almost exclusively against Germany and its allies. After the war ended, the illegals from the GRU and the PGU's predecessor were merged in 1947 into one component under the
Komitet Informatsii (Committee of Information), or KI. The PGU
retained many of the formerly GRU illegals even after the GRU
again began running its own illegals a few years later. The PGU and
its postwar sisters never ceased using this successful category of illegals, though their proportion in the total number of illegals gradually declined.

The "third generation" was born soon after World War II and
comprised PGU officers who were trained to be fluent in a Western
language and were documented as Westerners having no ties to the
Soviet bloc. These illegals were sent abroad for the rest of their ac-

tive lives, and their mission was to act as "sleepers." In case of war, when the Soviet Union's diplomatic relations with the West would be broken and its legal stations would cease to function, they would replace the PGU officers who were acting under legal cover. In the early 1950s, however, Moscow began using these illegals as communications officers for its most sensitive intelligence agents in the West. PGU colonel Rudolf Abel, who in 1957 was convicted of espionage in New York and five years later was exchanged for U-2 pilot Francis Gary Powers, was a typical example. In 1948 he arrived in Quebec on the SS *Scythia* with a passport identifying him as Andrew Kayotis, a naturalized American living in Detroit. The real Kayotis had died the year before while visiting his native Lithuania. Once the new Kayotis had crossed the border into the United States, he destroyed that passport and became Emil Robert Goldfus, who carried a true birth certificate showing that he had been born in New York City on August 2, 1902, that he was a white male, and that his parents had originally been citizens of Germany. After Abel's arrest, it was determined that the real Goldfuss (sic) had died as a baby in New York City on October 9, 1903.

In the 1970s many in this category of illegals were highly educated in various technical fields and were primarily used for penetrating scientific and industrial targets that were out of reach of the legal stations. Johann, the DIE illegal officer documented as a native West German, who was used against the defector Constantin Mandache, was one of these. Johann had been secretly recruited as a future illegal when he was sixteen, and at the top of his class. When he graduated as a mechanical engineer, again at the head of his class, he was secretly promoted to captain in the DIE. For the next eight years the captain did nothing but train in safe houses—illegal officers never set foot inside headquarters—perfecting his French, a language he would need to authenticate his biography, as well as his German, the language of his target country. He became a good tennis and bridge player and was coached in all the latest PGU communications techniques. After he had been trained up to his eyeballs, he was given his new identity: the son of a German Protestant missionary who had spent most of his life in what had been a part of German East Africa and had since become the

French-speaking country of Burundi. There had, of course, been a real German minister whose name Johann had taken. The minister and his wife had, however, died there of yellow fever some thirty years earlier, along with their newborn baby boy. It had been no problem for the DIE and the PGU, which worked together on that case, to "revive" that dead baby boy in the chaotic records of the city of Bujumbura. The minister's wife had had a sister, who was still living in Munich. By then she was old and almost senile, but quite wealthy. When Johann wrote his first letter to her, which was mailed by the PGU from Rwanda, the woman was thrilled to learn that her only nephew was still alive, and soon she invited him to come visit her. When Johann arrived in Munich, he seemed to be a skinny and scared young man on his first trip outside Burundi, and the woman burst into tears at the sight of him. Four years later Johann had earned a doctor's degree in engineering from the Ludwig-Maximilians Universität in Munich. (A few days after I defected, Johann disappeared from West Germany, along with several dozen other DIE illegal officers who were documented as citizens of various Western countries.)

In 1978, when I was granted political asylum, more than 80 percent of the DIE's illegals belonged to Johann's generation.

Now let me return to the similarities between de Mohrenschildt and Sorge, that paragon of the second illegal generation. In the spring of 1944, when Stalin became certain that Germany would be defeated, he took a relatively large number of Soviet illegals who had been used against Germany and its allies and dispatched them to the countries of Eastern Europe, engaging them in his operation to seize the governments of those countries—Romania alone received some two dozen that we in the management of the DIE knew about. The rest, who were uncompromised and showed future potential in the West, were kept in place in order to prepare for the "inevitable" war between communism and imperialism predicted by Lenin, which would finally allow communism to triumph worldwide. The illegals who remained in the West had their backgrounds purged of Nazi ties and tuned to make them attractive to the new target, "American imperialism" and its allied "flunkies." These illegals were also urged to find better professions that would provide them long-term cover in the West.

Sorge was no longer around to be recycled—he was executed on November 7, 1944, the day Moscow celebrated the twenty-seventh anniversary of the Russian Revolution. In the investigative documents about de Mohrenschildt's past, however, I found evidence showing that he had indeed been recycled toward the end of the war. In 1944, de Mohrenschildt enrolled at the University of Texas, where, according to his own statement, "with a fantastic effort and speed I succeeded in getting my master's degree in petroleum geology and minor in petroleum engineering in 1945, I think." While at the University of Texas, he again came under FBI scrutiny (during the war he had been suspected of Nazi sympathies), this time for alleged Communist sympathies. A declassified CIA summary of records on de Mohrenschildt states that during that same period he was also the subject of an investigation by the Office of Naval Intelligence, but no details are provided about the reason for the investigation or its results.

In 1946, de Mohrenschildt turned up at the Rangely oilfield in Colorado and applied for a job with the companies that were developing it. Interestingly, he there gave an entirely different version of his background. Now he claimed that his father had been a Russian engineer in the Ploesti oilfields in Romania and that his father had been captured there by the Soviet army and executed. In that connection it is worth noting that in 1945 the Soviets captured the archives of the foreign companies that had been operating in the Ploesti oilfields area of Romania—I learned that for a fact when I was in Romania—and therefore the PGU and GRU had no difficulty inserting new names into those companies' personnel records.

De Mohrenschildt's new background also stated that he had worked for the Shell Oil Company in Holland before emigrating to the United States; that during the war he had risen in the Polish underground to the rank of lieutenant colonel; and that he had spent most of the wartime in London serving as a liaison officer.

22

TRAINED TO MAKE FRIENDS, NOT MONEY

THROUGH my familiarity with the pattern of PGU illegal operations, I can recognize a number of other points, besides his family background, which suggest that George de Mohrenschildt was indeed a Soviet illegal of the 1930s variety. For one thing, there is his apparent status as an important businessman, though there seems to be no factual evidence that he ever engaged in any successful business venture. According to the relevant PGU manuals, the key to General Berzin's success with illegal operations lay in his ability to create impressive social standing for his illegals and his ingenuity in finding credible cover for the money the GRU issued them for achieving and maintaining that status. In a written confession to the Japanese police, Richard Sorge neatly summed up Berzin's new concept of illegal operations: "My group and I escaped because we had legitimate occupations which gave us good social standing and inspired confidence in us. I believe that all members of foreign spy rings should have occupations such as newspaper correspondents, missionaries, business representatives."

Even to the inexperienced eye of Gary Taylor, who was at one time married to de Mohrenschildt's daughter Alexandra, his father-in-law had "always been something of a mystery," having traveled around the world yet having "no visible means of support except his wife's earnings." De Mohrenschildt himself claimed his only money-making ventures for many years had been a couple of investments he had made abroad before becoming an American citizen. Neither of those ventures could be independently checked. One was, as he testified to the Warren Commission, in the mid-1930s, while he was a student in Belgium, where he "had an interest in a sport shop with a girlfriend of mine. . . . It was a very successful operation, this business, Sigurd." His other supposedly successful investment was in Mexico, to which he fled in 1941 after being arrested for sketching the Coast Guard facility in Texas. "I visited a sugar company there, and the manager of the sugar company told me to invest some money in that outfit, because it was going to—the stock was going to go up, which I did. I made some nice money out of that investment."

De Mohrenschildt's known business history in the United States was, however, replete with unproductive ventures and could not justify his apparent financial and social standing. According to the PGU book, that was a problem with most of the second-generation illegals, because they had no idea how capitalism worked and usually had no other professional training or experience besides having been Communist functionaries. Based on his own assertions, after de Mohrenschildt immigrated to the United States he began looking for a job—"very unsuccessfully, if I may say so. In New York in those days, in 1938. I even started selling perfumes, I remember for a company called Chevalier Garde," and fabrics for Schumacher and Company. When those sales jobs did not work out, he tried to become an insurance salesman, but he sold "not a single policy . . . [and] even didn't pass my broker's examination." Finally, "having had that background of the oil industry in my blood, because my father was the director of Nobel Enterprises, which is a large oil concern in Russia, which was eventually expropriated and confiscated . . . I decided to come and try to work for an oil company." All he could find in 1939, however, was manual work on a rig in Louisiana—"lifting pipes, cleaning machinery." Then he "had an accident on the rig, was badly cut up—something fell on my arm, and then I got dysentery. Frankly, I do not recall whether they fired me or I resigned myself."

In 1950, after several other unsuccessful jobs and a master's degree in geology that he acquired with the help of a "bequest" from

a friend of his wife's sister—"$10,000, I guess"—de Mohrenschildt
decided that "I should go in the oil business on my own, really in
the oil business, drilling and producing, which was interesting to
me." By remarkable coincidence, de Mohrenschildt claimed to have
used a similar amount of funds from his mother's estate, "maybe
$4,000 or $5,000" but reportedly perhaps as much as $10,000, to
start up the sporting goods business with his girlfriend in Belgium,
and then after dissolving the business in Belgium he had brought
"something like $10,000" with him when he came to the United
States. It may be noted that the GRU illegal Leopold Trepper was
dispatched to Belgium in 1938 with $10,000 and "the mission of
setting up secure commercial cover for an espionage net in France
and the Lowlands," which he accomplished by investing in a clothing export business. In 1962, when I became a deputy chief of the
DIE, the maximum amount of funds that either I or the DIE chief
could approve on our own was $10,000; for anything beyond that
we needed higher approval. Perhaps $10,000 was the GRU's limit
in the 1930s and 1940s.

Using the money "inherited" from his wife's sister's friend, in
1950 de Mohrenschildt set up a partnership with one of his wife's
relatives in New York, but "our first well was a dry hole, a disastrous dry hole." The next wells proved to be no better, and three
years later the partnership was terminated. "To make the story
short," he told the Warren Commission, "our first venture was quite
a failure." De Mohrenschildt's next venture was with his wife's uncle, "but we didn't do anything spectacular because he never could
provide any large amounts of money for anything spectacular. We
did small things. It was a small operation," which was terminated
two years later. From the time of that failure until the Warren Commission hearings and apparently until his suicide, de Mohrenschildt
claimed to be engaged in successful business activities outside the
United States once again. In spite of his claims, the new foreign
ventures seemed even more nebulous than the earlier ones and
proved similarly impossible to confirm. "In 1956 I took a job in
Haiti for a private—for some private individuals connected with Sin-
clair Oil Company," he told the Warren Commission, and later he
"started getting a lot of foreign jobs. . . . All in all, I visited and I did

foreign work, which means preparations for taking of concessions and suggestion of what areas should be taken for an oil and gas concessions—it was in Nigeria, in Togoland, in Ghana, in France," as well as in Mexico, Cuba, Yugoslavia, and Haiti.

Richard Sorge's professional background closely resembled de Mohrenschildt's. In Tokyo, Sorge passed himself off as a successful journalist who cavorted among high society and could afford almost any extravagance, from expensive restaurants and motorcycles to hordes of girlfriends. In fact, however, he earned almost nothing from his jobs. Although Sorge posed as a press attaché at the German embassy in Tokyo, he never figured on the embassy's payroll. With the outbreak of the war in Europe in September 1939, he started doing volunteer work for the embassy out of "patriotic duty." He took over editing a news bulletin compiled from the official Berlin news service and was given a small office at the embassy, where he would work from six to ten every morning. Nevertheless Sorge "had no official status in the Embassy," and he "refused on a number of occasions, to become a member of the staff." According to his testimony to the Japanese after he was arrested, the "Foreign Office in Berlin pressed [Ambassador] Ott to take me on in a fairly high position, in charge of information and press relations, but I continued to refuse."

Toward the end of the 1930s Sorge also established impeccable credentials for himself as the special Japan correspondent for the prestigious *Frankfurter Zeitung*. After his arrest, however, an official German inquiry into his relations with that newspaper established that in fact he was just a voluntary contributor. "As regards any contractual relationship between the paper and Mr. Sorge," the editor testified, "this can be said to have been non-existent." The editor of the *Algemen Handelsblad*, a Dutch financial newspaper for which Sorge also reportedly worked, responded similarly: "He was not in our service, but wrote articles for us regularly."

After Sorge was arrested, "the Japanese police, with bureaucratic thoroughness, made an inventory of items seized" at his house, which were to "form the first grim and material skeleton in the chain of proof to be forged against him." Among those items were "sixteen notebooks with details of contracts with agents and with finance," clearly showing that Sorge's money had in fact come from Moscow. Relieving him of the need to make money at it, the profession of journalist was ideally suited to Sorge the illegal, allowing him broad access to information as well as a flexible daily schedule. (In that context it is interesting to note that de Mohrenschildt apparently claimed at one time to have traveled around Europe as a correspondent for the Polish news service at the time he was living in Belgium.)

De Mohrenschildt's unusual "sexual athleticism" is another clue that he might have been a Soviet illegal of the 1930s. Quite a few times I heard the PGU chief, General Sakharovsky, regret that he did not have Sorge's penis in his museum for illegal operations. "They say its gland looked like a cat's head," he explained. Having a king-size penis was another "Berzin rule" for the illegals of the 1930s—a rule that still held true in 1972 when I began supervising the DIE component for illegal operations. PGU manuals for illegal operations put it this way: a regular foreign intelligence officer had an official position, a diplomatic passport, and a country behind him; an illegal had only his penis—that was his cover, his source of information, his immunity. The PGU was unquestionably a male chauvinist enterprise pushed to the limit; even so, only illegals documented as Westerners were allowed to have amorous adventures. Their handling officers could be reprimanded for merely talking about such things. The sexual freedom allowed to the illegals, which collided head-on with the puritanical rules imposed on the rest of the bloc's intelligence apparatus, was kept a deep dark secret—even the "recommendations" in regard to an illegal's sexual endowment and the size of his penis were included in separate instructions directed only to the management of the illegals department.

After de Mohrenschildt immigrated to the United States he had three brief marriages, each of which opened new doors for him. In 1943 he married the seventeen-year-old Dorothy Pierson, the daughter of an Italian "countess" and a wealthy "real estate man." This marriage suddenly propelled de Mohrenschildt into the aristocratic circles of New York and Palm Beach. One year later he divorced and went "on a vacation to New York," where he "met a very pretty girl," Phyllis Washington, "and she was willing to follow me," as he told the Warren Commission. By coincidence her father was a high-ranking State Department employee, and "she gave up the possibility of going to Spain, where her father was appointed chargé d'affaires at the time." Soon after becoming her husband, de Mohrenschildt got his American citizenship, "but then I realized that I could not remain married to Phyllis, because she was a girl of—who needed money, who needed a good way of life, needed luxury—she was used to luxury." The parents of his next wife, Wynne Sharples, were "very wealthy" and "socially prominent." She was just graduating from medical school, and "we fell in love with each other and decided to get married." It was this marriage that eventually propelled de Mohrenschildt to the very top of American political life. "It turned out to be that both of our children had cystic fibrosis—it is a terrible illness of genetic nature," he told the Warren Commission. Together with his wife, he "started a foundation, National Foundation for Cystic Fibrosis in Dallas, of which Jacqueline Kennedy was the honorary chairman." As with his previous marriages, this one too was short. "By the way, the reason for our divorce, in addition to whatever disagreements we had, which was not very important, was the fact that we both obviously have a tendency for cystic fibrosis, and the children from such a marriage have a very poor chance to survive."

Sorge was a similarly successful lady-killer, though he did not marry his conquests. According to the *razvedka* advisers, his intelligence career had been based "more on his penis than on his training," just as that of de Mohrenschildt seems to have been. Sorge left a German wife in the Soviet Union—she later divorced him—and never married again, but, according to those *razvedka* advisers, he was always surrounded by mistresses "ready to give their lives for him." The PGU manuals indicated that Sorge was able to get a job and an office at the German embassy in Tokyo because one of his numerous affairs was with the wife of the German military attaché, Col. Eugen Ott. The woman had fallen head over heels in love with him and did not wish to lose him. Four years later, in April 1938, Ott became a general and was named ambassador in Tokyo, and Sorge was given "free run of the embassy day and night." Sorge himself estimated that 60 percent of the intelligence sent by his spy ring to Moscow originated in the German embassy. On one occasion

Ott actually used Sorge as an embassy courier, sending him to Manila, Canton, and Hong Kong—thereby giving the GRU fortuitous access to the German diplomatic pouch.

Lilia Pardo Larin, an alleged Mexican citizen who in the early 1940s was closely associated with de Mohrenschildt, was one of his many female conquests who served his operational purposes. Larin was with de Mohrenschildt in 1941 when he was stopped as he was sketching the Coast Guard installation in Texas. After the American authorities searched their car, the couple were allowed to continue on their way to Mexico. De Mohrenschildt had already come under suspicion that year when he had attempted to join the newly formed OSS, the predecessor of the CIA, and had been turned down because of "suspected ties to Nazi and Polish intelligence." On October 8, 1942, the Department of State placed a "lookout" in de Mohrenschildt's file at the passport office, noting he was an "alleged Nazi agent" and cross-referencing his file to Larin's. Evidently frightened by the official American accusations against him, de Mohrenschildt remained in Mexico for some nine months, when the Mexican government declared him persona non grata and expelled him back to the United States. In his testimony to the Warren Commission, de Mohrenschildt described Larin as "the love of my life," but his story about how they had first met was almost as fuzzy as the one about how he had first met Oswald. "I met her through a Brazilian friend of mine," he told the commission. "I forgot his name . . . a rich Brazilian medical doctor." Then he remembered the name, Dr. Paolo Machado, an "enormously wealthy Brazilian, who calls himself the banana king, who liked American girls, the good life, and very good businessman at the same time." He and Machado "got into a fistfight" over Larin, and "the best man won, as it goes in the book, and Lilia and I fell in love."

All the above facts amount to nothing more than circumstantial evidence against de Mohrenschildt. In espionage investigations, however, everything is circumstantial until the spy is actually caught with his hand in the cookie jar. Even then it is often difficult to prove that the "cookies" in his hand legally constitute espionage material. It can prove almost impossible to obtain hard, prosecutable evidence against a Soviet-style illegal acting under "foreign flag."

Although the House Select Committee on Assassinations remained suspicious of de Mohrenschildt because of the many and varied allegations of his intelligence connections, it evidently did not suspect him of ties to Soviet intelligence, much less of being a Soviet illegal officer. Nor was Sorge suspected of being Moscow's man. Even after two members of Sorge's network had fully confessed, the Japanese government still had a hard time believing that a man with such a high reputation as a journalist and such high standing with the German embassy could be a Soviet intelligence officer. Even after Sorge himself had confessed, the Japanese did not really know what to make of him. "We were wondering whether Sorge was really a spy for Germany, and using the communists in Japan, but actually spying for the Nazi regime," Professor Mitsusada Yoshikawa, who interrogated Sorge, told two American researchers after the war. "That was one question. The second question was whether Sorge was a double agent for both Berlin and Moscow. The third question was whether he was really a spy for Moscow, pretending to be a Nazi. Therefore . . . we took a very cautious attitude."

23

THE FRIEND'S PGU ROLE

I N 1947, Stalin joined the PGU and GRU into the Committee of Information (KI), charged with "demilitarizing" Soviet foreign intelligence and turning its cutting edge toward Moscow's new enemies, the "bourgeoisie" and its leader, the U.S. government. Four years later, when Stalin separated the two intelligence services again, most of the GRU illegals left in the West were taken over by the PGU and included in its army of "sleepers" prepared to run the Soviet Union's intelligence agents in their host countries in case of war. Learning from past experience, the PGU renounced the concept of illegal networks, which had generated numerous breaches of security and caused the loss of many illegals, including Sorge, during World War II. Now the rule was that a PGU illegal should operate on a strictly individual basis. That was thought to be the best formula for keeping him clean and ready to act whenever needed.

In the mid-1950s the PGU amended that rule by starting an offensive to create "illegal couples," in which the wife could be either another illegal officer who would assist her "husband" in carrying out an assignment, or a civilian employee who would handle his communications and other technical tasks, or just an intelligence agent assigned to provide cover and logistical support to her "husband." In the early 1960s the PGU urged its sister services to follow suit, arguing that "illegal couples" had proved more immune to compromise than illegals acting alone in the West.

It seems more than coincidental to me that, at about the same time the PGU was promoting illegal couples, de Mohrenschildt acquired a Russian wife, Jeanne Bogoiavlensky LeGon, whom he married in 1959. He remained married to her for the rest of his life. "Women find him fantastically attractive," Jeanne told the Warren Commission. "I don't. I like his personality." It is also remarkable that the background of de Mohrenschildt's fourth and last wife appears to have been cast in the same mold used to shape his own. Jeanne was also born in an uncheckable place on the fringes of the Soviet Union (the city of Harbin in northeast China), her parents were also described as White Russian aristocrats who had renounced their Soviet citizenship and unexpectedly came into money, and she had also arrived in the United States in 1938, the same year de Mohrenschildt did. In her testimony to the Warren Commission, she specified that her father "was in charge of the Far Eastern railroad . . . [f]or China. He was working directly with the Chinese Government and with Chinese officials, with Chinese people. And then in 1925, when the Chinese sold the railroad . . . to the Russians . . . [m]y father resigned. And he received quite a lot of money from that." Her father also "took a Chinese passport, and I cannot tell you whether he already had it when I was born, or whether he took one later. But I believe he took one later . . . when they sold the railroad to the Reds, you know." By coincidence, her parents also "just disappeared" after she left "China." And only in 1957 did she learn that "Father was killed by Communists. . . . I don't know which ones—the Chinese or Reds or Japanese—I don't know." Jeanne's first husband, whom she claimed she married in 1932, also had an uncheckable background. "From what I know, he was born in—I think in Russia—and brought out as a very, very little boy. And I never met his father. His mother was supposed to be dead when he was born. . . . He had two half-brothers, charming boys, and they were both lost in the war with China and Japan. We never could find them. One of them was with the British forces and another with the French forces." Based on Jeanne's same testimony, she and her first husband were "building houses together" in Harbin, and "I believe he was also working in the—the Japanese were building their airport" there, and "he was helping and surveying the grounds or something. . . . And then somebody mentioned that they didn't like the idea that we knew too much about the plants or something of the airport and said we better leave, and we just left with very, very few things" for Shanghai and then the United States.

Coincidentally, soon after Jeanne arrived in the West she began working in the same sportswear apparel business de Mohrenschildt claimed to have been involved with after he came to Belgium. It is also worth noting that Jeanne was with de Mohrenschildt in Yugoslavia while he was assigned there, and was with him when he tried to approach Tito's villa on the island of Brioni by boat and was shot at by the Yugoslav security forces. "We went another day again," Jeanne admitted to the Warren Commission when she was questioned about the incident, "and we saw a little island. We left the canoe . . . [and] we were swimming and all of a sudden he took my photograph in front of a beautiful cave, and I was taking his photograph standing in the water in front of another cave. It was beautiful—just like a curtain drape. And all of a sudden, boom, the cannon shot, about a yard from me in the water. So, of course, we went right under the water in the cave." It is an old trick for an agent to pretend to be taking photographs of an accomplice who just happens to be standing in front of an object of intelligence interest.

Another suggestion of Jeanne's intelligence affiliation occurred in connection with her first husband, the Russian with whom she had reportedly left China. Just before going to Yugoslavia she had argued bitterly with him, called him crazy, and ended up divorcing him: "I actually told him that is the end, and I am divorcing you, and that is it, and there will be no change back, nothing at all." Then, while she was away, her first husband reportedly sent letters to all the restaurants and department stores in New York where she had accounts and to all her business clients, publicly accusing "Eugenia Fomenko Bogoiavlensky, my ex-wife," of being a Communist spy and announcing he was not responsible for her debts.

It was Jeanne de Mohrenschildt's testimony to the Warren Commission that gave me the first hint that de Mohrenschildt might have been the PGU illegal who had served as Oswald's contact while Oswald was assigned to El Toro Air Base in California. I had long wondered how the very young and inexperienced Oswald could have made such remarkably good travel connections when he defected to the Soviet Union. Oswald was discharged from the Marine Corps on September 11, 1959, and on September 17 he arrived in New Orleans and immediately booked passage to Europe on a Lykes Line freighter that was, by a great stroke of "luck," scheduled to sail the following day. Jeanne's testimony reveals that she and de Mohrenschildt traveled from Panama to Haiti in 1960 "by Lykes Line," and one of her statements shows that in fact the de Mohrenschildts must have frequently traveled with that line. "They never know which port [they will arrive at]," she told the Warren Commission.

The de Mohrenschildts' frequent use of the Lykes Line, whose freighters could accommodate just a handful of passengers on each voyage, suggests that de Mohrenschildt could have been the "friend" who in 1959 met Oswald in Tijuana, located not far from El Toro, and could have given Oswald travel instructions for the Soviet Union. As noted earlier, John Donovan, Oswald's superior officer at El Toro, told the Warren Commission that Oswald had made a couple of trips to Tijuana. And Nelson Delgado, Oswald's closest friend at El Toro, recalled that on one occasion the two of them had gone to Tijuana for a weekend, and that once there Oswald had gone off on his own to meet "friends." It is difficult to believe that the solitary Oswald could have made any personal friends whom he would have been meeting in Tijuana. Rather, the PGU must have instructed him to go there for a personal meeting.

Oswald was only nineteen years old, and his only experience as a world traveler had been under orders from the Marine Corps. He needed instructions on how to apply to the Albert Schweitzer College in Switzerland, and he needed help on how to travel discreetly to Europe and how to continue on clandestinely to Moscow.

By a remarkable coincidence, the de Mohrenschildts did visit Mexico in 1959. And they just happened to be in Mexico City when Anastas Mikoyan, a Politburo member and the deputy prime minister, visited there in November that year. By another stroke of "luck," Jeanne was personally introduced to him. At that time it was not unusual for the PGU to maneuver a "second-generation" illegal who had some overt connection with the Soviet Union into meeting a visiting member of the Soviet Politburo, if appropriate cover for such a meeting could be provided. Meetings of that kind were seen as ways to help the illegal increase his social standing, to reward him for excellent operational results, or just to "recharge his batteries."

When asked about her well-publicized meeting with Mikoyan, Jeanne told the Warren Commission: "We were two weeks in Mexico City. George was on business. And there was also a Russian exhibit which we missed in New York." In regard to the Soviet mission, she said: "We didn't know that they were there, absolutely. . . . It just happens to be that Mikoyan was there. . . . And we happened to know about it because we had this friend, the [Mexican] presidential pilot." According to Jeanne, the pilot "said, would you like to see Mikoyan? I said, of course I would." In the beginning, "George wanted to go, too . . . [but] I said, 'You better don't go, because it will be misinterpreted [and] may hurt you businesswise' in Texas." Jeanne went first to the farewell reception for Mikoyan. "I did it out of sheer curiosity," she explained. Then her pilot friend took her to the airport "to say goodbye to Mikoyan, at the plane. They had the Russian plane standing there, the cameras, TV's. And he introduced me to Mikoyan, this is my friend Señora de Mohrenschildt. And I take his hand and said . . . in Russian, how are you, Tovarish[ch] Mikoyan."

Here it must be remembered that Oswald had arrived in Moscow the month before this and had presumably been providing the PGU with valuable military intelligence. Interestingly, the defector Yury Nosenko told researcher Gerald Posner that Oswald's "KGB file" showed Mikoyan had personally given orders that Oswald's request for political asylum in the Soviet Union be given careful consideration. Also worth noting is that Mikoyan represented the Soviet government at President Kennedy's funeral, and that during that visit to Washington he also gave the State Department a number of Soviet "documents" about Oswald's life in the Soviet Union.

If de Mohrenschildt did indeed help Oswald arrange his 1959 trip to Europe on a Lykes Line freighter and his enrollment at the school in Switzerland, it is no wonder that de Mohrenschildt could not reveal the true circumstances of their first meeting to the Warren Commission. It logically follows that de Mohrenschildt might also have serviced the locker at the Los Angeles bus terminal where, as noted earlier, Delgado had deposited Oswald's duffel bag containing fighter plane photographs. In 1959 the PGU was widely using its "sleeper" illegals as contact officers for its most important agents in sensitive Western countries, and it would have been only natural for de Mohrenschildt to have been given such a task. He was an American citizen who could move freely around the United States and Mexico, and his various "business ventures" were nebulous enough to allow him to travel wherever and whenever the PGU needed him. If de Mohrenschildt did indeed act as Oswald's contact when the latter was assigned to El Toro, de Mohrenschildt would have shared in the accolades given Oswald after he arrived in Moscow in October 1959 and provided the PGU with valuable intelligence. Jeanne's meeting with Mikoyan was perhaps one way the PGU expressed its gratitude.

Jeanne's testimony also contains indications that George de Mohrenschildt might have been charged by the PGU to help Oswald and his family settle in Dallas after leaving the Soviet Union. In the fall of 1961, de Mohrenschildt set up a project with the government of Haiti to review mining resources in that country. In October 1961, however, for no apparent reason, the de Mohrenschildts returned to Dallas, where they no longer had a home and where neither of them had a job. "We thought we are going to return to Haiti in 6 weeks," Jeanne told the Warren Commission. "The contract that my husband was negotiating was supposed to materialize within 6 weeks. And I was stupid enough to talk about it, tell everybody. So, naturally, I could not take [a] job for a short time, because designing [clothes] you are involved. You start and cannot drop it. And then it was dragging and dragging and dragging, and actually took a year instead of 6 weeks to materialize the whole thing."

In fact it was likely for a different reason that the de Mohrenschildts were forced to postpone their return to Haiti. As we have seen, Marina's final PGU training evidently occurred in October 1961, when she disappeared for several weeks, allegedly to visit her aunts in Kharkov. That suggests that by the end of October 1961 Oswald and Marina were ready to leave for the United States, and that could well explain why the de Mohrenschildts at that moment interrupted their stay in Haiti and returned to Texas. Oswald was scheduled to settle in the Dallas area, where his relatives lived. It would have been only natural for the PGU to ask de Mohrenschildt to help him, as de Mohrenschildt evidently already knew Oswald and had useful friends and business contacts in the Dallas area. Bureaucratic procedures within the U.S. State Department held up the Oswalds' departure for another half-year, however, thereby evidently also throwing the de Mohrenschildts' plans into a muddle.

There exists one good indication that Oswald and de Mohrenschildt already knew each other before they met in Texas. After Oswald returned to the United States, his first priority was evidently to establish a public relationship with this man whom he had earlier met secretly, perhaps in Mexico, perhaps even in Moscow. Having spent his first weekend settling in at his brother's house in Fort Worth, on Monday morning Oswald gathered up the manuscript on life in the Soviet Union that he had brought with him from Moscow and took it to the office of a public typist, Pauline Bates. She looked through the material and agreed to type it up for him, incidentally commenting that she found it fascinating. Oswald replied that a friend of his in Texas was going to help him get it published, adding that his friend was an engineer of Russian origin who was involved in the oil business.

The way de Mohrenschildt tried to help Oswald after his return to the United States suggests that de Mohrenschildt did not know exactly what tasks Oswald had been trained to perform. That would be consistent with the PGU practice of the time, which required that the intelligence personnel providing logistical support to a Thirteenth Department agent be unaware of the agent's specific tasks. De Mohrenschildt must have been told to give Oswald the same kind of assistance he himself had needed when he had first come to the United States: a home, a job, and contacts with people from whom he could extract valuable intelligence. For example, Edward Jay Epstein interviewed Adm. Henry C. Bruton and his wife, to whom de Mohrenschildt had introduced himself and then had introduced Oswald to Mrs. Bruton. Admiral Bruton, who at the time Epstein met him had not been interviewed by the Warren Commission or the FBI, had served as director of naval communications and played a key role in reorganizing the global system the navy used to "communicate with and control the movements of all its submarines, surface ships, airplanes and missiles and to pinpoint the location of enemy vessels."

According to what Epstein learned from the Brutons, de Mohrenschildt had first appeared as a total stranger at their front door in the summer of 1962 and proceeded to tell Mrs. Bruton that he had been drawn to the house "by fond memories of the good times he had had there when it was owned by a friend of his— Colonel Schurger." He related how he had helped build the swimming pool and the brick barbecue, and Mrs. Bruton never suspected that he might be inventing some of his own participation in the design of the house. In fact de Mohrenschildt was so convincing that in the end the Brutons invited him to use the swimming pool whenever he liked. On October 1, 1962, the de Mohrenschildts drove Marina Oswald and her daughter to the Brutons' house, allegedly to use the swimming pool, and Oswald later joined them there. Oswald, however, showed no interest in pursuing the contact with the Brutons. Unbeknownst to de Mohrenschildt, he was evidently bent on carrying out an entirely different kind of assignment.

The fact that the de Mohrenschildts went to such lengths to help Oswald is, in my view, another sign that they did so from a sense of professional obligation, not for charitable reasons, contrary to how the de Mohrenschildts later tried to portray their strange relationship with the Oswalds before the Warren Commission. George de Mohrenschildt testified: "my philosophy is not to bend in front of the strong and be very nice to the poor—as nice as I can. And [the Oswalds] were very miserable, lost, penniless, mixed up. So, much as they both annoyed me, I did not show it to them because it is like insulting a beggar—you see what I mean." Jeanne explained her unusual interest in Marina by explaining that she herself had once been "in such circumstances: I didn't know anybody, and I didn't want to know anybody when I came over [to the United States]." In regard to Oswald, Jeanne testified that "maybe I was the only one that understood him." She described him as being "like a puppy dog that everybody kicked," though "he worked very hard. . . . He didn't drink, he didn't smoke. He was just hard working, but a very difficult personality. And usually offensive at people because people had an offensive attitude to him."

U.S. authorities never charged George de Mohrenschildt with being a Soviet agent, nor did he ever confess to that. From the PGU's point of view, however, his association with Oswald precluded his future operational use. Furthermore the de Mohrenschildts would not have been allowed to return to the Soviet Union—that could have been interpreted as an admission of Soviet involvement with Oswald. In such cases it was PGU practice to leave the illegal abroad forever, but at the same time to provide him with sufficient moral and financial support to retain his allegiance.

During its investigation, the House Select Committee on Assassinations interviewed Joseph Dryer, a stockbroker with Loeb & Rhodes in Palm Beach, who had known de Mohrenschildt in Haiti. (The de Mohrenschildts had returned to Haiti in the spring of 1963.) Dryer testified that, though de Mohrenschildt claimed he came to Haiti to scout for oil, "I could never figure out what he did," and Dryer expressed the belief that de Mohrenschildt had "some intelligence connection," though he did not know with which country. In the interview Dryer also said he had heard from Clemard Joseph Charles, the president of a bank in Port-au-Prince, that a large amount of money had been placed in de Mohrenschildt's account in Charles's bank just before de Mohrenschildt left Haiti in 1967.

Dryer also stated that he had heard from another person that sometime after the Kennedy assassination a "substantial" sum of money, $200,000 or $250,000, had been deposited in de Mohrenschildt's account in a different Port-au-Prince bank, that the money had been withdrawn, and that de Mohrenschildt had left Haiti soon after. Dryer identified the primary source of this report as "the person who handed out the funds at the bank." Although the House committee noted this information, it apparently did not pursue it further or draw any conclusions from it. To me, however, Dryer's information is credible because it makes operational sense—it tallies with the PGU concept of keeping a close hold even on those illegals who were no longer operationally useful, in order to prevent them from "betraying" what they knew and later to be able to refer to their cases as examples for others.

When in the fall of 1964 the Warren Commission publicly declared that it had "developed no signs of subversive or disloyal conduct on the part of either of the de Mohrenschildts," the PGU should have been greatly relieved. The de Mohrenschildts had come safely through the long and difficult investigation, and now it was the PGU's turn to take care of them. Because for operational and security reasons neither of them would ever be able to retire to the Soviet Union, the PGU must have put together a retirement package for them in the West. To be on the safe side, the PGU waited a couple of years, keeping the de Mohrenschildts on the sidelines in Haiti. Then the PGU maneuvered to transfer "laundered" funds into de Mohrenschildt's account(s) and instructed the couple to leave the small world of Haiti, where they were too well known. In his manuscript de Mohrenschildt describes their departure: "Since nobody expected our immediate departure, we made a very secret deal with a small German line–plying the trade in the Carribean islands–using the good offices of the German Ambassador, and the little ship accepted us on board late in the evening." Then the account becomes more melodramatic. "How we avoided the customs etc? I still had a laissé passé from the President Duvalier and nobody bothered to stop our truck with our furniture and supplies and our personal car. Late in the evening the only person who came to say good-bye to us was the delightful Ambassador and his charming Austrian wife, we drank a few glasses of champagne and departed into the dark Carribean. Incidentally on the manifest of this ship we signed our names as follows: Jeanne–a cook; I–a deckhand." If this story can be believed, it could be that de Mohrenschildt was concerned not about shipping his car and household effects but about secretly removing from Haiti the funds he had received from the PGU, the provenance of which he would scarcely have been able to explain to the Haitian authorities.

Through my familiarity with Soviet-style illegal operations, I detect one other indication that de Mohrenschildt was a "second-generation" illegal, whose final assignment was evidently to help clear Oswald's name. The overwhelming majority of those illegals were fanatical Marxists who kept their faith and allegiance to the bitter end, no matter what befell them. A good illustration of that is "Eugen," a DIE illegal officer who also abruptly ended his intelligence career. He was a longtime professional Communist who was recruited by the DIE in the early 1950s, trained as an illegal officer, and sent to Israel to gather information on its intelligence and military services. After spending some years there, Eugen was arrested by Israeli counterintelligence while he was receiving an encoded radio message from the DIE. Caught red-handed, Eugen confessed to the Israeli authorities to some extent, but he never admitted he had been a spy—he called himself a political activist behind the front lines. Richard Sorge also consistently denied that he had been a common spy. "My aim," he wrote in his final confession to the Japanese police, "was to preserve peace between Japan and the Soviet Union."

De Mohrenschildt, like Eugen and Sorge, remained to the end faithful to his political creed, though of necessity indirectly, because he had never confessed to working for Moscow. In his final testimony, his manuscript, de Mohrenschildt writes: "He is gone now, God bless his Bible-quoting soul and his earthy personality," referring to Nikita Khrushchev, the last Soviet leader to whom he would have sworn allegiance as an officer. "His sudden bursts of anger and beating of the table with his shoe, are all gone and belong to history. Millions of Russians miss him."

Then, like Eugen and Sorge, de Mohrenschildt chose a political line of defense, in his case not for himself but for Oswald. De Mohrenschildt writes: "I hope that this book will correct the generally low opinion people in this country have had on Lee," whom he describes as a person with a "deep desire to improve relations between the United States and the Soviet Union. . . . [Oswald] might have been sometimes violent, like almost anyone amongst us, he might kill a person he hated, he might have been violent to a racist or a pseudo-racist, to someone who might want to hurt him and his family. But to assassinate the President he rather admired, just for the glory of it, is entirely foreign to his personality."

Furthermore, de Mohrenschildt seeks to buttress Moscow's misleading allegation that Oswald could not have killed President

Kennedy because he was a poor shot. "Whatever later testimony tried to prove, I knew that [Oswald] was not a particularly good shot. He did not have that cold stare in his eyes—incidentally he had rather attractive gray eyes—he did not have a very steady hand and a stiff stance which indicate to anyone familiar with things military a good marksman. . . . He did not have a decisive, self-assured, automatic attitude of a sharpshooter. On the contrary, he was nervous, jittery, poorly coordinated type, and, and I said before completely unathletic. Also devoid of any mechanical ability. I had observed boys and men of that type in my own regiment and they were totally unfit for military performance—and usually very poor shots."

Finally, de Mohrenschildt reached for the PGU's Operation Dragon itself in order to defend the Soviet Union's innocence in connection with Kennedy's assassination. "Notwithstanding [the] superficial conclusions, favored in the USA, the general opinion in other countries stopped accepting the thesis of Lee's guilt. Many people suspected LBJ [President Lyndon Baines Johnson], as a party which profited directly from the assassination and who always thoroughly disliked JFK and the whole Kennedy clan, who used to cold-shoulder him and his wife. . . . It's not for us to judge but the latest discoveries of FBI's finageling add some credence to this theory. After all LBJ was a most devious man."

Deniability is another characteristic of Soviet-style illegal operations, which have always been carried out "under foreign flags." For thirty-four years Moscow "indignantly disclaimed" any part in the kidnapping of Gen. Aleksandr Kutepov from Paris and any connection with Sergey Puzitsky, the Soviet illegal who was instrumental in that operation. Even after Richard Sorge and the members of his network confessed to working for Soviet intelligence, Moscow firmly denied any connection. "The German Ambassador in Tokyo must know all about the Sorge affair," the TASS (Soviet press service) correspondent in Tokyo wrote in May 1942, when the Sorge affair was made public. "The whole thing is a plot engineered by the fifth column of Hitler's Elite Guards and Special Police. Moscow knows nothing about it," the Soviet embassy in Tokyo declared.

After the 1957 arrest of the illegal officer Rudolf Abel in the United States, the PGU temporarily amended its policy in order to rebuild the morale of the several thousand illegals the bloc intelligence community had stationed in the West at that time, and to repair the black eye the PGU had received with its sister services. During Abel's trial in New York it came to light that he had been "betrayed" by another Soviet illegal officer, PGU lieutenant colonel Reino Hayhanen, who had defected to the United States and who had been in a position to identify Abel owing to an embarrassing breach of security. The trial also revealed an abundance of espionage paraphernalia found in Abel's apartment by the FBI. The Kremlin gave General Sakharovsky the assignment to fix the mess.

Although negotiations leading to his 1962 exchange had treated Abel as the East German he claimed to be, after Abel was safely back in Moscow Sakharovsky acknowledged that he was "one of ours" and started parading him around the sister services as a PGU hero who had withstood five years of "American torture" without confessing his true identity or his operational tasks. During that triumphal time I met Abel twice, but even at my level the PGU did not disclose Abel's true identity as William Fischer. That would be learned only from his gravestone.

In 1964 Moscow took another unusual damage-control measure: Richard Sorge was made a Hero of the Soviet Union and represented as a legendary Soviet illegal who had played an important role in the defeat of Nazi Germany. None of the officially approved biographies of Sorge, however, contained the whole truth about his path. One of them, *Who Are You, Mr. Sorge?*, which was sponsored by the PGU and widely disseminated within the Soviet bloc, even launched the idea that the real officer who had impersonated Sorge was not the man whom the Japanese had killed but a third person, who was still alive somewhere in the world, fulfilling yet another heroic mission. Finally, in 1965 Moscow sang the praises of one more Soviet illegal in order to increase the patriotic fervor ignited by Abel and Sorge and to deflect public attention from its previous failures in that field. A KGB obituary published in the *Krasnaya Zvezda* (Red Star) of September 22, 1965, casually admitted that Sergey Puzitsky had been a Soviet illegal, and that he had "carried out a brilliant operation in the arrest of Kutepov and a number of White guard organizers," for which he "was twice awarded the Order of the Red Banner and received Chekist decorations." Yet even that unique obituary did not disclose that Puzitsky had belonged to the foreign intelligence service, let alone that he had been an illegal—commissar of state security was the title the article gave him.

Only extremely rarely did the Soviets acknowledge their illegal officers, and then only if they had something to gain. The Soviets had absolutely nothing to gain from admitting that de Mohrenschildt had been one of theirs; such an avowal would most likely have aroused international disgust, at the very least. In his case the Soviets therefore returned to their old policy of denial. In his book *Case Closed*, Gerald Posner writes: "The KGB informed this author in 1992 that it had no file on de Mohrenschildt or his wife, Jeanne, indicating neither had worked for it." A year later Moscow took the ultimate step of representing de Mohrenschildt as "a CIA informant."

24

A SHIFT IN PLANS

O N October 8, 1962, Oswald walked away from his job in Fort
Worth. The following day he alone moved to Dallas, where
the PGU surely wanted him to be—it was much more likely for
Kennedy to visit Dallas than Fort Worth. At first Oswald stayed at
the YMCA, then in a private room, and finally, on November 3, he
rented a furnished apartment and had Marina and the baby come
join him. Various members of the Russian émigré community had
looked after Marina when he first moved to Dallas, and they again
took her in for part of November 1962, when they believed he was
mistreating her. She would permanently move back in with her husband on November 17, causing most of the émigrés to wash their
hands of the couple.

The first thing Oswald did on October 9 was to visit the Dallas
office of the Texas Employment Commission to look for a job.
There he took a general aptitude test, scoring high in verbal and
clerical skills and making an excellent impression: "Well-groomed
& spoken, business suit, alert replies—Expresses self extremely
well." The commission sent him to Jaggars-Chiles-Stovall, a graphics company that printed commercial advertisements as well as U.S.
government maps of the Soviet Union, and he began working there
on October 12.

Also on his first day in Dallas, Oswald rented box number 2915
at the main post office. At first he apparently used it to receive his
magazines and newspapers. After September 6, when Reznichenko
sent Marina's passport back to her, the Oswalds had ceased corre-

sponding with the Soviet embassy in Washington for the time being. Oswald evidently had nothing urgent to report to Moscow, and it seems probable that his regular open-code correspondence with Golovachev in Minsk was all he needed for the moment.

Then the PGU suddenly suffered a terrible setback in its assassination operations. As already noted, in October 1962, during his well-publicized trial in West Germany, Bogdan Stashinsky, the PGU officer who confessed to secretly killing two German citizens, described in detail not only the modus operandi of the PGU's Thirteenth Department but also Khrushchev's direct involvement in its operations. Only hours after Stashinsky's trial began in Karlsruhe, the chief *razvedka* adviser in Bucharest asked DIE chief General Doicaru to halt all DIE "wet" operations and to order all illegal officers in the West involved in such operations to destroy their incriminating commo gear immediately. "The Comrade is furious," the adviser explained. "One step forward, two steps back," Doicaru acknowledged—that was Lenin's famous survival tactic.

At that time the DIE's Group Z had only a handful of illegal officers and agents on missions abroad. One of them was Johann, who was involved with the operation to kidnap the defector Constantin Mandache from West Germany. In an emergency message, drafted by Group Z's *razvedka* adviser, Johann was ordered to put all his intelligence assignments on ice and to destroy all compromising materials and devices. He was allowed to keep only his Grundig radio receiver and his book by Goethe—both items that had originally been purchased by the DIE on the local West German market—and was ordered to switch immediately to his emergency commo plan. That meant that from DIE headquarters he would receive only radio transmissions, which he would now decipher by using his Goethe book, and that he would report to headquarters only by using open-code messages mailed to his accommodation addresses in Austria.

According to his emergency commo plan, the DIE was to send Johann radio messages only once a month, following a previously agreed-upon program. Each transmission was now introduced by the playing of a particular song, followed by a number. The song, also previously selected, was the signal telling Johann that the transmission was indeed intended for him, while the number indicated the page number of his code book that was to be used to begin decrypting that particular message. If the song was not followed by a number, Johann understood that headquarters had no message for him that day.

If Oswald carried communications paraphernalia of a strictly espionage nature with him when he arrived back in the United States in June 1962—as seems logical judging from other similar cases—after the Stashinsky trial he was certainly instructed to destroy everything that might be incriminating. There is no way to know how the unpredictable Oswald would have reacted to such an order. Among his effects found by the Dallas police after his arrest was a "small German camera and black case on chain and film," later identified as a Minox, and a "Russian .35 mm camera and brown case." The Dallas police also found a "Wollensak 15 power telescope," binoculars "Mikron 6X Coated," and two viewmasters. In his book on the assassination of President Kennedy, Gerald Posner states that the Minox camera did not belong to Oswald but to Michael Paine, an American engineer in whose house Marina and her children were living when Kennedy was shot. That may be of interest, but it does not necessarily have operational relevance. The PGU (and the DIE) seldom used Minox cameras, which were considered incriminating and had to be hidden, together with their unexposed films. Instead the PGU (and the DIE) favored 35 mm Soviet or East German cameras available on the Western market. When a small ring (the only camera part the agent had to conceal) was inserted between such a camera's body and lens, perfect microdots could be produced. (In the late 1960s a microdot ring was adapted to fit certain West German cameras as well.) That the optical and camera equipment Oswald left behind had any operational significance, however, is uncertain.

Nevertheless it can legitimately be assumed that if Oswald had indeed been dispatched to the United States by the PGU's Thirteenth Department, his commo plan after October 1962 should have been similar to Johann's. That means the PGU would have sent Oswald one-way enciphered messages, which he was now to decipher with the help of a certain book, an identical copy of which would have been used by the PGU for encoding the messages. In this context it is interesting to note that among the Oswalds' effects confiscated after Kennedy's assassination was a Russian book containing helpful hints for cooking and keeping house, entitled *Kniga Poleznykh Sovetov* (Book of Useful Advice). This book is described in Warren Commission documents as containing 865 pages, the first 18 of which are missing. If Marina's housekeeping book did indeed serve as a code book, it would have been standard PGU practice to destroy pages one by one after they had been used to decipher a radio message.

On the inside cover of Marina's book there appears an inscription, in English: "July 12, 1961 from Lee to Marina." Oswald received his American passport back from the U.S. embassy in Moscow on July 10, 1961, and the next day he and Marina returned to the embassy to initiate procedures for her admission to the United States as an immigrant. Those actions would have signaled to the PGU that it could proceed with the operation and could issue Oswald his code materials. Another indication of the housekeeping book's possible operational significance is that after Oswald's arrest there would be found in it a very important note. This will be discussed in the next chapter in connection with Oswald's attempt to kill American general Edwin Walker in Dallas on April 10, 1963. After Oswald's arrest, Marina did not at first mention this note, which was turned over to the Dallas police by Ruth Paine, at whose house Marina was staying at the time of the assassination.

The reverberations of the Stashinsky trial soon extended far beyond the commo gear of a few illegal officers and agents. Sometime before the end of 1962, most likely in early November, the chief *razvedka* adviser at the DIE was summoned by the PGU to an emergency meeting in Moscow. A week later, when he returned to Bucharest, he informed DIE management that the Soviet Politburo had for the first time analyzed the activity of the PGU's Thirteenth Department, whose future now looked "gray." According to the adviser, the Politburo had decided that the PGU's secret assassinations should no longer be a "normal" instrument of foreign policy. Therefore, the *razvedka* adviser reported, all of the Thirteenth Department's current operations had been placed on hold indefinitely. He brought with him the order that the DIE must do likewise.

Yury Nosenko, who was in Moscow at the time, has described this unprecedented event in basically the same terms, though obviously with no operational details about PGU cases—he was not in the PGU but in the domestic VGU. He did, however, indicate a slightly different time frame. Stashinsky's trial, Nosenko told the writer John Barron, had an enormous impact, and "in late 1962 or early 1963, the leadership [the Politburo, or ultimately Khrushchev] did drastically curtail the practice of assassination and told the KGB that henceforth people would be liquidated in peacetime only in special circumstances."

In December 1962, Romania's Politburo adopted a similar top-secret resolution, formally prohibiting assassinations abroad. The entire DIE management participated in that Politburo meeting. The adopted resolution was not binding, however, because the Politburo continued to have no right to control the operations of the DIE. The future would show that the PGU continued secretly killing political opponents outside the Soviet bloc. Nevertheless, by the end of 1962 both the PGU and the DIE had for the time being frozen all their "wet" operations.

If the PGU had indeed planned to use Oswald for the killing of President Kennedy, the operation would certainly have been stopped in October 1962, or by November 1962 at the latest. By then Khrushchev may have realized that he was in enough political hot water abroad and could not risk another assassination that might implicate him. There is also reason to suppose that Sakharovsky, during that extremely difficult period for the PGU, would not even have risked a personal meeting with Oswald in order to explain to him the reasons for this unexpected decision. Johann had no personal meetings with his DIE case officer until one year after the Politburo meeting. Most likely the PGU acted like the DIE, sending Oswald a terse enciphered message simply instructing him "for reasons of security" to stop "all, repeat, all" operational activity and to destroy "all, repeat all" compromising commo devices "immediately, repeat immediately." It surely would have hit Oswald like a bolt from the blue.

Of course there is no way of knowing what really passed through Oswald's fanatical mind when he received such a message, suddenly ringing down the curtain on his "historic" mission without even offering him an explanation. It is not likely that he was familiar with the details of the Stashinsky trial, if indeed he had heard anything at all about it. In those days the American media were overwhelmed with another topic, one much closer to home: the Cuban Missile Crisis.

25

KHRUSHCHEV'S FINAL HUMILIATION

EARLY IN 1962 the management of the DIE learned that Khrushchev hoped to go down in history as the Soviet leader who exported communism and Soviet nuclear power to the American continent. According to General Sakharovsky, this was now almost a done deed. The PGU chief predicted that "the Pig" (Kennedy) would suffer a heart attack when he realized that Soviet rockets were now only ninety miles away from the United States.

During the critical days of the Cuban crisis, Gheorghiu-Dej was back in Moscow again. On the morning of October 23, 1962, returning home from a state visit to Indonesia and Burma, Dej stopped off in Moscow for a couple of hours to inform Khrushchev about the results of his visits. And there he stayed. Just before that, Kennedy had publicly warned Moscow to refrain from dangerous adventures in Cuba, and Khrushchev—who at critical moments always reached out for an audience—needed someone around to whom he could vent his anger.

According to Gheorghiu-Dej, the Soviet leader was tired and unusually irascible. Although their meeting was held before noon, Khrushchev already stank of vodka. Shortly after Dej entered Khrushchev's office, Marshal Rodion Malinovsky, the Soviet minister of defense, came in and reported that the American navy had been placed on alert, and that according to Soviet electronic monitoring the Pentagon was preparing a blockade of Cuba. Khrushchev flew into a rage, yelling, cursing, and issuing an avalanche of contradictory orders, and when Malinovsky dared to object to some of them, Khrushchev slammed his fists into him.

Without even asking Dej what his program for the day was, Khrushchev commanded a state luncheon and festive evening at the opera to be held in Dej's honor, ordering both events to be attended by the entire Presidium and to be widely publicized by the Soviet media as a display of Communist unity.

The rest of that day Khrushchev acted more irrationally than Gheorghiu-Dej had ever seen him behave, changing his mood from one minute to the next. During the state luncheon, for instance, Khrushchev swore at Washington, threatened to "nuke" the White House, and cursed loudly each time anyone pronounced the words *America* or *American*. At the end of the performance at the opera, however, he went out of his way to extend personal congratulations to an American singer who had performed in *Boris Godunov*.

The next morning Gheorghiu-Dej was having breakfast with Khrushchev when Gen. Vladimir Yefimovich Semichastny, the new chairman of the KGB, presented the Soviet leader with a PGU cable from Washington stating that Kennedy had canceled his official visit to Brazil and ordered a naval "quarantine" to prevent the eighteen Soviet cargo ships heading toward Cuba from reaching their destination.

According to Dej's account, when Khrushchev finished reading that cable his face was purple. He looked inquiringly at Semichastny, and, when the terrified general nodded, Khrushchev "cursed like a bargeman." Then he threw Semichastny's cable on the floor and ground his heel into it. "That's how I'm going to crush that viper," he cried. The "viper," Dej explained in telling the story, was Kennedy.

Goading himself on, Khrushchev grew increasingly hysterical, uttering violent threats against the "millionaire's whore" and his CIA masters. "If Kennedy had been there, the lunatic would have strangled him dead on the spot," Dej declared when he was back in Bucharest.

As I later learned, no sooner had Dej left Moscow than Khrushchev found a new victim in William Knox, the president of Westinghouse Electric International, who happened to be visiting Moscow that same day. Khrushchev summoned him to the Kremlin "for three hours of threats, complaints, and peasant jokes." As the scene was described by former U.S. official William Hyland:

> Khrushchev appeared in a state near exhaustion, but he warned that if a Soviet ship were sunk, Soviet submarines would go into action. Perhaps Khrushchev thought Knox would sound the alarm to the American Embassy, which in turn might warn Washington to veer from its perilous course.

During the night of October 25, Khrushchev received a joint PGU/GRU report that U.S. military forces had been put on worldwide alert, and that "the largest invasion force mounted since World War II" was massed in Florida. That intelligence report (Sakharovsky showed it to me a few years later) concluded that an attack on Cuba could take place within two or three days. I also learned from Sakharovsky that early on the morning of October 28, Khrushchev received a cable from Anatoly Dobrynin, the Soviet ambassador in Washington, containing the text of a letter signed by President Kennedy and handed to him by Robert Kennedy, the president's brother. The letter warned that time was running out, and that the United States was prepared to take strong and overwhelming retaliatory action by the end of the week if Moscow did not immediately agree to withdraw its missiles from Cuba.

It did not take Khrushchev long to make up his mind. Around midnight, Moscow time, about a dozen of the Soviet ships turned away from the confrontation. The Kremlin also publicly announced that all Soviet missile bases in Cuba were to be dismantled and that inspections would be permitted.

On the evening of that same Sunday, October 28, I went to Gheorghiu-Dej's residence to report the end of the Cuban crisis. "The greatest defeat in Soviet peacetime history," Dej said.

That day also happened to be my birthday, and Dej celebrated both events with caviar and champagne. Although it was true that Kennedy had won, Dej remarked, he would not give a penny for his skin. "He won't die in his bed," Dej predicted. Although he took secret pleasure in Khrushchev's "apocalyptic" humiliation, Dej was also troubled. "The lunatic can easily fly off the handle and start a nuclear war!"

26

OSWALD GOES IT ALONE

THE Cuban Missile Crisis of October 1962 was slow in building, but when it ended Oswald's "brilliant" Khrushchev had been personally and monumentally humiliated by the "millionaire's kid." That should have made the PGU's order to cease his operational activity appear at least strange to Oswald's eyes. Why? Was someone sabotaging the proletarian revolution even in Moscow?

It is important to remember that Oswald was not a disciplined and experienced professional in the espionage business. Unlike Johann, who had spent most of his mature life in a safe house or carrying out special intelligence tasks in the West, Oswald was a headstrong, individualistic American who had never shown much respect for authority. The evidence shows that he chose to ignore the PGU's order to drop everything, and that instead he decided to take matters into his own hands. Systematically, step by step, he planned what he had to do in order to fulfill his "historic" mission by himself.

Oswald's first step was to give his handlers in Moscow the impression that he had understood their order, was happy with it, and had even taken additional security measures. In late December 1962, Marina Oswald suddenly resumed her correspondence with the Soviet embassy in Washington, which she had broken off after receiving her passport from Reznichenko on September 6. Now Marina sent Reznichenko "and all employees of the Soviet Embassy" a greeting card with warm wishes for the New Year. In a letter dated December 31 (in which the greeting card was perhaps enclosed), she further informed Reznichenko that she and her husband now had box number 2915 at the main post office in Dallas, and very cordially ("not strictly officially, but in a simple, informal manner") reiterated her wishes for Reznichenko's health and success in the New Year. As before, this letter was internally routed to Gerasimov at the Soviet embassy. The friendly tone of these notes to Reznichenko is startlingly different from that of Marina's formal letters sent the preceding summer regarding her passport.

One other step Oswald took at this time was to prepare for his own escape from the United States. In January 1963 he made his final payment to the State Department on the loan it had advanced him for return travel. After that he would be free to apply for a new passport, which he could keep on hand. (The passport issued him in Moscow was good only for the trip from the Soviet Union back to the United States.)

Oswald also now moved to create a cover identity for himself that he could use for various operational activities. On January 14, 1963, he enrolled in a typing course in the night school at Crozier Technical High School in Dallas, which he attended irregularly until about March 28. That may have provided him an excuse for staying late or varying his working hours at Jaggars-Chiles-Stovall, enabling him after hours to use his employer's equipment to fabricate the cover identity documents he needed for his operational purposes.

Found in Oswald's wallet upon his arrest were a false certificate of service in the Marines and a Selective Service notice, both in the name of Alek James Hidell, which were established to have been essentially photocopied from his own documents. Also found among Oswald's effects was an international vaccination certificate for himself on which "Dr. A. J. Hideel" had falsely signed that Oswald had been vaccinated for smallpox on June 8, 1963—that was around the time Oswald applied for a new passport and wrote the Soviet embassy that he wanted to return to the Soviet Union. As we shall see, Oswald also used the name Hidell in connection with his Fair Play for Cuba activities in New Orleans that summer.

Oswald's brother Robert noted that Oswald often formed fictitious names by combining the names of people he knew. Oswald had known a Marine at Atsugi named John Rene Heindell, who was also from New Orleans and who was called by the nickname "Hidell." "Alek" was probably taken from the name Oswald himself often used in the Soviet Union, Alek or Aleksey. Sometime after opening the post office box in Dallas, Oswald also authorized Marina and A. J. Hidell to receive mail there—the date of authorization is unfortunately no longer available. (He would later also authorize Marina and Hidell to receive mail at the two other post office boxes he would open, in New Orleans and then back again in Dallas.) Although Marina would testify to the House Select Committee on Assassinations and also tell her biographer that she had noted a similarity between the names Fidel and Hidell, pointing out that Fidel Castro was Oswald's hero, there is no reason to believe her remark is relevant.

The primary reason for Oswald's fabrication of the Hidell documents was undoubtedly to enable him covertly to order the guns he needed to fulfill his "historic" mission. (Assuming that he had been ordered to cease all operational activity, he could no longer expect the PGU to supply him with an untraceable murder weapon, as would probably have been the original plan.) On January 27, 1963, Oswald, using the Hidell identity, ordered a Smith & Wesson .38 caliber revolver from a mail-order house in Los Angeles. He enclosed $10 in cash and paid the balance of $21.22 to Railway Express when the gun arrived at the post office box in Dallas, on about March 25. He also used the Hidell identity to order the Mannlicher-Carcano rifle that would be used in the Kennedy assassination, which arrived at Oswald's post office box in Dallas at about the same time as the revolver.

Oswald's next step was to try to establish a secure shelter for his wife and daughter back in the Soviet Union, using the pretexts that Marina was unhappy in a country where she could not speak the language, and that in the United States he could not find a job to support his family. That would put his wife and child out of the reach of Western authorities, and it would allow Oswald greater freedom of movement. On February 17, Marina wrote a brief—but certainly significant—letter to Reznichenko at the Soviet embassy in

Washington, which would as usual be routed to Gerasimov. Her letter reads in its entirety, as translated from the original Russian:

> Dear Comrade Reznichenko!
>
> I beg your assistance to help me return home to the USSR, where
> I can again feel like a full-fledged citizen. Please let me know what
> I should do for this, i.e., perhaps I will need to fill out a special ap-
> plication form. Since I am not presently working (because I lack
> knowledge of the English language and have a small child), I ask if
> you can possibly extend me some material assistance for the trip.
> My husband will remain here, since he is an American by national-
> ity. Once again I beg you not to refuse my request.
>
> > Sincerely yours,
> > [s] Marina Oswald

After Oswald's order for a revolver, this letter represents the
clearest evidence that Oswald was positioning himself to carry out
an operational plan on his own, and that he wanted first to see Marina and the baby leave safely for the Soviet Union. According to
Marina's testimony, it was Oswald who insisted that she leave him,
handing her pencil and paper and instructing her to write the Soviet embassy for permission to return.

On February 22, 1963, only days after Marina had written this
letter, some of George de Mohrenschildt's international friends
gave a party where the Oswalds first met Ruth Paine. She was a
Quaker who had been active in Quaker-sponsored exchanges and
correspondence between young Soviets and Americans, and in this
connection she had become interested in the Russian language.
Paine, a compassionate woman who had two young children, suggested she and Marina could get together for Russian conversation.
Thus began a friendship between the two women that would prove
highly convenient for Oswald. Whenever he needed freedom of
movement, Paine could be counted on to take Marina in. (The Russian émigrés who had earlier given Marina shelter from her supposedly brutal husband had by this time drifted away from the Oswalds.) Paine, who had room to accommodate Marina and June in
her modest house in suburban Irving, was a gregarious woman who
was in the process of separating from her husband and was appar-

ently happy for Marina's companionship. Rather than claiming Oswald was beating her, as she had done with the émigrés, Marina would flee to Paine for sympathy by alleging that Oswald no longer loved her and was trying to get rid of her by sending her back to the Soviet Union.

One of the first things Marina confided to Paine was that her husband had forcibly insisted she write the Soviet embassy, asking to be taken back. It seems that neither Moscow nor Marina was eager for her to take that irreversible step. Consul Reznichenko sent Marina a bureaucratic reply dated March 8, 1963, telling her to fill out an enclosed questionnaire and supply certain other papers, including letters from the relatives in the Soviet Union with whom she would live upon her return. On March 17, in a two-line letter, Marina specifically requested "a visa for entry in the USSR" and sent the requested documents to the Soviet embassy, without, however, mentioning letters from relatives, as far as can be determined. On April 18, Reznichenko replied, asking Marina to tell the embassy in a visit or in writing why she wished to go back. All these letters were routed to Gerasimov.

In early February 1963 George de Mohrenschildt introduced Oswald to a visiting German geologist named Volkmar Schmidt, a student of political ideology. The two men talked for hours, Oswald candidly and passionately describing the reasons for his Marxist beliefs. When the subject turned to President Kennedy, Oswald launched into a violent attack on his foreign policy, citing in particular Kennedy's "imperialist" interventions in Cuban affairs.

Realizing that Oswald held extreme and unyielding views that were not worth arguing about, Schmidt changed the subject and gave him a brief, admittedly melodramatic picture of Maj. Gen. Edwin A. Walker, a right-wing extremist living in Dallas who was then in the news for his racist activities at the University of Mississippi. Schmidt described Walker as a fascist and compared him to Hitler. Oswald seized on the subject and seemed to grow very excited.

The discussion with Schmidt may have given Oswald the idea of using General Walker to rehearse the operational plan he was working out in his own mind toward the fulfillment of his "historic" mission. On January 27, 1963, Oswald had just sent away for the

Smith & Wesson revolver, and he may have been looking for a target to try it on.

Oswald's clumsy attempts at secrecy during the early months of 1963 were not of the professional quality one would have expected from an operation being run by the PGU's Thirteenth Department. In most of its known political assassination operations, the weapon to be used was selected and supplied by Moscow. When Nikolay Khokhlov was dispatched to kill the émigré leader Georgy Okolovich in 1954, Khokhlov defected instead and then led American authorities to a dead drop located in a forest outside Munich, where they found a modified electric pistol and poisoned dumdum bullets. For both of the murders Bogdan Stashinsky committed, the PGU had supplied him in East Berlin with the special firing devices that would emit a charge of prussic acid, and he himself had been able to carry them into West Germany—on one occasion concealed in a tin of sausage. Similarly, after Anton was trained in sabotage techniques, he understood that, if he needed to blow something up, he would be directed to explosives already cached in Canada. And after his practice at a firing range, his Thirteenth Department case officer told him, "If a need for a weapon develops, one will be provided."

In Oswald's case, on the other hand, the fabricated Hidell documents were rather primitively altered copies of Oswald's own documents, and after Oswald's arrest it would not take the Dallas police long to figure out that the revolver and rifle ordered in Hidell's name in January and March 1963 had been delivered to a post office box that Oswald had opened in his own name. It seems clear that after the PGU told him to cease all operational activity, Oswald decided to go it alone.

27

THE DRY RUN

O N March 3, 1963, the Oswalds moved to 214 West Neely Street in Dallas. Oswald found the apartment and, according to Marina, said they should move there because it had a porch where the baby could play. But she felt he had really wanted to move there because of the little "office" where he could uninterruptedly go about his "work." It was in that little office that he would, according to Marina, put together his plans for the Walker attack.

On about March 10, Oswald took photographs of Maj. Gen. Edwin A. Walker's house and a stretch of railroad track running nearby. The photographs turned up in Ruth Paine's garage after Oswald's arrest and could be dated by the status of construction work being done at Walker's house that appeared in the background. It was evidently on that occasion that Oswald realized that the Smith & Wesson revolver he had already ordered would not be appropriate for taking a shot at Walker from outside his house. On March 12, Oswald therefore ordered the Mannlicher-Carcano rifle (the weapon later used to assassinate Kennedy) and paid for it with a $21.45 money order. Oswald was probably able to pick up both the rifle and the revolver at the post office on March 25, both having been shipped to "Hidell" on March 20.

On about Sunday, March 31, Oswald had Marina take pictures of him in their backyard with his old Imperial Reflex camera. He posed with the revolver on his hip and holding the rifle in various positions. In some of the pictures he is holding up copies of *The*

Militant and *The Worker*, two Communist publications to which he subscribed. From the dates when Oswald would have received those particular issues of the newspapers, it was determined that the photographs must have been taken after March 27. At first Marina volunteered nothing to the Warren Commission about the photographs or the incident connected with General Walker, which occurred on April 10. But after the photographs and other evidence pertaining to Walker were turned in by Ruth Paine, Marina testified that she had taken the pictures of her husband with his guns on a Sunday about two weeks before the Walker incident. The photographs were likely taken on or about Sunday, March 31, by which date Oswald would have had in his possession the two guns and both the publications depicted with him. After Kennedy's assassination, expert testimony confirmed that the photographs had been taken with Oswald's Imperial Reflex camera, and that the depicted rifle was probably the one that had been used to kill the president.

After Oswald's arrest, the Dallas police showed him an enlargement and then a small print made from the recovered negative of one of these photographs. Oswald denied having seen the picture before and claimed that someone who had taken his picture when he was arrested must have superimposed his head on a larger photo, then reduced it to make the smaller one. Oswald then went into a long harangue, saying he knew all about photography and how that could be done. Thus he revealed nothing about the photograph in question but a great deal about his own photographic training, most likely in the hands of the PGU. (As noted earlier, the PGU was extremely proficient at doctoring photographs and falsifying documents. Also, it routinely instructed its illegal officers and agents to admit to absolutely nothing in the event they were arrested in the West.)

Oswald must have wanted to have those photographs of himself for several reasons. He was probably planning to assemble a portfolio showing how he had committed a "perfect crime" and to find a way of getting it to the PGU. Thereby he might gain approval for his real mission and persuade the PGU to take care of his wife and child and see that they got back to the Soviet Union in case something happened to him. Oswald's plan of action and the photographs of himself with his guns would go nicely with the casing photographs of Walker's house. Marina would eventually testify that three days after the Walker incident, Oswald showed her a notebook containing the photographs of Walker's house and a map of the area where it was located; she added that he had destroyed the notebook at her insistence. More convincing than her testimony, however, is the corroborated fact that six months later Oswald similarly put together a show-and-tell notebook trying to convince the Cuban embassy in Mexico City of his revolutionary zeal. As we shall see, the notebook on the Walker incident was most likely submitted to the PGU, not destroyed.

Undoubtedly Oswald also believed that his name was destined to go down in history, and he perhaps envisioned those photographs of him eventually being reproduced in newspapers around the world. Ironically, they would indeed be widely reproduced, but not in a context he would have wished. He would never realize his dream of entering the annals of history as a Marxist hero, and even the Soviets would definitively dump him after the Kennedy assassination. Marina later claimed that he dedicated one of these photographs of himself to his baby daughter, June, and that he sent another to *The Militant*, but neither claim can be substantiated. As already noted, George de Mohrenschildt had in his possession one other copy of that series of photographs.

On April 6, Oswald was fired from his job at Jaggars-Chiles-Stovall, "ostensibly because of his inefficiency and difficult personality," but it appears that he himself brought about his discharge by flaunting his knowledge of Russian and his pro-Communist sympathies. That company, which did classified work for the Army Map Service, would have been concerned not to keep a pro-Communist on its payroll. As for Oswald himself, he could have wanted to get himself fired so that he would be free to carry out his operational plans.

On the evening of April 10 a rifle shot narrowly missed hitting General Walker's head as he was seated at his desk at home. The incident was reported in the news and the bullet was recovered, but no evidence turned up at the time that could help identify the shooter. After Oswald's arrest for the assassination of Kennedy and

Marina's eventual admissions about her husband's earlier attempt to shoot Walker, the bullet taken from Walker's house was examined by ballistics experts, who indicated that it could have been fired by Oswald's Mannlicher-Carcano rifle.

On December 2, ten days after Kennedy's assassination, Ruth Paine turned over to the police some of the things she had found in her garage belonging to Oswald, including the previously mentioned *Book of Useful Advice*. Inside that book was an undated note in Oswald's handwriting. From internal evidence, and as later confirmed by Marina, it must have been written just before Oswald took the shot at Walker on April 10. The note consists of instructions in Russian to Marina about what to do if he were arrested, or worse. It reads in entirety, in my wife's translation (emphasis in the original):

1. This is the KEY to the *mailbox* of the main post office, found in the *city*, on ERVAY street the same street where the drugstore is where you always stood. 4 blocks from the drugstore on the same street to the post office there you will find our box. I paid for the box last month so don't worry about it.

2. Send the *embassy* the information about what happened to me and also clip from the newspaper, (if anything is written about me in the paper) I think the embassy will quickly help you when it knows everything.

3. I paid for the house on the 2nd so don't worry about that.

4. I also paid for the water and gas not long ago.

5. It is possible there will be money from work, they will send to our box at the post office. Go to the *bank* and change the check into cash.

6. My *clothes* etc. you can throw out or give away. *Do not keep them.* But my PERSONAL *papers* (military, factory, etc. I prefer that you *keep*.

7. A few of my documents are in the blue small valise.

8. The address book is on my table in the study, if you need it.

We have *friends* here and the *Red Cross* will also help you. (Red Cross [sic] in English)

10. I left you money *as much as I could*, 60$ on the 2nd, and you and June can live on 10$ a week. 2 months more.

11. If I am alive and they have taken me *prisoner*, the *city jail* is located at the end of that bridge that we always rode over when we went into town. (the very beginning of the city after the bridge.)

Although at first glance this note may appear rather cold and impersonal, if Marina was at least generally aware of her husband's operational work for the PGU and of her own role in supporting him and covering for him, the note can be read as in fact showing considerable concern for her. The key to the post office box and the address book would have been important to her because they would have represented her way of staying in touch with the *"friends."* The word "friends" was always standard jargon throughout the Soviet bloc for any element of the KGB (or the GRU). "Red Cross" was a euphemism Oswald had used elsewhere in apparent reference to the PGU, in this context probably to be understood as PGU headquarters in Moscow, as opposed to the *"friends here"* at the Soviet embassy in Washington. (The English words for Red Cross might have been included for Marina to use in conversation with Americans, if necessary.)

As it turned out, Oswald evidently succeeded in firing a shot at Walker and getting away without attracting attention, just as he must have hoped. Marina would tell the Warren Commission that "[w]hen he fired, he did not know whether he had hit Walker or not," and that, when he learned from the paper the next day that he had missed only because Walker had chanced to move his head, Oswald "was very sorry that he had not hit him." The fact that he evidently fired only once (and narrowly missed) tends to support the theory that this was primarily a test exercise for Oswald, to prove that he would be able to escape cleanly from a future assassination. He would now have been ready to arrange a personal meeting with the PGU.

28

A GAME OF JAI ALAI

B ETWEEN April 13, 1963, when the de Mohrenschildts reportedly last visited the Oswalds' Dallas apartment, and April 24,
when Ruth Paine went there to pack up Marina and the baby and
move them to her house in Irving, there is no verifiable information
about Lee Oswald's whereabouts. Upon arrival at the apartment,
Paine found Oswald already packed and ready to take the bus for
New Orleans, where he said Marina had suggested he try looking
for work, since he had been unsuccessful with his job hunting in
Dallas. Beyond his visit to the employment commission in Dallas
on April 8, however, the only indication of his job hunting lies in
statements by Marina. She testified to the Warren Commission that
soon after the Walker incident "Lee lost his job—I don't know for
what reason. . . . And he looked for work for several days. And then
I insisted that it would be better for him to go to New Orleans
where he had relatives. I insisted on that, because I wanted to get
him further removed from Dallas and from Walker." If she had really been so worried about repercussions from the Walker incident,
why would she have waited two weeks before urging her husband
to leave town? Furthermore, the Texas Employment Commission
did not refer Oswald to any potential employers after April 8, and
it wrote him on April 16 disallowing the unemployment claim he
had submitted on April 12.

One strong piece of evidence indicates that in this period Oswald made a trip to Mexico City, never disclosed by Marina, besides
his later September/October trip documented by the Warren Com-

mission. On the bus he took from Nuevo Laredo to Mexico City on September 25–26, 1963, Oswald talked to two Australian girls, Patricia Winston and Pamela Mumford, telling them about his stay in the Soviet Union, which he claimed had been for the purpose of studying there. Upon arrival in Mexico City he recommended the Hotel Cuba to the girls, saying it was "clean and cheap" and claiming he had stayed there before himself. (In September he would stay at a different hotel, the Hotel del Comercio.) In 1976, Edward Jay Epstein interviewed employees of the Hotel Cuba, showing them photographs of Oswald, and he "found a chambermaid, Maria Segura, who was certain Oswald had stayed there."

Another strong piece of evidence shows that Marina went to great lengths to protect the secrecy of that first mysterious trip to Mexico City, which should have taken place between April 14 and April 23, when Oswald's whereabouts are otherwise unaccounted for. After Oswald shot President Kennedy, Marina advanced an otherwise inexplicable story about having locked Oswald in the bathroom at the Neely Street apartment on April 21 so that he would not carry out his intention of shooting at former vice president Richard Nixon. Marina told this story to Robert Oswald in January 1964 but did not mention it when she first testified to the Warren Commission the following month. Having learned about this supposed incident from Robert Oswald, the commission questioned Marina about it when she returned to testify in June 1964. At that time she stated that, a few days before her husband's departure from Dallas to New Orleans on April 24, 1963, he had finished reading a morning newspaper, put on a good suit, and taken his pistol. When she asked where he was going, he answered: "Nixon is coming. I want to go and have a look," adding that he would use the pistol if the opportunity arose. Marina said she then shut him up in the bathroom and began to cry. When questioned about how she could have prevented him from leaving, she said she might have been confused about shutting him in the bathroom, but "there is no doubt that he got dressed and got a gun." After extensive questioning, Marina said she was confused—perhaps Oswald had not intended to go out at all, perhaps he had not mentioned Nixon, but the one thing she insisted on was that the incident had taken place about three days before her husband left for New Orleans on April 24.

Marina also told this story to her biographer, melodramatically embellishing the incident and firmly dating it Sunday, April 21. At the same time she filled in more of the time gap by now saying that Oswald retrieved his rifle on April 14, handed out pro-Castro leaflets on the street soon after that, wrote the Fair Play for Cuba Committee asking for more pamphlets, which were mailed him on April 19, and on April 20 went along on a family picnic with Ruth Paine and her children. When asked about the alleged Nixon incident in 1978 by the House Select Committee on Assassinations, Marina could not remember the exact date except that it was after the Walker incident.

Contrary to Marina's claim, in April 1963 the Dallas papers mentioned nothing about a Nixon visit to Dallas. Nixon himself said the only time he was in Dallas in 1963 was November 20–21. Perhaps it was in November that Oswald made an unfavorable remark about Nixon to Marina, which she might have remembered when she later felt the need to account for her husband's supposed presence in Dallas during his undeclared trip to Mexico City.

There is one more indication of an earlier trip to Mexico. When Marina was being interviewed by the House Select Committee on Assassinations and the period just after Kennedy's assassination was under discussion, Marina stated: "I was very grateful to Mrs. Ruth Paine. . . . I was very embarrassed about the fact that if she finds out I knew about all this, the trips [sic] to Mexico and the rifle and things like that, it was very embarrassing for me to admit to myself that she has been used." In that revealing statement, Marina not only referred to *trips* to Mexico in the plural, she also connected them in her mind with Oswald's rifle that had been stored in Paine's garage and was used to shoot Kennedy—"things like that" perhaps meaning operational matters connected with Oswald's PGU mission. On the surface there would appear to be no reason for Marina to associate Oswald's rifle with his trip(s) to Mexico. (In this connection I note that Francis Gary Powers, the U-2 pilot who had been shot down over the Soviet Union, was concerned not to give the Soviets confirmation that there had been earlier U-2 overflights.

In his book he writes that he had to "watch my answers, weighing carefully to make sure not to make a slip. Just the use of the plural rather than the singular–'overflights' instead of 'overflight'–could give away everything.")

On balance it therefore seems likely that in April 1963 Oswald traveled to Mexico City. Marina's tenacity in trying to persuade her biographer and the Warren Commission that her husband did not leave Dallas at that time suggests that she was covering for him, and that in fact Oswald went to Mexico City to pass the PGU the package of operational documents that Marina claimed he had destroyed at her request. Those documents would have shown how successfully Oswald had carried out his self-initiated shooting of General Walker without incurring any security problem whatsoever. In his package Oswald also likely included an operational plan he had drawn up for fulfilling his "historic" mission, as well as the photograph of him holding a rifle in one hand and copies of *The Militant* and *The Worker* in the other, which would illustrate his political motivation.

Oswald had paid off his loan from the State Department, so a visit to Mexico should have presented no difficulties for him at the border. He did not yet have a passport for travel abroad, since the old one had been stamped valid only for his return to the United States; but he could probably have gone to Mexico just on the strength of his birth certificate, as he would do in September 1963 even after he had acquired a new passport.

In the 1950s and 1960s the PGU's favorite places for meeting agents were Vienna, Helsinki, New Delhi, and Mexico City, the four major capitals outside the Soviet bloc where the PGU and its sisters could operate with great freedom. Even in the 1970s, PGU agents living in the United States were usually met in Mexico City, as was the case in 1975–1976 for meetings with the agent Andrew Daulton Lee, who was giving the PGU information on classified American satellite systems being obtained by his friend Christopher Boyce in California.

As noted earlier, in September 1961 Valery Vladimirovich Kostikov, an identified officer of the PGU's Thirteenth Department, was assigned to Mexico City under cover as a consular officer.

Possibly Kostikov had met Oswald during his PGU training in Moscow and later was assigned to Mexico City in order to maintain contact with him and provide him with logistical support. In any case, Oswald would have had "iron" meeting arrangements that he could use for making an unscheduled or emergency meeting, whether with Kostikov or with an unknown PGU officer.

Assuming Oswald did go to Mexico City in April 1963, he probably went there by bus. He went everywhere by bus; he would even take a bus to leave the scene of Kennedy's assassination. He could not have afforded to fly to Mexico City because he had little cash to burn. After his return to the United States from the Soviet Union, there is no indication that the PGU gave him any substantial operational funds, much less any salary payments, but that would have been standard PGU practice with agents recruited for ideological reasons. (His salary from the PGU would have been regularly deposited to an escrow account held for him in the Soviet Union.)

Even if Oswald had not already met Kostikov in Moscow, he would have had some recognition phrase to use with any stranger from the PGU. (The Thirteenth Department's Anton was, for example, told to obey any orders given to him by a man who would ask him: "Were you by any chance in Brno?" Four years would pass before Anton would answer the phone one evening and hear those words.) According to notations in the Spanish-English dictionary and map of Mexico City that were found among Oswald's effects, it appears that he "intended to attend a jai alai game" in Mexico City, but in September/October 1963 he "almost certainly did not do so." Perhaps the jai alai arena was Oswald's "iron" meeting site, where he may have met Kostikov in April 1963. The Soviet-bloc services usually selected a public place, such as a movie house, museum, or sports arena, for the initial countersurveillance check and recognition meeting with an agent, to be followed perhaps an hour later with a meeting on a secluded street or at a back table in an out-of-the-way restaurant, where a private discussion could be held.

Kostikov would certainly have been surprised by Oswald's operational package. After hearing him out, it would have been normal for Kostikov (as for a DIE officer in a similar position) not to have expressed any opinion but simply to have said that he would check with Moscow headquarters on the matter. Another meeting would have been set for a couple of days later. Kostikov would have returned to the Soviet embassy and cabled the results of his meeting to Moscow on the special channel used by the Thirteenth Department.

When Oswald's proposed operational scenario arrived in Moscow, it must have set off an explosion. For one thing, the bad publicity stemming from the Stashinsky trial in October 1962 was a continuing embarrassment to the Kremlin, whose paramount concern at that time was to avoid any possibility that the Soviet Union's hand might be discerned behind another political assassination. By the spring of 1963, Shelepin had been promoted to Central Committee secretary responsible for all intelligence and security organizations, but his replacement as KGB chairman was his protégé Vladimir Semichastny, a political appointee who had been brought in from the Komsomol. Together Shelepin, Semichastny, and Sakharovsky (who was still head of the PGU) would have been politically astute enough to recognize that Oswald represented a grave potential for new international embarrassment. Even the bureaucrats in the Thirteenth Department, whose only concern was how to "neutralize" political adversaries, should have realized the inherent dangers of conducting any operation along the lines of the Walker incident, in which the target would be shot with a potentially traceable rifle and the perpetrator would escape by taking the bus home. A shot taken at the president of the United States would unleash such a concentrated manhunt that the perpetrator would be unlikely to get away. To have Oswald, a former defector to the Soviet Union, arrested in such a scenario, particularly after the publicity of the Stashinsky trial, would be suicidal for the Thirteenth Department as well, especially if Oswald were to confess his PGU connections.

I can well imagine how Sakharovsky exploded—during the years I worked under him I learned how violently he would react to unprofessional and undisciplined officers. I can also hear him telling General Fadeykin, chief of the Thirteenth Department: "We should get rid of him before it's too late." That was exactly what I heard Sakharovsky say in June 1962, during a long conversation he had with Doicaru and me after a dinner in Constanta with Khrushchev. Sakharovsky was referring to Stashinsky, who had given him a very black eye. I had been waiting for something to happen, and here it was: "We should get rid of that traitor before it's too late." The final decision to "neutralize" Oswald, however, could have been made only by Khrushchev. Not even Sakharovsky would have dared to order the killing of an American in the United States without the Kremlin's approval—to say nothing of an American who had previously defected to the Soviet Union and had been trained to assassinate the American president. Still, General Fadeykin would have immediately begun to look for someone he could use, so that when the order to "neutralize" Oswald came, he would be ready.

Very likely, Khrushchev was never informed of Oswald's proposal. Not only would the PGU have considered the plan dangerously unworkable, but by April 1963 the quixotic ruler in the Kremlin was no longer interested in having Kennedy killed. After the Cuban Missile Crisis, Khrushchev tried to represent his defeat as a "historic landmark," because for the first time in history the Americans had been forced to pledge not to invade one of their neighbors. "We behaved with dignity," Khrushchev would write in his memoirs, "and forced the U.S. to demobilize and to recognize Cuba." In fact Moscow was by then more preoccupied with Khrushchev's fate than with Kennedy's. Rumors circulating among East European leaders in the spring of 1963 had it that Khrushchev's single-handed mismanagement of the missile crisis had persuaded most of the Politburo to replace him with Frol Kozlov, his chief rival. Kozlov suddenly took sick, however, forcing the Politburo to postpone Khrushchev's replacement. But they compelled Khrushchev to place more emphasis on collective leadership. Marshal Moskalenko, who had been fired by Khrushchev because he had opposed the Cuban missile gamble, was restored to his position as head of the Soviet strategic rocket forces, and Khrushchev was forced to relax tensions with the United States. Plans were made for the two world leaders to sign an arms limitation agreement, which Khrushchev badly needed to improve his domestic political position. For the moment, in other words, Moscow probably needed Kennedy alive, at least long enough to see through the arms agreement.

The Thirteenth Department would most likely have cabled Kostikov that the order canceling all of Oswald's operational activity was now more valid than ever. Kostikov would probably have been instructed to reinforce Oswald's sense of discipline and loyalty, and above all to make sure he would take no further action toward his extremely risky assassination scenario. Most likely, however, Kostikov would also have been told not to rebuke Oswald in any way, so as not to provoke him into doing something that might damage the Soviet Union's current foreign policy concerns. Perhaps it was Kostikov, not Marina, who suggested that Oswald go to New Orleans to cool off.

The PGU should also have arranged an emergency contact with de Mohrenschildt and ordered him immediately to break off all relations with Oswald and return to Haiti. On April 19, 1963, the de Mohrenschildts abruptly left Dallas and disappeared from sight. They briefly returned to Dallas at the end of May, packed up their household effects in two days, and left again without saying goodbye to the Oswalds or talking to them at all. Then the de Mohrenschildts drove to Miami and flew on to Haiti, arriving there on June 2. They remained there until April 1964, when the Warren Commission brought them to Washington, D.C., to testify.

29

PLANS FOR KENNEDY'S VISIT

O N April 24, 1963, the headline in the *Dallas Times Herald* announced: "LBJ Sees Kennedy Visit–One-Day Texas Tour Eyed." On that day Ruth Paine arrived at the Oswalds' apartment in Dallas, expecting that the two families would spend the day together, perhaps on a picnic. Instead she found the Oswalds all packed and surrounded by a mountain of luggage. She understood they had decided to move to New Orleans, where Oswald had relatives and hoped he might have better luck looking for employment. He intended to go on ahead, then send for his family after he had found a job and an apartment for them. The ever-compassionate Paine felt sorry seeing that the pregnant and seemingly unloved Marina would be left alone to cope with a strange world where she could not even speak the language, and so Paine bundled up Marina and baby June and took them to live with her in Irving. Oswald took the bus alone for New Orleans. It would be two weeks before Marina would get a phone call from her husband and Paine would hear her joyfully tell baby June in Russian: *"Papa nas lubet"*–"Papa loves us." Oswald was ready for his family to join him in New Orleans.

It seems likely that Oswald came back from Mexico City more determined than ever to carry through with his plan for assassinating Kennedy (and then being allowed to return to the USSR). From Kostikov he probably now understood how extremely concerned the PGU was that he, with his known Soviet background and sympathies, not be connected with any action against Kennedy. But after his recent "success" against Walker, Oswald was presumably sure he could also carry out his "historic" mission without embarrassing Moscow. In the dry run against Walker, he had proved that he could both shoot straight and escape cleanly, and Oswald was probably confident he could repeat this performance when Kennedy came to Dallas. Even if the worst were to happen, Oswald was certain the PGU would not abandon him. In his initial training in Moscow he would have been told not to worry if he were arrested. It was a routine procedure for the PGU (and the DIE) to hammer into every illegal's head the idea that if he kept his mouth shut the PGU would make sure a clever lawyer would get him out. The note Oswald left Marina before he went out to shoot at Walker clearly suggests that this was what he had been told. In Oswald's mind, the important thing for him now was to dissociate himself from the city of Dallas and make sure he would be able to make a clean getaway after accomplishing his mission.

On April 24, the same day that Oswald must have read in the newspaper that Kennedy would be coming to Dallas (the news was also carried by local radio and television stations), he precipitately decided to move to New Orleans, and he wanted everyone who knew him to be aware of his move. When the time came, he could sneak back into Dallas unnoticed to accomplish the assassination, then run back to New Orleans to take his family to Mexico, from where they would all disappear into the impenetrable safe haven afforded by the Soviet Union. The authorities and his few friends and neighbors in the United States would understand that he had gone back because of his wife's homesickness and because of his own frustration over not having been able to find satisfactory employment. A perfect plan.

Upon arrival in New Orleans, Oswald telephoned an aunt, Lillian Murret, who, though unaware he had even returned from the Soviet Union, kindly agreed to let him stay at her house while he was looking for work. He spent the first Sunday locating his father's grave in the Lakeview Cemetery and feigned interest in looking for his roots, telephoning or visiting anyone who might be related to him. One aunt, Hazel Oswald, gave him a large picture of his father, which he later threw away—his motive in looking her up had undoubtedly not been filial piety but simply an effort to make his presence in New Orleans known to as many people as possible.

On April 26, Oswald went to the Louisiana Department of Labor in search of employment, stating that he was qualified as a commercial photographer, shipping clerk, or darkroom man. (As noted earlier, Oswald's known schooling and employment included no training as a photographer or darkroom technician. If he really had such skills, most likely he was taught them by the PGU in Moscow.) The interviewer noted that he made a good impression: "Neat. Suit. Tie. Polite." He was given a few leads, but they came to nothing. His aunt later testified that in the morning he would check through the newspaper advertisements and then spend all day job hunting. On April 29 he applied for reconsideration of his claim for unemployment compensation, which he eventually received after fraudulently listing fictitious companies where he had supposedly sought work.

On May 9, Oswald answered a newspaper advertisement and got a job oiling coffee machines for the William B. Reily Company. That same day he rented an apartment, with the help of another relative, and telephoned Marina to come join him. Ruth Paine bundled the Oswalds' household into her station wagon and set out for New Orleans, arriving on May 11. She and her children spent three days with the Oswalds before returning to Irving.

Oswald worked at Reily until July 19, when he was fired for inefficiency and inattention to his work. He had wasted too much of his working time loitering around the garage next door and chatting about guns with one of the owners. Thereafter he would live off unemployment, continuing to list fictitious job interviews on his claim forms. Presumably his plan was to remain unemployed for the rest of his days in the United States, both to support his cover story for his eventual return to the Soviet Union and to remain unencumbered by the restraints of a job so that he could act when the operational opportunity presented itself. (When the offer of a job at the Texas School Book Depository in Dallas later fell into his lap, it must have sounded simply too good to refuse, in view of the fact that the book depository building was located precisely along the route that the presidential motorcade would almost certainly take when Kennedy came to town.)

On May 14, Oswald closed his post office box in Dallas and directed that mail for it be forwarded to his street address in New Orleans. The next day both Oswalds signed a change-of-address form and sent it to the Soviet embassy in Washington, giving their new street address in New Orleans. On June 3, Oswald rented post office box number 30061 in New Orleans in his own name, authorizing his old fictitious friend Hidell to receive mail there too. The next time the Oswalds wrote the Soviet embassy, on July 1, they provided that new post office box address. (When he left New Orleans on September 25, Oswald closed that box and had the mail forwarded to Paine's address in Irving, Texas.)

During much of the time Oswald lived in New Orleans he very visibly engaged in activities for the Fair Play for Cuba Committee, a pro-Castro organization centered in New York. He formed a new chapter of the organization and falsely claimed to have rented an office for it, from which he was later supposedly evicted. He mostly ran his organization out of his post office box, using both his own name and the name of the fictitious Hidell, whom he made the president of his Fair Play for Cuba chapter. His Cuban activities would become particularly frenetic in August, when he was no longer tied down by a job, and after the Soviet embassy in Washington seemed to become coolly indifferent to him. On at least three occasions Oswald distributed pro-Castro handbills on the street, in one instance getting himself arrested for fighting with Cuban exiles and disturbing the peace. In jail Oswald was interviewed by the police and, at his request, by the FBI. His Cuban activities received some attention in the local press, and he twice spoke on the radio on behalf of the Fair Play for Cuba Committee. On an occasion arranged by one of his New Orleans relatives, he traveled to Mobile, Alabama, where he delivered a well-received talk to a group of Jesuits. In other words, Oswald apparently did everything he could think of to make his presence in New Orleans widely known, and to direct public perception toward his Cuban interests and away from his former Soviet connections. At the same time he should have enjoyed all this political activity, as he had always wanted to be seen as an openly militant Marxist. His publicly pro-Castro stance would generally be understood to hinder his attempt to find employment in New Orleans after he was fired from his first job there.

While he clearly admired Fidel Castro, there is no good reason to believe that Oswald ever shifted his real allegiance away from the Soviet Union. Even when he was arrested in New Orleans on August 9 for getting into a fight over Cuba, he told the police that he was a Marxist and had gone to the Soviet Union out of idealism, and that while he had been disillusioned with what he found there, he was nonetheless in America only temporarily and planned to return to the Soviet Union. That was when Oswald asked to see an FBI agent. The man who came, John Quigley, knew nothing about Oswald. Oswald told him some tall stories about his pro-Cuban organization, and Quigley left mystified about why he had been called. But FBI records would now show that Oswald was living in New Orleans.

On June 24, Oswald applied in New Orleans for a new passport, which was issued to him the following day. On the application he listed his approximate date of departure as "Oct–Dec 1963" and said he intended to leave New Orleans by Lykes Line ship (as he had traveled to the Soviet Union in 1959) on a tourist trip of three months to one year, visiting "England, France, Germany, Holland, USSR, Findland, Italy, Poland." He had already prepared himself an international vaccination certificate with the forged signature of "Dr. A. J. Hideel" (whose address was Oswald's post office box), who attested to Oswald's smallpox vaccination supposedly given on June 8, 1963. (In those days a U.S. citizen had to show such a certificate when leaving the United States, because it would be required for reentry.)

Now Oswald would have only one more logistical matter to attend to. He needed to talk Moscow into taking his wife and daughter, and eventually himself, back into the Soviet Union.

30

MOSCOW'S COLD SHOULDER

IN LATE June or early July Oswald told Marina that he wished to return to the Soviet Union with her. Marina told the Warren Commission that, as a result of that conversation, on July 1, 1963, she again wrote to Reznichenko at the Soviet embassy, replying to two letters he had sent her on April 18 (to Dallas) and June 4 (to New Orleans). Both contained the same message: she should visit or write the embassy explaining why she wished to return to the Soviet Union. Oswald enclosed a note in Marina's letter, emphasizing the urgency of her visa request and rather casually adding that he too wished to return. The full text of these two important letters is given below (Marina's in my wife's translation, Oswald's in the original English). The punctuation is as in the original.

Dear Comrade Reznichenko!

I received two letters from you in which you requested me to indicate the reason for my wish to return to the USSR.

But first of all, permit me to apologize for such a long silence on my part and to thank you for the considerate attitude toward me on the part of the Embassy. The reasons for my silence were certain family "problems" (so to speak), which stood in the way. That is also one of the reasons why I wish to return to the Homeland. The main reason is "of course" homesickness, regarding which much is written and spoken, but one learns it only in a foreign land.

I count among family "problems" the fact that at the middle or end of October I expect the birth of a 2nd child. This would

211

probably complicate matters for me, because I would not be able to work for the first few months. But there is no one I could expect to help me, for I have no parents. My relatives were against my going to America and therefore I would be ashamed to appeal to them. That is why I had to weigh everything once more before replying to your letter.

But things are improving due to the fact that my husband expresses a sincere wish to return together with me to the USSR. I earnestly beg you to help him in this. There is not much that is encouraging for us here and nothing to hold us. I cannot work for the time being, even if I did find a job. And my husband is often unemployed. It is very difficult for us to live here. We do not have the money for me to come to the Embassy, not even to pay for the hospital, etc. in connection with the birth of the baby. We both beg you very very much to help make it possible for us to return to live and work in the USSR.

In my application I did not specify the place where I would like to live in the Soviet Union. I earnestly beg you to help us obtain permission to live in Leningrad, where I grew up and went to school. There I have a sister and brother from my mother's second marriage. I know that I do not have to explain to you the reason for my wanting to live precisely in that city. It speaks for itself. I permit myself to write this without any wish to belittle the merits of our other cities. Moreover, it is easier for me to find a job in Leningrad, since there are more pharmacies there and they need more employees. For instance, when I came from Leningrad to Minsk, I could not find work in my field for quite a long time, because there were plenty of employees there.

These are the main reasons why my husband and I wish to return to the USSR. Please do not deny our request. Make us happy again, help us get back what we lost through our foolishness. We hope our second child will also be born in the USSR.

Sincerely and respectfully,
M. Oswald

P.S. I enclose with this letter my husband's application requesting permission to enter the USSR.

July 1, 1963
Dear Sirs

Please *rush* the entrance visa for the return of Soviet citizen Marina N. Oswald.

She is going to have a baby in *October*, therefore you must grant the entrance visa.

I make the transportation arrangements before then.

As for my return entrance visa please consider it <u>separatably</u>.

Thank you
Lee H. Oswald
(Husband of Marina Nicholeyev)

On July 8, Marina wrote Reznichenko again, briefly and urgently requesting an answer. On August 5, Reznichenko sent Marina a very formal reply (to the New Orleans street address, not the post office box) stating that her request to return to the Soviet Union for permanent residence had been forwarded to Moscow for review: "As soon as we receive an answer, we will immediately advise you." The copy of this letter retained at the Soviet embassy was routed to Gerasimov, as usual.

Besides their content, these letters also constitute proof that the correspondence between the Oswalds and the Soviet embassy in Washington involved operational matters of interest to the PGU, not consular matters of interest to the Ministry of Foreign Affairs. In late September and early October 1963, Oswald would visit the Cuban embassy in Mexico City and ask for a visa, claiming that he wished to visit Cuba en route to the Soviet Union. He also discussed his Soviet visa in a telephone call to the Soviet embassy in Mexico City. In other words, this Mexico City discussion of Oswald's Soviet visa was a matter of public record involving the foreign ministry of another country, Cuba; it therefore had to be handled in Soviet Foreign Ministry channels. When Yury Nosenko defected a few months later from the KGB's domestic security service, the VGU, he told the American authorities what he knew about Oswald from having read what he believed was *the* "KGB file" on him. Nosenko reported an awareness of Oswald's contact with the embassy in Mexico City but not of his contact with the embassy in Washington, a seemingly curious contradiction. The important point here is that the Cuban Foreign Ministry, the Soviet Foreign Ministry, and the KGB's VGU would all have been routinely aware of any Soviet visa request Oswald might have made (or pretended to have made) in Mexico City under those circumstances. The fact that Nosenko and the VGU knew of Oswald's visa request in Mexico City but were totally unaware of the Oswalds' protracted correspondence with the embassy in Washington concerning Soviet visas, even after Reznichenko had specifically written that the matter had been referred to Moscow, is a clear indication that the Oswalds' Washington correspondence was closely held within the PGU and was considered to be of a strictly operational nature. In short, Nosenko's information about these letters tends to confirm once more that Oswald was indeed acting as a PGU agent after his return from the Soviet Union.

Now let us return to Oswald. Although Kennedy's visit to Texas had been under consideration for some time, it was confirmed at a meeting of the president, Vice President Lyndon Johnson, and Texas governor John Connally, held on June 5 in El Paso. That was probably what gave Oswald the impetus to begin planning in earnest to carry out his mission and return to the Soviet Union. Oswald received his new passport and began working hard on the cover activities that would connect him with New Orleans, not Dallas, and would explain why he and his family would want to return to the Soviet Union. On July 1, after writing the Soviet embassy in Washington, he went to the New Orleans Public Library and borrowed William Manchester's biography of John F. Kennedy, *Portrait of a President*. When he returned that book he took out Kennedy's *Profiles in Courage*. Oswald was always a voracious reader, and during the waiting period in New Orleans he would read a book on Louisiana demagogue Huey Long's murder, a portrait of Mao Zedong, and an analysis of Khrushchev's policies, as well as books on politics, espionage, communism, and science fiction.

By July 1963 Oswald was ready, but was Moscow? As noted, it would have been suicidal for Khrushchev to have allowed the PGU to go ahead with Kennedy's assassination, and Khrushchev was not the man to stand on principle with his political survival at stake. By this time Khrushchev had made several dramatic openings toward his archenemy. The "hot line" teletype link with Washington had been activated, and in the works was the Nuclear Test Ban Treaty, which he, Kennedy, and British prime minister Harold Macmillan would formally sign on August 5—the very day that Reznichenko would write to put Oswald on permanent hold.

This time, in reply to her visa request, Marina did not receive a friendly note from Reznichenko. She had to wait more than a month before hearing from Reznichenko at all, only to be told stiffly on August 5 that the matter had been referred to Moscow for review.

This must have been an incomprehensible blow to Oswald. Here he had presumably spent almost six years, the formative years of his young manhood, doing everything the PGU had asked of him, constantly dreaming up new ways to please his PGU friends, receiving the Soviet Union's highest accolades, and now, when he was ready to offer the leader of his adopted country the ultimate sacrifice, the head of his deadliest enemy, now Oswald received an idiotic note from a bureaucrat in Washington saying, in effect, "Don't call us, we'll call you."

Oswald plunged into a whirl of Fair Play for Cuba activities while evidently trying to think of ways to get the PGU to listen to him. He probably felt completely confident of accomplishing the assassination—had he not proved its feasibility in the dress rehearsal with Walker? (According to Marina, after learning from the newspaper that Walker's life had been saved because he moved his head, Oswald had "said only that he had taken very good aim, that it was just chance that caused him to miss.") What Oswald evidently still needed, however, was final approval to proceed and assistance with an escape plan for himself and his family. He seems to have thought that if he could just sit down with the PGU for a real discussion, things could be straightened out and he would be given the final go-ahead. The problem was, where could such a meeting be held? Kostikov in Mexico City had undoubtedly been polite but firm in his refusal to enter into further discussion about Kennedy's assassination, and Oswald had no hopes there. The Soviet embassy in Washington was, of course, too closely watched by the FBI.

Cuba, on the other hand, was a safely Communist country that could easily be reached from Mexico City, and Oswald's open support of Cuba would surely persuade its embassy in Mexico to issue him an entrance visa. Perhaps back in Moscow the PGU had even mentioned Cuba to Oswald as a possible escape route. In any case, he seems to have believed that, if he could just get to the Soviet embassy in Havana, it would be an ideally secure place to talk things out with the PGU.

31

DISAPPOINTMENT IN MEXICO CITY

I N July, after Marina had written her friend Ruth Paine that Oswald was again talking about sending her back to the Soviet
Union, Paine had generously invited Marina to come live with her,
either permanently or at least for the birth of her baby, expected in
October. Now, on August 11, when Oswald perhaps began planning
for the time he would leave New Orleans to slip unnoticed back
into Dallas, he had Marina write Paine and again cry on her shoulder. Paine was traveling, but as soon as she learned that Oswald had
run out of jobs and money, she wrote back on August 25 promising
to arrive in New Orleans on September 20.

When Oswald learned that Paine would come to take Marina off
his hands, he began putting his plans into action. On August 31 he
wrote *The Worker* in New York City, saying that he and his family
would be relocating to that area in a few weeks. That same day he
also wrote to the Socialist Workers party in New York saying he and
his family would be moving to the Baltimore-Washington area in October. And on September 1 he wrote to the American Communist
party, also telling them of his move to the Baltimore-Washington
area. The PGU had probably told him that the FBI read all the mail
addressed to those organizations, and that he could therefore use letters to them to throw the FBI off his trail. (Along with Reznichenko's
address, Oswald may have been given the address of *The Worker* by
the PGU while he was still in Moscow, judging from a note found in

his effects.) When Paine arrived in New Orleans, he told her he was going to look for work in Houston, or possibly Philadelphia.

All these various stories seem to have been designed primarily to muddy the waters and leave behind no clear indication of where Oswald might go after leaving New Orleans. Should he eventually reappear in the Soviet Union, it would be assumed that all his job hunting in the United States had proved fruitless, and that he had gone back to the place where at least he knew that he could find employment.

Beginning on September 13, the two Dallas newspapers provided a steady stream of information on the president's anticipated visit to Texas, including a stop in Dallas, and the news spread nationwide. Oswald apparently decided to try to force the PGU's hand. On September 17, just before Paine's arrival, he applied at the Mexican consulate in New Orleans for a tourist card, declaring his wish to visit Mexico for two weeks and using his birth certificate as his proof of nationality. At the same time he assembled a package of materials evidently designed to impress the Cuban embassy with his devotion to Marxist principles and his support for Fidel Castro's Cuba: a few letters from the Soviet embassy in Washington and from the Communist party in the United States; his 1959 passport showing that he had spent more than two years in the Soviet Union (as well as his new passport to use for the trip to Cuba); his Soviet work permit; his certificate of marriage to a Soviet; membership cards and clippings related to his work for the Fair Play for Cuba Committee; and a "prepared statement of his qualifications as a Marxist." He must have been confident that this collection would be sufficiently impressive to ensure his welcome in Cuba.

Paine arrived as promised on September 20 and left three days later, taking with her Marina and June and the Oswalds' modest household effects. Included in the luggage was Oswald's rifle, disguised as "camping equipment," and presumably the revolver as well. On September 25, before leaving New Orleans, Oswald listed Paine's Irving, Texas, address as the forwarding address for mail coming to his post office box, and he cashed his latest unemployment check.

On September 25, Oswald took a bus for Houston, where that evening he telephoned the home of Horace Twiford, a Socialist Labor party member who had once mailed him some literature. Learning from Twiford's wife that her husband was away, Oswald said he was sorry to have missed him but he had to catch a plane to Mexico. That night he boarded a bus for Nuevo Laredo, where he changed to one for Mexico City. During the trip he remained mostly to himself, but he did mention to other passengers that he was the New Orleans secretary of the Fair Play for Cuba Committee and that he was on his way to Cuba, where he hoped to meet Fidel Castro. (He also talked to the Australian girls to whom he recommended the Hotel Cuba in Mexico City, as noted above in connection with his possible trip in April 1963.)

On balance it seems quite likely that Oswald intended his openly documented interest in Cuba to be the cover story for his real wish to talk with the PGU at the Soviet embassy in Havana. Marina would, however, support Oswald's interest in Cuba *per se* in her testimony to the Warren Commission, claiming that Oswald had told her his sole intention was to reach Cuba, and that his statements to the Cuban and Soviet embassies in Mexico City about wanting to visit Cuba only in transit to the Soviet Union were "deceptions designed to get him to Cuba." To her biographer she would go so far as to allege that she had been afraid she might never see her husband again after she kissed him goodbye in New Orleans.

When the bus arrived in Mexico City on Friday morning, September 27, Oswald checked in at the nearby Hotel del Comercio, where he would stay throughout his visit. (He may first have called Cubana Airlines, whose telephone number and address were found in his address book, but if so he would have learned that he had to have a Cuban visa before the Mexican authorities would permit him to fly to Havana.)

At the Cuban embassy Oswald spoke first to a local consular employee, Silvia Tirado de Durán, who was favorably impressed by his portfolio, filled out a visa application for him, and told him to come back with portrait photos, indicating a nearby shop where he could have them made. When Oswald returned with the photographs, Durán introduced him to the Cuban consul, Eusebio Azcue

López, who, upon learning that Oswald wished to visit Cuba for two weeks on his way to the Soviet Union, insisted that Durán check with the Soviet consulate. (Oswald apparently claimed that the Soviet embassy had just approved his Soviet visa.) Without mentioning any names on the phone, Durán did so and was told that the Soviet visa would take some four months. Oswald then got into a heated argument with Azcue, who was angered by Oswald's arrogant insistence on being given an instant Cuban visa and on being allowed to pick up his Soviet visa afterward at the Soviet embassy in Havana. They also argued about the Cuban Revolution, and Azcue ended up telling Oswald he was not the kind of person Cuba wanted to have come visit anyway. Azcue had been the Cuban consul in Mexico City for eighteen years and was about to retire to Havana; his replacement, Alfredo Mirabal, had already arrived and was in fact the one who would sign Oswald's visa application.

The comments written on Oswald's Cuban visa application (provided by the Cuban government) read (in translation): "The applicant states that he is a member of the American Communist Party and secretary in New Orleans of the Fair Play for Cuba Committee, and that he lived in the Soviet Union from October 1959 to June 19, 1962, and that he married a Soviet citizen there. He displayed documents as proof of his membership in the aforementioned organizations and a marriage certificate. He appeared at the embassy of the USSR in this city and requested that his visa be sent to the Soviet Embassy in Cuba. We called the consulate of the USSR and were told that they had to await authorization from Moscow in order to give the visa and that it would take about four months." (In 1978 Durán would testify to the House Select Committee on Assassinations that she evidently was mistaken about Oswald's membership in the Communist party, having been misled by letters he displayed.)

Ironically, it is possible that Oswald might have procured a visa to visit Cuba if he had not falsely claimed that he had, or was about to get, a Soviet visa because he was en route to the Soviet Union. He evidently believed that his past Soviet connections would impress the Cubans and make it easy for him to hop over to Havana for a few days. In fact they had the opposite effect of making the Cuban consul want to be very sure of the Soviets' relationship with Oswald before deciding to issue him a visa. Having gathered from Durán's veiled telephone call to the Soviet embassy (the Cubans and Soviets would have assumed that their telephones in Mexico City were tapped) that the Soviets had no special interest in Oswald, Azcue would have cabled Oswald's visa request to the Foreign Ministry in Havana, where it would have been cabled to the Soviet Foreign Ministry in Moscow and there brought to the attention of the KGB's VGU (and Nosenko). In other words, by lying about having just applied for a visa at the Soviet embassy in Mexico City, Oswald inadvertently set off all kinds of alarm bells.

There is no reason to believe that Oswald ever visited the Soviet embassy in Mexico City. He was not observed there at any time during his stay, though at that time the CIA had surveillance cameras trained on the entrance to the embassy. Instead, as we shall see, Oswald apparently met Thirteenth Department officer Valery Kostikov somewhere away from the embassy, as perhaps before in April 1963. How they met this time is not known, because Kostikov was not expecting Oswald, according to what Oswald would later write to the Soviet embassy in Washington, but Oswald's "iron" meeting arrangements would still have been valid. After the commotion Oswald caused at the Cuban embassy on September 27, however, the PGU station in Mexico City would in any case soon have learned of his presence, both directly from the Cubans and presumably also in a cable from Moscow sent through special Thirteenth Department channels. (The VGU's negative recommendation on Oswald's visa request, later related by Nosenko to American authorities, would have been transmitted separately through Soviet Foreign Ministry channels.) After leaving the Cuban embassy, Oswald might have taken the initiative and activated an emergency signal arrangement to call a meeting with Kostikov, hoping to get Soviet backing for his Cuban visa. (Oswald was reportedly not visited by anyone at his hotel.) Kostikov might have held a brief clandestine meeting with Oswald on Saturday, September 28–the date on which Oswald would a few days later say he had met Kostikov–at which time Kostikov would have agreed to check with Moscow and then meet

Oswald the following day or so. A free guide booklet for that week in Mexico City (*This Week–Esta Semana*, September 28–October 4, 1963), later found among Oswald's effects, shows the Soviet embassy's telephone number underlined, the Soviet consulate's number and the names *Kosten* and *Osvald* in Cyrillic noted on the page listing "Diplomats in Mexico," and check marks next to five movie theaters on the preceding page. Perhaps Kostikov (whom Oswald evidently also knew as "Kostin," as he would indicate in a letter to the PGU in Washington) held a brief meeting with Oswald at the movies, arranging then to meet him perhaps the following day at the bullfights, which in Mexico City were normally held at 4:30 on Sunday afternoon. In the back of his Spanish-English dictionary Oswald wrote "buy tickets for bull fight," and the Plaza México bullring is encircled on his Mexico City map. Also marked on Oswald's map, besides the bus terminals and the Cuban and Soviet embassies, is the Palace of Fine Arts, a favorite place for tourists to assemble on Sunday mornings for the Ballet Folklórico. There Oswald might have passed Kostikov one of the bullfight tickets he could have bought ahead of time, so that they could later meet as if by chance sitting next to each other at the Plaza México.

However they may have connected, it seems likely that Kostikov and Oswald did meet over the weekend of September 28–29. If so, it would have been normal for Kostikov to meet him twice, the second time after communicating with Moscow. From the tone of Oswald's last known message from the PGU, Reznichenko's letter of August 5, a good assumption is that the PGU instructed Kostikov to inform Oswald that for the time being he should sit tight and take *no* operational action—least of all against Kennedy. (Public statements made after 1992 by three Soviet consular officers assigned to Mexico City in September 1963, concerning their alleged contacts with Oswald, cannot be corroborated and should be read as Operation Dragon disinformation. The three Soviets, Pavel Antonovich Yatskov, Oleg Maksimovich Nechiporenko, and Kostikov himself, were all identified PGU officers at the time.)

Judging by the letter Oswald would later write to the Soviet embassy in Washington about his meeting with Kostikov, it appears that Kostikov must again have been instructed to listen sympathetically to Oswald but to prohibit him firmly from taking any action.

By this time the PGU had evidently realized there was no way the obsessive Oswald could be dissuaded from attempting to kill Kennedy, so to be on the safe side it had already set in motion measures to "neutralize" him. Meanwhile the PGU's only course would have been to keep Oswald believing that the Soviets were his friends, in order to ensure that no matter what happened he would not compromise the PGU's connection with him.

Oswald probably spent most of Monday, September 30, fighting off his discouragement, as he went about making his bus reservations to return to the United States, now directly to Dallas. The following day he again visited the Cuban embassy, trying one last time to obtain a visa. Again he claimed the Soviets had approved his visa, and at his request Durán telephoned the Soviet embassy. A guard, Ivan Obedkov, answered, and Durán passed the receiver to Oswald. In Russian, Oswald asked if a telegram had come in about his visa. When Obedkov asked whom he had talked to about it, Oswald said "Comrade Kostikov," on September 28. The guard suggested he talk to Kostikov about it again, and Oswald said he would be "right over." CIA coverage of the embassy did not pick him up, however. At that point Oswald must have given up, for he knew better than to go directly to the Soviet embassy. He left Mexico City early the next morning, Wednesday, October 2, surely a bitterly disappointed man. This visit to Mexico City was apparently the last PGU contact with Oswald.

After obtaining a new post office box in Dallas on November 1, Oswald wrote the Soviet embassy in Washington one last time while spending the long holiday weekend of November 9–11 at Ruth Paine's house in Irving. His wife and children were still staying there—his second daughter, Rachel, had been born on October 20. Paine would later testify that Oswald worked hard over this letter, apparently rewriting it several times before typing it on her typewriter, and one handwritten draft was found among his effects after the assassination. (Marina would testify that it was the envelope he retyped "ten times.")

The text of Oswald's final letter follows, with earlier draft versions also indicated in brackets:

FROM: LEE H. OSWALD, P.O. BOX 6225, DALLAS, TEXAS
MARINA NICHILAYEVA OSWALD, SOVIET CITIZEN
                          TO: CONSULAR DIVISION
                          EMBASSY U.S.S.R
                          WASHINGTON, D.C.
                          NOV, 9, 1963

Dear sirs;

This is to inform you of recent events since my meetings with comrade Kostin [in draft: "of new events since my interviews with comrade Kostine"] in the Embassy of the Soviet Union, Mexico City, Mexico.

I was unable to remain in Mexico [crossed out in draft: "because I considered useless"] indefinily because of my mexican visa restrictions which was for 15 days only. I could not take a chance on requesting a new visa [in draft: "applying for an extension"] unless I used my real name, so I returned to the United States.

[In draft: "I and Marina Nicholeyeva are now living in Dallas, Texas, you already ha"—last three words crossed out.]

[In draft, paragraph about FBI is located here.]

I had not planned to contact the Soviet embassy in Mexico as they were unprepared, [In draft: "It was unfortunate that the Soviet Embassy was unable to aid me in Mexico City, but I had not planned to contact the Mexico City Embassy at all so of course they were unprepared for me."] had I been able to reach the Soviet Embassy in Havana as planned, the embassy there would have had time to complete our business. [Crossed out in draft after *planned*: "I could have contacted the Soviet Embassy there for the completion of—would have been able to help me—assist me—get the necessary documents as I required." Not crossed out in draft: "would have had time to assist me, but of course the stuip Cuban Consule was at fault here, I'm glad he has since been replaced by another."]

Of course the Soviet embassy was not at fault, they were, as I say unprepared, the Cuban consulate was guilty of a gross breach of regulations, I am glad he has since been replced.

The Federal Bureau of Investigation is not now interested in my activities in the progressive organization "Fair Play for Cuba Committee", of which I was secretary in New Orleans (state Louisiana) since I no longer reside in [crossed out: "am no longer connected with"] that state. However, the F.B.I. has visited us here in Dallas, Texas, on November 1st. Agent James P. Hosty warned me that if I engaged [in draft: "attempt to engage"] in F.P.C.C. activities in Texas the F.B.I. will again take an "interrest" in me.

This agent also "suggested" to Marina Nichilayeva that she could remain in the United States under F.B.I. "protection", that is, she could defect from [in draft: "refuse to return to"] the Soviet Union, of course, I and my wife strongly protested these tactics by the notorious F.B.I..

Please inform us of the arrival of our Soviet entrance visa's as soon as they come.

Also, this is to inform you of the birth, on October 20, 1963, of a DAUGHTER, AUDREY MARINA OSWALD in DALLAS, TEXAS, to my wife.

> Respectfully,
> [s] Lee H. Oswald

This document is of great interest for several reasons. In the telephone conversation made to the Soviet embassy from the Cuban embassy in Mexico City, Oswald clearly said he had met with "Comrade Kostikov." The fact that he calls Kostikov "Kostin" in this letter is undoubtedly a reference to an operational alias by which Oswald knew him, perhaps going back to when they might have first met in Moscow. The fact that Oswald used an operational alias in referring to Kostikov confirms that Oswald's meeting with Kostikov in Mexico City was conducted in a PGU operational context, and that his correspondence with the Soviet embassy in Washington was too. Although Oswald had only a two-week Mexican tourist card, issued in the garbled name "Lee, Harvey Oswald," the real reason he did not stay in Mexico City longer was probably that he realized it was "useless" to try to "complete our business" with Kostikov, who was "unprepared for me." Oswald seems still sincerely to believe he could have straightened everything out if only he could have reached the PGU in Havana. The reference to "the necessary documents as I required" may mean that he had asked for alias documentation for himself, to use in his escape after the assassination. (That could have been the meaning of his July 1 request that his visa be processed *"separtably."*) The comments on the FBI in this letter seem designed to reassure the PGU that in Dallas Oswald was not under FBI suspicion—while fallaciously alleging that the FBI was still up to its usual dirty tricks. At the end of the letter, Oswald quietly and almost plaintively reminds the PGU that he and his family need visas so they can come home to the Soviet Union. In sum, in this letter the normally arrogant and abrasive Oswald seems to be trying his very best to appear polite and diplomatic and dutiful.

It would not help him. Undoubtedly his fate had already been sealed.

32

THE LONE ASSASSIN

WHEN OSWALD returned to Dallas on October 3, he may have been disappointed that he had not been able to sit down with the PGU in Havana, but evidently he was not totally discouraged. Quietly and all alone, he systematically set about accomplishing the mission he surely believed Nikita Khrushchev desired of him—and that some stupid bureaucrats were hindering. Then he and his family would be welcomed back to the Soviet Union.

It was still mid-afternoon when Oswald's bus pulled into Dallas, and the first thing he did was to visit the employment commission to say he was looking for work and to file for unemployment compensation. He spent the night at the YMCA, registering as a serviceman so he would not have to pay. The next day he applied for a job at the Padjett Printing Company. He was not hired, because the company checked with his previous employer, Jaggars-Chiles-Stovall, and received an unfavorable response. It being a Friday, he then finally called Marina at Ruth Paine's house, tried without luck to have Paine come pick him up, and eventually hitchhiked to Irving for the weekend. It was all vintage Oswald: cheating a little on the room rent, applying for work but making sure he was not hired, sponging off a kindhearted friend.

On Monday, October 7, Oswald went back to Dallas and rented a room at 621 Marsalis Street for that week. Since the end of September the local newspapers had been reporting that the president intended to make a two-day visit to Dallas, allowing him time to ride through the city in a motorcade. Oswald resumed his job hunting, probably at the same time exploring the possible routes a presidential motorcade might take. When he went back to Irving for the weekend of October 12–13, Paine found him extremely discouraged because his wife was expecting a baby any moment, he had no job prospects in sight, and he had just received the last of his unemployment checks. Paine could not have known about another matter that must have weighed even more heavily on his mind: he had heard nothing further from the Soviet embassy in Washington, and he still had no approved plan of escape back to the Soviet Union.

On Monday, October 14, Paine drove Oswald into Dallas and helped him move to a room at 1026 North Beckley Avenue. He gave her the telephone number there, but he did not tell her that he had registered in the name O. H. Lee. It seems likely that Oswald did not intend to find employment for the time remaining until Kennedy's visit, in order to keep himself unhindered when the opportunity presented itself. He would have had a little money left after his trip to Mexico City, and he knew how to live quite frugally. He had probably decided to keep a very low profile in Dallas for the next month, and then simply to disappear.

No one would really remember that Lee Harvey Oswald had even been in Dallas that fall, except for Marina and Ruth Paine, and they would not think it unusual if he suddenly took off for some other city in search of a job. (Marina would most likely have known that Oswald had to complete some PGU assignment before the family could leave for the Soviet Union, but she would not have known the specifics.) Oswald's plan contained two major flaws, however. One was that Marina gave birth to a new baby on October 20, and he apparently cared too much for his family to be able to stay away from his wife and daughter June, and from baby Rachel. (The baby would be registered as Audrey Marina Rachel. Oswald reportedly did not like the name Rachel, and that was presumably why he wrote the embassy that her name was Audrey Marina. But from the start the baby would be called Rachel, a name Marina liked.) The other flaw was that, unless the PGU came through for him, Oswald had literally nowhere to go except back to Marina and Paine—at the time of his arrest he had all of $13.87 in his pocket, which might have taken him to Irving but no farther.

Then, unexpectedly, Ruth Paine, well-meaning busybody that she was, found a job offer that was simply too tempting for Oswald to refuse. When she returned to Irving on October 14, after seeing Oswald settled into a new boardinghouse, she visited with some of her neighbors and bemoaned Oswald's jobless plight. One of the neighbors, Linnie Mae Randle, remarked that her brother, Buell Wesley Frazier, who lived with her and was working at the Texas School Book Depository in Dallas, had said there might be an opening there. Paine immediately telephoned the superintendent of the book depository, Roy Truly, who agreed to consider Oswald for the job if he would come in for an interview. When Oswald telephoned the Paine house that evening, Paine told him about the job possibility. Oswald went to see Truly the next day and was hired to begin work filling book orders on Wednesday, October 16. The book depository was located precisely along the route that the presidential motorcade was most likely to take, at the point where cars leaving the traditional parade route of Main Street had to make a turn to get onto the freeway. Moreover the upper six stories of the book depository building had rows of windows facing the street, behind which were irregular piles of cartons filled with books. It would be hard to imagine a more ideal setting for a sharpshooting assassin.

Oswald had established a pattern of spending weekdays in Dallas, at first job hunting and visiting the library, later working at the book depository during the day and reading in his room on North Beckley Avenue in the evening. On Friday evenings he hitched a ride to Irving with Frazier, returning to Dallas with him on Monday mornings. On November 1 he rented post office box number 6229 in Dallas, indicating that it would also be used to receive mail for the Fair Play for Cuba Committee and the American Civil Liberties Union, which he had meanwhile joined. On November 1 and 5 an FBI agent visited Ruth Paine to ask about Oswald's whereabouts, but she, perhaps truthfully, said she did not know his current address. (She did not give the FBI the telephone number she had for Oswald, apparently in the sincere belief that the FBI was hounding him unfairly. Marina would testify that he had used another name to register at the rooming house because he did not want the FBI to know where he was living, since he felt the FBI was making it difficult for him to find a job.) Oswald gave the Soviet embassy in Washington his new post office box number in his letter dated November 9, which was actually postmarked on November 12. That letter was, as usual, routed to Gerasimov; he signed off on it on November 18, but the PGU still sent Oswald no word about his "Soviet entrance visa's."

Even without the embarrassment brought on by the Stashinsky trial, there was no way for the Thirteenth Department to agree with Oswald's plan—the PGU had long ago forsaken bullets as too risky and had shifted instead to poisons and radioactive substances that induced natural-looking cardiac arrest and cancer. Moreover the PGU certainly knew that Kennedy's assassination was no longer desirable.

After his latest performance in Mexico City, when he had presumably insisted to Kostikov that he would be able to assassinate Kennedy with a rifle shot and make a clean getaway, the PGU must have intensified its plans to silence Oswald. At about the same time, PGU chief Sakharovsky must have decided to make Oswald appear to be acting as a tool of the American far right, in the event he should be arrested in connection with Kennedy's visit to Dallas. On October 23, Oswald apparently attended a rally at which General Walker was the speaker; it will never be known whether he attended out of curiosity or perhaps in response to a suggestion from Kostikov in Mexico City that he look into what the ultra-right "enemy" was up to. A letter ostensibly written by Oswald and mentioning his attendance at that rally came to the attention of the Warren Commission. The undated letter was postmarked November 1 and addressed to Arnold Johnson, director of the Communist party's information and lecture bureau in New York.

Johnson testified that he had received the letter after the assassination. It seems likely that the letter was a PGU forgery planted after Oswald's death as part of Operation Dragon, to suggest that Oswald might have come under rightist influence. The letter does not even sound like Oswald, when it says "political friction between 'left' and 'right' is very great here" and asks for advice on the "general view we have on the American Civil Liberties Union," whose meeting Oswald had attended with Michael Paine on October 25. Oswald was always an outspoken Marxist, sure of his own beliefs—superficial as they may have been—and it would have been totally uncharacteristic for him to have philosophized about friction between "left" and "right" to a party bureaucrat in New York, to say nothing of asking him for advice on what to think.

Another letter ostensibly from Oswald also appears to have been a PGU fabrication prepared in connection with Operation Dragon. That letter, though dated November 8, 1963, did not surface until 1975, when it was anonymously mailed from Mexico City to a researcher working on conspiracy theories involving various elements of the U.S. government in Kennedy's assassination. It is a brief, handwritten note addressed to "Mr. Hunt" asking for information about "my position," and it is signed Lee Harvey Oswald. Although the handwriting resembles Oswald's, he would not have been looking for employment in November 1963 as he was already ideally situated at the book depository. Moreover the grammar is awkward ("I am suggesting that we discuss the matter" rather than the "I suggest we discuss" that a native American would be more likely to write). The note is, however, nicely ambiguous in its use of "Mr. Hunt" and "position." By 1975, when some conspiracy advocates were attempting to implicate the CIA in Kennedy's murder, the name of the CIA's E. Howard Hunt was well known from the Watergate affair. Meanwhile it had also been determined that right-wing Dallas oilman Nelson Bunker Hunt had helped finance a black-bordered ad in the Dallas morning newspaper attacking Kennedy on the day of his assassination. Both of these were, from a technical point of view, completely within the PGU's capability, and from their contents they appear likely to have been floated as part of the Operation Dragon disinformation campaign designed to deflect attention away from the Soviet Union in connection with Oswald.

The one weekend Oswald did not go to Irving was November 16–17, the weekend before the assassination. Marina would later testify that she suggested on the telephone that Lee not come that weekend, because Ruth Paine was having a birthday party for one of her children; the father, Michael, would be there, and Marina testified that Oswald did not like Michael. She also said she told her husband he should not wear out his welcome at Paine's house, pointing out that he had spent three days there the preceding weekend. Paine would testify that she did hear Marina tell Oswald on the telephone about the birthday party. Marina and Paine tried to telephone Oswald at his rooming house on Sunday, November 17, but were told there was no one there by that name. The next day Oswald allegedly telephoned Marina to explain why he had registered as "Lee," but she would testify that she was angry and hung up on him.

That Thursday, November 21, Oswald hitched a ride home to Irving with Frazier, saying he wanted to pick up some curtain rods that were among his effects stored in Paine's garage and bring them back for his room in Dallas. Both Marina and Paine testified that when Oswald walked in the door that evening, they believed he had come home "to make up after the fight on Monday." Early the next morning he left to meet Frazier before the others were awake, leaving his wedding ring in a cup on the dresser and his wallet containing $170 in one of the drawers in the room where he and Marina slept. He carried a long brown package that he told Frazier held the curtain rods.

As established by the Warren Commission, that package contained Oswald's Mannlicher-Carcano rifle, with which at 12:30 on the afternoon of November 22, 1963, Oswald fired from a window on the sixth floor of the Texas School Book Depository, killing President John F. Kennedy and, presumably unintentionally, wounding Governor John B. Connally. Because the building was immediately surrounded by the police, Oswald was evidently forced to leave his rifle behind, but he himself managed to talk his way out of the building and make it back to his rented room, after taking evasive action by bus and taxicab and on foot. There he put on a jacket, picked up his revolver, and walked out again.

At 1:15 p.m. Oswald was confronted on the street by police officer J. D. Tippit, who had just gotten out of his squad car, where he had presumably heard the radioed alert for the assassin. At that point Oswald apparently panicked. He shot and killed Tippit, threw away his jacket, and ran into a movie theater, where the police arrested him a few minutes later, having been directed there by spectators. Oswald was taken to Dallas police headquarters and arraigned for the murders of first Tippit and then Kennedy. The Warren Commission coordinated the excellent investigative resources of local and federal authorities into a comprehensive and entirely credible account of how Lee Harvey Oswald, acting alone, had shot and killed President John F. Kennedy and police officer J. D. Tippit.

Between the time Oswald was brought back to the Dallas Police Department building, at about 2 p.m. on Friday, November 22, and when he was shot by Jack Ruby at 11:15 a.m. on Sunday, November 24, in the corridor of that building as he was about to be moved to the county jail, he was interrogated for approximately twelve hours. Most of the questioning was conducted by Capt. J. Will Fritz, head of the homicide and robbery bureau, but as many as twenty-five other persons were present or participated; inside Fritz's office there was constant going and coming, and as many as a hundred newsmen continuously swarmed outside his door. No stenographer or recording machine was available, so the only records of these interrogations are the memoranda later written up by Fritz and a few of the other interrogators. Of course the interrogators had no way of knowing that this would be their last chance to talk with Oswald.

According to Fritz, Oswald talked quietly and gave his questioners no trouble, but every time Fritz asked a question "that meant something, that would produce evidence," Oswald refused to comment. According to Fritz's report, Oswald denied owning a rifle; denied having rented the room on Beckley under the name of O. H. Lee, saying the landlady must have misunderstood him; denied having told Frazier anything about bringing back curtain rods; denied he had ever lived on Neely Street, where the photographs of him holding his guns had been taken. During the interview Oswald repeated several times that he was "a Marxist, but not a Leninist-Marxist." Thomas J. Kelley of the Secret Service, who was present when Fritz interviewed Oswald, wrote that Oswald sneered at the photographs showing him with his guns, insisting they were composite fakes.

James W. Bookhout of the FBI, who was also present during Fritz's interview of Oswald, confirmed that Oswald denied having told Frazier he was going to pick up some curtain rods in Irving;

denied he had kept a rifle in Paine's garage; denied he had ever owned a rifle; refused to take a polygraph test; and denied having shot President Kennedy, saying he had nothing against him personally. To postal inspector H. D. Holmes, Oswald denied that anyone besides himself, or perhaps occasionally his wife, had ever received mail at post office box number 2915 in Dallas; denied having ordered a rifle to be received at that box; denied having put a long package on the back seat of Frazier's car the morning of November 22, claiming the only bag he had taken along that day held his lunch; denied ever having heard the name Hidell before; and when asked about the Hidell identity document that had been found in his wallet said: "You have the card. Now you know as much about it as I do."

Thus Oswald followed the standard practice of PGU illegal officers and agents not to admit anything whatsoever if they were picked up by the police in a foreign country. The Romanian DIE operated on the same principle. The greatest concern was that an arrested illegal officer or agent not reveal the hand of the Soviet-bloc country running him. In 1981 two French citizens were arrested in Munich after stabbing Radio Free Europe employee Emil Georgescu twenty-two times and almost killing him. In describing this case, West German authorities wrote: "The perpetrators were . . . sentenced to several years in prison. They stubbornly refused to give any information on who had hired them."

In January 1985 I visited the French domestic security service, the DST (*Direction de la surveillance du territoire*), as guest of its director, Yves Bonnet, and among other things I discussed this 1981 attack on Emil Georgescu, which had been carried out by two French citizens. In the DST documents on them I recognized that one of the two perpetrators was "Sandu," a French drug smuggler who had been granted asylum in Romania, where he became a DIE agent and was trained in terrorist operations by the DIE's Group Z. It was only then that I could explain for a fact to the DST what had motivated the two arrested French mercenaries to maintain their absolute silence. In October 1976, while I was still in Bucharest, the DIE had dispatched Sandu and another French professional killer to Munich, with instructions to kill the same Emil

Georgescu by staging a car accident. For several weeks before leaving for Munich, both mercenaries were intensively trained in how to behave in case of arrest, being subjected to a string of simulated but tough interrogations to test their endurance. Both were told that this unpleasant exercise was for their benefit: as long as they kept their mouths shut in the event of arrest, the DIE would continue to deposit their salaries in their escrow accounts, take care of their families, and secretly bring them back to Romania after they were freed. Both were also told that, if they should ever betray their intelligence connections, the DIE would find them wherever they might try to hide.

Several times after he was in custody, Oswald tried to reach the New York attorney John Abt, but Abt could not be located. Abt later testified that he had been out of town, and that he had never heard of Oswald before the assassination. Oswald said he did not know Abt personally but wanted him to take his case because he had defended "the Smith Act case about 1949–1950." The Smith Act, a federal law passed in 1940, was used by the government after World War II to prosecute a series of leaders of the Communist party and the Socialist Workers party who were accused of advocating the violent overthrow of the government. Some of them were defended by Abt. Oswald may have learned Abt's name from his readings, though he did not seem very clear about who Abt was, but it is most likely the PGU would have given Abt's name to Oswald before he left Moscow. Abt himself would not have been told anything about Oswald at the time. In 1957, after PGU illegal Rudolf Abel was arrested and asked if he knew a lawyer who could represent him, Abel asked to be put in touch with John Abt. Abt did meet once with Abel but said he was too busy to take the case. The Romanian DIE also occasionally supplied such names of recommended lawyers to its illegals.

When Oswald's brother Robert saw him briefly at the police station on November 23, and asked him what was going on, Oswald said, "I don't know what they're talking about. Don't believe all this so-called evidence." When Robert asked about Marina and the two children, Oswald said, "My friends will take care of them." "Do you mean the Paines?" Robert asked. "Yes," Oswald said, according to

Robert, "indicating by his reaction that he was a little surprised that I knew of the Paines."

To Oswald, "friends" probably meant the PGU, as it did generally to anyone in operational contact with the PGU (in some cases it might mean the military service, the GRU). No wonder he looked surprised when Robert understood it to refer to the Paines. Although he had been dumped by the PGU, Oswald was still loyal to Moscow and hoped for its help. When he was arrested, he was still carrying Reznichenko's name and the address of the Soviet embassy in Washington in his wallet.

33

THE SILENCE OF THE GRAVE

O N SUNDAY, November 24, 1963, two days after he was charged with assassinating the president of the United States, Lee Harvey Oswald was silenced forever: fatally shot in front of television cameras, he died without regaining consciousness.

Jack Ruby, the man who shot and killed Oswald, did not do so spontaneously, as he steadfastly claimed, but instead committed a carefully premeditated crime. Upon judicious examination, the evidence assembled by the Warren Commission and the House Select Committee on Assassinations in investigating President Kennedy's death shows in fact that Ruby had closely followed Kennedy's visit to Dallas and hung around the police station where Oswald was being interrogated, and that afterward he lied about his reason for having shot Kennedy's assassin.

Here are the facts. In November 1963, Ruby was anticipating an assassination attempt against President Kennedy to take place during his visit to Dallas. On the morning of November 22, when Kennedy's plane was scheduled to land in Dallas, Ruby positioned himself in a place where he could almost instantly hear any news bulletins: the offices of the *Dallas Morning News*, just a few blocks from the route the president's motorcade would take. Ruby arrived at the newspaper between 11 and 11:30 a.m., reportedly to place weekend advertising for his two nightclubs, but he seemed more preoccupied with Kennedy's visit than with the advertisements. According to John Newnam, an employee of the paper's advertising department, Ruby was very concerned about and critical of the black-bordered ad headlined "Welcome Mr. Kennedy" that had appeared in that morning's paper. The ad welcomed the president to "a city that rejected your philosophy and policies in 1960" and will do so again "even more emphatically than before." The ad alleged that it was sponsored by "The American Fact-Finding Committee," but the Warren Commission was later unable to identify such an organization. As noted earlier, this ad was republished in Romania's newspaper *Scienteia* on November 26, 1963, at Moscow's request. It seems that Ruby was informed to look for it.

Ruby remained in the newspaper's building for no apparent reason after completing his advertising business. (Eva Grant, Ruby's sister, would also testify that he had telephoned her earlier that morning to call attention to the black-bordered ad.)

At about 12:45 p.m., a newspaper employee entered the office where Ruby was still loitering and announced that shots had been fired at the president. Newnam remembered that Ruby responded with a look of "stunned disbelief." Another employee recalled that Ruby appeared "obviously shaken, and an ashen color—just very pale" and sat for a while with a dazed expression. A few minutes later Ruby called his assistant at the Carousel Club, one of his two nightclubs, and said that "if anything happens we are going to close the club." Then he told Newnam: "John, I will have to leave Dallas." Ruby later explained to the Warren Commission: "I don't know why I said that, but it is a funny reaction that you feel. . . . I left the building and I went down and I got in my car and I couldn't stop crying." The evidence, however, would show a totally different reason for his thoughts about leaving town.

What Ruby did from that moment on can best be explained only by the premise that he was prepared to kill Oswald if the president was hit by a gunshot and Oswald was indeed arrested for it.

Let the facts speak for themselves. Seth Kantor, a local newsman who knew Ruby, reported to the police and later testified to the Warren Commission that on Friday, November 22, he had encountered Ruby at Parkland Hospital, where Kennedy had been brought after being shot. Although Kantor was not sure of the time, he believed it was just after 1:30 p.m., when a presidential press secretary announced that the president was dead. According to Kantor, Ruby stopped him momentarily inside the main entrance to the hospital and asked if he should "close my places for the next three nights, do you think?" Ruby later denied having gone to Parkland, and the Warren Commission concluded that Kantor was mistaken.

The House Select Committee on Assassinations, however, reinvestigated the above incident and "determined" that Kantor had remembered correctly. The House committee was also impressed by the opinion of Burt W. Griffin, the Warren Commission counsel who had directed the Ruby investigation and had written the Ruby section of the Warren report. Griffin told the committee he had come to believe, in light of evidence later uncovered, that "the [Warren] Commission's conclusion about Kantor's testimony was wrong."

As soon as Ruby learned that President Kennedy had died and that his presumptive assassin had been arrested, he began calling his closest friends and relatives. His former girlfriend, Alice Nichols, who had dated Ruby for eleven years, "was surprised to hear from him on November 22 since they had not seen one another socially for some time." Eileen Kaminsky, Ruby's sister who lived in Chicago, described her brother as "completely unnerved and crying about President Kennedy's death" when he phoned her. Alex Gruber, a boyhood friend who was living in Los Angeles, testified that when Ruby called him he "apparently lost his self-control during the conversation and terminated it." Cecil Hamlin, a friend of many years, said that on the phone Ruby had sounded very "broken up." In the afternoon Ruby visited his sister Eva Grant, who testified: "When he was leaving, he looked pretty bad. This I remember. I can't explain it to you. He looked too broken, a broken man already." Although Ruby normally attended religious services only on the Jewish High Holy Days, that evening he drove to his synagogue, arriving near the end of the two-hour Friday evening service that had begun at 8 p.m. Rabbi Hillel Silverman, who greeted him among the people leaving the services, testified that Ruby "appeared depressed."

It seems likely that Ruby had for some time been prepared to kill Oswald, and that now, when the moment had actually arrived, he wished to say goodbye to his closest friends and relatives before doing something that would change his life forever. In a way I can understand him, because on the evening before I was to leave Romania for good, I went around in somewhat the same fashion saying goodbye to the people and things I specially cared about: my daughter, the graves of my parents, the church where I had been baptized, the schools I had attended, my violin, my favorite books, and my art collection. When I was reunited with my daughter some eleven years later, she told me that I had not slept a single wink "during that last night in Bucharest," and that my eyes had been wet as I held her in my arms.

After Ruby left the synagogue, he purchased eight sandwiches and ten soft drinks from a delicatessen and drove downtown to the police station where Oswald was being detained. He later testified that, as he was driving toward town, a radio announcement that the Dallas police were working overtime had given him the idea of taking the people at police headquarters something to eat.

It seems likely, however, that Ruby actually hoped to use the snacks as a plausible reason for contacting the police officers who were interrogating Oswald. According to the Warren Commission, at about 11:30 p.m. Ruby was seen on the third floor of the Dallas Police Department, where reporters were congregated near the homicide bureau. He passed by the crowd of newsmen and walked "around the corner" toward the office where Oswald was being interrogated. Videotapes confirm Ruby's statement that later that night he was present on the third floor when Chief Jesse E. Curry and District Attorney Henry M. Wade announced that Oswald would be made available to the newsmen at a press conference in the basement. Ruby's presence at the midnight news conference was confirmed by television tapes and by at least twelve witnesses. When Oswald arrived, Ruby, together with a number of newsmen, was standing on top of a table on one side of the room.

One incident that took place during that news conference strongly raises the suspicion that Oswald was not unknown to Ruby, contrary to what Ruby consistently claimed, and that Ruby was in fact well informed about his intended victim. In answer to one question from reporters, Wade mistakenly stated that Oswald belonged to the "Free Cuba Committee," whereupon Ruby corrected him by shouting out, "Henry, that's the Fair Play for Cuba Committee."

It is, to say the least, surprising for Ruby to have already known about Oswald's connection with the Fair Play for Cuba Committee, which had been operating primarily in New Orleans, not Dallas, since Ruby had supposedly never heard of Oswald before that day.

One quite plausible explanation is that the PGU had given Ruby the task of killing Oswald, and that, in accordance with standard PGU procedures of that time, Ruby had received background information on his intended target. The Cuban espionage service, DGI, seems to be the logical instrument Moscow would have used to involve Ruby in this crime—it will later be demonstrated that Ruby had secret ties to Cuba. Here it may be recalled that, when Oswald visited the Cuban embassy in Mexico City on September 27, he displayed a file containing press clippings and correspondence documenting his activities in New Orleans on behalf of the Fair Play for Cuba Committee.

If Ruby had premeditated Oswald's killing, one obvious question is, why did he not shoot Oswald then and there at the press conference on the night of November 22? In an FBI interview on December 25, 1963, Ruby said he had been carrying a pistol during this encounter with Oswald, but when questioned by the Warren Commission about that pistol, he said: "I will be honest with you. I lied about it. It isn't so. I didn't have a gun."

There may have been one other reason for Ruby's hesitation. After I made my decision to defect, I postponed the actual moment several times. From my experience I know that it takes extraordinary internal willpower to accept the idea that tomorrow the people you have spent your life working with will call you a traitor, and to consent voluntarily to consign all your friends and all the many long years of your life into memories. So it was perhaps with Ruby. During that news conference, District Attorney Wade announced that Oswald could again be seen by the journalists a couple of days later, when he would be moved to the county jail. Ruby must have breathed more freely on hearing that.

I remember very well how I felt when told on July 26, 1978, that a U.S. military plane was waiting to take me to Washington from

West Germany, where I had asked for political asylum: much as I
wanted to reach the safe haven of the United States, I postponed
that irreversible step for one more day, until July 27. Evidently I
wanted to spend a few more hours living in my old, familiar skin. I
rationalized my hesitation to myself and to the American authorities by pretending that I had to wait one more day in order to learn
the details of a new DIE operation.

Ruby perhaps justified the postponement of his fatal action by
persuading himself that he needed to learn if Oswald was really
Kennedy's assassin. According to Wade's testimony, Ruby followed
him out of the news conference and introduced himself. Then Ruby
managed to have Wade interviewed within his hearing by two separate newsmen and one radio station. From the Police Department,
Ruby went to a local radio station where he "expressed satisfaction
that the evidence was mounting against Oswald." Danny Patrick
McCurdy, a radio station employee, testified that during that night
Ruby "looked rather pale to me as he was talking to me and he kept
looking at the floor."

Ruby returned to his apartment at about 6 a.m., but after only
two hours' sleep he was up again and agitating around in connection with the assassination. The investigation pursued by the Warren
Commission established that Ruby spent most of that Saturday trying to identify the Bernard Weissman who had signed the black-bordered advertisement that had been published in Friday's *Dallas
Morning News*. Stanley Kaufman, a friend and attorney who had
represented Ruby in civil matters, testified that "Jack was particularly impressed with the [black] border as being a tipoff of some
sort—that this man knew the President was going to be assassinated."
Ruby, who must have believed he had been betrayed, told Kaufman
that he had spent the day unsuccessfully trying to locate Weissman.
That evening Ruby called other old friends and invariably ended up
talking about the Kennedy assassination. One of these friends, Breck
Wall, testified that Ruby "was very upset the President was assassinated." Ruby's sister Eva Grant, whom he talked to on the telephone
after midnight, recalled that he was "in a depressed mood."

Elnora Pits, Ruby's cleaning lady, testified that on Sunday she
called Ruby sometime between 8:30 and 9 a.m. to learn if he

wanted her to clean his apartment that day. She said that "there was something wrong with him the way he was talking with me." Pitts explained that, though she had regularly been cleaning Ruby's apartment on Sundays, Ruby had seemed not to comprehend who she was or the reason for her call, and she had had to repeat herself several times.

It seems that by then Ruby had decided he would kill Oswald that day, and his mind must have been far away from his domestic chores. George Senator, Ruby's roommate, testified that during that morning Ruby was "mumbling, which I didn't understand. And right after he got dressed he was pacing the floor from the living room to the bedroom, from the bedroom to the living room, and his lips were going. What he was jabbering I don't know. But he was really pacing."

In July 1978, as I was about to leave Romania and my old life behind me forever, the only picture I took with me was that of my daughter, Dana, the only human being I cared about at the time. On his last trip, Ruby took along one of his beloved dogs, which he referred to as his children. The Warren Commission established that a few minutes before 11 a.m. on Sunday, November 24, Ruby left his apartment together with his dachshund Sheba. He took the revolver that he normally carried in a bank moneybag in the trunk of his car and placed it in his pocket. Listening to a portable radio he had brought along, he drove downtown. He parked his car in a lot near the Police Department, placed his keys and billfold in the trunk, and put the trunk key in the glove compartment. Ruby left Sheba in the car but did not lock the car doors.

Carrying the revolver, more than two thousand dollars in cash, and no personal identification, Ruby walked from the parking lot to the Western Union office, where he filled out forms for sending twenty-five dollars to one of his striptease dancers. The Western Union clerk who dealt with Ruby remembered that afterward he had promptly turned, walked out the door, and proceeded in the direction of the Police Department. The evidence accumulated by the Warren Commission showed that Ruby entered the police building through the auto ramp in the basement and stood behind the front rank of newsmen and police officers who were awaiting Oswald's transfer to the county jail. When Oswald emerged from a basement office, Ruby moved quickly forward and, without speaking, fired one fatal shot into Oswald's abdomen before being subdued by an onrush of police officers.

Ruby consistently claimed he had killed Oswald out of sorrow for President Kennedy's widow and children. A handwritten note from Ruby, however, which was disclosed by his lawyer in 1967, convinced the House Select Committee on Assassinations to consider "Ruby's explanation for the Oswald slaying as a fabricated legal ploy." The note was addressed to his attorney, Joseph Tonahill, and told him about the advice Ruby had received from his first lawyer, Tom Howard, in 1963: "Joe, you should know this. Tom Howard told me to say that I shot Oswald so that Caroline and Mrs. Kennedy wouldn't have to come to Dallas to testify. OK?"

* * *

A closer look at Oswald's killer shows him to have been as controversial as his victim. Jack Ruby (né Rubenstein) was born in Chicago into a family of Russian Jews who had immigrated to the United States in the early twentieth century. When Jack was ten years old his parents separated, and he was placed in various foster homes by the Jewish Social Service Bureau, for reasons of "truancy and incorrigible at home." His formal education apparently ended in 1927, when he completed the eighth grade and began working as a vendor. Over the years he sold anything he could, from carnations in dance halls and chocolate at burlesque shows to "hot" music sheets in violation of copyright laws and tip sheets for horseraces. As a teenager Jack was called "Sparky," reportedly because of his volatile nature, and later he became known as a man with a hot temper. Records of the Dallas police showed that between 1949 and November 1963 he had been arrested eight times for reasons such as disturbing the peace, carrying a concealed weapon, and violating a peace bond, as well as for simple assault. On some fifteen occasions since 1950 he had reportedly beaten with his fists, pistol-whipped, or blackjacked patrons of his nightclubs.

After World War II, Ruby and his three brothers ran a small manufacturing business in Chicago, which they owned jointly. Because thin profits led to frequent arguments, in 1947 Jack moved to Dallas, changed his name to Ruby, and started managing a nightclub owned by his sister, Eva Grant. By the time he killed Oswald, Ruby owned two nightclubs in that city and was close to "numerous underground figures," such as Joseph Civello, who allegedly headed Mafia operations in Dallas, and Harold Tannenbaum, a New Orleans nightclub figure linked to organized crime, with whom Ruby was considering going into partnership in the fall of 1963. "Two persons of questionable reliability" reported to the Warren Commission that "Ruby's consent was necessary before gambling and narcotics operations could be launched in Dallas." Although those two reports were not confirmed by other sources, most of Ruby's friends and partners described him as being himself addicted to gambling. Alice Nichols, Ruby's longtime girlfriend, testified that his refusal to give up gambling was one reason she never seriously considered marrying him.

The House Select Committee on Assassinations made an extensive computer analysis of Ruby's telephone records for the month before the president's assassination, revealing that he "either placed calls to or received calls from a number of individuals who may be fairly characterized as having been affiliated, directly or indirectly, with organized crime." These included associates of convicted criminals in the Chicago Teamsters Union, the Louisiana Mafia, and Florida's Cosa Nostra. There is no substantiated reason to believe that Ruby killed Oswald on behalf of any of these underground contacts. Nevertheless Ruby's long association with the world of crime suggests that violence and murder were not unfamiliar commodities for him.

34

THE CUBAN CONTRIBUTION

A FEW HOURS after Ruby killed Oswald, when Moscow ordered that the two DIE stations in the United States be put on extreme alert, the management of the DIE entertained no doubt that this latest killing had also been masterminded by Moscow, this time with Havana's help—in those days Cuba was one of Moscow's closest satellites. The top management of the Yugoslavian, Hungarian, and Bulgarian foreign intelligence services shared our belief. Today I can supply a great deal of evidence supporting that conclusion.

Ruby lied under oath about his connections with Cuba. He testified to the Warren Commission that he had visited that country only once, as a tourist, in August 1959. Fourteen years later, however, the House Select Committee on Assassinations obtained records of the U.S. Immigration and Naturalization Service "indicating that Ruby left Cuba on September 11, 1959, traveling to Miami, returned to Cuba on September 12, and traveled to New Orleans on September 13, 1959." These documents were later supplemented by tourist cards the committee obtained from the Cuban government, which showed "Ruby entered Cuba on August 8, 1959, left on September 11, reentered on September 12 and left again on September 13, 1959." The Cuban government did not certify that the commercial airline flights given in the INS records were the only ones Ruby had taken during the period.

In connection with these newly discovered trips, the chief counsel of the House committee, Robert G. Blakey, wrote: "we established beyond reasonable doubt that Ruby lied repeatedly and willfully to the FBI and the Warren Commission about the number of trips he made to Cuba and their duration." In its final report the committee concluded that "vacationing was probably not the purpose for traveling to Havana, despite Ruby's insistence to the Warren Commission that his one trip to Cuba in 1959 was a social visit." Indeed, the fact that Ruby obtained so many Cuban entry visas in so few days, during a period when Havana was not eager to have American visitors, indicates that he was in favor with the Castro government.

Information provided after Kennedy's assassination by Mary Thomson, the sister of a gun smuggler, shows that Ruby was involved in smuggling arms to the Cuban "revolutionary" forces of Fidel Castro. According to Thomson, in June 1958 she and her daughter traveled to the Florida Keys, where her brother introduced them to a man named "Jack." The women were told that Jack owned a nightclub in Dallas and was a member of "the syndicate" that was running guns to Castro in Cuba. Mary Thomson's story was reportedly given to the FBI and corroborated by FBI informant Blaney Mack Johnson, who stated that in the late 1950s Ruby was active in arranging illegal flights of weapons to the Castro forces, and who named Edward Browder as one of the pilots operating for Ruby. According to Florida court documents, Browder was implicated in a large theft of arms from an Ohio National Guard armory, which, according to federal authorities, appeared to be part of a massive gun-running operation to Cuba. No hard evidence proves Ruby's arms smuggling to Cuba, and after so many years it might be difficult to find. But there is quite strong evidence showing that during that same year of 1959 Ruby was engaged in other illicit dealings with the Castro government.

Other records obtained by the House committee indicated that Ruby was in Dallas at times during the period between August 8 and September 13, 1959. The committee wrote: "He apparently visited his safe deposit box on August 21, met with FBI agent Charles W. Flynn on August 31, and returned to the safe deposit box on September 4. Consequently, if the tourist card documentation, INS, FBI and bank records are all correct, Ruby had to have made at least three trips to Cuba" during the period between August 8 and

September 13 alone. Moreover the records, while apparently accurate, were clearly incomplete. The committee could not, for example, determine whether on the third trip "Ruby traveled by commercial airline or some other means," and it consequently concluded that it "could not rule out the possibility that Ruby made more trips during this period or other times."

Strong threads of suspicion connect these trips to Lewis McWillie, an underground figure who operated gambling establishments in the United States and Cuba, whom Ruby said he "idolized." From 1940 until 1958, McWillie lived in Dallas, where he managed several gambling operations, including the Top of the Hill Terrace and the Four Deuces in nearby Fort Worth. Somehow he became Ruby's protector and one of his closest confidants. Law enforcement files showed that McWillie had business and personal ties to major organized-crime figures, including Santos Trafficante. In the summer of 1958, McWillie relocated to Havana, where he eventually became manager of "the largest nightclub in the world," the Tropicana casino, owned by Trafficante, who was also the leader of the Florida branch of the Cosa Nostra. (During my official trips to Havana in the 1970s I was often taken to the Tropicana—by then an immense open-air variety show—by the head of the DGI, who told me that the Tropicana was a "purely" DGI operation.)

On June 6, 1959, Trafficante, together with other underground figures who controlled extensive gambling interests in Cuba, was arrested by Castro's police and held in Trescornia, a minimum-security detention camp outside Havana. There is sufficient reason to believe that McWillie appealed to Ruby for help to free his boss, and that he did so because he knew that Ruby was already secretly dealing with the Castro authorities. According to various testimony, soon after Trafficante was arrested in Cuba, Jack Ruby contacted convicted Texas arms smuggler Robert Ray McKeown in the United States. In the 1950s, McKeown had owned a manufacturing plant in Santiago, Cuba, but he had been forced to leave the island in 1957, reportedly after failing to pay kickbacks to Cuban dictator Fulgencio Batista. In 1958, McKeown was convicted by U.S. authorities of conspiring to smuggle arms to Castro and received a two-year suspended sentence and five years on probation. His arms-smuggling activities brought McKeown into personal contact with Fidel Castro, together with whom he was photographed during the Cuban leader's visit to Houston in 1959.

According to Robert McKeown's testimony to the Warren Commission, in 1959 Ruby contacted him by telephone, identifying himself as "Jack Rubenstein of Dallas," and told him he represented Las Vegas interests that were seeking the release of three prisoners in Cuba. Ruby offered $5,000 each for help in obtaining their release. McKeown told the caller he would accept the offer if the money was forthcoming. About three weeks later Ruby visited McKeown at his business near Houston. Ruby said he had access to a large number of jeeps in Shreveport, Louisiana, which he was about to sell in Cuba. He offered McKeown $25,000 for a letter of introduction to Castro. Again McKeown asked for money up front, and he claimed that Ruby "never returned."

On August 8, 1959, Ruby traveled to Havana. He testified to the Warren Commission that this was his only journey to Cuba, called it a "pleasure trip," and stated that he left Havana after eight days because he was "not interested in its gambling activities." The House Select Committee on Assassinations, however, developed circumstantial evidence showing that in fact Ruby traveled to Cuba in connection with the arrest of Santos Trafficante, who had long been recognized by law enforcement officials as "one of the Nation's most powerful organized crime figures." In 1976, in response to a Freedom of Information action, the CIA declassified a cable received from London on November 28, 1963, and sent it to the committee. It read:

> On 26 November 1963, a British journalist named John Wilson, and also known as Wilson-Hudson, gave information to the American Embassy in London which indicated that an "American gangster-type named Ruby" visited Cuba around 1959. Wilson himself was working in Cuba at that time and was jailed by Castro before he was deported.
>
> In prison in Cuba, Wilson says he met an American gangster-gambler named Santos who could not return to the U.S.A. . . . Instead he preferred to live in relative luxury in a Cuban prison. While

Santos was in prison, Wilson says, Santos was visited frequently by an American gangster type named Ruby.

After receiving this information, the CIA noted that there were reports that Wilson-Hudson was a "psychopath" and unreliable, but the Warren Commission was apparently not informed of this cable. The House committee was not able to locate John Wilson-Hudson, who apparently had died by the time of its investigation, but it was able to develop corroborative information to the effect that Wilson-Hudson had been "incarcerated at the same detention camp in Cuba as Trafficante." For example, Trafficante himself—who denied ever having met Ruby—testified to the House committee that he could re-call an individual fitting the description of John Wilson-Hudson among the men held in his section at Trescornia. In his testimony to the House committee, McWillie acknowledged that Ruby had visited him in Havana "for about a week" but claimed he "could not clearly recall much" about his visit. Jose Verdicia, a witness made available for a House committee interview by the Cuban government, had been the warden at Trescornia in August 1959. Verdicia told the committee he could not recall the name John Wilson-Hudson, but he could remember that one of the prisoners was a British journal-ist who had worked in Argentina, as had Wilson-Hudson. In 1978 the author Anthony Summers talked with the superintendent of the Trescornia prison, who confirmed that the "English journalist" was indeed held in the same area as Trafficante. He also confirmed that Trafficante had received special meals from one of the Havana ho-tels. (According to Ruby's travel documents, he stayed at the Capri Hotel, where Trafficante also held a major interest.)

This story was reportedly confirmed by Gerry Hemming, who allegedly was serving with Castro's forces in 1959 and claimed to have seen Ruby at that time in a meeting with Castro leader Capt. William Morgan discussing "efforts to release Trafficante from prison." According to documents supplied by the Cuban govern-ment, Trafficante was released from Trescornia on August 18, 1959, ten days after Ruby arrived in Havana.

It is worth noting that while he was involved in such dealings with Cuba, Ruby managed to establish a contact with the FBI. A

February 27, 1964, memorandum from FBI director J. Edgar Hoover to Warren Commission general counsel J. Lee Rankin (made public only in 1975) states:

> For your information, Ruby was contacted by an Agent of the Dallas Office on March 11, 1959, in view of his position as a nightclub operator who might have knowledge of the criminal element in Dallas. He was advised of the Bureau's jurisdiction in criminal matters, and he expressed a willingness to furnish information along these lines. He was subsequently contacted on eight occasions between March 11, 1959 and October 2, 1959, but he furnished no information whatever and further contacts with him were discontinued. Ruby was never paid any money, and he was never at any time an informant of this Bureau.

According to FBI agent Charles W. Flynn, who met with Ruby and later testified to the House Select Committee on Assassinations, the first contact between Ruby and the FBI was initiated by Ruby, who said he wanted to assist the FBI by supplying—on a confidential basis—criminal information that had come to his attention. Flynn said he opened a file on Ruby, but over the next seven months Ruby gave him only "a small bit of information" about thefts and related offenses. On November 6, 1959, Flynn wrote that Ruby's information had not been particularly helpful and that further attempts to develop Ruby as an informant would be fruitless, and he concluded that the file on Ruby should be closed.

The House committee staff was intrigued by Ruby's initiative to establish a contact with the FBI during the period when he was making trips to Cuba. The committee's chief counsel, Robert G. Blakey, a professor of law and director of the Notre Dame Institute of Organized Crime, who had also spent four years in the organized crime and racketeering section of the Kennedy Justice Department, wrote:

> Ruby could, of course, have contacted the FBI with no ulterior motive, and it could have been wholly unrelated to his Cuban activities. . . . We [the committee staff] believed, however, that Ruby's behavior was consistent with the pattern of seasoned offenders, who

often cultivate a relationship with a law enforcement agency during a period when they are engaging in a criminal activity in the hope that, if they are caught, they can use the relationship to secure immunity from prosecution.

Shortly after Ruby killed Oswald, the Secret Service established that in early 1959 Ruby had bought more than five hundred dollars' worth of miniaturized tape-recording equipment. The saleswoman contacted by the Secret Service recalled that Ruby had bought "a wristwatch which held a microphone for the equipment, and also an instrument to bug a telephone [and a] tie clip and attaché case." The House committee also noted that on April 27, 1959, soon after Ruby had bought the equipment, he rented safety deposit box number 448 at Merchants State Bank in Dallas, where he maintained a small business checking account. From the time Ruby acquired the safety deposit box through the fall of 1959, "researchers have discerned a pattern—both before and after making a trip to Cuba, Ruby would enter his deposit box and contact the FBI."

Ruby's initiative to establish a contact with the FBI and his purchase of miniaturized recording equipment are consistent with standard PGU (and DIE) practice. Both organizations instructed their foreign agents used for smuggling and similar illicit tasks to make contact with local counterintelligence and police services to try to learn their current methods of operation in such matters and whether the agents themselves were under suspicion. The PGU would go to great lengths to record such discussions between its agent and a Western counterintelligence or police officer, in the belief that PGU headquarters would be in a much better position than the agent to get a true feeling for the situation. The PGU could, of course, issue those agents professional miniaturized recording equipment, and in a few special cases it did so. The PGU rule, however, was to instruct the agents to purchase such equipment in local stores, so that if it should be found on them it could not be considered incriminating evidence.

In fact Ruby's case looks just like that of "Felix," a DIE agent who was arrested by the FBI soon after I was granted political asylum in the United States. Felix (real name Fred Kolman, né Alexandru Scárlátescu), an American citizen born in Romania with business interests very similar to Ruby's, had become a DIE agent in 1969. A professional smuggler, Felix had been arrested at the Romanian border with Bulgaria because he tried to smuggle a Romanian citizen out of the country with a counterfeit American passport. During his interrogation by the *Securitate*, Felix agreed to become an informant of the Romanian political police. He later admitted to being connected with the American Mafia, thereby causing his case eventually to be transferred to the DIE. At that time the DIE was deeply involved in smuggling drugs to the West, and experience showed that Mafia-connected smugglers were significantly more successful than others.

The DIE did not, however, involve Felix in smuggling drugs, as he soon proved to be much more useful than that. Over the next two years Felix provided the DIE with samples of miniaturized monitoring devices reportedly used by the CIA and the FBI. He also turned over numerous secretly recorded audiotapes containing his discussions with American law enforcement officers on various subjects requested by the DIE, which proved to be of great operational interest to the DIE's counterintelligence component. For both activities Felix was generously rewarded with cold cash.

There is a strong possibility that Ruby might have become an agent of the Cuban DGI in mid-1959, when he dashed over to Havana and reportedly approached Castro's representatives with an offer to smuggle American jeeps into Cuba in exchange for Trafficante's release. That offer, together with Ruby's apparent involvement in smuggling arms to Castro's forces, his connections with the American underworld, and particularly his contact with the FBI, might have formed the basis for a DGI attempt to recruit him as an intelligence agent and use him for other smuggling operations. Ruby's addiction to gambling and his constant need for money could have motivated him to agree to become a DGI agent. (In 1973, when I accompanied Ceausescu to Havana for the first time, I was present when Castro told the Romanian dictator that the DGI had long before set up its own drug-trafficking networks, described by Castro as "an important instrument for destabilizing Western imperialism." In an effort to persuade the avaricious Ceausescu to join him in this venture, Castro added that in the end his drug smuggling was bound to pay off handsomely–both politically and financially.)

It is significant that the Cubans released Trafficante from jail while Ruby was still in Havana, and that three days after Trafficante was freed Ruby apparently returned secretly to the United States, where he is known to have met his FBI contact, Flynn. It is also significant that before and after that meeting, Ruby visited his safety deposit box. It seems likely that he took his miniaturized recording equipment from that box, recorded his discussion with Flynn, put his equipment back in the safety deposit box, and returned to Cuba with the tape proving that he was indeed connected with the FBI. By that time the DGI was already involved in operations against anti-Castro exiles living in the United States. Any connection with the FBI could have proved extremely useful to the DGI in that regard.

No evidence indicates that Ruby traveled to Havana after September 1959, but if he was already recruited by then, the DGI would no longer have wanted to see him in Cuba. If it should have needed him there for some reason, it would have brought him into Havana "black." Felix never made an overt trip to Romania after he had been recruited by the DIE. He always entered the country clandestinely–a few times on private planes registered in Western Europe that were used by the DIE. In fact, fewer than 1 percent of the DIE's agents recruited in Romania who were not involved in official business demanding such travel were allowed to make further open visits there after they became intelligence agents.

It would have been quite out of character for the Cuban DGI–which followed the same PGU pattern as the DIE did–to allow an agent in the United States to continue openly visiting Cuba, much less to vegetate and do nothing. Beginning in the early 1960s, the DGI was intensely interested in smuggling in Western arms that Cuba could use in terrorist operations abroad in connection with Castro's export of the revolution, and Ruby must have seemed to be just the right man for such a job. (During my 1971 visit to Cuba I visited what proved to be the bloc intelligence community's largest factory for manufacturing double-walled suitcases and other concealment devices for use in secretly transporting weapons into various non-Communist countries. Sergio del Valle, head of the Cuban security forces, told me that arms smuggling was one of their main jobs at the time.)

Conceivably Ruby came to the PGU's attention in the spring of 1963, when the chief of the PGU's Thirteenth Department, Gen. Ivan Fadeykin, began searching for an agent able to "neutralize" Oswald. (Oswald's reckless behavior in the General Walker incident on April 10 was sufficient cause for George de Mohrenschildt to drop Oswald at once, and Oswald's probable meeting with the PGU in Mexico City shortly thereafter would have confirmed the need for the Thirteenth Department to prepare for the worst.) Ruby's compromising record as an intelligence agent and his Mafia connection could well have made him eligible for the job.

Once again, Ruby's case looks to me like a duplicate of Felix's. In April 1978 I accompanied Romanian president Ceausescu on his last official visit to Washington, where he was castigated by American congressmen and the press in connection with his refusal to allow the family of a DIE defector, Constantin Rǎutǎ, to emigrate to the United States. Later that same day, Ceausescu asked me, "Where is the Mafioso?" Ceausescu knew who almost all the important DIE agents were, but he could never recall their code names and made up his own names for them. The Mafioso's code name was Felix. A few days later Felix was secretly brought to Romania and confidentially told that new information concerning a defector who was now in Washington, D.C., Constantin Rǎutǎ, showed that he might have indirectly learned about Felix's cooperation with the DIE. Before defecting, Rǎutǎ had worked as an engineer in a DIE component responsible for developing new operational techniques based on CIA samples provided by Felix.

Gen. Gheorghe Maxim, the chief of Brigade U (illegals), who was in charge of killing Rǎutǎ and was introduced to Felix as "General Manea," told Felix that the DIE had unfortunately only now found a report attesting that Rǎutǎ had been given "more information than necessary" about the source who had provided the CIA samples. The officer who wrote that report was dead, Manea explained, and therefore the DIE could not get to the bottom of the story.

This could be dangerous for "both you and us," Manea concluded, and he then asked Felix to help the DIE "neutralize" Ráutá. In exchange the DIE would "royally" reward him with tax-free money and would provide political asylum in Romania for him and his family in case he should be suspected of having done the deed, or if his smuggling and Mafia operations should ever bring him into conflict with U.S. law. For secrecy reasons, General Maxim changed Felix's code name to "Leman," purged his file of all information relating to his real identity, and took over the direct handling of his case.

From an operational standpoint, Ruby represented all that Felix did. Ruby had the additional advantages of living in Dallas, the city where Oswald would most likely attempt to shoot at President Kennedy, and of having long-standing connections with the local Dallas police owing to his nightclubs.

In accordance with the PGU pattern at that time, Ruby would have been summoned to a personal meeting in a third country, most likely Mexico. There he would have been indoctrinated to understand that the Soviet bloc had great admiration for Kennedy, and he would probably have been given a long story about how the DGI (or possibly the PGU) had obtained information indicating that "reactionary American forces" hated Kennedy because he wanted to end the cold war, and that those forces had decided to get rid of him. Ruby might have been told that the American plotters had given the job to the CIA, which was planning to use as a hit man one of its agents, Lee Harvey Oswald, who had previously been dispatched on a mission to the Soviet Union under cover as a defector and had later been brought back home. In that way, Ruby's DGI case officer would have explained, the CIA intended to kill two birds with one stone: to knock off Kennedy and to blame the Soviet Union for his death. To top it all off, the case officer would have said, the CIA had tried to involve Cuba as well, by having Oswald noisily support the Fair Play for Cuba Committee and by recently sending Oswald to the Cuban embassy in Mexico City, where he had asked for an "urgent" visa to visit Havana and had raised a huge ruckus when it had been refused, just to make sure that no one would forget his Cuban connections.

Ruby would have been told that, if Oswald did indeed succeed in assassinating Kennedy, it was important for Oswald to be killed before he could slander the Soviet Union and Cuba as being behind the assassination. The DGI case officer would have coached Ruby to claim that he had acted spontaneously in killing Oswald, because that would get him a light sentence. After serving it, he would be given political asylum in Cuba or anywhere else he chose within the Soviet bloc, where he could "live like a king." He could even spend the rest of his life in South America, under a new identity. At the end of the session, Ruby would have been given a documentary file on Oswald to review, and any questions he might have had about Oswald would have been answered. The above scenario, or something similar, would explain all of Ruby's moves on the day of Kennedy's assassination as well as his interest in sticking as close to the arrested Oswald as he could, and it would certainly be consistent with PGU practice.

In June 1978, Felix gave the DIE photographs of Ráutá that he had secretly taken in Washington, and he submitted a detailed operational plan to have him killed in an "accident" that would land him at the bottom of the Potomac River. Ceausescu personally approved the assassination plan, but a few days later I defected to the United States, and that ended Felix's intelligence work for the DIE. He was arrested in New York. Initially he refused to acknowledge any connection with Romanian intelligence, but he broke his silence after learning that his interrogators were familiar with all the details of his plan to kill Ráutá, including the go-ahead code signal that would alert him to proceed. As I would learn, soon after that Felix jumped out the window of the high rise where he was being questioned by the FBI. (The information about Felix that was contained in the *Securitate* and DIE files was recently disclosed in a book published in Bucharest.)

Although there is no hard proof that Ruby killed Oswald on behalf of the Cuban DGI, circumstantial evidence indicates that after his arrest Ruby was terrified of having his secret connection with Havana discovered by the American authorities. According to Wally Weston, the Carousel Club's emcee, who visited Ruby at the Dallas County Jail not long after his conviction in 1964, Ruby said to him: "Wally, you know what's going to happen now? They're going to find out about my trips to Cuba and my trips to New Orleans and the guns and everything." In 1966, while awaiting a new trial, Ruby repeated the same thing to his lawyers.

In regard to his mention of New Orleans, recall that Oswald relocated there at the end of April 1963, just when the PGU must have begun looking for someone to "neutralize" him if he insisted on going though with his assassination plans. There, for the next few months, Oswald very visibly promoted the Fair Play for Cuba Committee.

Equally interesting are the parallels between Ruby's remarks about why Kennedy was killed and the PGU's Operation Dragon. In the fall of 1964, while awaiting the outcome of his conviction appeal, Ruby is said to have written a sixteen-page letter to a fellow prisoner who was about to leave the jail. That letter, which reportedly ended up in the hands of Penn Jones, a researcher into the Kennedy assassination, accused Lyndon Johnson of the deed and used almost the same words found in the Dragon: "The only one who gained by the shooting of the president was Johnson, and he was in a car in the rear and safe when the shooting took place. What would the Russians, Castro or anyone else have to gain by eliminating the president? If Johnson was so heartbroken over Kennedy, why didn't he do something for Robert Kennedy? All he did was snub him."

35

NOSENKO'S TESTIMONY

I N February 1964, before the start of the Warren Commission investigation, the U.S. government had an unexpected source of
information about Oswald's stay in the Soviet Union fall into its
lap–the KGB defector Yury Ivanovich Nosenko. When Nosenko
left Moscow on an official trip and arrived in Geneva on January
20, 1964, he immediately contacted the CIA, with which he had
been in contact on a previous trip abroad in 1962. Now, he said, he
wished to defect. One of the first things Nosenko told the CIA in
Geneva was his knowledge of Oswald.

Nosenko insisted that he had been the KGB officer who had supervised Oswald's file while Oswald had been in the Soviet Union,
and that he had also been assigned to make a complete investigation into the Oswald affair after Kennedy's assassination. According to what Nosenko said he knew from the KGB file and from
hearsay, Oswald was an unstable person of no intelligence value
who had never been contacted or debriefed by any branch of the
KGB. He had merely been passively monitored until his return to
the United States. On February 4, 1964, Nosenko was accepted as
a defector and brought to the United States, where the FBI reviewed with him in greal detail his knowledge of Oswald, his story
remaining essentially the same.

Immediately a great controversy arose within various elements
of the U.S. government over Nosenko's credibility. FBI director
Hoover, who always took a legalistic approach to Soviet espionage
and showed little interest in or understanding of the complexities of

Soviet foreign intelligence deceptions, accepted Nosenko's information at face value. Hoover concluded that the KGB had not been involved in Kennedy's assassination, and that the FBI had therefore not been remiss in its coverage of Oswald after his redefection to the United States.

Meanwhile at the CIA, the subject of counterintelligence was jealously guarded by James Angleton, who had headed its Counterintelligence Staff for many years. By this time Angleton had descended into an irrational paranoia, the legacy of which severely crippled the CIA's counterintelligence capability for many years. Angleton, who at the time represented the CIA in dealing with the Warren Commission, insisted that Nosenko's statements about Oswald were incredible, and that Nosenko must be a KGB plant dispatched to conceal the KGB's true role in the assassination of President Kennedy. Therefore the CIA's counterintelligence experts persuaded the director of central intelligence, Richard Helms, to have Nosenko placed under in-house arrest. This led to the incarceration of Nosenko for almost three years in a cell specially built for him by the CIA, during which time he was allowed to see no one but his jailers and guardians.

The net result of this controversy has been that serious investigators into the Kennedy assassination have basically ignored Nosenko's information in reaching their conclusions.

Before examining Nosenko's reports, I should state that I know for a fact that he was a genuine defector who caused serious damage to the Soviet government. (The U.S. government has also long since recognized him as a bona fide and valuable defector.) Nosenko was not only a KGB captain but the son of a former high-ranking Soviet official (minister of the shipbuilding industry and alternate member of the Central Committee), at whose funeral Khrushchev himself had led the honor guard and who lay buried in the Kremlin wall along with other Soviet heroes. According to General Sakharovsky, the operational damage to the KGB by Nosenko's defection was without precedent; working for the VGU, the domestic security service, he compromised hundreds of cases of Westerners who had been contacted by the VGU while visiting Moscow, some of whom were later transferred to the PGU.

I deeply respect Nosenko's loyalty to the United States, which he has never criticized in spite of the terrible treatment he received after defecting. True, Nosenko tried to embellish his position before his debriefers by claiming higher military rank than he actually had, or inventing a nonexistent KGB cable in order to pressure the CIA into speeding up his defection. And he sometimes took a broad-brush approach to the facts, being less than specific in describing how and when he might have learned them. Such behavior was, however, quite common among the privileged "golden youth" he had lived among in the Soviet Union.

In my view, nonetheless, Nosenko's information about Lee Harvey Oswald is generally credible. But the conclusions to be drawn from it are just the opposite of what Nosenko intended and of what he certainly believed. The problem with his information lies not in its content but in the inability of various Western analysts to place it in proper context.

In the 1960s, as is still the case now, Americans generally considered the KGB to be a single entity. Any member of that organization, they thought, should know everything about its operations. In fact, the operational side of the KGB (like that of its Romanian counterpart, the *Securitate*) was divided into two separate and quite different organizations, the domestic political police and the foreign intelligence service, both of which went to great lengths to preserve the secrecy of their own operations from the other. Nosenko never worked for the PGU. Except for a brief early period in the military GRU, where he was assigned in the Soviet Far East and was mainly involved with Japanese prisoners of war, Nosenko spent his intelligence career at the headquarters of the KGB's domestic VGU. This was the equivalent of the Romanian *Securitate*'s Third Directorate (counterespionage), the main task of which was to monitor, in Romania, the embassies and other official representatives of non-Communist countries, as well as businessmen and tourists from those countries. In 1959, when Oswald arrived in Moscow, Nosenko held the position of deputy chief of the First Section of the VGU's Seventh (tourist) Department; that section was responsible for monitoring tourists from the United States and British Commonwealth countries.

In 1964, when Nosenko defected to the United States, he held a position in the domestic KGB similar to the one I had held in the Romanian equivalent organization, the *Securitate*, in 1955, before I was transferred to the DIE. At that time I was sure I knew the intelligence business inside out, but when I set foot in the DIE I realized that I had entered an entirely different world, operating under entirely different rules. Foreign intelligence was a universe of unimaginable secrecy, which did everything it could to conceal even its own existence—to say nothing of the identity of its agents recruited in the West.

Of course I was prepared to see new things at the DIE, but I did not expect that everything there would come as a revelation. Even my own identity was disguised.

As soon as I crossed the DIE threshold my name was changed into Mihai Podeanu, and Podeanu I remained for all the twenty-three years I worked there. I received a complete new set of identity documents to authenticate my new name. No one in the *Securitate* was ever to know that I now belonged to the foreign intelligence service. Everyone outside the DIE, including my wife and my small daughter, I was told, should understand that I had been transferred to the Council of Ministers—one of the DIE's covers at that time.

This secrecy, which held true throughout the Soviet bloc, was even more dominant when it came to agents recruited in the West. "Once the *Securitate* knows about your agent, you can kiss him goodbye," was the theme song of the DIE's *razvedka* advisers from the PGU. They used to preach that, in the PGU's experience, the officers of the domestic directorates were notorious for openly discussing their operations among one another and for their habit of sharing whatever they knew about a foreign target with the regional KGB officers temporarily involved in monitoring him, and even with the militia officers responsible for covering a specific district, block, or hotel.

Therefore, following PGU policy, whenever a DIE component had to bring one of its foreign agents to Romania, it also had to submit for approval the measures it planned to take to prevent *Securitate* officers from learning about his DIE connections. It was as if the CIA wished to bring one of its foreign agents into the United

States without arousing the FBI's suspicion—except that in a police state the trick requires elaborate planning because of the pervasiveness of domestic security controls.

With practice the bloc espionage services grew skillful at deceiving their domestic rivals in order to protect the secrecy of their cases. Malek, a case mentioned earlier, is a good example of how far the DIE went to avoid arousing *Securitate* curiosity. In 1977, Malek was secretly brought to Romania, where the DIE wanted to foist an agent off on him as his girlfriend, then use her to lure him gradually into recruitment. The greatest threat to the case was the *Securitate*'s Third Directorate (counterintelligence)—the equivalent of Nosenko's VGU. In order to prevent its officers from interfering with Malek, the DIE obtained Nicolae Ceausescu's approval to have the minister of chemical industry sign a fictitious contract showing that Malek was engaged in secret consulting work for that ministry. Also with Ceausescu's approval, the minister of chemical industry "leaked" to the chiefs of the Third Directorate (which was responsible for monitoring Western tourists and businessmen) that in fact Malek was working for Ceausescu's wife, Elena, who was the director of the Central Institute for Chemical Research, and that she wanted the *Securitate* to keep its hands off her "technical adviser." Until 1978, when I defected, all the *Securitate* knew about that case was what the DIE wanted it to know: that Malek was an unstable, wealthy skirt chaser who had given everyone in Romania nothing but headaches. Behind that innocuous façade, Malek was actually one of the DIE's most important agents, his activity directed by Nicolae Ceausescu himself.

An excellent example of this pattern of compartmentation within the KGB can be found in the case of Geoffrey Arthur Prime. Prime was also a *serzhant* assigned abroad—a corporal in the British Royal Air Force who served as a voice radio operator at Gatow in West Berlin. Like Oswald, Prime was a loner who had studied Russian and persuaded himself that communism would solve the world's problems. One day in 1968, when crossing through a Soviet checkpoint in Berlin, Prime handed a Soviet officer a note with instructions how Soviet intelligence might contact him. The officer passed the note to that element of the KGB he normally dealt with, the Third Directorate, which had responsibility for security in the Soviet armed forces. Instead of turning the lead over to the PGU as it should have, the Third Directorate elected to run the case itself. After Prime was routinely separated from the RAF later that year, the Third Directorate brought him clandestinely to Soviet military headquarters at Karlshorst, outside East Berlin, for training in such tradecraft as photography, secret writing, and radio, then successfully ran him in England for the next fourteen years, most of that time as a penetration of the Government Communications Headquarters (the equivalent of the American NSA), where he had secured a job as a linguistic specialist. So good was the Third Directorate's security in this case that for years the defector Oleg Gordievsky knew nothing about it, even though in 1981 he had been on the British desk at PGU headquarters and after January 1982 had been the PGU station chief in London. Only in November 1982, when Prime was incidentally arrested for sexual offenses and confessed to espionage, did Gordievsky learn that Prime was a KGB agent.

There is no doubt in my mind that Nosenko believed what he told the CIA and the FBI. But he was misinformed about Oswald, just as Gordievsky was misinformed about Prime. In fact Nosenko's information on Oswald conforms perfectly with what the PGU could be expected to have wanted the domestic VGU to believe, in order to protect the PGU's valuable *serzhant*–that Oswald was an unstable young student with no interest for the KGB. Oswald's "Historic Diary" reflects complete agreement with how Nosenko and the VGU viewed him, for Oswald writes that upon his arrival in Moscow on October 16, 1959, an Intourist guide took him to the Hotel Berlin, where he "Reges. as. 'studet,'" and then on October 21 he slashed his wrist and ended up in the "Insanity ward" of the hospital.

Despite Nosenko's unawareness of the pattern used by the PGU to protect its most important agents from being known to the domestic KGB, I have reason to believe that he has consistently spoken in good faith. Nevertheless his earliest statements on Lee Harvey Oswald, given in 1964 to the CIA and the FBI, appear to be the most reliable.

Over the years Nosenko appears to have embellished his story, perhaps influenced by what he learned about Oswald from other sources. For instance, in his 1964 original testimony to the FBI, Nosenko expressly stated that he "did not know whether [Oswald's evaluation as unstable] was based on a psychiatric examination or was merely an observation of the hospital medical staff." A few years later, when Nosenko was debriefed by the House Select Committee on Assassinations, he reported that his superiors had concluded that Oswald should be independently examined by two psychiatrists. According to the committee's report, "Nosenko had an opportunity to read both reports and said that both psychiatrists found Oswald to be 'mentally unstable.'" In 1993, Nosenko told the researcher Gerald Posner that the KGB had ordered Oswald transferred to a psychiatric ward at the Botkin Hospital, where he was kept for three days. "We had two psychiatrists, neither of whom was a KGB doctor, examine him," Nosenko recalled. "One was on the Botkin staff and the other came in from outside. I read their reports. Both concluded he was 'mentally unstable.' It made us feel one hundred percent that he should be avoided at all costs."

Allowing for human failings and for the vagaries of memory, the information reported by Nosenko remains remarkably consistent.

36

A TANGLED WEB
OF DECEPTION

NOSENKO'S testimony is of great value not for any new facts about the years Oswald spent in the Soviet Union but because it provides proof of the PGU's secret connections with Oswald. It is extremly significant that "Nosenko had no knowledge that OSWALD ever directed a communication of any type to the American Embassy in Moscow," according to the FBI debriefing report. In other words, the KGB file on Oswald that Nosenko knew, which he believed was the *only* KGB file on that target, contained no record of the many letters Oswald exchanged with the U.S. embassy in Moscow between 1959 and 1962. At least eleven such letters are a matter of record in the Warren Commission files.

I was intimately familiar with the Soviet-style mail censorship system as I supervised one such unit for six years. I can state with certitude that there was no way the KGB could have missed *all* those letters between Oswald and the U.S. embassy, since that embassy was by far the most important mail censorship target in the Soviet Union. Nor would it have been possible for any KGB officer to have simply thrown away such letters. Nothing was considered more incriminating for anyone under observation—as Nosenko says Oswald was—than for him to correspond with the U.S. embassy, and there were hard and fast rules requiring that every photocopy of such correspondence be registered and kept in the target's file.

There is one obvious explanation for the fact that Nosenko knew nothing of Oswald's correspondence with the U.S. embassy: it was being monitored by the PGU, not by Nosenko's domestic KGB component, the VGU. It is equally meaningful that Nosenko was unaware that Oswald had visited the U.S. embassy in Moscow in October 1959, though Nosenko has consistently claimed he was the only officer responsible for overseeing Oswald's file. These points again indicate that in fact the VGU did not know what was really going on in Oswald's case.

In 1959, when the PGU brought Oswald into the Soviet Union, its first concern would have been not to let the domestic KGB get the slightest whiff of the PGU's future plans for him. According to the testimony provided by Nosenko to the FBI in March 1964, he first learned about Oswald when one of his subordinates presented him with a two-page report from an Intourist interpreter and KGB informant working at the Hotel Berlin, showing that Oswald "desired to remain permanently in the USSR and to become a Soviet citizen." During the same FBI debriefing, Nosenko pointed out that the VGU's Tourist Department was routinely notified "immediately upon issuance of a visa to a person to visit the USSR." That had evidently not happened in Oswald's case, however, because Nosenko and his department learned about Oswald only after he was already in Moscow. This would confirm the argument that the PGU brought him in "quietly," either on a false passport or with an "invisible" loose-leaf visa.

The PGU's intention of keeping Oswald's visit to the Soviet Union a secret was evidently blown by the restive Oswald himself. Faced with the determination of his PGU handlers to send him back to the West as a student, Oswald tried to force their hand by injuring himself, as he had done more than once before in order to achieve his goals. The PGU then apparently moved him out of a safe house and into a hotel, as the first step in making his presence in Moscow public, both to the VGU and to the U.S. embassy, so as to avoid future unpleasantness over his treatment. According to Nosenko's 1964 testimony, Oswald asked his Intourist guide for help, and then hotel employees found him bleeding from self-inflicted wounds and took him to a medical institution believed by

Nosenko to have been the Botkin Hospital in Moscow. A hospital report Nosenko recalled having seen stated that Oswald had attempted suicide because he had not been granted permission to remain in the Soviet Union. The report also included the evaluation that this indicated mental instability. Nosenko told the FBI that the VGU chief had accepted Nosenko's recommendation that Oswald's request be refused, and Nosenko had directed the Intourist interpreter to inform Oswald that he would have to leave the Soviet Union upon the expiration of his visa.

Nevertheless the decision was made to allow Oswald to remain in the Soviet Union. Nosenko did not know who had made this decision or why, but he speculated that Oswald had been allowed to stay in the Soviet Union so as to avoid another suicide attempt that might cause bad publicity for the Soviet Union. In his testimony to the FBI, Nosenko suggested that "either the Soviet Red Cross or the Ministry of Foreign Affairs made the decision to permit Oswald to reside in the USSR and also made the decision to assign him to Minsk." Evidently Nosenko was unaware that the Soviet Red Cross was a PGU cover organization—that was a closely held secret—or that the Ministry of Foreign Affairs had no right to grant permanent residence to a Westerner, much less to an American Marine.

For many years I was one of the two vice chairmen of Romania's National Commission for Visas and Passports, which had to approve *every* request for immigration to Romania or emigration from that country; the chairman of that commission was the minister of interior, and the other vice chairman was the deputy minister of foreign affairs. (In the Soviet Union, the chairman of the corresponding commission was the chairman of the KGB.) The unwritten but strongly enforced rule, based on the Soviet system, was that no person could immigrate or emigrate without approval by either the DIE or a domestic *Securitate* directorate. Since the Soviet VGU did not sign off on Oswald, as Nosenko has testified, there could be just one explanation: the PGU did.

According to Nosenko's testimony to the FBI, after this decision had been made, the VGU's Tourist Department sent its file on Oswald to the Minsk KGB, with written instructions to take no action concerning him "except to 'passively' observe his activities." In a more recent interview with Gerald Posner, Nosenko detailed those instructions: "The Minsk KGB was prohibited from any 'active surveillance' of Oswald. They could not detain or arrest him, blackmail him, or attempt to recruit him *without the permission of the chief of the Second [Chief] Directorate, as well as the chairman of the KGB.*" I have emphasized the latter part of the VGU's instructions because that was word for word the formula used by the PGU—and the DIE—to protect its illegal officers and agents who were temporarily in the country's home territory to work out their biographies or fulfill some other operational demand.

Nosenko did not hear of Oswald's case again until 1963. Then, after serving in the VGU's American Embassy Section, he returned to the Tourist Department, now as deputy department chief, and learned that Oswald had applied in Mexico City for a reentry visa for the Soviet Union. According to his FBI testimony, Nosenko learned about that "from an oral inquiry of Nosenko's department by M. I. Turalin, Service Number Two (counterintelligence in foreign countries), First Chief Directorate," or PGU. This counterintelligence service was the only PGU component (as was true with its DIE counterpart) legally allowed to maintain contact with the domestic KGB (in Romania, with the *Securitate*). Nosenko testified he had remembered the case because of the unusual circumstances surrounding the earlier decision to allow Oswald to remain in the Soviet Union, but Nosenko was unaware that Oswald had meanwhile married and left the Soviet Union. The VGU's Tourist Department recommended that the reentry visa be refused.

Nosenko told the FBI that he next heard about the case after Oswald had been accused of assassinating Kennedy. The VGU's Tourist Department checked its records and established that Oswald's file was still being held in Minsk. On instructions from Gen. Oleg Gribanov, chief of the VGU, Nosenko telephoned the KGB office in Minsk and had it dictate a summary of the Oswald file. This summary ended with the statement that the KGB at Minsk had endeavored "to influence OSWALD in the right direction." That statement, according to Nosenko, had greatly disturbed Gribanov, "since the KGB headquarters had instructed that no action be taken concerning OSWALD except to passively observe his activities."

Gribanov therefore directed that Oswald's entire file be flown by military aircraft to the VGU in Moscow. Nosenko testified to the House Select Committee on Assassinations that it had been a large file—seven or eight volumes—and that he had examined the first one, page by page. That was the critical one, he said. "If there had been any KGB recruitment of Oswald, evidence of it would have appeared in Volume One." Based on his review of that first volume, Nosenko stated unequivocally that no KGB officer had ever spoken to Oswald, much less recruited him.

Nosenko was misled by all of the PGU's disinformation about Oswald because foreign intelligence was a world essentially unknown to that VGU officer when he defected. One more good indication of that is to be found in Nosenko's 1964 testimony to the FBI, where he states that "the KGB did not know of OSWALD's prior military service," and even "had such information been available to him, it would have been of no particular interest or significance to the KGB." To Gerald Posner, Nosenko later clarified: "If he had been a Marine guard at the U.S. embassy, then we would have been very interested. But that wasn't the case with Oswald."

This statement makes it clear that Nosenko's only intelligence horizon was that of the VGU, whose most important target was the U.S. embassy in Moscow. "I am surprised that such a big deal is made of the fact that [Oswald] was a Marine," Nosenko remarked to Posner. "What was he in the Marine Corps—a major, a captain, a colonel? We had better information already coming from KGB sources than he could ever give us." Obviously Nosenko never heard of the PGU's *serzhant* mania that was raging at the time. Certainly he did not know that in fact those low-level *serzhanty* over time provided the PGU and its sister services with the most valuable military information they ever received.

A curious footnote to the investigation of Oswald's stay in the Soviet Union is also tied to Nosenko. After Edward Jay Epstein's request to interview alleged witnesses to Oswald's life in the Soviet Union was refused, he met informally with the Soviet press attaché in Washington, Igor Agou. Agou suggested that Epstein "might speak to Nosenko, who had defected from the Soviet Union to the United States in 1964." Epstein had already interviewed Nosenko, but he found this "an extraordinary suggestion, coming from a Soviet official." As press attaché, Agou was likely engaged precisely in the PGU's Operation Dragon, aimed at shifting suspicion in the matter of President Kennedy's assassination away from the Soviet Union. If the PGU was confident that Nosenko (and the rest of the VGU, with the possible exception of the chief) had indeed been successfully misinformed about the PGU's real relationship with Oswald, Agou's suggestion does not sound at all extraordinary. What could be more beneficial for the PGU than to have a defector unwittingly spin your propaganda line?

37

DEATH OF A HIT MAN

O N October 5, 1966, the Texas Court of Criminal Appeals overturned Jack Ruby's death sentence for "murder with malice" and ordered a new trial. This might likely have ended by sentencing Ruby to a short term in jail for murder without malice and soon allowed him to walk free. On December 6, however, Ruby was moved to Parkland Hospital after he complained of persistent coughing and nausea. A day later he was diagnosed as suffering from advanced lung cancer, and he conveniently died on January 3, 1967.

Ruby's unexpected death is not known to have aroused any suspicion within the U.S. government. On the other side of the Iron Curtain, though, the management of the DIE and our Hungarian, Bulgarian, and Yugoslavian counterparts were convinced that Ruby must have been killed by the PGU. We had good reason to think so.

In 1957, General Sakharovsky, the new head of the PGU, brought to Bucharest a PGU operational plan for "neutralizing" Oliviu Beldeanu, a Romanian émigré who was being held in a Swiss jail. Beldeanu had been the leader of a 1955 attack on the Romanian Legation in Bern, Switzerland, that had ended with the capture of voluminous DIE classified documents. Beldeanu surrendered to local authorities together with the captured DIE documents, and received a four-year sentence. The DIE was Sakharovsky's creation, and his prestige had been seriously besmirched by the incident. Now he wanted Beldeanu's scalp.

Sakharovsky told us that his experts had just produced "the ultimate weapon" for "wet affairs," a substance that would cause the "target" to die of radiation poisoning without leaving any trace in his body. The plan was to mix that odorless substance with food and insert it in a package sent to Beldeanu in prison by one of his friends. A couple of months later Sakharovsky canceled this plan without explanation. Of course, that did not stop him from going after Beldeanu (in 1958, after his release from prison, Beldeanu was secretly kidnapped to Romania in a joint DIE-Stasi operation directed by Sakharovsky), but the operational conditions had changed. We learned that Sakharovsky had unsuccessfully tried that same "ultimate weapon" on a Soviet "traitor," Nikolay Khokhlov, and that the failure of that operation had set off a public outcry.

As noted earlier, in 1955 Khokhlov had been sent to West Germany to kill Georgy Okolovich, an anti-Communist Russian émigré sentenced to death by Khrushchev. Instead Khokhlov defected and displayed an electrically operated gun, concealed inside a cigarette pack, which would fire cyanide-tipped bullets. Later Khrushchev had wanted the "traitor" killed, and Sakharovsky had obliged.

What happened was this. In 1957, Khokhlov fell ill after drinking a cup of coffee at a public reception in West Germany. In his blood were found traces of thallium, a metallic substance sometimes used as rat poison—but the treatment for rat poison had no effect. A few weeks later, when Khokhlov was close to death, a doctor at the U.S. Army hospital in Frankfurt/Main solved the enigma: the thallium found in his coffee had been previously subjected to radiation, which had caused the metal to disintegrate slowly in Khokhlov's body and to generate a fatal form of radiation poisoning. The doctor estimated that by the time Khokhlov would have died, the thallium would have entirely disintegrated, and the autopsy would have shown no sign of poisoning. Fortunately Khokhlov lost his hair but not his life.

Eight years later Gheorghe Gheorghiu-Dej, Romania's leader, died of an unexpected form of virulent cancer, and the whispered rumor making the rounds at the top levels of our intelligence community was that he had been secretly killed by the PGU with a new generation of its thallium weapon. On Sunday, February 25, 1965, I paid my last visit to Dej's winter residence in Predeal. He had just come back from a Warsaw Pact meeting in Poland, and as usual I found him with his best friend, Chivu Stoica—the pro forma president of Romania. Dej complained of feeling weak, dizzy, nauseous. "I think the PGU got me," he said, only half in jest. "They got Togliatti. That's for sure," Stoica squeaked ominously.

Palmiro Togliatti, head of the Italian Communist party, had died suddenly of an alleged brain hemorrhage on August 21, 1964, while on a visit to the Soviet Union. The buzz going around in the highest circles of the bloc foreign intelligence community was that Togliatti had been irradiated on Khrushchev's order while vacationing in Yalta. There he had written a "political testament" in which he had questioned Khrushchev's political honesty and had suggested the need for fundamental change in the Soviet Union's foreign policy. The facts that Brezhnev had attended Togliatti's funeral in Rome, and that in September 1964 *Pravda* had published portions of Togliatti's "testament" that were critical of Khrushchev, were viewed as confirmation of these rumors.

Now, at Dej's residence in 1965, I saw him shiver. He was also at war with Moscow. On October 14, 1964, Khrushchev had unexpectedly been dethroned in a Politburo coup. Dej had concluded that the Kremlin was in a rout and had decided to take advantage of the confusion. On October 21 he told the Soviet ambassador that he wanted the PGU advisers recalled from Romania. At Dej's request, the KGB counselors had already been withdrawn from the domestic *Securitate*—he was afraid the KGB might frame him as a Western spy, as it had done with former rulers of Czechoslovakia, Hungary, and Bulgaria. Moscow had swallowed that pill because it had other ways of influencing Romania's domestic policy. But the PGU advisers in the DIE had been enabling the Kremlin to control Romania's tentative new independence in foreign policy, and Moscow now reacted violently. KGB chairman Gen. Vladimir Semichastny sent a scathing letter to his Romanian vassal, Minister of Interior Alexandru Draghici, urging that the PGU advisers be kept in place. A similar letter signed by Sakharovsky landed on Doicaru's desk. In November Sakharovsky arrived in Bucharest on two hours' notice. "Semichastny is boiling mad," he said. "He's ready to tear *him* limb from limb with his own two hands." *Him* meant Dej. "Iron Shurik" was also furious, Sakharovsky added, referring to Aleksandr Shelepin, the former KGB chairman, who had by then become a full Politburo member with responsibility for the Red Army and the KGB. Then Semichastny himself put in an appearance in Romania.

In the end Dej got his way. In December 1964 the DIE became the first foreign intelligence service in the Warsaw Pact community to function without PGU advisers—and, to the best of my knowledge, it remained the only one until the 1989 revolutionary wave changed the face of Eastern Europe.

During the March 12, 1965, elections for Romania's Grand National Assembly, Gheorghiu-Dej still looked vigorous and full of life. On March 19 he was dead.

"Assassinated by Moscow," Romania's new leader, Nicolae Ceausescu, whispered to me a few months later. "Irradiated," he murmured in an even lower voice, claiming that this was "firmly established by the autopsy." The subject had come up because Ceausescu had ordered me immediately to obtain the best Western radiation detection devices and have them secretly installed throughout his offices and residences. (These devices were still in use in 1978 when I broke with communism.) When I discussed this subject with Ceausescu's personal physician, Dr. Abraham Schechter, he expressed full agreement that Dej had been irradiated. "I have the proof," the physician said.

In an earlier book I mentioned that in the 1970s Ceausescu had received a lethal irradiated substance from Moscow, to use against political dissidents. Ceausescu baptized it with the code name "Radu," from the Romanian *radiere* (radiation), and gave the new weapon to Dr. Schechter to study and recommend measures for protecting Ceausescu. In February 1973 the *Securitate* secretly purloined from Dr. Schechter's apartment a letter and its attached documents attesting to Dej's irradiation and providing a technical description of the PGU's Radu, described as being a new generation of the radioactive thallium unsuccessfully used against Khokhlov. The minister of interior, Ion Stanescu, informed Ceausescu that electronic coverage of Schechter had showed he was secretly intending to send the letter and the documents to Radio Free Europe. On March 15, 1973, Dr. Schechter just happened to "fall" out of a window. Ceausescu was sure that the PGU had killed his physician after learning about his intentions from its agents in the *Securitate*. Ceausescu fired the minister of interior on the spot, summoned the ministry's executive bureau (to which I belonged), and ordered it to find out what happened with Dr. Schechter. Our investigation concluded that he had indeed been murdered.

On the unforgettable day of July 22, 1978, Ceausescu ordered me to "give Radu" to Noel Bernard, the director of Radio Free Europe's Romanian program, who was exposing my boss's political crimes. I may have done many reprehensible things in my years as a Soviet-bloc intelligence officer, but I had never been involved in operations that led to a loss of life. The next day I flew to Bonn to deliver a message from Ceausescu to Chancellor Helmut Schmidt. Once in West Germany, I asked the U.S. government to grant me political asylum.

On December 23, 1981, Noel Bernard died of a galloping form of cancer. Nestor Ratesh, a former director of RFE's Romanian program, who spent two years researching *Securitate* archives, has recently established that Bernard was definitely killed by the Romanian intelligence service. The details of his research will be the subject of a book soon to be published by RFE.

Twenty-five years after Bernard's death, Alexander Litvinenko, a former KGB officer living in Great Britain, where he had received political asylum, was killed with an irradiation weapon. Litvinenko was also guilty of *lèse majesté*–intentional disrespect for "Sovereign Authority," which has been branded as a political crime in Russia ever since tsarist times. In a 2001 book published in London, Litvinenko provided evidence that the FSB–the successor to the KGB, whose former officers were then, as now, ruling in the Kremlin–had coordinated a 1999 Moscow apartment bombing that killed more than 300 people, whereas Russian officials blamed the explosions on Chechen separatists. In a 2003 television interview, Litvinenko had also revealed the identities of two so-called Chechen terrorists involved in a 2002 Moscow theater siege, who were in fact working for the FSB. More than 150 people died during the botched FSB rescue operation.

On November 1, 2006, Litvinenko fell ill and was hospitalized. Three weeks later he died in terrible pain. The autopsy established that he had been poisoned with polonium-210, an extremely expensive ($2 million to $3 million for the dose that killed Litvinenko) and strictly controlled substance used to trigger nuclear weapons. The British government documented that the polonium-210 had been furtively brought into England by a former KGB officer (Andrey Lugovoy) living in Moscow, and it ruled that Litvinenko had been assassinated. Russia refused to cooperate with the British criminal investigation, which also established that some 130 people who happened to be in Litvinenko's vicinity during the day he was irradiated tested positive for polonium-210, and that 16 of them might develop cancer.

By the mid-1960s Moscow certainly had the capability to inflict upon its enemies a rapid-growing and fatal form of cancer. Even though Jack Ruby had been misled about why Oswald should be killed, the PGU could not risk having him set free on the streets to babble about what he knew.

38

OPERATION DRAGON
LIVES ON

L ESS THAN a year after Kennedy was assassinated, Nikita
Khrushchev was accused of "harebrained schemes, immature
conclusions, hasty decisions, bragging, and phrase-mongering," and
was toppled. But his Operation Dragon lives on.

In 1992 the British Secret Intelligence Service exfiltrated retired
PGU officer Vasili Mitrokhin from Russia, also bringing out six
cases of notes he had made in the course of twelve years, describing top-secret KGB files. The FBI characterized these notes (totaling some 25,000 pages) as "the most complete and extensive intelligence ever received from any source."

According to Mitrokhin's documents, the PGU forged American
papers and manipulated Western books in order to divert public attention for the killing of President Kennedy away from Moscow and
toward the United States itself. The very first American book on the
assassination to appear was published in 1964 by Carlo Aldo
Marzani, a longtime PGU agent code-named Nord, as identified in
the Mitrokhin material. An Italian-born American who in 1947 was
sentenced to prison for falsely denying under oath his membership in
the Communist party, Marzani owned the Liberty Book Club (code-
named Sever by the PGU) and its commercial bookselling network,
the Prometheus Book Club, both in New York. In the early 1960s the
PGU paid Nord a total of $80,000 for producing pro-Soviet books,
plus an annual $10,000 for aggressively advertising them.

Nord's book on the Kennedy assassination, published in a record five weeks, was *Oswald: Assassin or Fall-Guy?* by the German writer Joachim Joesten. A member of the German Communist party who had spent 1932–1933 in the Soviet Union, Joesten supported Moscow's line by blaming the assassination on a conspiracy of right-wing extremists, including "oil magnate H. L. Hunt." The book describes Oswald as "an FBI *agent provocateur* with a CIA background," who was murdered to prevent him from giving evidence.

The American lawyer Mark Lane soon came to the KGB's attention as the most talented of the conspiracy theorists researching the assassination. Joesten dedicated his book to Lane, but, according to the Mitrokhin archive, the KGB did not wish to risk contacting him directly. The PGU *rezidentura* in New York sent Lane $1,500 through someone identified in the archive only as a "trusted contact," and in the same way provided $500 for a trip to Europe, but PGU headquarters did not agree to Lane's request to visit Moscow to discuss the material he had found. There is no indication that Lane knew the ultimate source of these funds. Soviet journalists encouraged Lane in his research, and in 1966 he published the bestseller *Rush to Judgment*, alleging complicity in the Kennedy assassination at the highest levels of the U.S. government.

As noted earlier, in the mid-1970s a letter addressed to "Mr. Hunt" turned up that was dated November 8, 1963, and signed by "Oswald." It aroused suspicion in the United States because of its belated appearance, unnatural wording, and strange content (asking for "information concerning my position"). The Mitrokhin archive now documents that it was forged by the PGU during the Watergate scandal. Immediately after the assassination, the PGU had concentrated on blaming right-wing Texas oil barons such as H. L. Hunt in its propaganda, but when former CIA officer E. Howard Hunt began making news as a Watergate conspirator, the PGU took advantage of the name similarity to make the CIA the main culprit in Kennedy's death. E. Howard Hunt was given the code name Arlington. Before disseminating the Hunt letter in the United States, the PGU had the forgery twice checked for "authenticity" by the KGB's Technical Operations Directorate (OTU). In 1975 three photocopies were mailed out to conspiracy buffs in the United States, with anonymous covering letters saying the director of the FBI had been given the original. (I know that only photocopies of counterfeited documents were allowed to be used in disinformation operations, to avoid close examination of the originals.) After a couple of years of quiet disappointment for the KGB, the Hunt forgery finally caused a stir with publication in Texas. The *New York Times* reported that three handwriting experts had authenticated it as having been written by Oswald. His widow also identified his handwriting.

The Hunt letter forgery inspired numerous imaginative writers to produce books attributing Kennedy's assassination to the CIA and other elements of the U.S. government. Thirty-some years later the majority of Americans still view the CIA as the main culprit in that crime.

In April 1977, shortly after the publication of the Hunt letter, Chairman Yury Andropov informed the party's Central Committee that the KGB was launching a new campaign of *activnyye mery* (active measures, or "dirty tricks") to further implicate the "American special services" in the Kennedy assassination. After that, the Mitrokhin archive is unfortunately silent on the subject.

In 1992, soon after the collapse of the Berlin Wall, I visited the once-familiar headquarters of the *Stasi*, the former East German political police. To my amazement, its archives, comprising a total shelf-length of 200 kilometers (roughly 125 miles), each kilometer containing some 15 million pages—for a grand total of some 3 billion document pages—were still stacked in the same rotating file holders that the *Stasi* had obtained from the Romanian *Securitate* when I had been at its helm. At its peak the *Stasi* was bloated with 85,000 operations officers. The KGB, on the other hand, had 500,000, so its archives should contain at least five times more documents than the *Stasi*'s. The 25,000 pages of the Mitrokhin archive, fascinating as they are, thus open just a miniscule window on the enormous sea of KGB documents still hidden in Russia.

In 1993, as the United States commemorated the thirtieth anniversary of Kennedy's death, Moscow sought to wash its hands of the case definitively. *Passport to Assassination: The Never-Before-Told Story of Lee Harvey Oswald by the KGB Colonel Who Knew*

Him, a Russian book written for an American, not a Russian, audience, claimed that a thorough investigation into Oswald had found no Soviet intelligence involvement with him whatsoever. Its "author," Oleg M. Nechiporenko, was a "retired" PGU officer who, if necessary, could be said to be speaking purely for himself, not officially. That was another PGU pattern from the old days, used so that the Soviet government could not be held responsible if the statements were proven untrue.

Nechiporenko was serving under consular cover at the Soviet embassy in Mexico City when Oswald visited there in the fall of 1963. Oswald himself claimed to have been met by Valery Kostikov, alias "comrade Kostin," who was a Thirteenth Department officer; but in this book Nechiporenko states that it was he who met Oswald and knew all about what little Soviet involvement there was with him. Even more conclusively, Nechiporenko claims that he also studied all the KGB files on Oswald. "I turned for help to the new leadership of the Russian Foreign Intelligence Service (FIS), the Russian Ministry of Security (MBRF), and the Belarus KGB. All three organizations were extremely supportive and directed me to the relevant archival materials," but in them he could find nothing incriminating.

According to Nechiporenko, the "definitive" answer to the never-clarified allegations about Moscow's involvement in Kennedy's assassination came from Gen. Vladimir Semichastny, KGB chairman during the years Oswald lived in the Soviet Union. Semichastny, of course, is the man who would be held accountable for the killing if the KGB should ever be found to have had a hand in it. (He too is now retired, and therefore his statements cannot damage the Russian government either, in case they should be proven false.) In an alleged interview with Nechiporenko, General Semichastny is said to have stated categorically that General Sakharovsky, "head" of the "First Chief Directorate of the KGB, responsible for foreign intelligence, similar to the CIA," had told him: "Oswald was of no interest to [foreign] intelligence. A week later the same opinion was expressed by the Second Chief Directorate, responsible for counterintelligence within the Soviet Union. When I asked him how to proceed, he answered, 'Who the hell needs Oswald?'" To make the record even clearer, Semichastny is said to have added: "We had no relations with Marina; Oswald found her himself. Why he married her was incomprehensible to us; Marina was also of no use to us."

Once he had "firmly" established that the KGB had no role whatsoever in Kennedy's killing, Nechiporenko considered it his duty to help America look in the right direction. "In the author's view," he writes, there were three "more plausible versions. The first is that his assassination was organized by the CIA. Next, Kennedy's death was the result of a conspiracy of right-wing extremists, in which the billionaire E. Howard Hunt played a special role. [Note that here Nechiporenko has completely merged Texas billionaire H. L. Hunt with CIA and Watergate veteran E. Howard Hunt.] Oswald, due to his Communist sympathies, was perfect for the killer's role. Finally, the military-industrial complex was responsible, since it preferred to have Johnson as a president. Oswald was a pawn, used, then eliminated." In the conclusion of "his" book, Nechiporenko writes: "As far as solving the 'enigma' is concerned, I have a feeling that our former American intelligence adversaries still have a good deal to offer on this matter."

Except for a fictionalized biography of Nechiporenko, this book looks to me like nothing more than another manifestation of the plan for Operation Dragon that I wrote out by hand in Bucharest back in 1963. Khrushchev's hard and fast rule that Moscow should never acknowledge its involvement in assassinations abroad seems to hold as true in post-Soviet Russia as it ever did when he was reigning in the Kremlin.

CONNECTING THE DOTS

THIS SUMMARY of Khrushchev's behind-the-scenes war against President Kennedy, and Soviet intelligence's manipulation of Lee Harvey Oswald in the course of that war, is based upon verifiable and reasonably postulated information from Western sources. The bracketed material contains comments drawing on the author's knowledge of relevant activity patterns of the Soviet PGU and its surrogate counterpart, the Romanian DIE, as well as a few factual reports from other sources.

October 18, 1939   Lee Harvey Oswald is born in New Orleans. He spends a lonely childhood being dragged around the country by his dysfunctional mother, reading about Marxism in public libraries. He completes ninth grade, tries to join the Marines, is told to wait a year, works at odd jobs.

October 24, 1956   At age seventeen, Oswald enlists in the Marine Corps in Dallas, is assigned to various bases in California, Florida, and Mississippi, is trained as a radar operator. He studies Russian by himself.

December 21, 1956   Oswald qualifies as a sharpshooter, the middle level of three qualifications on the Marine scale of marksman–sharpshooter–expert.

September 12, 1957   Oswald arrives in Japan, is assigned as radar operator at MACS-1 at Atsugi Air Base (which also has a U-2 plane unit), near Tokyo. [In 1956, recruiting military personnel at

U.S. bases in West Germany and Japan—the display windows for the most modern American weapons—became a PGU priority. Wiesbaden (West Germany) and Atsugi (Japan)—both of which handled U-2 flights—topped the list. As higher ranks proved difficult to recruit, the main target was a *serzhant*, including enlisted men and local civilians. In 1957 I became the Romanian DIE station chief in West Germany, and my mission directive—written by PGU advisers—concentrated almost exclusively on recruiting American servicemen.]

October 1957   Oswald begins going to local bars near Atsugi Air Base, where—because of his Marxist and pro-Soviet views—he is probably quickly spotted and recruited by the local PGU, as suggested by later remarks to his brother Robert and other Americans. Oswald dates a Japanese hostess from the expensive Queen Bee nightclub in Tokyo. Soon he begins going to Tokyo on unexplained two-day leaves. [The Queen Bee hostess looks like the equivalent of my DIE's "Mimi."]

October 18, 1957   Oswald is told that his unit is to be shipped out to the South China Sea and the Philippines. He likes his life in Japan, where the local PGU station has been nice to him, and he tries to remain at Atsugi by marginally injuring himself. [The PGU's Tokyo Station would have wanted to keep him on its own agent roster in Japan rather than turning him over to another PGU station.]

September 1958   Oswald stages an incident on Formosa to get himself sent back to Japan. In these two incidents, Oswald is trying to force the hand of the Marines. (He will use a similar ploy in Moscow in 1959, to try to prevent the PGU from sending him back to the United States.)

September 1958   Oswald has a short tour at Iwakuni Air Base, located several hundred miles from Tokyo. He studies Russian with an attractive Eurasian woman. [As with the high-class hostess in Tokyo, this woman was most likely a PGU agent. In this isolated area she may have been Oswald's only contact with the PGU.]

November 2, 1958   Oswald leaves Japan, takes leave in the United States.

December 22, 1958   Oswald is assigned as a radar controller at MACS-9 at El Toro Air Base in Santa Ana, California. He studies Russian by himself and likes being called "Oswaldovich." In 1959 he visits Tijuana, Mexico, with a fellow Marine, then goes off alone to meet "friends" there. [During this period, the PGU–and the DIE–used Mexico for personal meetings with their agents living in the United States. Both George and Jeanne de Mohrenschildt were PGU illegals who were probably involved with Oswald from this time on. They traveled extensively in Mexico in 1959 and could have met Oswald there. From DIE records it seems clear that George de Mohrenschildt was connected with the PGU; later he would become Oswald's "best friend" in the United States.]

1959   On an unspecified date in 1959, Oswald pays a fellow Marine to deposit a duffel bag with classified documents and airplane photos in a bus station locker in Los Angeles. [At this time the PGU had its agents in the United States use train and bus station lockers as dead drops for the passage of bulky materials. Such drops were normally serviced by PGU illegals. In the summer of 1959, DIE headquarters urgently asked my station in West Germany to verify "unconfirmed" information just obtained by the PGU giving the U-2 flight altitude as "about 30,000 meters" (roughly 90,000 feet). It is likely that this "unconfirmed" information was from Oswald, who as a radar operator at Santa Ana had learned this flight altitude for the U-2. Downed U-2 pilot Francis Gary Powers later confirmed that this Marine base had access "not only to radar and radio codes but also [to] the new MPS-16 height-finding radar gear."]

February 25, 1959   Oswald takes a Russian test, is rated "poor"–but not bad for someone who has had no formal training in this difficult language.

March 19, 1959   Oswald applies to Albert Schweitzer College in Churwalden, Switzerland, "to broaden my knowledge of German." [Moscow recommended a college in Switzerland, to be out of the reach of American and West German counterintelligence. Oswald could not have afforded a Swiss college on his own, as his total savings after three years in the Marine Corps was $950. Evidently the PGU was paying for it.]

March 23, 1959   Oswald passes high school equivalency tests, enabling the Swiss college to accept him.

August 17, 1959   Oswald requests early dependency discharge, which is approved.

September 4, 1959   At Santa Ana, Oswald applies for a passport, which is issued on September 10. He states his intention to attend schools in Switzerland and in Finland, as well as visit various countries.

September 11, 1959   Oswald is honorably discharged. [His discharge was changed on September 13, 1960, to "undesirable," after the navy learned of his defection and statements to the press in Moscow. After his return to the United States, he tried unsuccessfully to have the "undesirable" changed, and finally solved the problem by simply lying that he had received an honorable discharge. [The PGU stressed to its agents that their overt records should be very clean, so as not to arouse the suspicion of the FBI or other counterintelligence organizations.]

September 1959   A U-2 plane malfunctions and crashes at Atsugi—the same plane Francis Gary Powers will fly on May 1, 1960. [In the summer of 1959, GRU (Soviet military intelligence) officer Petr Semenovich Popov told the CIA that the Soviets had technical information on U-2 flights. The CIA suspended U-2 flights after October 1959, both because of Popov's report and because on October 31, 1959, Oswald told the U.S. embassy in Moscow that he had given the Soviets his radar information.]

September 20, 1959   Oswald sails from New Orleans to Le Havre on *SS Marion Lykes*, an unlisted freighter that has only three other passengers on board. Oswald has apparently made up his mind to defect to the Soviets, and he writes a kind of farewell to his mother before sailing. [George de Mohrenschildt repeatedly used

Lykes Line ships. These freighters carried only a handful of passengers and had irregular schedules, making them unlikely targets of hostile intelligence.]

October 8, 1959   Oswald arrives at Le Havre, does not accompany the other passengers to London, and is not seen again until October 31 in Moscow. [He was probably met in Le Havre by the PGU and taken "black" to Moscow. A record of travel presumably performed by a PGU "double" shows an "Oswald" arriving in London on October 9 and intending to stay one week before going on to a school in Switzerland—evidently the story planned to cover a one-week clandestine visit to Moscow. (It was common PGU—and DIE—practice to have a "double" stay at a hotel and send home pre-signed postcards to cover an agent's clandestine visit to Moscow or Bucharest.) After Oswald compromised his presence in Moscow on October 31, apparently the PGU retroactively forged travel records showing he flew on to Helsinki on October 9—though there were no flights he could have taken there from London that day—then stayed at the luxury hotels Torni and Klaus Kinki in Helsinki and visited the Soviet embassies in Helsinki and Stockholm, obtaining a six-day Soviet tourist visa on October 14. He allegedly took the train on October 15, arriving in Moscow the next day. (The PGU had an entire department responsible for fabricating such travel records.)]

October, 1959   In Moscow, Oswald slightly slashes one wrist when told he will not be allowed to remain permanently in the Soviet Union. [Oswald probably arrived clandestinely in Moscow for a week of debriefing and instructions. (Such "black" visitors were usually brought in via Aeroflot or Soviet ships, using diplomatic passports issued in false identities.) There he faked suicide in another attempt to force someone's hand, in this case the PGU's, and be allowed to stay in the USSR instead of attending school in Switzerland and/or Finland in preparation for a new intelligence assignment.]

October 31, 1959   Oswald visits the U.S. embassy in Moscow on a Saturday, saying he wants to renounce his citizenship and leaving his passport at the embassy. He says he has already offered radar information to the Soviets. The embassy thinks he is probably a nut and tells him to come back during normal hours. [By allowing Oswald to visit the U.S. embassy on a Saturday, when it was closed to the public, the PGU was trying to ensure that nothing indicating an agent relationship with Oswald became known either to the Americans or to the working level of the VGU (KGB domestic counterintelligence directorate). The consular section of the U.S. embassy was extensively covered by microphones, and the PGU would have arranged to learn what Oswald said on this visit. After this episode, the PGU realized it needed better control of Oswald and could not yet send him back to attend school in the West.]

October 31, 1959   Oswald is observed at the Hotel Metropole by U.S. journalists. [According to PGU practice, Oswald would have been kept in a safe house, then moved to a tourist hotel (controlled by the KGB) after he made public his presence in Moscow.]

November 1959   The de Mohrenschildts are in Mexico City at the time of an official visit by senior Soviet Politburo member Anastas Mikoyan, and either Jeanne or both of them are introduced to him. [If security allowed, PGU illegals were in those days sometimes personally commended by a senior Soviet official for special accomplishments. Mikoyan, who was close to Khrushchev, appears elsewhere in Oswald's story as representing the Soviet government at JFK's funeral, at which time he brought the U.S. government some innocuous "documents" on Oswald.]

November 3, 1959   Oswald writes to the U.S. embassy in Moscow, again asking to renounce his citizenship. The embassy tells him to appear in person.

November 8, 1959   Oswald writes his brother Robert, saying, "I have wanted to do this for well over a year."

November 13, 1959   Oswald is interviewed at the Hotel Metropole in Moscow by Aline Mosby of UPI. [The interview with a "friendly" reporter was certainly organized by the PGU, as was the one my DIE arranged for "Hans," when he refused to leave Romania in 1959.]

November 16, 1959   Oswald is interviewed at the Hotel Metropole by Priscilla Johnson from North American Newspaper Alliance. [Another "friendly" interview arranged by the PGU. Oswald was coached by the PGU to reinforce the legend that he had traveled to the Soviet Union by himself, and such interviews provided good publicity for the Soviets.]

November 26, 1959   Oswald writes to his brother Robert saying he wants to remain in the Soviet Union for the rest of his life.

December 17, 1959   Oswald writes to break off all contact with his brother Robert, saying he is starting a new life and does not wish to have anything to do with the old life.

April 9, 1960   American U-2 flights are resumed from Adana, Turkey. [In June 1960 I learned from Khrushchev and PGU chief Sakharovsky that the PGU had received reliable information on the U-2's flight altitude in late 1959, but the Soviet Air Defense Command had not been able to test its accuracy until this flight in April 1960. This information had come from a "defector." I also learned that after this April 9 flight the Soviets were ready to shoot down the next U-2.]

April 30, 1960   Found in Oswald's effects after his death were flashcards for learning German and a handmade calendar giving the alphabet in old German and dating from October 16, 1959 (his arrival in Moscow as shown by the PGU's fabricated stamps in his passport) through April 1960. [This indicates that until April 30, 1960, the PGU still intended that Oswald learn German, in preparation for being sent out to attend the college in Switzerland, as planned. After May 1, 1960, when the U-2 was downed, he became a hero in the eyes of the PGU. For the time being the PGU canceled its plans to send him to Switzerland. As of early 1961 the PGU was preparing him for a more important assignment in the United States.]

May 1, 1960   U-2 pilot Francis Gary Powers is shot down over USSR. Oswald's "Historic Diary" places him in Minsk at the time, but later in the United States he tells a co-worker that he viewed the May Day parade in Moscow.

July 18, 1960   When arrested in 1963, Oswald had in his possession a one-year hunting license issued to him in Minsk on this
date, as well as a membership certificate in the Belorussian Society
of Hunters and Fishermen and a gun permit, both issued in the
summer of 1960. In the United States, Oswald is proud of these
documents and of his marksmanship. [According to Soviet law,
such documents could not be removed from the Soviet Union without special approval. These documents were thus no doubt provided to Oswald by the PGU as evidence of his supposed residence
in Minsk. At an unknown date, but perhaps as early as the summer
of 1960, Oswald must have been turned over to the PGU's Thirteenth Department (assassination and sabotage) to begin training
for a possible, but as yet unspecified, new assignment. He would
have been trained at a Moscow safe house, in marksmanship and in
clandestine communications.]

August 17, 1960   On February 15, 1962, Oswald wrote his
brother that he had seen U-2 pilot Powers in Moscow (most likely
at the show trial on August 17, 1960). [The PGU, and my DIE, liked
to reward their sources by allowing them, if possible, secretly to attend public events in which they had played a role.]

November 7, 1960   Kennedy is elected president. Khrushchev
is at first glad Nixon has lost; as a gesture he releases downed RB-
47 pilots five days after Kennedy takes office in January 1961. But
later that month the honeymoon comes to an end when
Khrushchev learns from "reliable PGU sources" that Washington
intends an assault on Cuba. [The de Mohrenschildts spent the first
four months of 1961 in Guatemala, where the CIA was then training the Cuban invasion force.]

February 13, 1961   The U.S. embassy in Moscow receives an
undated letter, postmarked from Minsk, in which Oswald says he
wants to return to the United States. The embassy replies that he
should appear in person. (His "Historic Diary" for January 4, 1961,
says that Oswald is reconsidering his wish to stay in the USSR.) [In
January 1961 the KGB chief directed the Soviet bloc to prepare a
"diversion in Washington." The DIE was instructed to provide the

PGU with trusted officers and agents who spoke American English and could be sent to the United States with sabotage and diversion tasks.]

March 10, 1961   Oswald interprets for a U.S. tourist group in Minsk, including Katherine Mallory, and says he wants to spend the rest of his life in Minsk. [The PGU moved Oswald to Minsk in preparing his biography for a return to the United States. The PGU probably regretted having allowed Oswald to speak with the American group, as his comments contradicted his letter to the U.S. embassy sent one month earlier.]

March 20, 1961   U.S. embassy gets a letter from Oswald, saying he is in Minsk and cannot come in person. The embassy replies that the Soviet government does not interfere with visits from U.S. citizens—confirming that he is still considered a U.S. citizen. [It was important for the PGU's plans to find out if Oswald was still regarded as an American citizen, as that would allow him free movement once back in the United States.]

April 17, 1961   U.S. fiasco at the Bay of Pigs in Cuba. [Khrushchev exultantly declared war on Kennedy. The PGU ordered its satellite services, such as my DIE, to "throw mud" on "the Pig," the new KGB code name for the American president.]

May 5, 1961   Date of Oswald's letter to his brother Robert, saying he married on April 30 and that his wife was born in Leningrad. Oswald does not say he wants to return to the United States.

May 25, 1961   The U.S. embassy in Moscow receives a letter, postmarked from Moscow, in which Oswald says he has married, that his wife was born in Leningrad, and that he wants to take his wife with him to the United States. [When the U.S. embassy in Moscow received Marina's passport, issued July 19, 1961, it showed she was born in the remote town of Molotovsk, where a background check would have been virtually impossible.]

June 2–3, 1961   Khrushchev meets Kennedy in Vienna, and his hatred is reinforced. The Berlin crisis escalates. [Khrushchev was at the peak of his war with Kennedy. He sent a letter to Romanian leader Gheorghiu-Dej (and probably to the other satellite leaders) saying the president was a puppet of the CIA and the American military-industrial complex.]

July 8, 1961   Oswald appears at the U.S. embassy, again on a Saturday. He is told to come back.

July 10, 1961   Oswald visits the U.S. embassy, retrieves his old passport, and files for renewal as well as for a visa for Marina.

August 10, 1961   Oswald appears in a photo taken by American tourist Monica Kramer in Minsk. They do not talk, however. [The PGU probably wished to display Oswald as being in Minsk, but after his uncontrolled behavior on an earlier occasion, his PGU case officer was probably on hand to ensure that he did not converse with any Americans.]

August 13, 1961   Khrushchev increases tension over Berlin. The Berlin Wall is built.

October 1961   The de Mohrenschildts return to Dallas. According to Jeanne, they planned to return to Haiti, where they were then living, in about six weeks, but "certain negotiations" dragged on and it actually took a year. [The PGU may have sent de Mohrenschildt to Dallas to help Oswald get settled there. The Oswalds' Soviet exit permission was reportedly granted in December 1961, but for bureaucratic reasons the U.S. embassy did not issue their final papers for more than six months. Later de Mohrenschildt would claim he first met Oswald through émigré circles in Dallas/Fort Worth because they had both lived in Minsk, but no one could confirm his several versions of how it had happened. They may in fact have first met in Moscow, or more likely even earlier, when Oswald was stationed at Santa Ana.]

February 15, 1962   Recorded birthdate of June Lee Oswald.

May 24, 1962   Oswald and Marina get their final papers at the U.S. embassy.

June 1, 1962   Oswald gets a loan from the U.S. embassy, then he, Marina, and June take the train for Holland. Travel is arranged by the U.S. embassy.

June 13, 1962   The Oswalds arrive in Hoboken, New Jersey, on the *SS Maasdam*.

June 14, 1962   The Oswalds fly to Fort Worth, Texas, with money sent them by his brother Robert. They stay with Robert.

June 1962   Oswald begins to meet Russian émigrés, as an entrée using a manuscript about life in the Soviet Union he has brought out with him.

June 26, 1962   FBI interviews Oswald but notes nothing of significance.

July 1, 1962   Marina sends her address to the Soviet embassy in Washington. [The letter, later made available to the Warren Commission, was routed to Vitaly Gerasimov, a PGU officer under consular cover. It was common practice for PGU and DIE agents sent abroad in true identity to inform their handlers in this way that they had arrived safely at their destination and were not under suspicion.]

July 1962   The Oswalds move to an apartment with his mother. Through an employment office, Oswald gets a job at the Leslie Welding Company.

August 1962   The Oswalds move to a furnished apartment at 2703 Mercedes Street in Fort Worth.

August 16, 1962   FBI again interviews Oswald.

August 1962   Oswald writes to the Soviet embassy in Washington, sending his new address and asking for Russian newspapers and bulletins put out for "your citizens living, *for a time* [my emphasis], in the U.S.A." [On many occasions Oswald indicated that he and Marina were in the United States only temporarily and intended to return to the USSR. Also, it was common practice for agents to have numerous newspapers and other publications sent to them, where the PGU could insert pre-established messages, such as in innocuous advertisements.]

September 1962   De Mohrenschildt visits Oswald at his apartment. (Later he gives conflicting stories about how they first met.) De Mohrenschildt tries to help Oswald get a better job, without success. [It was usual for an illegal such as de Mohrenschildt to provide support to an agent without knowing the agent's tasks. Throughout his intelligence career de Mohrenschildt himself had been assigned to collect military and political information, and he apparently assumed that Oswald would wish to make contacts allowing him access to such information.]

October 9, 1962   Oswald quits his job. De Mohrenschildt moves Oswald alone from Fort Worth to Dallas, while Marina moves in with kindly émigrés. Oswald opens P.O. Box 2915 in Dallas in his own name, later adding the name Hidell as another mail recipient.

October 11, 1962   Oswald gets a job at Jaggars-Chiles-Stovall graphic arts company in Dallas. Later he makes identity documents there for both Hidell and Lee. In his address book, Oswald notes "microdot" next to the name of Jaggars-Chiles-Stovall, and explains to an employee this espionage technique for reducing several documents to a dot that can be hidden under a postage stamp. [Oswald is not known to have actually used microdots, but they were a popular PGU technique at the time; it was a closely held secret that some were indeed hidden under postage stamps. Oswald on several occasions claimed to be a photographer, though he is not known to have had any overt training. In Moscow the PGU would have trained him in various communications techniques, including microdots.]

October 22–28, 1962   In the Cuban Missile Crisis, Khrushchev backs down and removes the missiles—a huge loss of face.

October 1962   Trial of PGU illegal officer Bogdan Stashinsky in West Germany, at which he publicly announces that Khrushchev decorated him for murdering the Soviet Union's political enemies in the West. Another major humiliation for Khrushchev, who abandons thoughts of political assassinations abroad. [The PGU ordered all Soviet-bloc illegal officers sent to the West with assassination tasks to halt their operational activity and destroy their commo gear and special weapons. It is unknown what commo gear Oswald might have had. Found among his effects after his death was a Russian 35-millimeter camera that could have been used as commo gear. The PGU (and DIE) did issue Soviet and East German cameras for making microdots by using a special ring–which was kept concealed and was the only incriminating part.]

December 1962   The Oswalds send a cordial New Year's card to the Soviet embassy in Washington. [This card, like all other mail from the Oswalds, was routed to PGU officer Gerasimov.]

January 14, 1963   An émigré helps Oswald enroll in evening typing class, but his attendance is irregular. [Oswald would later use his typing skills to fabricate identity documents for himself.]

January 27, 1963   Oswald orders a Smith & Wesson revolver in Hidell's name. [PGU agents were not permitted to procure weapons abroad for use in assassination assignments. They were told the PGU would provide them. Oswald's use of the Hidell name, which was easily traceable to himself, strongly indicates that Oswald was acting on his own, not under PGU guidance. It also indicates that Oswald was eager to complete his assignment so that he could return to the Soviet Union.]

February 17, 1963   Marina writes to the Soviet embassy in Washington saying she wants to return to the Soviet Union. [This letter suggests that Oswald wanted to see Marina and June safely back in the Soviet Union before he went ahead with what he believed was still his PGU task.]

February 22, 1963   De Mohrenschildt introduces Oswald to various people, through whom on this date Oswald meets Ruth Paine at a party. [The goodhearted Paine would be used by the Oswalds, but she was certainly unwitting of any PGU connection.]

March 3, 1963   The Oswalds move to 214 West Neely Street in Dallas, allegedly because Marina likes the porch. Oswald has his own small room, which he can lock and use as a private work area. According to Marina, this is where he will prepare a folder when planning his attempt to assassinate Gen. Edwin Walker on April 10, 1963. [In this room Oswald could also have listened for open-code or encoded radio messages from the PGU, a practice widely used at that time.]

March 8, 1963   The Soviet embassy in Washington sends Marina a bureaucratic reply asking for much paperwork. [This is another indication that the PGU wished to discourage Oswald from continuing with his original assignment.]

March 10, 1963   Probable date on which Oswald takes surveillance photos of General Walker's house.

March 12, 1963   Oswald orders Mannlicher-Carcano rifle in Hidell's name. [This is the rifle he would use to assassinate Kennedy. Again, the Hidell name was a very flimsy cover, and in any case the PGU would have forbidden him to order an operational weapon.]

March 17, 1963   Marina again asks the Soviet embassy for a visa to return to the Soviet Union.

March 25, 1963   Rifle arrives at post office box (and revolver at about the same time, since both are shipped on March 20).

March 31, 1963   Marina claims that on this day she takes photos of Oswald in the backyard, holding a rifle, revolver, and political magazines. Two different photos with the rifle exist; another is allegedly destroyed in his mother's presence after Oswald's arrest. [The date is consistent with the dates of the magazine issues shown in the photos. After his arrest, Oswald claimed the photo was a fabrication. The PGU always instructed its agents never to admit to anything if arrested, because "once you say A, you can be forced to say Z."]

April 5, 1963   Marina inscribes one photo of Oswald with guns and gives it to the de Mohrenschildts, who are visiting the Oswalds at the Neely Street apartment. This photo later turns up in de Mohrenschildt's possession after Oswald's death. [After Oswald's death, both the de Mohrenschildts and Marina kept changing their stories about who signed the back of the photo and when it was given to the de Mohrenschildts.]

April 6, 1963   Oswald is fired from Jaggars-Chiles-Stovall—he talked too much about Russia.

April 8, 1963   Oswald visits employment office for work, but nothing is available. Applies for unemployment.

April 10, 1963   Oswald takes one shot at General Walker, but Walker moves slightly and is unharmed. (After Oswald's death, the recovered bullet tends to confirm that Oswald was the attempted assassin.) Before leaving for Walker's house, Oswald writes Marina an operationally important note telling her what to do in case he is arrested, reminds her they have "friends" who will help her, as will the Soviet Red Cross. [Throughout the Soviet bloc, "friends" was used as a euphemism for the PGU or other friendly intelligence services. The Soviet Red Cross is documented as having been used as cover by the PGU for the payment of agents.]

April 13, 1963   De Mohrenschildts visit the Oswalds for the last time. On April 19 the de Mohrenschildts suddenly leave Dallas for Haiti, without saying goodbye to the Oswalds. [It was reliably reported that, sometime after the Kennedy assassination, $250,000 was deposited in de Mohrenschildt's account at a Port-au-Prince bank. De Mohrenschildt withdrew the money in 1967 and soon thereafter left Haiti. He avoided customs controls by using a *laissez-passer* from President Duvalier and with help from the German ambassador. This was evidently a lump-sum payoff by the PGU, which after the assassination would have broken all regular contact with de Mohrenschildt, who was compromised by his known association with Oswald.]

April 14–23, 1963   Oswald probably travels to Mexico City to show the PGU how well he planned the attempt on Walker. [This speculation is based on a postmortem report that Oswald once stayed at the Hotel Cuba on an earlier trip to Mexico City, and on references in Marina's testimony to more than one trip to Mexico. An agent like Oswald would have had emergency meeting arrangements for contacting the PGU in Mexico City, away from the Soviet embassy. Clearly he was unable to persuade the PGU to allow him to complete his original mission and return to the Soviet Union. In fact the PGU seems to have told him to move away from Dallas.]

April 18, 1963   The Soviet embassy in Washington continues to stall Marina, writing to ask for more bureaucratic information about her desire to return to the USSR.

April 24, 1963   Marina moves in with Ruth Paine in Irving, Texas. Oswald takes the bus to New Orleans and moves in with his aunt.

April 26, 1963   Oswald applies for work at the employment office in New Orleans, receives some unemployment money.

May 9, 1963   Oswald applies for work at the William B. Reily Company, oiling coffee machines, and begins work the next day. He rents an apartment at 4905 Magazine Street in New Orleans and phones Ruth Paine's house, asking Marina to come join him.

May 11, 1963   Paine drives Marina to New Orleans, and leaves on May 14 to return to Irving.

May 14, 1963   Post office box in Dallas is closed.

June 11, 1963   Oswald opens P.O. Box 30061 in New Orleans in his own name, also listed to Hidell and Fair Play for Cuba Committee.

June 24, 1963   Oswald applies for a passport and gets it the next day; states he wants to visit England, France, Germany, Holland, Italy, Finland, Poland, and Russia as tourist. He already has forged himself a vaccination certificate from "Dr. Hideel." [Although there is evidence that the PGU instructed Oswald in photography, particularly in making microdots, the PGU would not have trained him to forge his own identity documents. Forging documents was a specialized technique done only at PGU headquarters. If Oswald had needed alias documents, they would have been securely sent to him. By this time, however, Oswald was acting on his own, without PGU support.]

July 1, 1963   Oswald has Marina write the Soviet embassy in Washington to ask for permission for both of them to return to the USSR. Oswald asks for *"rush"* handling because Marina is pregnant and wants to have the baby in the Soviet Union, and asks that his

visa be issued *"separtably."* [This letter confirms that Oswald intended to send Marina and child back to the Soviet Union as soon
as possible, and that he himself planned to escape to Moscow after
accomplishing his task.]

July 8, 1963   Marina again writes to the Soviet embassy, asking to expedite her requests.

July 19, 1963   Oswald is fired from Reily for inattention to
work. He has spent too much time discussing guns at the Crescent
City Garage next door.

August 5, 1963   The Soviet embassy coldly informs Marina
that her request has been sent to Moscow for review.

August 9, 1963   Oswald has a fight with anti-Castro Cubans,
spends a night in jail, and at his request is interviewed by the FBI.
[The FBI was mystified by Oswald's request, but his possible purpose was to create a record that he was not in Dallas and not interested in Soviet affairs.]

August 1963   Oswald appears on TV news passing out pro-
Castro literature (August 16), gives radio interview (August 17), has
radio debate on Cuba (August 21). [All these actions are apparently
designed by Oswald to establish his presence in New Orleans and
his surprising new interest in Cuban affairs.]

September 20, 1963   Ruth Paine arrives in New Orleans,
spends three nights with the Oswalds. Marina returns to Irving with
Paine to await the birth of her second baby, taking household effects with her.

September 25, 1963   Oswald leaves New Orleans, probably
by bus to Houston. Known to have taken the bus that same day
from Houston to Mexico City.

September 26, 1963   Post office box in New Orleans expires.

September 27, 1963   Oswald arrives in Mexico City, gets a
room at Hotel del Comercio as O. H. Lee, probably visits the Cuban
embassy twice. He says he wants to visit Cuba on his way to the

Soviet Union. Cuban embassy employee Silvia Durán phones the Soviet embassy to ask about this, without giving any name, and is told the local Soviets must check with Moscow. [The CIA surveillance camera at the Cuban embassy was out of order, but Oswald's visits there were later credibly confirmed by Silvia Durán. There is no record Oswald visited the Soviet embassy.]

September 28, 1963   Oswald again visits the Cuban embassy, on a Saturday. No record he has visited Soviet embassy, as claimed. Later, in a letter to the Soviet embassy in Washington, Oswald claims he met "Comrade Kostin" on this date in Mexico. [The PGU knew its embassy in Mexico was under CIA surveillance and would never have met Oswald there. Markings on tourist materials for Mexico City found among Oswald's effects after his death indicate he may have met his PGU case officer at public places, such as a movie theater, the bullring, the folklore ballet theater. Normally the PGU would have met him at a "brush pass" to check for hostile surveillance, then met again for a conversation, probably agreed to check with Moscow, and then arranged to meet again the next day.]

September 29–30, 1963   Oswald takes his meals at his hotel, but there is no other record of him. He will bring back postcards depicting bullfights and tourist attractions.

October 1, 1963   Oswald goes to the Cuban embassy. At his request, Durán phones the Soviet embassy and gives him the receiver to talk to a guard there. Oswald gives his name and says he will be right over to talk to Kostikov. [There is no record that Oswald visited the Soviet embassy on this date or any other, but his phone conversation was recorded.]

October 2, 1963   Oswald takes the bus back to Texas, having booked a seat the previous day.

October 3, 1963   Oswald arrives in Dallas, stays at the YMCA.

October 4, 1963   Oswald hitchhikes to Paine's home in Irving, returning to Dallas on October 7.

October 7, 1963   Oswald rents a room at 621 Marsalis Street in Dallas. Says he cannot find a job.

October 12–13, 1963   Oswald spends the weekend at Paine's. His unemployment runs out. [Oswald did not want a job, as he wanted to be free to pursue his operational task. Kennedy's visit to Dallas had already been announced.]

October 14, 1963   Paine drives Oswald to Dallas and helps him rent a room at 1026 North Beckley Avenue, where he uses the name O. H. Lee. Back in Irving, Paine learns from a neighbor about a job at the Texas School Book Depository. When Oswald calls her that evening, she tells him to visit superintendent Roy Truly there the next day about the job.

October 15, 1963   Oswald talks to Truly, gets the job, and begins work the next day. Oswald arranges to ride to Irving on weekends with Wesley Frazier, the brother of Ruth's neighbor who told her about the job opening.

October 20, 1963   Birth of Audrey Marina Rachel Oswald in Dallas.

November 1, 1963   Oswald opens P.O. Box 6225 in Dallas in his own name.

November 1, 1963   FBI interviews Ruth Paine, and again on November 5. She is evasive, trying to protect Oswald from the "nosy" FBI.

November 9–11, 1963   Oswald is at Paine's for the long weekend. On November 9 he works on a letter to the Soviet embassy in Washington, saying he has been unable to complete his business with "Comrade Kostin" in Mexico; complains about treatment at Cuban embassy; says the FBI is not bothering him in Dallas. [Valery Kostikov, whom Oswald called "Comrade Kostin" in his letter to the Soviet embassy, was an identified officer of the PGU's Thirteenth Department ("wet affairs"), who had been assigned to Mexico under consular cover in September 1961. It is possible that Oswald first met Kostikov as "Comrade Kostin" in the Soviet

Union, in preparation for Kostikov's assignment to Mexico City as Oswald's Thirteenth Department contact officer.]

November 19, 1963   The *Dallas Times-Herald* publishes the precise route of President Kennedy's visit to Dallas. The School Book Depository is on that route.

November 21, 1963   Unusually for a Thursday, Oswald rides to Irving with Frazier, gets his Mannlicher-Carcano rifle, concealed in a package as "curtain rods," and returns back to Dallas with him the next morning.

November 22, 1963   *Dallas Morning News* publishes a veiled, black-bordered threat to Kennedy in the form of an ad, allegedly placed by right-wingers in the United States. [This ad is PGU disinformation designed to draw attention away from Oswald should he stubbornly try to proceed with his plans. On the day after the Kennedy assassination, the DIE received the same article from the PGU, which asked that it be republished in Romania. It appeared on November 26 in *Scinteia*, the official party newspaper, as a bulletin "from Washington."]

November 22, 1963   Oswald kills the president with shots from the window of the Texas School Book Depository, escapes, and then kills Dallas patrolman J. D. Tippit when confronted. Oswald is arrested and taken to Dallas police headquarters. He denies owning the Mannlicher-Carcano rifle; denies having seen a photo of himself with the rifle and insists it is a fake; denies knowing who Hidell is; denies having brought any package but his lunch to Dallas that day; and asks to see a lawyer. He tries several times to reach the lawyer John Abt in New York. [Abt was known for having defended Communists, and the PGU (and DIE) occasionally gave its illegals the name of a lawyer who could defend them, should they be arrested in a foreign country. Later Abt credibly claimed he had never before heard of Oswald.]

November 24, 1963   Nightclub owner Jack Ruby shoots Oswald at the Dallas police station. [Circumstantial but credible evidence showed that Ruby was connected with Cuban, not Soviet, intelligence, and that he was coerced into killing Oswald, believing Oswald had been used by the CIA to kill Kennedy.]

January 3, 1967   Ruby dies in jail of a virulent form of cancer, just before his release is to be considered. [In September 1957 the PGU attempted to assassinate the defector Khokhlov in West Germany by using a substance designed to generate a galloping cancer. Khokhlov lost his hair but escaped alive. In 1970 the Romanian *Securitate* received an improved irradiation weapon; Moscow claimed it would kill the target in less than a month.]

March 29, 1977   De Mohrenschildt commits suicide at his former sister-in-law's house in the fashionable town of Manalapan in Palm Beach County, Florida, just before he is to be questioned by the writer Edward Jay Epstein and later by members of the House Select Committee on Assassinations. [De Mohrenschildt has been an enigma for most researchers of the Kennedy assassination and even for his friends. In 1963 I learned for a fact that de Mohrenschildt was a PGU asset, and in the book I make the case that he was a Soviet illegal of the famous Richard Sorge generation.]

NOTES

ABBREVIATIONS USED IN THE NOTES

WC Report. The summary report of what has become known as the Warren Commission, published as *Investigation of the Assassination of President John F. Kennedy: Hearings Before the President's Commission on the Assassination of President Kennedy* (Washington, D.C.: United States Government Printing Office, 1964), volume entitled Report.

WC Vol. Testimonies published by the Warren Commission in the twenty-six numbered volumes documenting the investigation.

WCE. Exhibits of documents also published in the twenty-six volumes of the Warren Commission investigation.

HSCA Report. The summary report of the House Select Committee on Assassinations, published as *Investigation of the Assassination of President John F. Kennedy: Hearings Before the Select Committee on Assassinations of the U.S. House of Representatives: Ninety Fifth Congress: Second Session* (Washington, D.C.: U.S. Government Printing Office, 1979), Volume of Findings and Recommendations.

HSCA Vol. The twelve Kennedy volumes of Hearings and Appendices published by the House Select Committee on Assassinations.

HCE. Exhibits of documents also published in the twelve Kennedy volumes of the House Select Committee on Assassinations investigation.

PREFACE

page

xi   "a great national and international leader": *President Nicolae Ceausescu's State Visit to the USA: April 12–17, 1978,* English version (Bucharest: Meridiane Publishing House, 1978), 78.

1. KENNEDY KILLED BY A "*SERZHANT*"

5   "Moscow cautioned us to be vigilantly circumspect": Arkady Shevchenko, *Breaking with Moscow* (New York: Alfred A. Knopf, 1985), 123.

5   DGI: *Dirección General de Inteligencia*, the Cuban foreign intelligence service.

5   "seal all DGI files": Edward Jay Epstein, *Legend: The Secret World of Lee Harvey Oswald* (New York: Reader's Digest Press, McGraw-Hill, 1978), xi–xii.

7   "in some crises short of war": Christopher Andrew and Oleg Gordievsky, *KGB: The Inside Story of Its Foreign Operations from Lenin to Gorbachev* (New York: HarperCollins, 1990), 522–523.

8   "explosive in a Volkswagen car": Vladimir Kuzichkin, *Inside the KGB: My Life in Soviet Espionage* (New York: Pantheon Books, 1990), 215–218.

9   "died of natural causes in 1983": Norman Polmar and Thomas B. Allen, *The Encyclopedia of Espionage* (New York: Gramercy Books, 1997), 276. In Romania I knew only that Ignatyev had disappeared from sight, and we assumed that he had been killed.

9   "died of a stroke after an argument with Stalin": Polmar and Allen, 180. While in Romania I was given to understand that Dzerzhinsky had died of heart failure shortly after giving a speech before the plenum of the Central Committee. Apparently his argument with Stalin immediately followed that speech.

10   "WELCOME MR. KENNEDY TO DALLAS": WCE 1031, reproduced in WC Report, 194.

10   "Weissman . . . had served in the U.S. Army in Munich": WC Report, 295. The Warren Commission established that Bernard Weissman had served "in the U.S. Army in Munich, Germany in 1962." He testified to the commission that in Munich he and two friends, who would also be involved with the black-bordered statement, had "planned to infiltrate various U.S. rightwing organizations" so as eventually to get "elected or appointed to various higher officers in these organizations, and by so doing this bring in some of our own people, and eventually take over the leadership of these organizations."

2. MOSCOW'S OPERATION DRAGON

17   "dispel the notion that the Soviet Union was somehow behind the assassination": Oleg Kalugin, with Fen Montaigne, *The First Directorate: My 32 Years in Intelligence and Espionage Against the West* (New York: St. Martin's Press, 1994), 58.

17   "to propagate the Soviet point of view": Kalugin, 36.

17   "to improve relations with Russia": Kalugin, 58.

17   "Johnson, along with the CIA and the Mafia, had masterminded the plot": Shevchenko, 124.

17 "attempts against people's lives, terrorism, subversion": HSCA Vol. 2, 250–251.

17 "the KGB . . . had nothing to do with Kennedy's assassination": Kalugin, 58.

3. FIRST HARD EVIDENCE OF THE PGU'S HAND

19 "worldwide publicity to the way in which [Khrushchev's] 'peaceful coexistence' really works": John Barron, *KGB: The Secret Work of Soviet Secret Agents* (New York: Reader's Digest Books, 1974, reprinted by Bantam Books), 429.

19 "no evidence to indicate that either Lee Harvey Oswald or Jack Ruby was part of any conspiracy": WC Report, 21.

20 "many entries seemed to have been written long after the fact": WC Report, 258–259.

20 "Alferd is a Hungarian chap": entry for May 1, 1960, WCE 24.

20 Rosa is "very merry": entry for October 23, 1959, WCE 24.

20 Ella refuses Oswald's "dishonourable advanis": entry for January 1, 1961, WCE 24.

20 "I am in the Insanity ward": entry for October 22, 1959, WCE 24.

20 McVickar . . . did not assume that position until almost two years later: Epstein, *Legend*, 109–110.

21 "Historic Diary" must have been written in one or two sittings: Epstein, *Legend*, 109.

21 Correspondence between Yugoslav leader Tito and Stalin: Andrew and Gordievsky, 463–464. The authors describe several bogus memoirs produced by the Agayants department, noting that the fraudulent Litvinov book was "sophisticated enough to deceive even such a celebrated Soviet scholar as E. H. Carr, who in 1955 contributed a foreword" to it.

22 "a huge sum!!" from the "Red Cross" in Moscow: entry for January 5, 1960, WCE 24.

22 Salary supplement from the Red Cross given to Oswald in Minsk: entry for January 13–16, 1960, WCE 24.

22 Proof that Soviet Red Cross was used to fund espionage activities: William R. Corson and Robert T. Crowley, *The New KGB: Engine of Soviet Power* (New York: William Morrow, 1985), 302–304.

22 Oswald supposedly lived in Minsk for almost two and a half years: WCE 92.

22 Oswald says it took him "almost two years" to realize the Red Cross money had come from the "M.V.D.": WCE 24, 1B.

23 Marina "lied . . . repeatedly on matters which are of vital concern": Epstein, *Legend*, 24.

23 Marina falsely denied knowing about Oswald's trip to Mexico City: Epstein, *Legend*, 24.

23 Chief Justice Warren ruled out lie detector test for Marina: Epstein, *Legend*, 25.

25 House committee believed Soviet government not involved in assassination: HSCA Report, 99.

4. RECRUITING A *SERZHANT*

26 Sergeant Johnson in a position to supply the PGU with valuable documents on ciphers: Andrew and Gordievsky, 460–462.
26 Sergeant Mintkenbaugh provided the PGU with rocket fuel samples: Andrew and Gordievsky, 461–462.
27 Sergeant Dunlap provided the Soviets with materials from the National Security Agency: Andrew and Gordievsky, 459.
27 Sergeant Johnson received written congratulations from Khrushchev himself: Andrew and Gordievsky, 462.
27 Chief Warrant Officer Walker's information given the PGU had "devastating consequences for the United States": John Barron, *Breaking the Ring* (Boston: Houghton Mifflin, 1987), 148, 212.
30 Balthasar arrested by West German police: Jack Anderson, "The Ante Rises Over Radio Free Europe," *Washington Post*, July 25, 1981, B7.

5. A "DEFECTOR"

33 Operation Mill is described in detail in Ion Mihai Pacepa, *Mostenirea Kremlinului* (The Kremlin's Legacy) (Bucharest: Editura Venus, 1993), 228–232.

6. RECRUITMENT IN JAPAN

36 Oswald assigned to MACS-1 at Atsugi Air Base outside of Tokyo: WC Report, 683.
36 Function of MACS-1 was to direct U.S. planes by radar: Epstein, *Legend*, 53–55.
36 U-2 pilots apparently requested wind speeds at ninety thousand feet: Epstein, *Legend*, 66.
37 "disappear to Tokyo on a two-day leave": Epstein, *Legend*, 68–71.
38 Drummond received a life sentence: Barron, *KGB*, 189.
38 Oswald involved with hostess at expensive bar in Tokyo: Epstein, *Legend*, 71.
39 In Moscow, Oswald told American journalists he had been planning defection for two years: WC Report, 256.
39 "I have waited for 2 year [sic] to be accepted": WCE-24, 1.
39 Oswald wanted "to see for himself how a revolutionary society operates": WC Report, 390.
39 "some Communists in Japan . . . got me excited and interested . . . in going to Soviet Russia": WC Report, 256.
40 Old lady in New York handed Oswald a pamphlet on the Rosenbergs: WC Report, 695.

40 Philby gave a triumphant press conference: Andrew and Gordievsky, 435.

40 Oswald and his unit headed for the Philippines: Epstein, *Legend*, 72–73.

41 "I've seen enough of a democratic society here in MACS-1": Epstein, *Legend*, 77–79.

42 "waited to do this for well over a year": WC Report, 694.

7. AN IDEAL AGENT

43 Born two months after the death of his father: Unless otherwise noted, the description of Oswald's early years is based on the findings of the Warren Commission, particularly WC Report, 375–385.

44 "intellectual functioning in the upper range of bright normal intelligence": WC Report, 381.

44 No "neurological impairment or psychotic mental changes": WC Report, 379–380.

44 "I still remember it for some reason, I don't know why": WC Report, 388.

44 "the first victims of American fascism": Andrew and Gordievsky, 480.

45 "vocabulary made him quite articulate": WC Report, 10.

45 Asking for information on youth groups: Epstein, *Legend*, 61–62.

46 Only young men of higher-than-average intelligence: testimony on May 5, 1964 of John E. Donovan, who was at one time in command of a radar crew that included Oswald, WC Vol. 8, 291.

46 To San Diego for basic training: Epstein, *Legend*, 62.

46 An excellent shot compared with the average civilian male his age: WC Report, 191–192.

46 Squirrel and rabbit hunting with his brother Robert: WC Report, 192.

46 "always did like hunting and fishing": Robert L. Oswald, with Myrick and Barbara Land, *Lee: A Portrait of Lee Harvey Oswald by His Brother* (New York: Coward-McCann, 1967), 82.

46 Bought a rifle: Robert Oswald, 74.

46 Relatives in New Orleans: Epstein, *Legend*, 65.

47 Seventh in his class of thirty: Epstein, *Legend*, 64–65.

47 "a very rare breed": Andrew and Gordievsky, 440–441.

48 Sold documents to the PGU through his father: Barron, *Breaking the Ring*, 219.

49 "radar height-finding antennas": Epstein, *Legend*, 69. Wilkins was interviewed by Epstein.

49 Keen interest in classified briefings at Atsugi: Epstein, *Legend*, 68.

8. WORKING FOR THE PGU

50 "Oswald liked Japan and wanted to stay": Epstein, *Legend*, 80–82.

50 Half-Russian who was teaching Oswald the Russian language: Epstein, *Legend*, 82–83.

51 Reported for duty at El Toro Air Base in Santa Ana, California: WC Report, 684.

51 "had his mind made up": Donovan testimony, WC Vol. 8, 301.

52 Had apparently achieved some proficiency in that difficult language: Epstein, *Legend*, 85–86.

53 Gave Delgado two dollars to stuff photos into bus station locker: Epstein, *Legend*, 89.

53 Most highly classified secret about the U-2: Francis Gary Powers, with Curt Gentry, *Operation Overflight: The U-2 Spy Pilot Tells His Story for the First Time* (New York: Holt, Rinehart, 1970), 357.

53 Went off on his own, allegedly to meet "friends": Epstein, *Legend*, 87–88.

53 "took a couple of trips down to Tijuana": Donovan testimony, WC Vol. 8, 301.

54 Interest in visiting the Cuban consulate in Los Angeles: Epstein, *Legend*, 88.

54 "to transfer radio-radar and radio signals over a great distance": Donovan testimony, WC Vol. 8, 298.

54 Albert Schweitzer College in Churwalden, Switzerland: WC Report, 688; WCE 228.

55 His savings totaling only some $950: Epstein, *Legend*, 91, 287n.

55 He had a mere seven hundred dollars: Epstein, *Legend*, 93.

55 "without a given magic college degree": Donovan testimony, WC Vol. 8, 295.

55 "healty climate and a Good moral atmosphere": WC Report, 688; WCE 228.

55 Equivalent of a high school diploma: WC Report 687.

55 Deposit sent to the school: WC Report, 688; WCE 234.

55 "I know what I want to be and how I'm going to be it": Epstein, *Legend*, 90.

9. A SECRET TRIP TO MOSCOW

57 "specifics of the U-2 program": Epstein, *Legend*, 117.

57 "suspended all U-2 flights anyway": Epstein, *Legend*, 118.

58 "radar operation, as he possessed": WC Report, 747; WCE 908.

58 PGU penetration of British foreign intelligence who knew about the Popov case: Andrew and Gordievsky, 437–438, 474.

59 Mother's injury the previous December: WC Report, 688.

59 Large candy jar had fallen on her nose: Robert Oswald, 93.

59 Might travel to . . . Russia, Cuba and the Dominican Republic: Epstein, *Legend*, 90.

59 Passport was issued on September 10, 1959: WCE 946.

59 "my values are very different from Robert's or yours": WC Report, 689–690.

60 Took a freighter for France, docking at Le Havre on October 8: Epstein, *Legend*, 91–93.

60 "arriving at Helsinki on Saturday, October 10, 1959": WC Report, 258; WCE 2676, 2671, 946.

60 "left Helsinki on a train destined for Moscow on October 15": WC Report, 258; WCE 2676, 2711, 946, 2677.

60 One week in England before going on to college in Switzerland: Epstein, *Legend*, 93.

61 Did not recall seeing Oswald on that train: Epstein, *Legend*, 93.

61 No flight arriving in Helsinki within this travel window: Epstein, *Legend*, 93, 287–288n.

61 Passport would show arrival in Moscow: Epstein, *Legend*, 93; WC Report, 258; WCE 946, 2676.

61 Hotel Klaus Kurki for the next five days: Epstein, *Legend*, 91–92.

61 Did not leave customary tip when he disembarked: Epstein, *Legend*, 93, 288n.

61 Hotel in Mexico cost him only $1.28 a night: Epstein, *Legend*, 235.

61 Highly regarded PGU agent: Andrew and Gordievsky, 432–433.

10. SOVIET CITIZENSHIP DENIED

66 Visa allegedly issued by the Soviet embassy in Helsinki: WC Report, 258.

66 Slightly slashing his left wrist: WC Report, 260; entry for October 21, 1959, in Oswald's "Historic Diary," WCE 24.

66 Wound on left wrist was "not very deep": Epstein, *Legend*, 106; WCE 2778.

67 Did not give "any indication that he had recently received medical treatment": WC Report, 260; WC Vol. 5, 260, testimony of consular official Richard E. Snyder.

67 Documents Soviet government provided to Warren Commission: WCE 985, doc. 1C-2, 1C-3.

67 Leeway in choosing the date he would be allowed to go: WCE 913.

67 Took a taxi to the embassy: entry for October 31, 1959, in Oswald's "Historic Diary," WCE 24.

68 "information concerning the Marine Corps and radar operation": WC Report, 262; WCE 908.

68 Listening devices mounted in key sections of the U.S. embassy in Moscow: Epstein, *Legend*, 301n.

68 "lodge a formal protest regarding this incident": WCE 912.

68 Deliver any message to him at his hotel: WC Report, 749.

69 Unable to reach him at the hotel that day, however: WC Report, 693–694.

69 Best, he said, to continue his education: WCE 1385.

69 "touching in his eagerness to stay in Russia": Priscilla Johnson McMillan, *Marina and Lee* (New York: Harper & Row, 1977), 3, 5.

69 "extraordinary" commitment to communism in light of his age": testimony of Priscilla Johnson McMillan, WC Vol. 11, 449.

70 "Lee was vastly relieved": McMillan, 69–70.

70   "used as a tool in its military aggressions": WC Report 391–392; WCE 295.

70   "anything to do with the old life": WC Report, 697; WCE 297.

11. BOGUS DOCUMENTS

71   Four more times in 1961 and 1962: WC Report, 693.

71   A few American journalists: WC Report, 693–694,

71   Gave interviews to two of them: WC Report, 695–696.

71   Seen in Minsk by American tourists: WC Report, 268, 702.

71   Spoke with a Leningrad accent: information from George Bouhe, obtained in an interview by McMillan and published in her *Marina and Lee*, 197–198.

71   Minsk, where Oswald allegedly lived after his defection: staff report on George de Mohrenschildt, HSCA Vol. 12, 75.

71   Suicide attempt soon after his arrival in Moscow: WC Report, 259–260.

72   "asking the Russian Government to document our suspicions": Epstein, *Legend*, 25.

72   Warren Commission complied: Epstein, *Legend*, 25.

72   "sources, including defectors from the KGB": HSCA Report, 100–103.

72   "none . . . desired to be interviewed": Epstein, *Legend*, 294.

72   "nor were there any surveillance reports": HSCA Report, 100–103.

72   After their arrival in the United States in 1962: WCE 986.

73   Treatment at the Botkin Hospital in Moscow: WCE 985.

73   Lived for almost two and a half years: WCE 92.

73   Statement of Oswald's political philosophy: WCE 25.

73   Question-and-answer paper: WCE 100.

73   "wave and motor vibration existed": Epstein, *Legend*, 309.

73   "Historic Diary," which he brought with him to the United States in 1962: entire diary can be found in WCE 24 and WCE 101.

73   "details of Oswald's activities" in the Soviet Union: WC Report, 258–259.

73   "written in one or two sessions": Epstein, *Legend*, 109, 298*n*.

74   "a country I hate," as he wrote his brother Robert: WCE 294.

74   "waited for 2 year to be accepted": entry for October 21, 1959, WCE 24.

74   "don't want to live in the U.S.": entry for October 31, 1959, WCE 24.

74   "I explaine I am a communist, etc.": entry for October 17, 1959, WCE 24.

74   "give vauge answers about 'great Soviet Union'": entry for October 21, 1959, WCE 124.

74   "this sign of my faith in them": first four pages of "Historic Diary," WCE 24.

75   "till some solution is found with what to do with me": entry for November 16, 1959, WCE 24.

75   "not have to leave the Soviet Union": WCE 294.

75 "sending me to the city of 'Minsk'": entry for January 4, 1960, WCE 24.

12. KHRUSHCHEV DECLARES WAR ON KENNEDY

76 Released five days after Kennedy took office: *"Aircraft Downed During the Cold War and Thereafter,"* created and maintained by David Lednicer, revised June 23, 2001, 9, as published on http://www.silent-warriors.com/shootdown_list.html.

77 Sabotage the nerve centers of Western governments: Andrew and Gordievsky, 522–523.

79 "either gradually or by force": Theodore C. Sorensen, *Kennedy* (New York: Harper & Row, 1965), 592.

80 "divisive activity of imperialist agent Beria": Fyodor Burlatsky, "Khrushchev: Sketches for a Political Portrait," *Literaturnaya Gazeta*, February 24, 1988, cited in Andrew and Gordievsky, 423–424.

80 "generals who were waiting in the next room": Nikita Khrushchev, *Khrushchev Remembers*, translated and edited by Strobe Talbot (Boston: Little, Brown, 1970), 337. (This is the first volume of Khrushchev's memoirs, hereafter designated Khrushchev I.)

81 Beria shot as a Western spy: Andrew and Gordievsky, 424–425.

81 Put a human face on his father: Sergei N. Khrushchev, *Nikita Khrushchev and the Creation of a Superpower* (College Park: Pennsylvania State University Press, 2000).

13. MAY DAY IN MOSCOW

82 Wished to return to the United States: WCE 931.

82 "anything to do with the old life": WCE 297.

82 "Director of the factory": entry for January 13–16, 1961, WCE 24.

83 "I have had enough": entries for January 1–31, 1961, WCE 24.

83 "I might have had in the U.S.": WC Report 391; WCE 295.

83 Did not spend money . . . even on his wife: WC Report, *passim*.

83 Considered his return there to be only temporary: WC Report, *passim*.

83 "did not want them to become Americanized": WC Report, 417.

83 Planned to return to Russia: Epstein interviewed the police officer in question, Lt. Francis Martello. Epstein, *Legend*, 226, 320.

84 A few words in German and Russian: WCE 18.

84 Flash cards for learning German: WCE Potter-A-1.

84 Otherwise not known to have visited: Epstein, *Legend*, 160.

85 "didn't open fire soon enough": Nikita Khrushchev, *Khrushchev Remembers: The Last Testament*, translated and edited by Strobe Talbot (Boston: Little, Brown, 1974), 442–444. (This is the second volume of Khrushchev's memoirs, hereafter designated Khrushchev II.)

86 "to make sure it couldn't escape": Khrushchev II, 442–444.

86   After he returned to the United States: Epstein, *Legend*, 121, 300*n*.
86   "by sleeping in in the morning": Entry for May 1, 1960, WCE 24.
87   Aleksandr Shelepin, chairman of the KGB: Powers, 99–111.
87   "took him to Dzerzhinsky Square [KGB headquarters], and made
     their own report": Jerrold Schecter and Peter Deriabin, *The Spy Who
     Saved the World: How a Soviet Colonel Changed the Course of the
     Cold War* (New York: Charles Scribner's Sons, 1992), 119. Deriabin
     was the editor of Penkovsky's memoirs.
87   Centered on the flight altitude of the U-2: Powers, 99–111.
87   A U-2 that had crash-landed there: Powers, 118.
87   Other reconnaissance besides weather: David Wise and Thomas B.
     Ross, *The U-2 Affair* (New York: Random House, 1962), 54.
87   RB-47 . . . flights, but he said he did not: Powers, 118.
88   In the vicinity of Novaya Zemlya on July 1: Wise and Ross, 232.
88   Trouble with his oxygen equipment: Powers, 139.
88   "the pilot had been captured alive": Khrushchev II, 446.
88   "attempt to violate Soviet airspace": Powers, 140–141.
88   "we would reveal to the world": Khrushchev II, 446–449.
88   Spy mission over the Soviet Union: Powers, 140–141.
89   Out of prison just to show him the display: Powers, 141.
89   Blaming . . . not President Eisenhower for the incident: Khrushchev
     II, 447.
89   "distasteful but vital necessity": Powers, 141.
89   "kicking it as hard as we could": Khrushchev II, 447–449.
89   "justified rebuff to the world's mightiest state": Khrushchev II,
     454–461.
89   Later showing on television and in movie theaters: Powers, 160–162.
89   Ten years' imprisonment: Wise and Ross, 212.
89   Exchanged for the PGU illegal officer Rudolf Abel: Wise and Ross, 4.
89   Not . . . admitting he was a Soviet citizen: Wise and Ross, 237–238.
90   "when I saw him in Moscow": WCE 315.
90   "$2,000 to spend on a holiday in Monte Carlo": Andrew and
     Gordievsky, 462.
90   Inducement to return to Romania: Additional details on this case are
     given in Ion Mihai Pacepa, *Red Horizons* (Washington: Regnery
     Gateway, 1987), 307–308.

14. ASSASSINATION BECOMES A TOOL
OF FOREIGN POLICY

97   "Semtex to last 150 years," Havel estimated: Craig R. Whitney,
     "East's Archives Reveal Ties to Terrorists," *New York Times*, July 15,
     1990, 6.
97   Right up to the fall of the Berlin Wall: John O. Koehler, *Stasi: The
     Untold Story of the East German Secret Police* (Boulder, Colo.: West-
     view Press, 1999), 324.

15. TESTING THE WATERS

99   "dropping of any legal proceedings against me": WCE 931.

99   "request for the return of my American passport": WCE 931.

99   No indication that he had written the embassy that December: WC Report, 752.

100   "at no time insisted that I take Russian citizenship": WCE 931.

100   "writing rather than calling in person": WCE 931.

100   Before the status of his American citizenship could be determined: WCE 1084.

101   Close to the American president's family: summary of information about George de Mohrenschildt, HSCA Vol. 12, 63.

101   Connections with Jackie Kennedy: testimony of Marina Oswald, WC Vol. 1, 31.

101   "knew Jackie Kennedy before she was married to John Kennedy": testimony of Marina Oswald Porter, HSCA Vol. 2, 206–319.

101   "find out what had happened to Minsk": manuscript de Mohrenschildt was working on at the time of his suicide in 1977, HSCA Vol. 12, 75.

102   Spend the rest of his life in Minsk: Epstein, *Legend*, 129–130, 301*n*.

102   Did not exchange conversation: Epstein, *Legend*, 301*n*. Kramer's photograph is reproduced in WC Report, 268.

102   "in some cases other means must be employed": WCE 940.

102   "American citizens in the Soviet Union": WCE 1085.

16. PRELUDE TO REPATRIATION

103   Local figures who were supposed to be his close friends: WCE 2609, 2612; Epstein, *Legend*, photographs following 192.

104   Golovachev was probably his closest friend in Minsk: testimony of Marina Oswald Porter, HSCA Vol. 2, 213.

104   "Twice hero of USSR in W.W.2": WCE 24.

104   General's existence was evidently confirmed by the CIA: Epstein, *Legend*, 112, 294*n*.

104   Showing him as he "repairs hi-fi": Epstein, *Legend*, photographs following 192.

104   "worked in the same factory as Lee did": testimony of Marina Oswald, WC Vol. 1, 38.

104   "the closest friend he ever had": McMillan, 95–96.

104   "I do not remember exactly from whom": testimony of Marina Oswald Porter, HSCA Vol. 2, 214.

104   Letter dated September 15, 1962: WCE 132.

105   Engaged Philby for writing projects or training courses: Andrew and Gordievsky, 541–543.

105   Especially stiff and unnatural: reproduced in Epstein, *Legend*, following 192.

105   Refused Edward Jay Epstein permission to interview: Epstein, *Legend*, xiii, 340*n*.
105   The case of "Anton Sabotka" is discussed in Barron, *KGB*, 434–446.
105   "special" tasks in a time of "crisis": Barron, *KGB*, 439.
106   Retrieved by persons unknown to him: Barron, *KGB*, 437, 440.
106   Qualified as a commercial photographer: WC Report, 725.
106   When applying for a Mexican tourist card: WCE 132.
106   Microdot hidden "under a postage stamp": Epstein, *Legend*, 195–196.
106   Entry for Jaggars-Chiles-Stovall: WCE 18.
107   Occasionally outshot his instructor: Barron, *KGB*, 438.
107   "such a bad shot, they often had to give him game": Nosenko's statement to the HSCA, HSCA Vol. 2, 464.
108   Hunting license valid for one year: WCE 1964, 1984.
108   In his wallet on the day of his arrest: WCE 1964; WC Report, 274.
108   "vulnerabilities to sabotage": Barron, *KGB*, 437.
109   "comrade Kostin": Epstein, *Legend*, 236–237; WC Report 285, 309; WCE 15.
109   Kostikov was an identified officer of the PGU's Thirteenth Department: The information on Kostikov's Thirteenth Department affiliation is from the FBI, according to Epstein, *Legend*, 16. The CIA identified Kostikov as a known KGB officer in WCE 2764. The date of Kostikov's assignment to Mexico City is given in Mark Lane, *Plausible Denial: Was the CIA Involved in the Assassination of JFK?* (New York: Thunder's Mouth Press, 1991), 47, citing CIA document CD 928 sent to the Warren Commission but not published in the commission's report.
109   Anton understood that he might sometime be given tasks in the United States: Barron, *KGB*, 436.
110   "difficult but honorable": Barron, *KGB*, 426.
110   "special" tasks in a time of crisis: Barron, *KGB*, 439–440.
110   "obey whatever orders he conveyed": Barron, *KGB*, 439.
110   "it would have saved many lives": WC Report, 406.
110   Kennedy's "papa bought him the presidency": McMillan, 413.
111   "a copy of *Life* magazine with a cover photo of the President": McMillan, 194.
111   A toy truck in which the PGU had concealed . . . a Minox camera: Barron, *KGB*, 440.
111   Went through customs in Hoboken, New Jersey: WC Report, 713.

17. MARINA

112   "was born in the city of Leningrad": WCE 298.
112   "be persecuted for any act pertaining to this case": WCE 252.
112   "encourages me to do what I wish to do": entries for March 18, March 18–31, April 30, and May and June 1961, WCE 24.
113   Born in "Molotovsk"... in "Archangel *oblast*": WCE 129–131.

113 Gulags holding anti-Soviet prisoners: Louis Begley's review of *The Island* by Gustaw Herling, *New York Times Book Review*, December 27, 1992, 1.

114 Found to be scarcely credible: McMillan, 40–41.

114 "definitely [moral] degeneration": testimony of Jeanne de Mohrenschildt, WC Vol. 9, 323.

114 "Cubans I met in Minsk were just as attractive": George de Mohrenschildt manuscript, HSCA Vol. 12, 99–100.

114 "After all, a pharmacist": testimony of Jeanne de Mohrenschildt, WC Vol. 9, 324.

115 "prerevolutionary officer or some tsarist official": George de Mohrenschildt manuscript, HSCA Vol. 12, 101, 104.

115 "for nonpayment of dues": HSCA Vol. 12, 512.

115 Who had helped get her exit visa: WC Report, 278–280.

115 "granted Soviet exit visa's": entry for December 25, 1961, WCE 24.

115 "helped his niece to get out of Russia": George de Mohrenschildt manuscript, HSCA Vol. 12, 103.

115 VGU: *Vtoroye Glavnoye Upravleniye*, or Second Chief Directorate of the KGB, responsible for domestic security and counterintelligence.

116 Meeting that also began "in a subway station": George G. Church, "Crawling with Bugs," *Time*, April 20, 1987, 14–24.

116 An attractive Soviet cook and her Uncle Sasha: Molly Moore and David B. Ottaway, "2nd Ranking Embassy Marine a Suspect in Security Breach," *Washington Post*, April 1, 1987, A1, A19.

116 Had just recently become pregnant: entry for September–October 1961, WCE 24.

116 Visiting two aunts in Kharkov: McMillan, 128.

117 Names and positions of her relatives: WCE 49.

117 Cause her husband to defect: Barron, *KGB*, 427–428.

118 "failed to respond to my request for cooperation": William Manchester, *The Death of a President: November 20–November 25, 1963* (New York: Harper & Row, 1967), xii.

118 Memory of almost all events in her life with Oswald: testimony of Marina Oswald Porter, HSCA Vol. 2, 206–319.

118 Did not answer the question: testimony of Marina Oswald Porter, HSCA Vol. 2, 290.

118 Numerous questions about Leningrad: McMillan, 196–198, based on conversation with George Bouhe.

118 Crucial role in Oswald's future actions: WC Report, *passim*.

118 "Not even Marina knows why I have returned to the United States": Epstein, *Legend*, 171.

18. A FOOTHOLD IN TEXAS

120 Procedures for Marina's immigration were initiated: WC Report, 706.

120 Travel arrangements had been made by the embassy: WC Report, 711–712.

120   To Fort Worth on June 14: WC Report, 712–713.
120   Furnished apartment of their own: WC Report, 715.
121   "that he himself could not buy": WC Report, 401.
121   After Thanksgiving also with his brother: WC Report, 401.
121   Work as a Russian translator: WC Report, 400.
121   Entrée to people he wanted to meet: WC Report, 714.
121   At the Fort Worth Public Library: WC Report, 281.
121   Others in the local Russian émigré community: WC Report, 281; Epstein, *Legend*, 161.
122   Russian conversation practice with Marina: WC Report, 281–282.
122   "lest he lose his own fluency in Russian": McMillan, 195, based on Paul Gregory's statement to the Warren Commission, WC Vol. 2, 341.
122   Changed to "undesirable": WC Report, 386–387, 710.
122   An effort to clear his record: WC Report, 387, 710, 769.
122   One of the first things Oswald brought up: WC Report, 714.
122   Navy refused to change its decision: Epstein, *Legend*, 161.
122   Money for a lawyer even if he should succeed: WC Report, 325; Epstein, *Legend*, 221.
123   Claimed that he had been honorably discharged: WC Report, 715.
123   With the Texas School Book Depository: WCE 431.
123   Moved to Dallas the next day: WC Report, 402, 715–716.
123   Fired from jobs on April 6 and July 19, 1963: WC Report, 403–404.
123   Claiming he had been turned down at job interviews: WC Report, 727.
123   Could "always go back to Russia": Testimony to the Warren Commission of Denis Hyman Ofstein, WC Vol. 10, 203, as cited in McMillan, 276.
123   "no longer had any source of income": WC Report, 737.
124   With the exception of the de Mohrenschildts: WC Report, 281–282.
125   "Minsk, where I had spent my early childhood": George de Mohrenschildt manuscript, HSCA Vol. 12, 89.
125   "stray dogs" that the unconventional de Mohrenschildt and his wife Jeanne took in: McMillan, 214.
125   When she was still a girl: George de Mohrenschildt manuscript, HSCA Vol. 12, 89.
125   Job leads that de Mohrenschildt suggested to him: WC Report, 717–718.

19. THE COMMO PLAN

128   Hidden compartment of a briefcase: Corson and Crowley, 361–362.
128   Microdot reader, and a Minox camera: Barron, *KGB*, 440.
128   "in a floor, wall, or dry cellar": Barron, *KGB*, 438–439.
128   Letters to his father in Czechoslovakia: Barron, *KGB*, 439.
129   Mail some magazines in the near future: WCE 42.
129   Will soon send more: WCE 132.
130   Interview had gone "just fine": WC Report, 715–716.

131 Arrived on schedule and without mishap: WCE 986.
131 Routed to "Comrade Gerasimov": WCE 986.
131 Of particular interest to the FBI: Epstein, *Legend*, 165.
131 Internally routed to Gerasimov: WCE 986.
131 Reznichenko's name and address in his wallet: WC Report, 616.
131 "living, for a time, in the U.S.A.": WCE 986.
131 Asked to be sent other party literature: WC Report, 287.
131 To send him literature: WC Report, 189.
132 Friendly to the Soviet embassy: McMillan 364.
132 Cuban literature from New York: WC Report, 290–292.
132 In the basement of his house to decipher them: Barron, *KGB*, 441.
132 Lock the door and "do all of my own work there": McMillan, 266–267.
132 Between . . . arrival in Canada and March 1965: Barron, *KGB*, 441.

20. OSWALD'S BEST FRIEND

133 Described him to another émigré as "Lee's best friend": testimony of Katherine Ford, WC Vol. 2, 301.
133 "he liked de Mohrenschildt . . . but only de Mohrenschildt": WC Vol. 1, 10–11.
133 "for whom Oswald had appreciable respect": WC Report, 282.
134 "all the support that Oswald needed for his new life in Dallas": Epstein, *Legend*, 189, based on interview with Gary Taylor.
134 "big, fat women, working in a brick factory": WC Vol. 9, 225.
134 "what type of mushrooms you find, that type of conversation": WC Vol. 9, 241.
134 "a certain understanding between us": WC Vol. 9, 241–242.
135 "Czarist officer of some kind—you see what I mean?": WC Vol. 9, 229.
135 "he immediately parted company with Oswald": Edward Jay Epstein, "Who Was Lee Harvey Oswald?" *Wall Street Journal*, November 22, 1983, 34.
135 "last time he talked to George de Mohrenschildt was in the fall of 1961": HSCA Vol. 12, 54.
135 "out of our minds completely, because so many things happened in the meantime": WC Vol. 9, 225.
135 "I don't recall that," de Mohrenschildt told the Warren Commission: WC Vol. 9, 225.
135 "would like to know, myself, now, how it came about," she said: WC Vol. 9, 307.
136 Not been present at the original meeting between de Mohrenschildt and Oswald: Epstein, *Legend*, 314*n*, based on interviews with George Bouhe and Max Clark.
136 "drove to this slum area in Fort Worth and knocked at the door": WC Vol. 9, 225.
136 "the two were already well acquainted": Epstein, *Legend*, 175–176, based on interview with Lawrence Orlov.

136   Through the Dallas Aid Society—but no such organization existed at that time: Epstein, *Legend*, 176, based on interview with Jim Savage.
136   "met the Oswalds in Orlov's company": Epstein, *Legend*, 314n.
136   "didn't know a damn thing about it" . . . told the Warren Commission under oath: WC Vol. 9, 250.
136   "when my wife saw his gun": WC Vol. 9, 248.
136   "that fool husband of mine used it to buy a rifle": Epstein, *Legend*, 319n, based on interview with Jim Savage.
137   "No, I didn't look at the gun": WC Vol. 9, 249.
137   Not to show him Oswald's rifle for identification: WC Vol. 9, 250.
137   "I see the gun standing there": WC Vol. 9, 315.
137   "started to laugh about it": WC Vol. 9, 317.
137   "I don't remember that": WC Vol. 1, 14.
138   "did not consider this a crazy occupation": HSCA Vol. 12, 198–199.
138   "he tried to take care of it himself": WC Vol. 1, 13–14.
138   "something to mask its presence in the room": WC Vol. 1, 13–14.
138   "Oswald disliked General Walker, you see": WC Vol. 9, 249.
138   "hates the man, it is a logical assumption you see": WC Vol. 9, 250.
139   "looks like a telescopic sight": WC Vol. 9, 249.
139   "what on earth" Oswald was "doing with a rifle": WC Vol. 9, 316.
139   "Not always—but in this case": WC Vol. 1, 18.
139   "I don't recall that incident": WC Vol. 9, 250.
139   "not to try any such crazy foolishness": HSCA Vol. 12, 202.
139   "ESP (extrasensory perception) which he had with Oswald": Epstein, *Legend*, 319n.
140   Insisted they were fakes: WC Report, 181.
140   Flushed the burned remains of the picture down the toilet: WC Vol. 1, 16; McMillan, 34; Epstein, *Legend*, 248.
140   Denied she had ever seen her husband with a rifle: Epstein, *Legend*, 248.
140   Before Oswald took a shot at General Walker on April 10, 1963: WC Vol. 1, 15–16.
140   Oswald's Imperial Reflex camera: WC Report, 127–128.
140   Confronted with two different views: WC Vol. 1, 16.
140   Ever taken in her life up to that time: HSCA Vol. 2, 334.
140   No copy of such a photograph has ever been uncovered: HSCA Vol. 2, 321.
140   De Mohrenschildt killed himself: Epstein, *Legend*, 319,
141   "a gift for us from beyond his grave": HSCA Vol. 12, 253–256.
141   "Are you sure of that?" she was asked once more. "Yes": HSCA Vol. 2, 338.
141   "I cannot claim it was his handwriting": HSCA Vol. 2, 243.
141   Probably the Mannlicher-Carcano he had used to kill Kennedy: HSCA Vol. 2, 320; HSCA Vol. 12, 52–53.
142   "show pictures like that to a friend": HSCA Vol. 2, 336.
142   Apartment on Neely Street for an afternoon visit: Gerald Posner, *Case Closed: Lee Harvey Oswald and the Assassination of JFK* (New York: Random House, 1993), 112.

142 "I completely mixed all the dates," she explained: WC Vol. 9, 314.
142 "hunter of fascists": Written on the back of the photograph is: "To my friend George from Lee Oswald, 5/IV/63"; in Russian, *"okhotnik za fashistami–kha–kha–kha–!!!"*; and "Copyright G. de M." HCE 133A.
143 "was fired upon by security guards": HSCA Vol. 12, 63; Epstein, *Legend*, 182.
143 "I was making drawings of the seashore": WC Vol. 9, 270.
143 "actually gathering intelligence on the oil potential of the area": Epstein, *Legend*, 182.
143 "known to Shell Oil Co. that I was a consulting geologist": WC Vol. 9, 211.
144 "all we knew about it": WC Vol. 9, 216.
144 Attack on the Bay of Pigs on April 15: Albert C. Person, *Bay of Pigs: A Firsthand Account of the Mission by a U.S. Pilot in Support of the Cuban Invasion Force in 1961* (Jefferson, N.C.: McFarland, 1990), 73.
144 "disloyal conduct on the part of either of the de Mohrenschildts": WC Report, 283–284.
144 "denied any other intelligence associations": HSCA Vol. 12, 49.
144 By various intelligence agencies under the Freedom of Information Act: Epstein, *Legend*, 313n.
144 Subpoena to testify before the House Select Committee on Assassinations: HSCA Vol. 12, 49; Posner, 119; Edward Jay Epstein, *The Assassination Chronicles: Inquest, Counterplot, and Legend* (New York: Carroll & Graf, 1992), 555–556.

21. THE BACKGROUND OF AN ILLEGAL OFFICER

146 "mixed-up family, of which there were so many in Russia," de Mohrenschildt explained: WC Vol. 9, 168–169.
146 "born in Mozyr, Russia, in 1911": Epstein, *Legend*, 177–178, from FBI records.
146 Described him as a "Greek Catholic" born in 1914: Epstein, *Legend*, 178, from FBI records.
146 That part was quietly dropped from his biography: F. W. Deakin and G. R. Storry, *The Case of Richard Sorge* (London: Chatto & Windus, 1996), 23; Harry Rositzke, *The KGB: The Eyes of Russia* (New York: Doubleday, 1981), 6–7.
147 Using at about that time to legalize other illegals: Anthony Read and David Fischer, *Operation Lucy: The Most Secret Spy Ring of the Second World War* (New York: Coward, McCann & Geoghegan, 1980), 50–51, 61.
147 World War II spy ring the Red Orchestra: Rositzke, 14.
147 Degree in international commerce from the University of Liege: WC Vol. 9, 177–178.
147 Passport issued by the Polish embassy in Brussels: Epstein, *Legend*, 177–178, from FBI records.

147   To Poland from time to time in the summer: WC Vol. 9, 175–176.

147   As "sergeant candidate officer," he supposedly left for study in Brussels: WC Vol. 9, 172–175.

148   To the United States on August 29, 1920, directly from Russia: WC Vol. 9, 177.

148   "typhoid fever which she contracted during this escape": WC Vol. 9, 173.

148   Killed in Germany at the end of World War II: WC Vol. 9, 197.

148   "cover as a writer for the *Soziologische Magazine*": Gordon W. Prange, *Target Tokyo: The Story of the Sorge Spy Ring* (New York: McGraw-Hill, 1985), 18.

149   Eligible to join the Sons of the American Revolution: WC Vol. 9, 183.

149   "the last Czarist Embassy here in Washington": WC Vol. 9, 173.

149   Baku, where Richard Sorge was born four months later: Prange, 35.

149   "more or less of a French orientation": WC Vol. 9, 173.

149   School in Belgium that had been founded by Napoleon: WC Vol. 9, 177.

150   "my understanding that it was French intelligence": WC Vol. 9, 183–184.

151   Underground White Guard organization in the Soviet Union: Andrew and Gordievsky, 151–152.

152   White Russian émigré communities throughout Europe: Andrew and Gordievsky, 152–154, 163.

153   Died as a baby in New York City on October 9, 1903: Louise Bernikow, *Abel* (New York: Trident Press, 1970), 15–16.

155   The twenty-seventh anniversary of the Russian Revolution: Deakin and Storry, 323.

155   "minor in petroleum engineering, I think": WC Vol. 9, 190.

155   Reason for the investigation or its results: Epstein, *Legend*, 180, 216*n*.

155   Captured there by the Soviet army and executed: Epstein, *Legend*, 181.

155   In London serving as a liaison officer: Epstein, *Legend*, 181.

22. TRAINED TO MAKE FRIENDS, NOT MONEY

156   "occupations such as newspaper correspondents, missionaries, business representatives": Deakin and Storry, 217.

156   "no visible means of support except his wife's earnings": Epstein, *Legend*, 190, based on interview with Taylor.

157   "very successful operation, this business, Sigurd": WC Vol. 9, 178–179.

157   "made some nice money out of that investment": WC Vol. 9, 186.

157   Fabrics for Schumacher and Company: WC Vol. 9, 179.

157   "didn't pass my broker's examination": WC Vol. 9, 180.

157   "work for an oil company": WC Vol. 9, 179.

157   "fired me or I resigned myself": WC Vol. 9, 180–181.

158   "$10,000, I guess": WC Vol. 9, 181, 184.
158   "drilling and producing, which was interesting to me": WC Vol. 9, 195.
158   Business with his girlfriend in Belgium: WC Vol. 9, 178–179.
158   "$10,000" with him when he came to the United States: WC Vol. 9, 179.
158   By investing in a clothing export business: Rositzke, 14.
158   "first venture was quite a failure": WC Vol. 9, 195.
158   "small operation," which was terminated two years later: WC Vol. 9, 199.
159   In Mexico, Cuba, Yugoslavia, and Haiti: WC Vol. 9, 201–202.
160   Sorge's money had in fact come from Moscow: Deakin and Storry, 102, 204–205, 218, 255, 334.
160   For the Polish news service at the time he was living in Belgium: Epstein, *Legend*, 178, from FBI records.
161   "children from such a marriage have a very poor chance to survive": WC Vol. 9, 188–200.
161   "free run of the embassy day and night": Prange, 218, footnoted to Wolfgang von Gronau, *Weltflieger: Erinnerungen 1926–1944* (Stuttgart: 1955), 267.
161   Originated in the German embassy: Prange, 221, footnoted to *Genday-shi Shiryo*, Vol. I, 251.
162   Access to the German diplomatic pouch: Andrew and Gordievsky, 239.
162   Allowed to continue on its way to Mexico: WC Vol. 9, 184–186.
162   "suspected ties to Nazi and Polish intelligence": Epstein, *Legend*, 180, from FBI records.
162   Cross-referencing his file to Larin's: HSCA Vol. 12, 50, footnoted to JFK Classified Document No. 172.
162   Expelled him back to the United States: HSCA Vol. 12, 51, 63.
162   "Lilia and I fell in love": WC Vol. 9, 184–185.
163   "we took a very cautious attitude": Deakin and Storry, 336.

23. THE FRIEND'S PGU ROLE

165   "I like his personality": WC Vol. 9, 296.
166   "for Shanghai and then the United States": WC Vol. 9, 285–289.
166   Same sportswear apparel business: WC Vol. 9, 293–294.
166   "went right under the water in the cave": WC Vol. 9, 300–301.
166   Not responsible for her debts: WC Vol. 9, 291–292.
167   "which port [they will arrive at]," she told the Warren Commission: WC Vol. 9, 305.
167   A couple of trips to Tijuana: WC Vol. 8, 301.
167   Off on his own to meet "friends": Epstein, *Legend*, 7–8.
168   "how are you, Tovarish[ch] Mikoyan": WC Vol. 9, 303–304.
168   Be given careful consideration: Posner, 52.
168   "documents" about Oswald's life in the Soviet Union: Oleg M. Nechiporenko, *Passport to Assassination: The Never-Before-Told Story of Lee Harvey Oswald by the KGB Colonel Who Knew Him*

(New York: Birch Lane Press, 1993), 110, 113, 115; Judie Mills, *John F. Kennedy* (New York: Franklin Watts, 1988), 288.

169   "a year instead of 6 weeks to materialize the whole thing": WC Vol. 9, 299.
170   Engineer of Russian origin who was involved in the oil business: Epstein, *Legend*, 159–160, 310*n*, based on interview of Pauline Bates.
171   "pinpoint the location of enemy vessels": Epstein, *Legend*, 313–314*n*, 175–177.
171   No interest in pursuing the contact with the Brutons: Epstein, *Legend*, 175–177, 183–185.
171   "like insulting a beggar—you see what I mean": WC Vol. 9, 241.
172   "an offensive attitude to him": WC Vol. 9, 309.
172   Did not pursue it further or draw any conclusions from it: HSCA Vol. 12, 57, 60–61.
173   "no signs of subversive or disloyal conduct on the part of either of the de Mohrenschildts": WC Report, 283.
173   "Jeanne—a cook; I—a deckhand": HSCA Vol. 12, 244.
174   "peace between Japan and the Soviet Union": Deakin and Storry, 346.
174   "Millions of Russians miss him": HSCA Vol. 12, 204.
174   "entirely foreign to his personality": HSCA Vol. 12, 305–306.
175   "usually very poor shots": HSCA Vol. 12, 262–263.
175   "LBJ was a most devious man": HSCA Vol. 12, 251.
175   Sorge affair was made public: Deakin and Storry, 346.
175   "Moscow knows nothing about it," the Soviet embassy in Tokyo declared: Prange, 539.
177   The title the article gave him: Andrew and Gordievsky, 153, 679*n*.
177   "neither had worked for it": Posner, 86*n*.
177   De Mohrenschildt as "a CIA informant": Nechiporenko, 160.

24. A SHIFT IN PLANS

178   Causing most of the émigrés to wash their hands of the couple: WC Report, 400–401 and *passim*.
178   Began working there on October 12: WC Report, 402–403.
178   Box number 2915 at the main post office: WC Report, 312.
178   Reznichenko sent Marina's passport back to her: WCE 986.
180   Binoculars "Mikron 6X Coated" and two viewmasters: WCE Stovall-A.
180   Paine, an American engineer in whose house Marina and her children were living when Kennedy was shot: Posner, 344*n*.
181   Book . . . containing 865 pages, the first 18 of which are missing: WCE 1971.
181   "July 12, 1961 from Lee to Marina": WCE 1971.
181   For her admission to the United States as an immigrant: WC Report, 706.
182   "liquidated in peacetime only in special circumstances": Barron, 430–431.

25. KHRUSHCHEV'S FINAL HUMILIATION

185 Singer who had performed in *Boris Godunov*: this event was reported on at length in the official Romanian newspaper, *Scinteia*, October 24, 1962, 1.

186 "might warn Washington to veer from its perilous course": William Hyland and Richard Wallace Shyrock, *The Fall of Khrushchev* (New York: Funk & Wagnalls, 1986), 56.

26. OSWALD GOES IT ALONE

188 Box number 2915 at the main post office in Dallas: WC Report, 312.

188 Routed to Gerasimov at the Soviet embassy: WCE 986.

188 Loan it had advanced him for return travel: WC Report, 330.

188 Attended irregularly until about March 28: WC Report, 723.

188 Identity documents he needed for his operational purposes: McMillan, 258.

188 Essentially photocopied from his own documents: WC Report, 571–577.

188 Fair Play for Cuba activities in New Orleans that summer: WC Report, 121–122, 313–314, 571–578.

188 By combining the names of people he knew: Robert Oswald, 232.

189 Called by the nickname "Hidell": McMillan, 329.

189 Name Oswald himself often used in the Soviet Union, Alek or Aleksey: WC Report, 122.

189 Boxes he would open in New Orleans and . . . Dallas: WC Report, 312–313.

189 No reason to believe her remark is relevant: testimony of Marina Oswald Porter, HSCA Vol. 2, 252, 255; McMillan, 329.

189 Revolver from a mail-order house in Los Angeles: WCE 790.

189 The gun arrived . . . on about March 25: WC Report, 174.

189 Mannlicher-Carcano . . . at about the same time as the revolver: WC Report, 118–121.

190 "Sincerely yours, [s] Marina Oswald": WCE 986.

190 Write the Soviet embassy for permission to return: WC Vol. 1, 35.

190 Get together for Russian conversation: WC Report, 284.

191 Sending her back to the Soviet Union: WC Report, *passim*.

191 Insisted she write the Soviet embassy, asking to be taken back: WC Report, *passim*.

191 Relatives in the Soviet Union with whom she would live upon her return: WCE 8, 986.

191 Sent the requested documents . . . as far as can be determined: WCE 9, 986.

191 Why she wished to go back: WCE 10.

192 Oswald . . . seemed to grow very excited: Epstein, *Legend*, 203–205, based on conversations with Schmidt.

192   Had just sent away for the Smith & Wesson revolver: WC Report, 174.
192   Modified electric pistol and poisoned dumdum bullets: Barron, *KGB*, 421.
192   Concealed in a tin of sausage: Barron, *KGB*, 424.
192   "If a need for a weapon develops, one will be provided": Barron, *KGB*, 438.
192   Box that Oswald had opened in his own name: WC Report, 121–122, 174.

27. THE DRY RUN

193   Uninterruptedly go about his "work": McMillan, 266–267.
193   Plans for the Walker attack: WC Report 404–406.
193   Walker's house that appeared in the background: WC Report, 185–186.
193   A $21.45 money order: WC Report, 118–121.
193   Shipped to "Hidell" on March 20: WC Report, 119, 174.
194   The one that had been used to kill the president: WC Report, 125–128.
194   All about photography and how that could be done: report of Capt. J. W. Fritz, Dallas Police Department, 10–11, as reproduced in WC Report, 608–609.
195   Destroyed the notebook at her insistence: WC Report, 185, 404–406.
195   Convince the Cuban embassy in Mexico City of his revolutionary zeal: WC Report, 734.
195   Neither claim can be substantiated: Epstein, *Legend*, 210, 319.
195   Flaunting his knowledge of Russian and his pro-Communist sympathies: WC Report, 403–404.
195   Classified work for the Army Map Service: Epstein, *Legend*, 192–193.
196   Could have been fired by Oswald's Mannlicher-Carcano rifle: WC Report, 183–187.
197   "the very beginning of the city after the bridge": WCE 1.
197   "very sorry that he had not hit him": WC Vol. 1, 17.
197   Fired only once (and narrowly missed): WC Report, 183.

28. A GAME OF JAI ALAI

198   Unsuccessful with his job hunting in Dallas: WC Report, 725.
198   "further removed from Dallas and from Walker": testimony of Marina Oswald, WC Vol. 1, 18.
198   Unemployment claim he had submitted on April 12: WC Report, 724.
199   Stay at a different hotel, the Hotel del Comercio: WC Report, 733.
199   Was certain Oswald had stayed there: Epstein, *Legend*, 235, 324–325*n*.
200   Before her husband left for New Orleans on April 24: WC Report, 187–189.

200 Picnic with Ruth Paine and her children: McMillan, 293–297.
200 Could not remember . . . except that it was after the Walker incident: testimony of Marina Oswald Porter, HSCA Vol. 12, 249.
200 Nothing about a Nixon visit to Dallas: WCE 1962, report from the Dallas FBI dated June 1, 1964, after checking the relevant newspapers for anything about Nixon.
200 Only time Nixon in Dallas in 1963 was November 20–21: WC Report, 188.
200 "admit to myself that she has been used": testimony of Marina Oswald Porter, HSCA Vol. 2, 278.
201 "'overflights' instead of 'overflight'–could give away everything": Powers, 102.
201 Even after he had acquired a new passport: WCE 2478.
201 Information . . . obtained by his friend Christopher Boyce in California: Andrew and Gordievsky, 530.
202 Take a bus to leave the scene of Kennedy's assassination: WC Report, 157.
202 Answer the phone one evening and hear those words: Barron, *KGB*, 440–441.
202 "attend a jai alai game" but "almost certainly did not do so": WC Report 735.
204 "forced the U.S. to demobilize and to recognize Cuba": Khrushchev II, 512.
205 De Mohrenschildts remained in Haiti until April 1964, when the Warren Commission brought them to Washington, D.C., to testify: WC Vol. 9, 299; HSCA Vol. 12, 204.

29. PLANS FOR KENNEDY'S VISIT

206 "One-Day Texas Tour Eyed": WCE 1972.
206 Ready for his family to join him in New Orleans: McMillan, 314–317.
207 Carried by local radio and television stations: WCE 1972.
207 Let him stay at her house while he was looking for work: WC Report, 725.
207 Locating his father's grave in the Lakeview Cemetery: Epstein, *Legend*, 216.
207 Visiting anyone who might be related to him: WC Report, 725.
207 Picture of his father, which he later threw away: WC Report, 402; Epstein, *Legend*, 216–217.
208 Fictitious companies where he had supposedly sought work: WC Report, 725–726.
208 With the Oswalds before returning to Irving: WC Report, 726.
208 Fictitious job interviews on his claim forms: WC Report, 726–727.
209 Mail forwarded to his street address in New Orleans: WC Report, 312, 633.
209 Giving the Soviet embassy their new street address in New Orleans: WCE 986.

209   Provided that new post office box address: WCE 986.
209   Mail forwarded to Paine's address in Irving, Texas: WC Report, 312, 633.
209   Cuban activities . . . well-received talk to a group of Jesuits: WC Report, 290–292, 728.
210   Fired from his first job there (in New Orleans): WC Report, 729.
210   Told the police . . . in America only temporarily and planned to return to the Soviet Union: Epstein, *Legend*, 226.
210   Quigley left mystified about why he had been called: Epstein, *Legend*, 225; McMillan, 346–347.
210   New passport, which was issued to him the following day: WC Report, 773–774.
210   Intended to leave New Orleans . . . visiting . . . "USSR, Findland, Italy, Poland": HCE 34.
210   Vaccination supposedly given on June 8, 1963: WC Report, 121–122.

30. MOSCOW'S COLD SHOULDER

211   He wished to return to the Soviet Union with her: WC Report, 412.
212   Marina's letter "requesting permission to enter the USSR": WCE 12, 986.
213   Letter requesting separate entrance visas, signed "Lee H. Oswald, (Husband of Marina Nikoleyev)": WCE 13, 986.
213   Wrote Reznichenko again, briefly and urgently requesting an answer: WCE 14, 986.
213   At the Soviet embassy was routed to Gerasimov, as usual: WCE 986.
214   Visit to Texas . . . confirmed at a meeting . . . held on June 5 in El Paso: WC Report, 28.
214   Biography of John F. Kennedy, *Portrait of a President*: McMillan, 337.
214   Took out Kennedy's *Profiles in Courage*: McMillan, 337.
214   Books on politics, espionage, communism, and science fiction: Epstein, *Legend*, 218, 321*n*.
215   The matter had been referred to Moscow for review: WCE 986.
215   "Just chance that caused him to miss": WC Vol. 1, 17.

31. DISAPPOINTMENT IN MEXICO CITY

217   For the birth of her baby, expected in October: WC Report, 727–728.
217   Paine . . . promising to arrive in New Orleans on September 20: Epstein, *Legend*, 225; McMillan, 346–347.
217   Telling them of his move to the Baltimore-Washington area: McMillan, 363–364.
218   Judging from a note found in his effects: HCE 62.
218   Look for work in Houston, or possibly Philadelphia: WC Report, 284.
218   Anticipated visit to Texas, including a stop in Dallas: WC Report, 40.
218   Using his birth certificate as his proof of nationality: WCE 2481, 2478; WC Report, 730.

218 "prepared statement of his qualifications as a Marxist": WC Report, 288, 730–731.
218 Oswald's rifle, disguised as "camping equipment": McMillan, 370.
218 Cashed his latest unemployment check: WC Report, 730–731.
219 Bus for Nuevo Laredo . . . Australian girls . . . in connection with his possible trip in April 1963: WC Report, 731–733.
219 "deceptions designed to get him to Cuba": WC Report, 299–301.
219 Kissed him goodbye in New Orleans: McMillan, 370.
219 Hotel del Comercio, where he would stay throughout his visit: WC Report, 731–733.
220 Mirabal . . . was in fact the one who would sign Oswald's visa application: The discussion of events at the Cuban embassy is based on WC Report, 301–305 and 733–735; and interviews of Silvia Tirado (by then divorced from de Durán) and Eusebio Lopez, HSCA Vol. 3, *passim*.
220 "it would take about four months": WCE 2564.
221 Cameras trained on the entrance to the embassy: Epstein, *Legend*, 16.
221 Oswald would later write to the Soviet embassy in Washington: WCE 986, letter of November 9, 1963.
221 Oswald's visa request, later related by Nosenko to American authorities: HSCA Vol. 2, 462–463.
221 Not visited by anyone at his hotel: WC Report, 305.
222 Movie theaters on the preceding page: WCE 2486.
222 "buy tickets for bull fight": testimony of Ruth Hyde Paine, WC Vol. 3, 12–13.
222 Bullring is encircled on his Mexico City map: WCE 1400.
222 Palace of Fine Arts: McMillan, 496.
222 Yatskov . . . Nechiporenko . . . Kostikov himself, were all identified PGU officers at the time: Posner, 183–196; Nechiporenko, *passim*.
223 To return to the United States, now directly to Dallas: WC Report, 736.
223 Oswald said he would be "right over": Epstein, *Legend*, 236–237.
223 Early the next morning, Wednesday, October 2: WC Report, 736.
223 The envelope he retyped "ten times": WC Report, 309, 739.
225 Text of Oswald's final letter . . . Respectfully, [s] Lee H. Oswald: WCE 986; first draft in WCE 103.

32. THE LONE ASSASSIN

227 Hitchhiked to Irving for the weekend: WC Report, 246–247, 737.
227 Room at 621 Marsalis Street for that week: WC Report, 737.
227 Ride through the city in a motorcade: WC Report 29, 40.
227 Oswald resumed his job hunting: WC Report, 737.
228 Received the last of his unemployment checks: WC Report, 737.
228 Registered in the name O. H. Lee: WC Report, 737.
228 Baby would be called Rachel, a name Marina liked: McMillan, 381.
228 Might have taken him to Irving but no farther: WC Report, 745.

229   Begin work filling book orders on Wednesday, October 16: WC Report, 738.

229   Along the traditional parade route . . . make a turn to get onto the freeway: WC Report, 31–40.

229   Irregular piles of cartons filled with books: WC Report, 477, 485, 723.

229   American Civil Liberties Union, which he had meanwhile joined: WC Report, 312.

230   Felt the FBI was making it difficult for him to find a job: WC Report 419, 738–739.

230   No word about his "Soviet entrance visa's": WCE 986.

230   Meeting Oswald had attended with Michael Paine on October 25: WC Report 293, 415–416.

231   In note addressed to "Mr. Hunt" . . . grammar is awkward, not what . . . a native American would be more likely to write: Jim Marrs, *Crossfire: The Plot That Killed Kennedy* (New York: Carroll & Graf, 1989), 196–197.

232   She was angry and hung up on him: WC Report, 416–420.

232   Long brown package that he told Frazier held the curtain rods: WC Report, 420–421.

233   Entirely credible account of how Lee Harvey Oswald, acting alone, had shot and killed President John F. Kennedy and police officer J. D. Tippit: WC Report, *passim.*

233   Memoranda of these interrogations later written up by Fritz and a few of the other interrogators: WC Report, 180, 196–202.

233   "Question that meant something, that would produce evidence," Oswald refused to comment: WC Report, 199–200.

233   "a Marxist, but not a Leninist-Marxist": Fritz's report is reproduced in WC Report, 599–611.

233   Insisting they were composite fakes: Kelley's report is reproduced in WC Report, 628.

234   Denied having shot President Kennedy, saying he had nothing against him personally: Bookhout's report is reproduced in WC Report, 621–624.

234   "You have the card. Now you know as much about it as I do": Holmes's report is reproduced in WC Report, 633–636.

234   Refused to give any information on who had hired them: *Betrifft Verfassungsschutz '82* (Bonn: Der Bundesminister des innern, April 1983), 210.

235   Kill the same Emil Georgescu by staging a car accident: See Pacepa, *Red Horizons,* 162–164.

235   "the Smith Act case about 1949–1950": WC Report, 210, 623.

235   Abt did meet once with Abel but said he was too busy to take the case: Bernikow, 116, 145.

236   "surprised that I knew of the Paines": Robert Oswald, 144.

236   Reznichenko's name and the address of the Soviet embassy in Washington in his wallet: The contents of Oswald's wallet are given in the

November 23, 1963, report of FBI agent Manning C. Clements, reproduced in WC Report, 614–618.

33. THE SILENCE OF THE GRAVE

238 Warren Commission was unable to identify such an organization:
WC Report, 297.
238 To call attention to the black-bordered ad: WC Report, 335.
238 "I got in my car and I couldn't stop crying": WC Report, 334–335.
239 Ruby later denied having gone to Parkland, and the Warren Commission concluded that Kantor was mistaken: WC Report, 335–336.
239 "Commission's conclusion about Kantor's testimony was wrong":
HSCA Report, 158–159.
239 "A broken man already": WC Report, 337–338.
239 Attended religious services only on the Jewish High Holy Days: WC
Report, 804.
239 Ruby "appeared depressed": WC Report, 340.
240 Oswald would be made available to the newsmen at a press conference in the basement: WC Report, 340–342.
240 Standing on top of a table on one side of the room: WC Report,
342.
240 Belonged to the "Free Cuba Committee": WC Report, 342.
241 "that's the Fair Play for Cuba Committee": Marrs, 416.
241 "It isn't so. I didn't have a gun": HSCA Report, 158.
242 "he kept looking at the floor": WC Report, 342–343.
242 "in a depressed mood": WC Report, 347–348.
243 She had had to repeat herself several times: WC Report, 353.
243 "But he was really pacing": WC Report, 353.
243 Did not lock the car doors: WC Report, 354, 804.
244 Shot into Oswald's abdomen before being subdued by an onrush of
police officers: WC Report, 354–357.
244 "Caroline and Mrs. Kennedy wouldn't have to come to Dallas to testify. OK?": HSCA Report, 158.
244 For reasons of "truancy and incorrigible at home": WC Report,
418.
244 Arrested eight times . . . as well as for simple assault: WC Report,
800.
244 Pistol-whipped, or blackjacked patrons of his nightclubs: WC Report,
804.
244 Business in Chicago, which they owned jointly: WC Report, 784–791.
245 Ruby owned two nightclubs in that city: WC Report, 791–795.
245 Close to "numerous underground figures": WC Report, 801.
245 Going into partnership in the fall of 1963: HSCA Report, 171.
245 Reason she never seriously considered marrying him: WC Report,
801.
245 Louisiana Mafia, and Florida's Cosa Nostra: HSCA Report, 154–156.

34. THE CUBAN CONTRIBUTION

246 Flights given in the INS records were the only ones Ruby had taken during the period: HSCA Report, 151.

247 "the number of trips he made to Cuba and their duration": Marrs, 394.

247 "trip to Cuba in 1959 was a social visit": HSCA Report, 152.

247 Appeared to be part of a massive gunrunning operation to Cuba: Marrs, 391–400.

248 "possibility that Ruby made more trips during this period or other times": HSCA Report, 151–152.

248 McWillie . . . whom Ruby said he "idolized": WC Report, 802.

248 Ties to major organized-crime figures, including Santos Trafficante: HSCA Report, 151.

248 McWillie relocated to Havana: HSCA Report, 151.

248 Manager of "the largest nightclub in the world," the Tropicana casino: Marrs, 394.

248 Leader of the Florida branch of the Cosa Nostra: HSCA Report, 153.

248 Held in Trescornia, a minimum-security detention camp outside Havana: HSCA Report, 153.

248 Contacted convicted Texas arms smuggler Robert Ray McKeown in the United States: Marrs, 395.

249 During the Cuban leader's visit to Houston in 1959: Marrs, 395.

249 Identifying himself as "Jack Rubenstein of Dallas": Marrs, 395.

249 Offered McKeown $25,240 for a letter of introduction to Castro: HSCA Report, 152.

249 He claimed that Ruby "never returned": HSCA Report, 152; Marrs, 395–396.

249 "not interested in its gambling activities": WC Report, 802.

249 "one of the Nation's most powerful organized crime figures": HSCA Report, 152.

250 "Santos was visited frequently by an American gangster type named Ruby": HSCA Report, 153.

250 "could not clearly recall much" about his visit: HSCA Report, 153–154.

250 "efforts to release Trafficante from prison": Marrs, 398–399.

250 Ten days after Ruby arrived in Havana: HSCA Report, 153.

251 Ruby "was never at any time an informant of this Bureau": Marrs, 398–399.

251 Concluded that the file on Ruby should be closed: HSCA Report, 151.

251 Blakey . . . spent four years in the organized crime and racketeering section of the Kennedy Justice Department: Marrs, 524.

252 "use the relationship to procure immunity from prosecution": Marrs, 399.

252 "Ruby would enter his deposit box and contact the FBI": Marrs, 399–400.

255 For more details on the Ráutá case, see Pacepa, *Red Horizons*, 276–279.

257 Information about Felix . . . was disclosed in a book published in Bucharest: Mihai Pelin, *Culisele spionajului românesc: DIE*

1955–1980 (Behind the Scenes of Romanian Espionage) (Bucharest: Evenimentul Zilei Press, 1997), 94–96.

258 Ruby repeated the same thing to his lawyers: Marrs, 392–393.
258 "why didn't he do something for Robert Kennedy? All he did was snub him": Marrs, 430–431.

35. NOSENKO'S TESTIMONY

259 His knowledge of Oswald, his story remaining essentially the same: Epstein, *Legend*, 7–11.
260 Basically ignored Nosenko's information in reaching their conclusions: HSCA Report, 101–102.
261 Pressure the CIA into speeding up his defection: Epstein, *Legend*, 13, 32–36.
261 Involved with Japanese prisoners of war: Epstein, *Legend*, 5.
261 Monitoring tourists from the United States and British Commonwealth countries: FBI debriefing of Nosenko in 1964 (JFK Exhibit F-5), HSCA Vol. 12, 508.
263 Activity directed by Nicolae Ceausescu himself: additional details on the Malek case can be found in Pacepa, *Red Horizons*, 40–41, 64–69, and Ion Pacepa, "La grande fauche" (The big rip-off), *L'Express*, Édition Internationale No. 1721, July 6, 1984, 22–28.
264 Did Gordievsky learn that Prime was a KGB agent: Andrew and Gordievsky, 524–530. Details of the Prime case itself are taken from Corson and Crowley, 356–366, based on the *Report of the Security Commission May 1983*, presented to Parliament by the Prime Minister by command of Her Majesty, May 1983 (London: Her Majesty's Stationery Office, CMnd 8876).
264 In the "Insanity ward" of the hospital: entries for October 16 and 22, 1959, WCE 24.
265 "or was merely an observation of the hospital medical staff": FBI 1964 debriefing of Nosenko, HSCA Vol. 12, 510.
265 "psychiatrists found Oswald to be 'mentally unstable'": Nosenko's statement to the HSCA, HSCA Vol. 12, 461.
265 "he should be avoided at all costs": Posner interview of Nosenko, Posner, 51.

36. A TANGLED WEB OF DECEPTION

266 "communication of any type to the American Embassy in Moscow," according to the FBI debriefing report: FBI 1964 debriefing of Nosenko, HSCA Vol. 12, 514.
266 Such letters are a matter of record in the Warren Commission files: The embassy received a letter from Oswald dated November 3, 1959. On November 6, 1959, the embassy wrote Oswald at his Moscow hotel and during that month sent him several registered letters, none of which he answered. On February 13, 1961, the embassy received an

undated letter from Oswald postmarked February 5 in Minsk. On February 28, 1961, the embassy wrote Oswald in Minsk. On March 20, 1961, the embassy received a letter from Oswald postmarked March 12 in Minsk. On March 24, 1961, the embassy wrote Oswald in Minsk. On May 25, 1961, the embassy received a letter from Oswald postmarked May 16 in Moscow. In 1961 the embassy received further letters from Oswald, dated July 15, August 8, October 4, and one undated letter received in August. There was an additional exchange of correspondence between the embassy and Oswald in 1962. (This information is from U.S. State Department reporting to the Warren Commission, WC Report, 749–758.)

267   "upon issuance of a visa to a person to visit the USSR": FBI 1964 debriefing of Nosenko, HSCA Vol. 12, 508.

268   Leave the Soviet Union upon the expiration of his visa: FBI debriefing of Nosenko, HSCA Vol. 12, 508–509.

268   Might cause bad publicity for the Soviet Union: Posner interview of Nosenko, Posner, 52.

268   "decision to assign him to Minsk": FBI 1964 debriefing of Nosenko, HSCA Vol. 12, 510.

268   "to 'passively' observe his activities": FBI 1964 debriefing of Nosenko, HSCA Vol. 12, 510.

269   "without the *permission of the chief of the Second [Chief] Directorate, as well as the chairman of the KGB*": Posner interview of Nosenko, Posner, 54.

269   "M. I. Turalin, Service Number Two (counterintelligence in foreign countries), First Chief Directorate": FBI 1964 debriefing of Nosenko, HSCA Vol. 12, 511.

269   Recommended that the reentry visa be refused: Nosenko's statement to the HSCA, HSCA Vol. 2, 463.

270   Flown by military aircraft to the VGU in Moscow: FBI 1964 debriefing of Nosenko, HSCA Vol. 12, 511–512.

270   No KGB officer had ever spoken to Oswald, much less recruited him: Nosenko's statement to the HSCA, HSCA Vol. 2, 463–464.

270   "of no particular interest or significance to the KGB": FBI 1964 debriefing of Nosenko, HSCA Vol. 12, 509.

270   "a Marine guard . . . but that wasn't the case with Oswald": Posner, 49.

270   "better information already coming from KGB sources than he could ever give us": Posner, 49.

271   "extraordinary suggestion, coming from a Soviet official": Epstein, *Legend*, 294.

37. DEATH OF A HIT MAN

272   Conveniently died on January 3, 1967: Marrs, 431–432.

273   Khokhlov lost his hair but not his life: Boris Volodarsky, "The KGB's Poison Factory," *Wall Street Journal* (Europe), April 7, 2005, A10.

274 Need for fundamental change in the Soviet Union's foreign policy: The complete text of Togliatti's "testament" appeared in "Text of Togliatti Memorandum on the Problems of World Communist Tactics," translated from the Italian by the *New York Times*, and published in the *New York Times*, September 5, 1964, 2.

274 Brezhnev had attended Togliatti's funeral in Rome: Robert C. Doty, "Togliatti's 'Will' Assails Moscow," the *New York Times*, September 5, 1964, 3.

274 Portions of Togliatti's "testament" that were critical of Khrushchev: Excerpts from Togliatti's "testament" were printed in *Pravda*, September 10, 1964.

276 "Radu," from the Romanian *radiere* (radiation): Pacepa, *Red Horizons*, 143.

276 Blamed the explosions on Chechen separatists: Alexander Litvinenko and Yuri Felshtinski, *Blowing Up Russia: The Secret Plot to Bring Back KGB Terror* (London: Encounter Books, 2001).

277 Died during the botched FSB rescue operation: Nick Lazaredes, "Terrorism Takes Front Stage," Australian TV *Dateline*, June 4, 2003.

277 Might develop cancer: Ann Curry, "The Last Days of a Secret Agent," *Dateline NBC*, February 25, 2007.

38. OPERATION DRAGON LIVES ON

278 "bragging and phrase-mongering": "The Man Between Two Eras," *Time*, September 20, 1971.

278 "ever received from any source": Christopher Andrew and Vasili Mitrokhin, *The Sword and the Shield: The Mitrokhin Archive and the Secret History of the KGB* (New York: Basic Books, 1999), 1.

278 For aggressively advertising them: Andrew and Mitrokhin, 226–227.

279 Spent 1932–1933 in the Soviet Union: Biography of Joachim Joesten, published on http://karws.gso.uri.edu/jfk/the_critics/joesten/joesten bio.html.

279 To prevent him from giving evidence: Andrew and Mitrokhin, 227, citing Joesten's book.

279 Highest levels of the U.S. government: Andrew and Mitrokhin, 227–228, 616*n*.

280 FBI had been given the original: Andrew and Mitrokhin, 228–229.

280 Identified his handwriting: Andrew and Mitrokhin, 229.

280 "American special services" in the Kennedy assassination: Andrew and Mitrokhin, 229.

281 No Soviet intelligence involvement with him whatsoever: Nechiporenko, 61–62.

281 Could find nothing incriminating: Nechiporenko, viii.

282 "Marina was also of no use to us": Nechiporenko, 61–62.

282 "a pawn, used, then eliminated": Nechiporenko, 135–136.

282 "a good deal to offer on this matter": Nechiporenko, 314.

INDEX

A NOTE ON THE AUTHOR

Ion Mihai Pacepa was born in Bucharest, Romania, and studied chemical engineering at the Polytechnic Institute in Bucharest. He was national security adviser to Romanian president Nicolae Ceausescu, acting chief of the Romanian foreign intelligence service, and state secretary in the Romanian Ministry of Interior. In 1978 he was granted political asylum by President Jimmy Carter, becoming the highest-ranking Soviet-bloc intelligence official to defect to the United States. He has also written *Red Horizons*, a book published in twenty-seven countries and serialized by Radio Free Europe.